ECONOMIC LIBERALIZATION AND
INDUSTRIAL PERFORMANCE IN BRAZIL

Economic Liberalization and Industrial Performance in Brazil

EDMUND AMANN

OXFORD

UNIVERSITY PRESS

OXFORD

UNIVERSITY PRESS

Great Clarendon Street, Oxford OX2 6DP
Oxford University Press is a department of the University of Oxford.
It furthers the University's objective of excellence in research, scholarship,
and education by publishing worldwide in

Oxford New York

Athens Auckland Bangkok Bogotá Buenos Aires Calcutta
Cape Town Chennai Dar es Salaam Delhi Florence Hong Kong Istanbul
Karachi Kuala Lumpur Madrid Melbourne Mexico City Mumbai
Nairobi Paris São Paulo Singapore Taipei Tokyo Toronto Warsaw

and associated companies in Berlin Ibadan

Oxford is a registered trade mark of Oxford University Press
in the UK and certain other countries

Published in the United States
by Oxford University Press Inc. New York

© Edmund Amann, 2000

The moral rights of the author have been asserted
Database right Oxford University Press (maker)

First published 2000

British Library Cataloguing in Publication Data

Data available

Library of Congress Cataloging in Publication Data
Amann, Edmund.
Economic liberalization and industrial performance in Brazil / Edmund Amann.
p. cm. — (QEH series in development studies)
Includes bibliographical references and index.
1. Industrial equipment industry—Brazil. 2. Brazil—Economic policy.
I. Title. II. Series.
HD9680.B72 A7 2000   338.981—dc21   00-029351
ISBN 0-19-829612-6

1 3 5 7 9 10 8 6 4 2

Typeset by Graphicraft Limited, Hong Kong
Printed in Great Britain
on acid-free paper by
Biddles Ltd, Guildford & King's Lynn

PREFACE

In the past ten years the Brazilian economy has experienced an unprecedented wave of market liberalization as import substitution has been progressively abandoned in favour of insertion into the global economy. While the nature of this changing policy environment has been widely discussed in the literature, its impact upon individual productive sectors has received far less attention. By focusing on the fortunes of one key industrial sector—the non-serial capital goods sector—this book sets out to partially fill this gap, shedding some light upon the consequences of rapid market liberalization for industrial performance and technological self-reliance. In addition to addressing this important policy issue, the book, through its focus on a pivotal industrial sector, aims to provide a panoramic viewpoint of an economy in transition.

This book is based upon a Ph.D. thesis which I completed at the University of Manchester in 1996. I should particularly like to thank my supervisors, Professor Fred Nixson and Mr Pat Devine for the constant and invaluable help and guidance they provided both before and during the carrying out of the research. While undertaking the fieldwork phase of the research, I was based at the University of Brasília and I should like to thank the Department of Economics, especially Professor José Sant'ana and Professor Steve de Castro for the warm hospitality and support that was extended to me throughout my stay. I also owe a particular debt of gratitude to Professor João Carlos Ferraz at the Federal University of Rio de Janeiro, Professor Ernani Teixeira Torres Filho at the BNDES, and Dr Manoel Fernando Thompson Motta for the considerable assistance provided in the course of the fieldwork. I should also like to express my thanks to ABDIB and IPEA for their valuable help. Finally, I should like to thank all those at the University of Oxford Centre for Brazilian Studies, the Latin America Centre, and Queen Elizabeth House who have done so much to make the completion of this book a feasible and pleasant project!

Centre for Brazilian Studies   E.A.
and Queen Elizabeth House,
University of Oxford

CONTENTS

LIST OF CHARTS
and their sources

xii   LIST OF CHARTS

LIST OF TABLES

LIST OF ABBREVIATIONS

ABDIB	*Associação Brasileira para o Desenvolvimento das Indústrias de Base* (Brazilian Association for the Development of Basic Industries)
ABIFER	*Associação Brasileira para a Indústria Ferroviária* (Brazilian Railway Industry Association)
ABNT	*Associação Brasileira para Normas Técnicas* (Brazilian Association for Technical Standards)
AFRMM	*Adicional ao Frete para Renovação da Marinha Mercante* (Merchant Marine Fund)
BEFIEX	*Comissão para Concessão de Benefícios Fiscais a Programas Especiais de Exportação* (Commission for Granting Fiscal Incentives to Special Export Programmes)
BNDE	*Banco Nacional de Desenvolvimento Economico* (National Economic Development Bank)
BNDES	*Banco Nacional de Desenvolvimento Economico e Social* (National Economic and Social Development Bank)
BNDESMAQ	Capital goods sector incentive scheme run by the BNDES
BNDESPAR	BNDES *Participações* S.A. (Equity participation programme operated by the BNDES)
CACEX	*Carteira do Comércio Exterior* (Foreign Commerce Department of the *Banco do Brasil*)
CAD	computer-aided design
CADE	*Centro de Articulação com a Demanda Por Bens de Capital* (Centre for the Coordination of Demand for Capital Goods)
CAPES	*Coordenação de Aperfeiçoamento de Pessoal de Nível Superior* (Coordinating Agency for the Improvement of High Level Personnel)
CDI	*Comissão de Desenvolvimento Indústrial* (Industrial Development Commission)
CEPAL	*Comissão Econômica para Amērica Latina e o Caribe* (Economic Commission for Latin America and the Caribbean)
CET	common external tariff
CIF	carriage, insurance, and freight
CNC	computer numerically controlled/computerized numerical control
CNI	*Confederação Nacional de Indústria* (National Confederation of Industry)

CNPq	*Conselho Nacional de Pesquisa* (National Research Council)
CPA	*Conselho de Política Aduaneira* (Council for Customs Duty Policy)
CRC	Convention on Reciprocal Credit
CTT	*Coordenação Técnica de Tarifas* (Technical Coordination of Tariffs)
DECEX	*Departamento de Comercio Exterior* (Department of External Commerce)
DNC	direct numerical control
ECLAC	Economic Commission for Latin America and the Caribbean
ERP	effective rate of protection
FDC	*Fundação Dom Cabral* (Dom Cabral Foundation)
FESBRASIL	*Friedrich Ebert Stiftung Brasil* (Friedrich Ebert Foundation Brazil)
FINAME	*Agência Especial de Financiamento Industrial* (Special Industrial Finance Agency)
FINAMEX	*Programa de Financiamento á Exportação de Bens de Capital* (Capital Goods Export Financing Programme)
FINEP	*Financiadora de Estudos e Projetos* (Finance Agency for Studies and Projects)
FINEX	*Fundo de Financiamento á Exportação* (Fund for Export Financing)
FMM	*Fundo de Marinha Mercante* (Merchant Marine Fund)
FOB	free on board
FRONAPE	*Frota Nacional de Petroleo* (National Petroleum Shipping Fleet)
FUNCEX	*Fundação Centro de Estudos de Comércio Extevior* (Centre for Foreign Trade Studies Foundation)
GATT	General Agreement on Tariffs and Trade
GEICON	*Grupo Executivo de Construção Naval* (Brazilian executive group for shipbuilding)
GEIMAPE	*Grupo Executivo da Indústria Mecânica Pesada* (Executive Group for Heavy Mechanical Industry)
GEIPOT	*Grupo Executivo para a Integração da Politica de Transportes* (Executive Group for the Integration of Transport Policy)
IBGE	*Instituto Brasileiro Geografia e Estatística* (Brazilian Government Statistical Service)
IBRE/FGV	*Instituto Brasileiro de Economia/Fundação Gétulio Vargas* (Brazilian Institute of Economics/Gétulio Vargas Foundation)
IBS	*Instituto Brasileiro de Siderúrgia*
ICM	*Imposto sobre Circulação de Mercadorias* (indirect sales tax on goods)

ICMS	*Imposto sobre a Circulação de Mercadorias e Serviços* (indirect tax on the sale of goods and services)
IEI-UFRJ	*Instituto de Economia Industrial-Universidade Federal do Rio de Janeiro* (Institute of Industrial Economics-Federal University of Rio de Janeiro)
IE-UNICAMP	*Instituto de Economia-Universidade Estadual de Campinas*
ILDES-FES	*Instituto Latinoamericano de Desenvolvimento Economico e Social-Friedrich Ebert Stiftung* (Latin American Institute for Economic and Social Development-Friedrich Ebert Foundation)
ILO	International Labour Organization
IMF	International Monetary Fund
INPI	*Instituto Nacional de Propriedade Industrial* (National Institute of Industrial Intellectual Property)
IPEA	*Instituto de Pesquisa Economica Aplicada* (Institute for Applied Economic Research)
IPI	*Imposto sobre Produtos Industrializados* (indirect tax applying to industrial products)
IPT	*Instituto de Pesquisa Tecnológico* (Institute of Technological Research)
ISI	import substitution industrialization
ISO	International Standards Organization
JIT	just in time
LANs	local area networks
LDC	less developed country
Libor	London Inter-Bank Offered Rate
MERCOSUL	*Mercado Comum do Sul* (Southern Common Market)
MRP	materials resources planning
NAI	*Núcleos de Articulação com a Indústria* (Centres for Interaction with Industry)
NBER	National Bureau of Economic Research
NTB	non-tariff barrier
OECD	Organization for Economic Co-operation and Development
OPEC	Organization of Oil Exporting Countries
PAF	*Programa de Acompanhamento de Fornecedores* (Programme of Supplier Partnership)
PBDCT II	*Plano Básico de Desenvolvimento Científico e Tecnológico II* (Second Brazilian Scientific and Technological Development Plan)
PBQP	*Programa Brasileiro de Qualidade e Produtividade* (Brazilian Quality and Productivity Programme)
PCI	*Programa de Competitividade Industrial* (Industrial Competitiveness Programme)

PIS/PASEP	*Programa de Integração Social/Programa de Formação de Patrimônio do Servidor Público* (Social Integration Programme/Programme for the Training of Public Sector Workers)
PND II	*Programa Nacional de Desenvolvimento II* (Second National Development Plan)
PROALCOOL	*Programa Nacional de Álcool* (National Alcohol Programme)
PROEX	*Programa de Financiamento as Exportações* (Export Financing Programme)
PUC-RJ	*Pontifica Universidade Católica do Rio de Janeiro* (Catholic University, Rio de Janeiro)
R&D	research and development
REER	real effective exchange rate
RFFSA	*Rede Ferroviária Federal S.A.* (Federal Railway Network)
SBE	*Sociedade Brasileira de Electrificação* (Brazilian Electrification Society)
SFP	single factor productivity
SNICN	*Sindicato Nacional para a Indústria de Comércio e Navegação* (National Syndicate for the Shipping Industry)
SUNAMAN	*Superintendencia Nacional de Marinha Mercante* (Merchant Marine National Superintendency)
TCP	technology capability programme
TFP	total factor productivity
TNC	transnational corporations
TQM	total quality management
UFRJ	*Universidade Federal do Rio de Janeiro* (Federal University of Rio de Janeiro)
UNCTAD	United Nations Conference on Trade and Development
UNICAMP	*Universidade Estadual de Campinas* (State University of Campinas)
UNIDO	United Nations Industrial Development Organization

1

Introduction

The past ten years have witnessed radical shifts in the character of Brazilian economic development. Inward-orientated growth strategies have been abandoned and the private sector given an ever greater role in production and allocation decisions. This movement towards liberalization has coincided with a return to democracy and an increased emphasis on regional integration. More recently, Brazil has finally succeeded in bringing inflation under control after two decades of chronic price instability. These profound changes in the economic environment provide the background for this book. Focusing on the 1982–95 period, this book sets out to analyse how one crucially important industrial sector—the non-serial capital goods sector*—reacted to the forces of liberalization as it was forced to compete in an increasingly open and private sector-dominated domestic market. In examining the response of the Brazilian non-serial capital goods sector to policy liberalization, a very important set of theoretical and empirical issues is addressed. These issues turn out to have very broad implications for the conduct of industrial and trade policy in other emerging market economies.

The key policy shifts encountered by the sector have been replicated in Latin America and across the world. By the mid-1980s, many developing nations emerging from the debt crisis were forced to recognize that the inward-orientated, state-led strategies that had underpinned their development were no longer sustainable. Faced with the fiscal exhaustion of the state, inefficiency among industrial sectors, and the urgent need to attract capital inflows through external adjustment, many economies embarked on ambitious liberalization programmes. In addition to trade liberalization and reduced public investment, the scope of industrial policy was drastically curtailed, deregulation introduced, and privatizations initiated. In Latin America the momentum of liberalization accelerated throughout the late 1980s, first embracing Mexico, then Argentina, and, finally, after 1987, Brazil. Latin America was by no means unique in its sudden and collective rejection of the traditional state-led development model. From the mid-1980s onwards a number of African economies embraced greater liberalization as they complied with the

---

* The term 'non-serial capital goods' denotes those capital goods that are made to order, do not always follow standardized designs, involve discontinuities in the production process, and are sometimes associated with long lead times. Non-serial capital goods are frequently employed in basic process industries such as steel making and oil refining or in the provision of power and water supplies. Good examples of non-serial capital goods would include heavy industrial equipment such as blast furnaces or distillation plant, ships, oil rigs, and generators for use in power stations. Non-serial capital goods can be contrasted with serial capital goods, the bulk of which can be classified as machine tools. Serial capital goods are produced in greater quantities, not necessarily to order, and are manufactured to standard designs using production-line techniques.

terms of World Bank structural adjustment programmes. Asia, too, was not immune from the process with significant moves towards liberalization occurring in several of the region's economies, notably India.

In the case of Brazil, the scope of policy liberalization was, by historic standards, drastic and, indeed, unprecedented. After two years of cautious opening up under President Sarney, the Brazilian economy, in 1990, was the object of a far more ambitious programme of liberalization. The newly elected President, Fernando Collor de Melo, engineered a radical restructuring of the role of the state in the economy. Public expenditure—especially on plant and equipment—was slashed, severely depressing demand in the non-serial capital goods sector's single most important market, that of the nationalized industries. At the same time non-tariff barriers were abolished and a rolling programme of tariff cuts launched. These trade measures were supplemented by additional tariff adjustments in the run-up to the launch of Mercosul in 1995. Despite the impeachment of President Collor de Melo in 1992, subsequent administrations have broadly maintained the programme of liberalization on track. For the majority of industrial sectors (including that of capital goods), tariff reductions have continued to be applied while public sector investment has remained depressed, not least because of the privatization of many public enterprises. For the Brazilian non-serial capital goods sector, these policy changes constitute no less than a revolution.

In theoretical terms, support for policy liberalization of this nature is underpinned by a core theoretical proposition deriving from neoclassical political economy. In essence, this proposition holds that trade and market liberalization are able to induce rapid and positive changes in the level of efficiency of industrial enterprises. These gains manifest themselves in terms of both static and dynamic efficiency.

Static efficiencies result as enterprises attempt to optimize production efficiency with respect to existing products and production techniques. At the same time, dynamic efficiencies result as firms engage in efforts to increase technical progress either through the development of new products or production processes. Despite the centrality of this theoretical contention to much of current industrial and trade policy-making, evidence concerning the actual (as opposed to predicted) impact of the resulting policy regimes has been somewhat thin on the ground. This is especially true in the case of Brazil where research into contemporary industrial issues has been rather restricted, especially in the English language. Given this background, the central objective of this book is to make a contribution towards a greater empirical understanding of the impact of policy liberalization on industrial efficiency. Although necessarily focusing on the specific case of the Brazilian non-serial capital goods sector, the book aims to draw out the broader implications of the sector's experiences for the current debate on industrial and trade policy liberalization.

In order to achieve its objectives, this book deliberately adopts a broad conception of industrial efficiency. In contrast to a number of other studies, an attempt is made to decompose industrial efficiency into its static and dynamic components and then trace the impacts of policy change on each. In drawing this conceptual distinction in its analysis of policy impacts, this book enables a rich interpretation of the nature of policy effects while allowing for a consideration of the inter-temporal implications of a liberalizing policy regime on industrial efficiency. In the case of the Brazilian non-serial capital goods sector, the results derived from this approach throw up an interesting set of policy conclusions whose implications extend very broadly. The applicability of these policy conclusions is seen to spread beyond the specific case under consideration towards other sophisticated industrial sectors undergoing policy liberalization. These sectors are not only located in Brazil but in many other parts of the world, particularly in Latin America and South and East Asia.

In order to provide the appropriate theoretical and empirical background for the book, the remainder of this chapter divides into two sections. Section 1.1 sets out the theoretical context of the study. Two critical theoretical issues are addressed in this section. First, attention is paid to the special role ascribed to the capital goods sector in the theoretical literature on industrialization and development. Secondly, the discussion focuses on the role of industrial and trade policy in inducing changes in industrial efficiency. The section concludes by setting out the key questions to be examined empirically in subsequent chapters. Following on from this, Section 1.2 outlines the methodological approach adopted in the course of the book, highlighting, among other issues, the concepts of industrial efficiency employed and the nature of the data used.

1.1 The Theoretical Context

1.1.1 CAPITAL GOODS AND ECONOMIC DEVELOPMENT

The development and rapid expansion of the Brazilian non-serial capital goods sector in the post-1945 period was, as Chapter 2 shall demonstrate, very strongly influenced by the developmental priorities of the state. The sector came to be perceived of as central to the process of self-reliant industrial growth and was accorded special status in the formulation and implementation of industrial policy. To this extent, the Brazilian experience had much in common with those of other newly industrializing nations such as South Korea, India, and Mexico, not to mention those of the centrally planned economies.

The special treatment directed at the sector in the course of the industrial development of Brazil and other nations rested on the belief that the sector had a particular role to play in the modernization of the industrial economy and, more generally, in the generation of economic growth. These special functions can be divided into 'quantitative' and 'qualitative' dimensions. The quantitative dimension refers to the direct role that capital goods can play in the process of accumulation and growth while the qualitative dimension concerns the relationship between the growth of the sector and technological progress. The latter dimension turns out to be synonymous with the generation and diffusion of dynamic efficiencies, themselves a primary focus of empirical investigation in later chapters.

(i) Capital Goods and Accumulation: The Quantitative Dimension

Theoretical approaches emphasizing the quantitative dimension have proved to be very influential in the formulation of development strategies around the world, particularly during the era of the centrally planned economies. Among the most important theoretical insights in this area are those offered by Feldman (1928) and Mahalanobis (1953). For both Feldman and Mahalanobis the major constraint on growth in the long term lies in the ability of developing nations to engineer increases in the capital stock. Given an insufficient capacity to import capital equipment due to external constraints, the capital goods sector should be prioritized in the process of industrialization. The prioritization of this sector rests on the fact that, in the absence of capital goods imports, it alone provides the means by which savings may be transformed into investment forms that facilitate growth and accumulation. With a given technology, it is possible to calculate the proportion of resources that should be utilized in the capital goods sector for any desired long-run growth trajectory.

The planning approaches typified by the work of Feldman and Mahalanobis have increasingly fallen out of favour as development economists have placed a greater and greater emphasis on decentralization and the market in the process of resource allocation. Despite the demise of the planning models, the capital goods sector has continued to receive special attention within the debate on development and industrialization. This has less to do with its traditional role as a motor of accumulation, than because of the fact that it possesses a unique set of technological characteristics.

(ii) Capital Goods and Technological Change: The Qualitative Dimension

Many authors have highlighted the important observation that the capital goods sector is unusually technologically intensive and produces a disproportionate number of innovations relative to its size. Using input–output analysis with reference to the US economy, Scherer (1982) examined inter-industry technology flows. He discovered that the capital goods sector is an unusually large net 'exporter' of R&D to other sectors in the economy (ibid. 231) and an unusually large proportion of innovations are used in the sector itself (ibid. 229). Similar findings for the UK economy were uncovered by Robson, Townsend, and Pavitt (1988). Five core sectors—chemicals, machinery, mechanical engineering, instruments, and electronics—accounted for 64.3% of all innovations (ibid. 3). Furthermore, innovations produced in these sectors were particularly widespread in their use in other sectors (ibid. 7). Stewart (1976: 199), Baark (1991: 907), and UNCTAD (1985: 3) also draw attention to the importance of the sector in generating technological change.

Rosenberg's classic 1963 article also draws attention to this characteristic and highlights one reason for its existence, namely that all innovations be they product or process will require new production equipment at some stage (Rosenberg 1963a: 188). Thus, even if the innovation originates outside the capital goods sector, the sector will have to become involved in technological change simply in order that the innovation can be incorporated into manufactured articles and commercially realized. Considerations of profitability and a desire to maintain buoyant markets for capital goods are also likely to contribute to the intensity of innovation in the sector. Because of the long physical life of some capital goods, it may be necessary to introduce deliberate technological obsolescence if markets are to be sufficient in the future. This may be particularly true after a cyclical upswing when stocks of capital goods are high and demand in the absence of upgraded products could be thin if not non-existent (Brown 1957: 410). Further reasons for the intensive nature of technological development in the capital goods sector may be seen in its relationship with other sectors of the economy.

One of the distinguishing features of the capital goods sector is the degree to which it is interrelated. This has two main dimensions. Most obviously, it takes capital goods to produce other capital goods. This implies that there will be considerable economic and technological interdependence between different components of the capital goods sector. Given the high technological literacy of purchasers of capital goods within the sector, user–producer relationships can be expected to be strong. This creates a favourable climate for technological development. Strassman (1959) points out that consumer good industries are different in this respect. They are linked to the supply side of the capital goods sector and other supplier industries but not to each other.

Given the characteristics of the capital goods sector highlighted above, it is not surprising that the sector plays a considerable role in diffusing technology to other sectors of the economy. This feature has been highlighted by Baark (1991: 905) and UNCTAD (1985: 3), while Rosenberg (1982: 71) also points to the role of the sector in raising productivity in sectors other than itself. Empirical basis for these observations is provided by Scherer (1982: 231, 244) and Robson, Townsend, and Pavitt (1988: 7). In addition to its role as a diffuser of technology, the sector may also convey positive externalities through its contribution to learning and human capital formation. This is due to the ability of the sector to generate a pool of indigenous technical knowledge and improve the efficiency of the production process. In particular, possession of an indigenous capital goods sector provides the capability to effectively select and assimilate technologies from overseas and possibly adapt them to suit local conditions. These issues will be examined below starting with that of learning.

Bell (1984) provides a detailed discussion of the implications of learning in an LDC (less developed country) context. Learning can occur through experience without any deliberate strategy involved. This is referred to as 'learning by doing' (Bell 1984: 188) and is the form of learning discussed by Arrow (1962). Alternatively, learning may result from more deliberate strategies such as training, outside hiring of skilled personnel, or technological upgrading of plant. Of particular significance to the present discussion is the idea that significant learning and consequent technological change can result from user–producer relationships which are characterized by feedback flows of information. These, of course, are of key significance in the capital goods sector. This point is emphasised by Baark (1991: 907). Accumulation of technology in the capital goods sector through this form of learning and the consequent implications for the rest of the economy provide one of the main justifications upon which any decision to raise domestic capability in the sector should be based (ibid. 907).

The accumulation of knowledge and technological capability through the existence of a capital goods sector could offer further benefits. These arise because the sector provides a platform upon which indigenous technological change can occur which in turn holds out the possibility of independence from the possible constraints imposed by importing technology. Two sets of issues will be examined here: first, the ability of the sector to facilitate the effective assimilation of technologies developed overseas, and secondly, the possibility that the sector could develop technologies appropriate to LDC conditions.

Mitra (1979) emphasizes the development of a skills base as one of the principle positive externalities generated by the presence of a capital goods sector. The skills used in capital goods production confer benefits on the rest of the economy in that they can be deployed to maintain and repair existing equipment in machinery-using sectors (Mitra 1979: 9). This has obvious positive implications for an LDC in that it may save on importing replacement equipment or sending equipment overseas for repair. The range of equipment which an LDC is able to purchase, operate, and maintain is also increased.

Most significantly, it can be argued that the possession of a skills base provides a favourable environment for effective selection and assimilation of capital goods technology produced overseas (ibid. 9). Ranis (1984: 97) develops this point further and argues that a key measure of the quality of indigenous technological activity is the ability to make sensible choices regarding purchase of overseas equipment and, once the choice has been made, to tinker, adjust, and eventually diffuse the technology throughout the economy. Stewart (1984: 81) also stresses this point.

One of the most influential arguments concerning the desirability of an indigenous capital goods sector in an LDC is that of appropriate technology. In the absence of a domestic capital goods sector, the LDC will be obliged to obtain its capital goods requirements from abroad. There may be disadvantages to this, however, in that overseas technologies may require factor intensities or possess characteristics that are inappropriate to local conditions. Of particular note in the literature is the possibility that imported equipment may be biased towards capital-intensive techniques. This may be of particular concern in countries where there is a substantial pool of unemployed or under-employed labour. One possible role of a domestic capital goods sector would be to produce or adapt (from foreign designs) equipment that was more appropriate to local factor endowments. This argument in favour of a domestic capital goods sector finds favour with a very wide spectrum of economists ranging from Stewart (1976) to Little (1982) to some dependency theorists, for example, Dos Santos (1978).

This section has attempted to outline the main technological character-istics of the capital goods sector. The intention has been to demonstrate the importance of the sector for technological development, thus providing an argument for its special consideration from a policy perspective. Any policy-maker, however, is faced with a complex question. This concerns the nature and extent of polices required to promote the development of the capital goods sector. This issue is examined below.

1.1.2 STATE INTERVENTIONS AND INDUSTRIALIZATION: THEORETICAL AND EMPIRICAL PERSPECTIVES

The previous section drew attention to various theoretical considerations that might justify the establishment of a capital goods sector in an industrializing economy. However, little attention was paid to the practicalities involved in such an undertaking, most particularly those relating to the role of the state. The purpose of the following discussion is to consider what light theory sheds on the role that the state might play in fostering an advanced industrial sector in a less developed country and the problems that might be encountered.

More specifically, the discussion attempts to pinpoint the types of market failure that justify particular types of intervention along with an assessment of the problems that such intervention might in turn produce. By consider-ing these issues it will prove possible to establish theoretically derived expecta-tions regarding the likely impact of a scaling down of state support for the non-serial capital goods sector in Brazil, a scaling down that encompassed reduced protection, support for technological development, and public pro-curement of non-serial capital goods. Subsequent chapters, in examining the empirical evidence, will attempt to establish whether or not these expecta-tions are borne out in reality.

The remainder of the section divides into two. First, the arguments sup-portive of an extensive role for the state in the development of advanced indus-trial sectors are discussed and analysed. Secondly, the possible problems that might result from such a role are considered alongside the potential benefits to be gained from liberalization.

(i) Arguments for State Intervention

(a) *Domestic considerations* In the previous section it was demonstrated that the capital goods sector is notable for its ability to internally generate tech-nical change and then transmit it through the rest of the economy. However, the role of the state in facilitating and promoting this process was not considered. The concepts of market failure and externalities, when applied to the technological activities of the capital goods sector, appear to suggest a number of possible areas where state intervention is justified.

Most fundamentally, the pool of technological knowledge generated by the processes of R&D and learning in the capital goods sector is likely to be of use to other sectors of the economy (Pack 1981: 229). Such knowledge may be conveyed either through being embodied in capital goods themselves, in the ability to repair and adapt existing machinery, in the provision of advice to clients, in the movement of skilled personnel to other firms, or through general diffusion of knowledge into the public domain. Even if there is little formal R&D, any learning that takes place within the capital goods sector has positive implications for other sectors of the economy as the results are felt through improved product quality and supplier experience leading to improved user productivity (Erber 1978: 116).

Roles for the state arise from the consideration that firms in the sector are not able to capture all the benefits that result from the diffusion of the fruits of their R&D and learning efforts, a phenomenon associated with the imperfect appropriability of knowledge and skills (Lall 1994: 649). For example, some of the results of innovation by the capital goods firm are likely to become generally available through reverse engineering or patent documentation. Such information which would then take on some of the character of a public good might provide help to rival producers in their innovation efforts. This frequently has the result that similar, though non-patent-infringing designs come to be produced by rivals.

Another possibility is that firms are unwilling to engage in 'socially optimal' levels of training for fear of losing expensively trained skilled personnel to rivals. Finally, capital goods firms are never able to feel all of the benefits that their innovations bring to user firms in terms of productivity, efficiency, and profit gain so their incentive to innovate is accordingly reduced. Thus, for a number of reasons, there could be a tendency for firms to under-invest in R&D and training and engage in sub-optimal levels of learning. The state could help to offset these tendencies by assisting R&D activity, facilitating training, and providing a favourable environment to learning. This could be achieved in a number of ways.

First, a direct subsidy could be granted to firms to engage in particular R&D projects thought to have particularly strong potential 'spin-off' effects. Secondly, the state itself could engage in R&D, providing R&D institutes, engineering consultancies, or standardized technical manuals (Mitra 1979: 29–30). Thirdly, support of R&D could be less specifically targeted through its favourable treatment in corporate taxation. Fourthly, the state can play a vital role in ensuring that there is a good supply of trained personnel able to carry out R&D through the provision of higher education or special institutes. Fifthly, credit could be made available on favourable terms to assist R&D.

Finally, the state can ensure a favourable environment for learning and R&D by encouraging large-scale production. This could be achieved through the implementation of macroeconomic policy that led to high levels of demand for capital goods. Fransman (1986: 33) goes further and suggests that the state has a more direct role to play as a procurer of capital goods in its own right.

The state, through the generation of demand and the specification of advanced technological requirements, may be able to induce rapid technological change within the capital goods sector. For example, the necessity to achieve extremely high precision in the machining of helicopter rotor blades for the US air force directly led to the development of numerical control for machine tools (ibid. 33). In the Brazilian case, the deep drilling requirements of the state-owned Petrobrás oil company led to the development of specialist technological capabilities in parts of the Brazilian non-serial capital goods sector (Tadini 1993).

So far it has been established that several roles can be justified for the state as a provider of support for R&D activity in the capital goods sector. However, the reasoning so far has ignored the very important issues of the impact of imports on the process of R&D and the choice between indigenous technological development and the licensing of foreign designs. It is to these that the discussion now turns.

(b) *International considerations* Constraints may be placed on domestic R&D not only by the operation of domestic externalities but also by the impact of competition from imports and the availability of foreign technologies for transfer whether in the form of intra-TNC (transnational corporations) transfers or in product designs developed abroad. These constraints are likely to be particularly acute where an emerging capital goods sector faces competition from the technologies and products of more technologically advanced foreign competitors. From a contemporary structuralist perspective, Lall (1994) argues that industries in less developed countries will tend to import fully packaged technologies, complete with proven designs and processes rather than engage in indigenous R&D because of the lower costs and risks involved (ibid. 649). Thus, a rationale is created for policies that restrict the import of technologies in embodied form and favour the operation of more disembodied forms of technology transfer such as certain forms of technology licensing which permit domestic learning (ibid. 649).

Stewart (1984: 83) points to the possibility that, in the absence of import controls and technology transfer restrictions, risk aversion and the desire to minimize costs would cause entrepreneurs to opt for foreign rather than locally generated capital goods technology when making investment decisions. More generally, Stewart hypothesizes that absence of import controls and increased competition from overseas leads to the predominance of process over product innovation (ibid. 83). In other words, innovations are encouraged that help reduce the cost of production without necessarily enhancing the intrinsic technological sophistication of the final product. For the capital goods sector such a situation is especially serious as long-run competitiveness is strongly reliant on constant product innovation (Pack 1981: 242). Stewart's hypothesis is highly relevant to the current study and subsequent chapters will examine the degree to which it appears to be supported in the Brazilian case.

Given the considerations outlined above, there would appear to be an argument for enhanced protection and technology transfer regulation of the capital goods sector if R&D is to proceed and its benefits to be felt throughout the economy. Given that the objective of the exercise is to raise indigenous R&D and innovation, blanket tariff or quota protection and technology-licensing restriction of the sector may not be appropriate. Some forms of capital good import would have to be restricted as they competed head on with local production. However some types of capital good, particularly of a more advanced nature, could continue to be imported freely if they were involved in an upgrading of technical knowledge in the indigenous capital goods sector. The issue of technological licensing is one in which there may also be a role for the state.

As the previous discussion has suggested, the assumption should not necessarily be made that domestic capital goods production involves exclusively domestic R&D. Much of the capital goods production that takes place in less developed countries relies on imported basic designs for which a licence fee is paid (Larrain 1989: 207). Unless restrictions are placed on the use of imported designs, domestic R&D is frequently limited to the modification of these basic designs and production equipment to facilitate local production. In other words, process innovation may come to dominate 'genuine' product innovation. Might there be any reasons why the state might wish to encourage more development of indigenous basic design and reduced reliance on licensing and, if so, what would the appropriate policy measures be?

Erber (1978) points to a number of considerations that would have to be taken into account in the making of any decisions. First, the nature of the foreign exchange constraint must be examined. The more critical this is, the less attractive extensive foreign licensing becomes (ibid. 123). Secondly, the risks and time taken to develop indigenous designs must be taken into account. If these are perceived to be excessive and foreign designs are available off the shelf, then there may be considerable private and social costs in the short run attached to indigenous relative to imported designs (ibid. 128).

However, the ongoing process of learning in the capital goods sector is likely eventually to reduce both the amounts of time and risk associated with opting for indigenous design (ibid. 129). Thirdly, the choice between licensing and self-reliance in basic designs involves considerations of positive externalities. These are likely to be higher when capital goods are entirely designed within the domestic economy as there is a much greater impact on the pool of technical knowledge existing within the sector which in turn will be diffused throughout the economy as a whole.

Another factor that might encourage preference for indigenous rather than foreign designs lies with the issue of appropriateness. This concept and its limitations are examined in Chapter 2. It is noted that capital goods designs originating in the advanced industrial nations might tend to have a capital-intensive bias. The promotion of local designs more appropriate to local factor conditions could form part of the justification for controls to be placed on the importation of certain designs. Once the state has decided that control of imported designs may be desirable in some cases then legislation can be put in place requiring firms to obtain permission before entering into licensing agreements with foreign firms. This would allow the state to screen the design in question so that its compliance with overall policy objectives could be assessed. Of course, for reasons that have already been discussed, it is very likely that the state's role would also have to encompass more direct support for indigenous R&D than restriction of foreign designs alone.

(c) User–Producer Linkages in the Capital Goods Sector: Roles for the State Baark (1991: 907) characterizes the accumulation of technology in the capital goods sector as a long-run process in which there is a reliance on feedback flows of information both from within the capital goods sector and between the sector and users. Baark believes that the contribution the capital goods sector can make to overall technological accumulation and growth is likely to depend on the strength of such linkages. In a similar vein, Bruton (1985: 94) argues that the capital goods sector must be fully informed about the content of the requirements of using firms, thoroughly familiar with existing technical knowledge, and know the environment in which other firms function. Neo-Schumpetarians cite such user–producer linkages as essential, particularly in the early days of a new technology (Schmitz and Cassiolato 1992: 5).

For all of these linkages to work smoothly requires a considerable investment in gathering information on behalf of firms in the capital goods sector. However, information is not always costless and not always readily available. The more imperfect the market for information, the less likely it is that firms will gather sufficient quantities to permit smooth user–producer interaction. There may be an argument, therefore, for the state to step in and improve the flow of information. This could be achieved by sponsoring or initiating industrial associations or simply by engaging in a regional policy that brought users and producers physically closer together. If the government were engaged in a programme of indicative planning then it would be in a position to act as a more direct conduit for information between users and producers.

(ii) Arguments for Liberalization

In the previous section it was demonstrated that a variety of interventions in the capital goods sector could be theoretically justified by market failure and the presence of externalities. Principally, roles lay for the state in the direct support of R&D, the regulation of technology transfer, public sector procurement of capital goods, and the protection of the market (of which public sector procurement policy may be an important component). The theoretical and empirical material discussed in this section, however, casts doubt on the efficacy and feasibility of much of this intervention. In particular, a number of propositions are made regarding the long-run impact of market protection, technology transfer regulation, and continued reliance on the state for orders. In examining the possible problems of such interventions, this section examines their potential consequences for productivity, static and dynamic efficiency within enterprises. The section concludes by reviewing recent empirical evidence on the linkages between trade liberalization and the development of industrial efficiency in emerging market economies.

The expansion of the domestic market through public sector procurement and its protection through the use of tariffs, quotas, and other measures have been one of the most widely employed methods of trying to raise self-reliance in advanced industrial sectors and were key to the development of the non-serial capital goods sector in Brazil. In previous sections, numerous theoretical justifications were identified for the implementation of such measures. However, disillusionment with the impact of such policies, particularly those associated with Latin American import substitution has led to the development of a substantial literature that is both critical of these measures and supportive of efforts to reduce them and foster greater integration into the world economy.

Given the Brazilian context in which public sector procurement has been substantially reduced, high barriers to capital goods imports have been replaced by a more liberal regime, and regulation of technology transfer and support for technological development have been curtailed, a brief review of these arguments is very much in order. In order to achieve this objective, the implications of the literature for a number of important themes are examined starting with productivity, moving on to specific aspects of static and dynamic efficiency, and concluding with exports.

(a) *Productivity*   Changes in productivity can be a very important indicator of alterations in economic efficiency and international competitiveness and may also act as an indicator of technical change (Weiss 1988: 228). In so doing, changes in productivity may reflect changes in underlying static and dynamic efficiencies. Productivity may be measured on the basis of a single factor of production (usually capital or labour) or using all factors of production to give total factor productivity (TFP).

The importance of capital goods sector productivity change as a very important determinant of productivity growth throughout the economy has already been demonstrated. However, there might be reason to suspect that infant industry, or any other form of protection combined with continuing primary reliance on public sector orders, may slow down productivity growth, especially if they last too long. This could lead to an internationally uncompetitive capital goods sector or, from an infant industry standpoint, one in which maturation is never realized. An explanation for this can be found in a consideration of Verdoorn's Law.

Verdoorn's Law demonstrates that a positive relationship exists between productivity change and the rate of growth in output (Nishimizu and Robinson 1984: 179). According to Kaldor, the fundamental reason for this is that expansion of output enables the achievement of scale economies, specialization and learning (ibid. 179). In many circumstances, the domestic market remains too small for the kind of output increases that would generate such rises in productivity. At the same time, protective mechanisms, overvalued exchange rates, and the uncompetitive nature of domestic firms make it difficult to expand output through exporting (Belassa 1980: 7). This can lead to a situation in which productivity and output stagnate behind protective barriers with firms remaining reliant on their traditional public sector sources of demand and unwilling and unable to export. At the same time, technology transfer restrictions may mean that access to foreign technology in the form of designs or capital goods is limited meaning that their potentially productivity-boosting effects are forgone.

Productivity growth is also restricted by the fact that competing with foreign firms in domestic or overseas markets can give rise to learning and incentives to innovate in process technology. In a situation where markets are protected and the public sector offers a guaranteed source of demand, risk aversion among managers is likely to mean that there is little likelihood that such efforts will be undertaken (World Bank 1987: 92). Policies that lead to a concentration of firms on the domestic market may also lead to a situation in which firms are unable to specialize in particular products because of small market size. This is particularly serious in the capital goods industry where considerable economies of scale derive from horizontal and vertical specialization, further restricting scope for productivity growth (Belassa 1980: 11). In the case of Brazil, the peculiar characteristics of public sector procurement policy have tended to accentuate this lack of specialization as Chapters 3 and 6 will make clear.

Disappointing productivity performance behind protective barriers has received considerable attention in the literature on Latin American industrialization. There is substantial evidence that the years of protection under ISI (import substitution industrialization) did little to raise levels of productivity and exploit economies of scale to a point where international competitiveness was achieved. Baer, for example, points to this 'market critique' of ISI as being relevant for key industries such as steel and automobiles across Latin America (Baer 1972: 102). Pack (1981: 231–2) indicates the presence of low plant-wide productivity in protected capital goods industries throughout the Third World and the particular problem of capacity under utilization that arises from small markets and production runs. Nishimizu and Robinson (1984: 198), in a survey of four countries and twenty-eight industries, find higher TFP growth in those countries which embarked on a policy of export expansion than those who selected protective measures and import substitution.

Such critiques, taken together with the more theoretical approaches that have been examined appear to lend support to the view that the scale of protection and public sector procurement for industry in general and the capital goods sector in particular should be scaled down rather than maintained or enhanced. However, recent empirical evidence concerning the impact of trade liberalization on productivity growth offers less than wholehearted support for these arguments.

In their survey of the literature, Clarke and Kirkpatrick (1992) point out that most cross-country studies have failed to find 'strong empirical evidence of a link between trade liberalization and productivity growth' (ibid. 58). In a study of the Mexican manufacturing sector conducted by Weiss (1992), a degree of support is found for the hypothesis that trade liberalization has favourably influenced productivity growth. Inter-temporally, however, there is no consistency as to which trade liberalization indicators are the most significant explanatory variables. Significantly, Weiss also stresses the importance of structural and technological factors as key determinants of productivity growth (Weiss 1992: 14). Among recent studies, only Papageorgiou, Michaely, and Choksi (1991) give strong support to the hypothesis that trade liberalization favourably influences productivity growth. In sum, the evidence concerning the relationship between trade liberalization and productivity does not lend unambiguous empirical support to the pursuit of trade liberalization, despite its broad acceptance throughout Latin America and beyond.

(b) *Static Efficiency*   In the literature sceptical as to the potential for efficient state interventions, the argument is often put forward that policy interventions designed to compensate for the imperfections of markets may actually lead to welfare losses. Many attempts have been made to assess the nature and extent of these losses, particularly those that arise from the use of tariffs or quota protection.

Given the practical difficulties of empirically attributing efficiency losses to either allocative or productive failings, much of the study of the impacts of protection assesses overall efficiency losses. In the majority of such studies, internationally prevailing prices and their associated production techniques (presumably emerging from conditions of maximum currently attainable efficiency) are employed to create a reference point against which calculations of the overall efficiency of protected activity can be compared. The most widely known analytical approach of this nature is that of the effective rate of protection (ERP).

The ERP assesses the total amount of protection given to a product by the entire structure of tariffs and quotas. In contrast to measures of nominal protection which measure only the impact of tariffs and quotas directly attaching to final output, the ERP takes into account the effects of import restrictions on input prices and estimates the amount by which value added is raised as a result (Little *et al.* 1970: 169; Ghatak 1986: 285). By employing measures of ERP it is possible to see the extent to which value added at domestic prices exceeds value added at world prices for any activity. If it is assumed that it is the structure of protection alone that permits this excess, then it is possible to use ERP as a measure of production inefficiency engendered by protection (Kirkpatrick and Nixson 1983: 16). However, the operation of other interventions, in particular, the granting of subsidies and the provision of privileged access to the public sector market, will also have the effect of raising the ERP. Very commonly, ERP is also used as a measure of the incentive for firms to move into a particular activity (Weiss 1988: 183).

Many studies have been conducted to examine the extent of ERP for various sectors in LDC industrial economies. Baer (1972), Little, Scitovsky, and Scott (1970), Soligo and Stern (1965), and Corbo (1988) all point to persistently high effective rates of protection associated with infant industries and import substitution. More recent studies demonstrate the existence of high ERP in many industrial activities even when formal import substitution has been abandoned (World Bank 1987). Interestingly however, much of the research reveals relatively low levels of ERP for the capital goods sector (Weiss 1988: 184). This reflects the fact that many countries, in their industrialization strategy, have allowed certain capital goods to be imported with low or non-existent tariffs and quotas, reducing the overall ERP of the capital goods sector. Indeed, in some cases subsidies on purchases of capital equipment meant that effective protection was actually negative. For reasons that shall be discussed in later chapters, for much of the post-1975 period, Brazil has been something of an exception to this pattern.

The structure of protection may also encourage a lack of competition between firms in domestic markets. Because of the small size of domestic markets there simply may not be room for a large enough number of competing producers to generate domestic competition. This could be expected to lead to the conventional welfare losses associated with monopolies. Liberalization of imports could be expected to remedy this situation by increasing the number of firms competing for the domestic market and reducing the deadweight loss.

Thus, there are a number of reasons to believe that the achievement of static efficiency could be prejudiced by the long-run application of protective and industrial policy measures. The obvious policy conclusion is that the structure of protection and the other policy measures should be scaled down once substantial inefficiencies manifest themselves. However, the impact of these policies may not be limited to their effects on static efficiency. Dynamic efficiency may also be affected by the incentives to innovate and learn in a protected and intervention-strewn market. It is to these issues to which the discussion now turns.

(c) *Dynamic Efficiency*   In previous sections it was shown that protection and selected interventions such as public sector procurement could be justified if they provided conditions under which a domestic technological capability is built up in the capital goods sector. However, a literature has emerged pointing to instances of limited learning and technological progress in developing country capital goods sectors affected by such policies (e.g. Chudnovsky *et al.* 1983; Fransman 1986; Schmitz 1984). Basic designs tend to be imported and local research and development is limited to adapting these designs to suit local manufacturing capability and reducing the costs of production. Thus, the positive externalities to be derived from more basic research and development are forgone. Is it possible that structures of protection and other interventions act as disincentives to larger-scale domestic research and development?

For Felix (1978), the riskier the R&D activity, the higher the output and the greater the overall economies of scale required. However, prior to liberalization, firms are likely to be faced with limited internal markets and export opportunities restricted by the incentive structure of protectionism. Thus, they may not be able to achieve the output and economies of scale required to make riskier, basic forms of R&D viable. For Felix this implies that firms will tend to import basic designs and carry out adaptive, process R&D. In time, such R&D and the process of learning may give rise to mastery of certain technologies where the international frontier of technological progress is stable. However, where the frontier is moving, such mastery is never achieved and the country remains technologically dependent (ibid. 20).

There may be reasons to believe that restricted market size is not the only impediment to technological progress engendered by protective measures. Bell, Ross-Larson, and Westphal (1984: 27) point out that technological change may be stimulated by increased competition in the product market. This may be due to the challenge-response mechanism induced by foreign competition in such markets (Nishimizu and Robinson 1984: 179). In other words, lack of competition, particularly foreign competition, reduce incentives for domestic producers to innovate. Domestic producers tend to be focused on supplying protected domestic markets, a process which involves the exploitation of long-standing relationships with established domestic clients, especially those in the public sector.

Unless specific policies enforce technological dynamism on these producers (for example, through public sector procurement policies explicitly aimed at raising technological capacity), the tendency will be for the maintenance of relative technological conservatism. The reduction of protective measures and the forcing away of domestic producers from their traditional markets might therefore be expected to raise technological dynamism.

To some extent, this view is echoed in the 1987 *World Development Report* (World Bank 1987). In particular, according to the report, the more outward-oriented trade policy is and the greater the involvement of firms in export markets, the more technologically dynamic firms are likely to be (ibid. 91).

In addition, exposure to export markets and interface with their technologically advanced users can also be a great stimulus to indigenous technological capability as a form of technology transfer takes place.

Competing in world markets may also have beneficial effects on quality levels within industry. This is likely to be increasingly true as many customers now request that industrial goods meet international quality standards set by the International Standards Organization, in particular ISO 9,000. Under conditions of protected home markets and 'cosy' arrangements with traditional domestic clients, the achievement of quality may not be a priority. During the era of import substitution in Latin America, for example, concerns were expressed at low quality levels and the need to compete in world markets (Hirschmann 1968: 24). The structure of protection may also restrict the availability of high quality imported inputs, further prejudicing overall levels of quality (Baer 1972: 104; Krueger 1985: 22).

(*d*) *Exports and Interventions*   From the preceding discussion it is clear that, at least according to critics of interventionism, exports have a valuable role to play in raising the static and dynamic efficiency of developing capital goods sectors. Exports allow for the development of specialization, efficiency, and productivity due to large-scale production. In addition, incentives for technological change and product improvement are offered by exports (Belassa 1971: 181). Therefore, there seems good reason to promote the growth of exports to assist the emerging capital goods sector. Unfortunately, it would appear that the operation of protective and other industrial policy measures could act as a hindrance to the achievement of export expansion.

There are circumstances under which the implementation of protective measures could effectively levy a 'tax' on exports. This might be expected to happen if a tariff raised the price of domestically produced goods subject to tariff protection but not exported (importables) relative to those domestically produced, unprotected, but exported (exportables). Under these circumstances there is an effective tax on exports, the effect of which on export volumes may be further exacerbated by higher domestic consumption of the relatively low priced exportables (World Bank 1987: 80).

Another route through which protection and the operation of certain interventions may have a harmful impact on export performance lies with considerations of efficiency and cost competitiveness. Protection of the domestic market and reliance on domestic public sector orders, for reasons already examined, would appear to take the pressure off firms to maximize efficiency and price at internationally competitive levels.

Given these circumstances, it is hard to conceive of firms managing to compete on price and penetrate export markets. The fact that there are profits to be made by engaging in inefficient production for the domestic market does not encourage firms to look further afield. Even if firms were willing to become more efficient and enter the export markets, tariffs and quotas on vital imported inputs may mean that it is impossible to get prices down to world levels (Little *et al.* 1970: 130). In terms of the capital goods sector, this is a particularly important consideration as attainment of international competitiveness may necessitate the importation of particular equipment unavailable domestically. A further obstacle may be provided by the overvaluation of exchange rates which have been frequently employed as part of a policy to increase industrial self-reliance (Fishlow 1990: 63).

Much of the empirical work conducted on the impact of import substitution in Latin America supports these theoretical perspectives regarding the impact of high tariff levels on export performance. Many writers point to the discrimination against exports that emerged through the pattern of protection (e.g. Corbo 1988: 160) and the fact that high ERPs diverted domestic resources into activities where exports were of secondary importance. Grunwald (1970: 840) points to the innate inefficiency of infant industries developed under protection as a cause of poor export performance while Hirschman (1968: 13) talks of import substitution being affected by 'seemingly congenital inability to move into export markets'.

(iii) Possible Problems of State Intervention in Advanced Industrial Sectors: Implications of the East Asian Experience

The previous section surveyed the predominantly neoclassical critique of state intervention in advanced industrial sectors such as that of capital goods. The critique consistently highlights the inability of the state to generate efficient industrial expansion through interventions in the sector due to the inappropriateness of policy instruments, the lack of suitable information, or the rational behaviour of firms faced with the moral hazards implicit in the operation of policy. This 'intervention pessimism' implicit in the critique is, however, challenged by some economists working within what might be termed the Contemporary Structuralist School. This challenge emerges from a reinterpretation of the process of industrialization amongst the countries of East Asia, particularly South Korea.

According to the critique of interventionism, the most consistent problem faced by efforts to build up static and dynamic efficiencies using protective policies and public sector procurement appears to lie in the inefficiencies and sub-optimal operational characteristics adopted by enterprises as they are shielded from external and possibly internal competition. However, according to the Contemporary Structuralists, the absence of such market pressures does not necessarily mean that the development of inefficiencies is inevitable providing that the state adopts appropriate and credible countervailing policy measures.

Thus, in the case of South Korea, policies of protection, public sector procurement, and subsidization were accompanied by intense scrutiny of the performance of targeted sectors with performance targets set and monitored rigorously (Amsden 1989). Performance targets consisted not only of measures of productivity, quality, and cost but also extended to the acquisition of technological self-reliance through the disembodied transfer of technology. The latter proved very effective in building up technological self-reliance in the shipbuilding sector (ibid. 274–5). Significantly, however, in more sophisticated capital goods sub-sectors, enterprises have proved unable to reduce reliance on imported product designs despite years of concerted policy interventions. Indeed, the majority of dynamic efficiency gains experienced within South Korean industrial sectors have been the direct result of process, rather than product, innovation.

Perhaps the greatest incentive to the achievement of efficiency targets was the eventual requirement that sectors be competitive internationally to the extent that they would survive and prosper following forced insertion into the export market as elements of the protective regime altered. Indeed, the South Korean case stands out as an unusual example of the effective operation of selective protection counterbalanced by strong pressures to export in certain sectors (Lall 1991: 133).

The development of strong South Korean export performance in certain non-serial capital goods sub-sectors, in particular shipbuilding, would appear to demonstrate that heavy state involvement in the development of the capital goods sector is not necessarily consistent with the persistence of static and dynamic inefficiencies. However, as previous discussion has made clear, according to Contemporary Structuralists, interventions are only likely to be effective if undertaken on a detailed, well-researched case-by-case basis, addressing the particular forms of market failure prevalent within the context of institutional, technological, and organizational specificities.

1.1.3 SOME CONCLUSIONS

The theoretical literature on the role of the capital goods sector in developing economies makes a number of powerful arguments for the prioritization of the sector in the process of industrialization. The arguments centre around the view that an expanded capital goods sector may be an especially effective agent in raising the long-run rate of growth (the quantitative dimension) and at increasing the rate of technological progress (the qualitative dimension). The discussion pointed to the increased emphasis that has been placed on the latter characteristic in more recent work.

The existence of unique developmental characteristics within the sector may create a number of potential roles for the state. According to the literature supportive of intervention in the sector, intervention can be justified by the existence of market failure and the need to enhance dynamic efficiency. In the absence of such interventions, the expectation is that long-run dynamic efficiency would be impaired as product innovation became subordinated to measures that emphasized the attainment of greater static efficiency. This would probably mean that the indigenous capital goods sectors would have difficulty in catching up with their counterparts in the advanced industrial nations.

The literature opposing such intervention does not deny that catching up and the achievement of dynamic efficiency are important objectives. However, it questions whether state intervention is the most suitable means of achieving them. In particular, any benefits that accrue to the capital goods sector through the means of interventions may be outweighed by the costs. These costs express themselves not only in conventional static terms but also through losses in dynamic efficiency. However, a portion of the literature advocating a greater role for the state suggests that some of these efficiency losses can be reduced through better policy design and tight monitoring of its implementation.

The policy implications of the analysis critical of an extensive role for the state are that the scale and scope of interventions should be substantially reduced in order to enhance long-run static and dynamic efficiencies. In particular, barriers to imports should be scaled down, the role of the state as a procurer of capital goods should be relatively reduced, and the sector should be forced to compete in the international market. This is precisely what has been happening to the Brazilian capital goods sector since 1990. A key objective of the following chapters is to examine the performance of the Brazilian non-serial capital goods sector within this context and to try and assess whether this conforms with the predictions and recommendations of the literature advocating a reduced role for the state with static and dynamic efficiency gains resulting. At the same time, the evidence will also be examined in an effort to establish whether the performance of the sector conforms, instead, to the expectations generated by the literature more favourable to state intervention in the sector which would predict static gains occurring at the expense of longer-run dynamic efficiencies.

In order to assess these competing theoretical perspectives in the light of the evidence, it will be necessary to develop a number of specific hypotheses derived from the literature that can be examined with the available data. The next section presents these hypotheses and sets out to explain how they are to be examined.

1.2 Data Sources and Analytical Approach

The previous sections illustrated the importance of the capital goods sector to a developing economy together with the potential benefits and costs that might arise from the presence or absence of government policy measures aimed at supporting the sector. Following on from this theoretical discussion, the next chapter will aim to trace the development of state intervention in the sector over recent years. The conclusion that will be drawn is that, especially since 1988, a combination of trade liberalization, cuts in public sector procurement, and a scaling down of other industrial policy measures have resulted in a substantially reduced role for the state and increased exposure to foreign competition.

The objective of the Chapters 3 to 6 will be to assess the performance of firms in the light of these developments and thereby consider whether the empirical evidence that emerges is in line with any of the theoretical expectations outlined in earlier chapters. Specifically, the remaining discussion would wish to assess changes in static and dynamic efficiency within the sector and whether and to what degree these have been positive or negative following the scaling down of trade barriers and state intervention.

(i) Data Sources

In investigating the Brazilian non-serial capital goods industry, perhaps the single greatest challenge lies in identifying and tapping relevant sources of data, a situation that in large part results from the lack of published sources. Virtually all of the data contained in the book is unavailable outside Brazil and much of it lies unpublished or outside the public domain within that country.

The data divide into three source categories. The first category consists of primary data in the form of quantitative enterprise performance indicators which have been assembled and made available to the researcher by ABDIB, the non-serial capital goods trade association. These data are available for the sub-sectoral level and have been calculated by aggregating data supplied by individual member enterprises. The sub-sectors covered are boiler making, mechanical equipment, electrical energy equipment, railway equipment, and shipbuilding. The number of enterprises forming the sample for each sub-sector is indicated below.

The data have been obtained from a sample of 56 enterprises which represents about 80% of ABDIB membership). Over the past fifteen years the sample size has dropped slightly due to the effects of mergers between enterprises in the sample (see Chapter 6 for more details). The sample is very

TABLE 1. Sample size used for ABDIB data*

Sector	Sample size (No. of Enterprises)
Boiler making	15
Mechanical equipment	26
Electrical energy equipment	9
Railway equipment	3
Shipbuilding	3

Note: * Economic and financial indicators in Annual Reports.

Source: Personal communication from co-ordinator of ABDIB Economics Department, 9 Aug. 1995.

representative and in fact reasonably closely approaches the population, ABDIB membership representing the vast bulk of installed capacity in the non-serial capital goods sector (interview). In addition to the ABDIB data, further primary quantitative data are available from IBGE (the government statistical agency) and ABIFER (the railway equipment industry trade association).

The second category of data comprises secondary data sources. Some of these are in the form of unpublished reports and documents which have been made available to the researcher. These contain useful qualitative assessments of the sector's situation as well as occasional items of quantitative data. In addition, some published material is included. The majority of this is in the form of published reports (most undertaken by BNDES and IPEA) whose remit touched on sector activity. Some material has been extracted from published trade journals and business magazines while a minority has been obtained from the Brazilian academic literature, the most significant source in this connection being the UNICAMP/UFRJ competitiveness survey of 1993. The latter source provides a useful account of the evolution of the electrical energy equipment industry.

The third and final category of data collected consists of primary data obtained by interview. In-depth structured interviews were conducted within enterprises themselves and with individuals with strong links to the sector. Interviews undertaken outside enterprises included interviews with the head of FINAMEX, the capital goods export finance arm of BNDES, Rio de Janeiro, the head of the Economics Department at ABDIB, São Paulo, a leading sector consultant in Rio de Janeiro, and two academic specialists at the Federal University of Rio de Janeiro (UFRJ).

The enterprises selected for interview were chosen for their importance and representativeness within the non-serial capital goods sector. Three enterprises were chosen, each being of equal size ranking within its respective subsector (electrical energy equipment, mechanical equipment, and shipbuilding). Throughout the text these enterprises are referred to as 'Enterprise A' (the electrical energy equipment manufacturer), 'Enterprise B' (the mechanical equipment manufacturer), and 'Enterprise C' (the shipbuilder). By choosing enterprises of similar significance, it was hoped that comparisons and contrasts would be easier to draw across sub-sectors.

During the visits to the enterprises, interviews were conducted not only with representatives of general management but also with engineers, technicians, and shop-floor operatives. The advantages of this interview strategy are twofold. First, such a strategy ensures that one's view of the enterprise is not formed by the information supplied by one individual alone. The second advantage is that the process of change and the impact of policy can be examined for all facets of enterprise operation and a more thorough overall assessment made. All visits included lengthy tours of the production facilities which provided the opportunity to become familiar with the manufacturing operation at firsthand. Such familiarization is especially indispensable for understanding certain aspects of enterprise behaviour such as plant layout and organization and the impact of automation.

(ii) Analytical Approach

Section 1.1 pointed to the theoretical controversy that has developed concerning the impact of protection and extensive state intervention on levels of productivity within the affected sector. In particular there seems to be some debate as to whether such measures restrict productivity growth by shielding enterprises from the effects of competition and reducing the need to become efficient or whether such measures may in fact promote productivity growth, at least in the short run, by generating conditions under which capacity expansion and learning can take place.

By examining the behaviour of productivity within the various non-serial capital goods sub-sectors both before and after the policy changes, it is hoped some light can be shed on this question. Following a detailed discussion of these policy shifts in the next chapter, this is the task of Chapter 3. The first stage in this inquiry is to present the changes in productivity that have occurred over the period in question so that any important trends may be identified. The measures of productivity employed are output per employee and per employee-hour, physical output per employee, and output per unit of assets. Having achieved this objective, attempts are made to explain why the changes in productivity have occurred. In particular, the discussion attempts to establish whether, and to what extent, changes in government policy have been responsible. This will involve tracing the relationship between government procurement and overall demand, tariff levels, output and productivity, and considering the influence of changing capacity utilization throughout the period.

As well as examining these quantitative relationships for evidence, qualitative data are also employed. In particular, the results of enterprise interviews are presented in an attempt to identify the motivation, at firm level, underlying attempts to raise productivity. The impact of the *Programa Brasileira de Qualidade e Produtividade*, a government policy initiative aimed at increasing productivity throughout industry, will also be considered. Finally, and very importantly, an attempt is made to understand the strategies employed to raise productivity drawing on both qualitative enterprise-level primary data and more aggregate secondary data. Two important issues are examined in this connection, the first being new forms of plant layout (in particular, production cells) and the second, investment in new equipment.

The discussion has already pointed out that one of the primary reasons for the establishment of a capital goods sector is its ability to generate particularly high rates of technical progress—a form of dynamic efficiency—the effects of which would diffuse throughout the economy. Theoretical arguments were developed supportive of a role for the state in supporting technological development in the sector, both directly through initiatives such as support for R&D

and indirectly through public sector procurement and protection from international competition. Before 1987, the sector faced relatively high levels of public sector demand, was relatively protected, and (albeit depleted) resources were made available to support technological development in the sector through agencies such as FINEP (*Agência Especial de Financiamento dos Estudos e Projetos*).

Since 1987, trade liberalization has been accompanied by a dramatic fall in such direct measures of support. Given this changing policy background, this book attempts to ascertain the extent to which patterns of firm-level technological progress have changed both in terms of process and product technology. In particular, the book tries to establish whether this more 'liberal' economic environment has encouraged enhanced innovation or, as much of the literature would tend to suggest, tended to downplay its significance at the expense of other competitive strategies, notably those related to static efficiency.

In examining this question, Chapter 5 draws on primary data gathered at firm level as well as material made available by ABDIB, IPEA, BNDES, and the 1993 competitiveness survey. A particular focus of the investigation lies in the consideration of the role of technology transfer over this period, which has traditionally provided Brazilian enterprises with the technologies required for the production of what are particularly technologically intensive and complex types of capital good. The chapter concludes with a consideration of the incentives and obstacles enterprises currently face with respect to any moves towards greater technological self-reliance.

The role of exports has been identified in the literature as having an important relationship with the evolution of static and dynamic efficiency. In particular, it is argued that exposure to international markets through exports is capable of inducing (or indeed requires) gains in static and dynamic efficiency such as advances in process technology, product technology, or plant organization. However, much of the literature critical of state intervention in the sector, in particular that hostile to a restrictive trade policy, points to the effects of such policies in restricting the growth of exports. Chapter 4 seeks to examine if, following the trade liberalization of 1988 onwards, there has been a change in the quantity and pattern of exports.

Additionally, the chapter aims to establish the relative contribution of trade liberalization, as against those of other influences, in the sector's changing export performance. In particular, the influences of falling government procurement and access to official government credit are considered. These issues are examined using quantitative trade data for imports and export values supplied by the United Nations and quantitative and qualitative data made available by FINAMEX. In addition, much additional secondary data and firm-level primary data are also examined in the course of the chapter.

In most cases, the impact of changing exposure to the export market on efforts to increase static and dynamic efficiency is discussed in the other chapters as appropriate. However, the linkage between export performance and one facet of efficiency, quality (an item that contains elements of both dynamic and static efficiency), is so strong that this issue merits discussion in the chapter on exports. Firm-level primary data enables a detailed discussion to be undertaken concerning the motivation for strategies to improve quality, the nature of the strategies, and their results. Such data are supplemented by available secondary quantitative and qualitative data to give a broader view of the evolution of quality issues within the sector. The role of the *Programa Brasileira de Qualidade e Produtividade* is also considered.

Following this discussion, Chapter 6 examines changing patterns of concentration within the sector, in an attempt to establish whether policy changes have tended to promote a more concentrated and specialized non-serial capital goods sector or a more diversified and atomized one. The implications of the findings for the development of static and, particularly, dynamic efficiencies are set out with special attention being paid to the issues of specialization and technological capability.

The chapter also attempts to evaluate alterations in efficiency with reference to indicators of financial performance which have been made available by ABDIB, the non-serial capital goods trade association. The data allow inter-sub-sectoral comparisons to be made with regard to return on capital, profitability, liquidity, and debt among other items. Consideration of the issues enables an assessment to be made of the impact of the strategies to raise static and dynamic efficiency on the 'bottom line' and also provides an indication of the resource constraints that firms operate under and which may colour the types of efficiency gains which they pursue.

Following the conclusion of the empirical investigation, Chapter 7 attempts to summarize the most important analytical results and consider their significance and implications in terms of existing theoretical perspectives. Specifically, the validity of the theoretical expectations is assessed in the light of the evidence and suggestions made as to why certain theoretical perspectives have proved to be deficient and whether this justifies any alterations or modifications in the theory itself. This exercise is undertaken with specific reference to the case study in hand. In addition, some general conclusions are drawn regarding the impact of economic liberalization on the non-serial capital goods sector in Brazil and their implications outlined for theory and practice in other industrialized LDCs with an established or emerging advanced industrial sector.

2

The Policy Environment

Introduction

The Brazilian non-serial capital goods sector is currently the largest in the developing world after that of China and is easily the largest in Latin America. The rapid ascendancy of the sector to its current position has been associated with policies that led to extensive state intervention and a concentration on the internal market. In recent years, however, the pattern of intervention has radically altered and the sector has been faced with a less protected market in which the state has played a less significant role. As a result, substantial changes have occurred within the industry and the sector has evolved new strategies to cope with the altered environment.

This chapter will seek to examine the nature of these policy changes and thus provide the background for the empirical investigation that follows in subsequent chapters. In surveying the policy changes, the discussion covers a great quantity of material, the vast bulk of which is Brazilian in origin. In doing so, the chapter offers—for the period in question—the only comprehensive study of the evolution of government policy towards the sector in either the English or Portuguese language. For reasons of thematic unity and coherence of presentation, those aspects of government policy directly focused on export promotion and technological development in the post-1980 period are largely omitted from the current chapter, being discussed instead in Chapters 4 and 5 respectively.

In order to achieve its objectives, the chapter is organized as follows. First, the emergence of the sector is put into historical context, focusing on developments up to the Second National Development Plan (PND II) in 1974. Given the objectives of the thesis and limitations of space this section is necessarily brief and offers a summary of the main developments rather than engaging in detailed discussion. Secondly, the period of rapid growth and heavy intervention (1974–80) is discussed in rather more detail, as it was during this period that the main instruments of government support for the sector were put into place. This is followed by a discussion of the difficult policy environment of the early to mid-1980s which followed the crisis at the beginning of the decade. In the same section, evolution of policy is brought up to date with a discussion of the deregulation, trade liberalization, and fiscal constraints that have characterized the period since 1986. It is the response of the non-serial capital goods sector to the transition to the latter policy environment that forms the focus of the remainder of the book.

2.1 The Emergence of the Sector: Policy Developments up to 1974

2.1.1 FROM THE COLONIAL PERIOD TO 1950

Although the emergence of much of the Brazilian non-serial capital goods sector has been concentrated into the last forty years, it is important to recognize that the origins of the sector go back much further in time. Indeed, precursors to the industry can be traced back to the colonial period of the sixteenth, seventeenth and eighteenth centuries when a rudimentary tool-making sector emerged in São Paulo state in response to the discovery of iron ore and other important minerals (Corrêa do Lago *et al.* 1979: 6). However, much of the demand for capital goods during this period was met through imports from Europe channelled through Portugal. During the Peninsula War in 1808, the Portuguese royal family were evacuated to Brazil by the Royal Navy heralding a period in which Brazilian ports were required to be open to British vessels. As a result, Brazil became increasingly dependent on the importation of British capital goods.

Following independence in 1820, the pursuit of a more protectionist approach to trade became possible and in 1844, despite pressure from England, tariffs were raised under Alves Branco (ibid. 10). During the 1840s, the first major non-serial capital goods enterprise was established in Brazil at Ponta da Areia by the Barão da Mauá. The enterprise produced steam engines, agricultural equipment, and steam vessels. In a pattern that would become familiar throughout the sector in later years, the enterprise was highly reliant on state orders and a protective trade régime. The enterprise exists to this day as the CCN shipyard.

Through the 1860s, 1870s, and 1880s the non-serial capital goods sector began to emerge in earnest as the growth of the coffee industry and the development of the railway network provided growing demand for equipment. The sector received a further incentive from a rise in import duties during the 1890s and the operation of the Law of Similars (see Section 2.2.1 for a description). The First World War limited Brazilian access to imports of capital goods and provided further stimulus to the sector. By 1920 a modest but diversified sector had emerged producing a range of basic non-serial capital goods such as steamships, boilers, turbines, railway vehicles, urban transport vehicles, and pumps (ibid. 53). The decade up to 1920 saw the establishment in Brazil of many of the most important enterprises operating in the sector today. Of particular note were the foundation of General Electric do Brasil, Bardella (1911), Villares (1918), and Dedini (1920) (Araújo *et al.* 1991: 75). Many of the 'Brazilian'-owned enterprises were founded by recently arrived Italian and German immigrants who brought their skills and capital from Europe.

During the 1920s, the city and state of São Paulo grew rapidly, propelled by the rapidly expanding coffee industry. The non-serial capital goods sector became increasingly concentrated in this region, particularly in the industrial

TABLE 2. Number of Capital Goods Enterprises Founded, 1900–1949

Type of Capital Good	Total	Up to 1900	1900–1909	1910–1919	1920–1929	1930–1939	1940–1942	1943–1945	1946–1948	1949	Date unknown
Mechanical equipment	684	14	6	22	58	119	77	120	190	64	14
Electrical and communications equipment	269	—	2	1	9	42	31	65	88	29	2
Transport equipment	481	4	8	3	34	72	42	56	149	59	14
Subtotal	1404	18	16	26	101	233	150	241	427	152	30
Manufacturing industry as a whole	68,591	532	309	1,320	4,252	11,335	7,022	10,306	20,655	9,284	3,376

Source: IBGE—Recenseamento Geral de 1950, Série Nacional, vol. iii, tomo 1, Brasil Censo Industrial, pp. 8–9 in Corrêa do Lago et al. (1979: 86).

suburbs of São Paulo city. This period also witnessed increasing multinational investments in the sector, particularly from US corporations. Perhaps the most significant policy developments the sector had faced up to that point emerged in the 1930s as Brazil took its first determined steps along the road to comprehensive import substitution industrialization (ISI). The move towards greater self-sufficiency and a more inward-oriented trade policy were prompted by the Depression of the early 1930s in which demand for Brazil's major primary product exports—among them principally coffee—collapsed. This meant that Brazil became unable to generate sufficient foreign exchange to meet its import requirements for capital goods, leading to a growing reliance on internal supply. At the same time, the government of Getúlio Vargas, which came to power in a military coup in 1930, introduced to Brazil, in the *Estado Novo*, a corporatist state much more ideologically committed to industrial policy and extensive state intervention than any of its predecessors.

The result of these developments was an environment conducive to the accelerated expansion of the capital goods industry in general and the nonserial sector in particular (Leff 1968). Tariffs were raised and a number of important infrastructural projects begun. The period also saw the establishment of a large steel industry as part of the intensified industrialization drive. Further shelter from the pressures of international competition was offered by the Second World War. Some idea of the expansion of the capital goods industry during this period can be gauged from Table 2 which shows the growth of the number of enterprises established per time period in the various sectors of the industry.

2.1.2 FROM 1950 TO 1974

The 1950s witnessed the most concerted attempt yet to achieve industrial self-sufficiency in Brazil. From 1956 to 1961 there was a substantial acceleration in the pace of industrialization as President Juscelino Kubitschek's *Plano de Metas* (Plan of Targets) went into effect (Leff 1968). The plan prioritized key industries such as the automotive, petrochemical, and steel sectors and supported their development with subsidies, enhanced tariff protection, and subsidized credit. The Brazilian non-serial capital goods sector expanded to meet the demand from the emerging new industries yet was not itself the object of such intensive support. Although it received added protection, following the creation of the CPA's *ad-valorem* tariff in 1957, a system of multiple exchange rates and government incentives encouraged the import of certain capital goods (Motta *et al.* 1994: 8). However, it is worth noting the importance of incentives to attract foreign capital into the sector which, taken together with the buoyant domestic market, encouraged the establishment of subsidiaries of major international (particularly European) producers of capital goods. During this period, for example, Indústrias Romi, Mecânica Pesada, Voith, and Siemens commenced operation in Brazil (ibid. 9). Some of these developments took place under the auspices of GEIMAPE (*Grupo Executivo da Indústria*

Mecânica Pesada), a government-sponsored organization established in 1959 to assist with the development of heavy industry. GEIMAPE played an important role in facilitating injections of capital into the industry through organized share subscriptions by affiliated financial institutions.

In addition it was able to provide clearance for duty-free imports of essential equipment and raw materials for the sector (Erber 1978: 241). GEIMAPE provided a forum for a group of organizations whose activities were later to prove vital in the development of Brazilian non-serial capital goods production, in particular, the BNDE (*Banco Nacional de Desenvolvimento Economico*), the state-owned national economic development bank, CACEX (*Carteira do Comércio Exterior*), a state organization that administered the non-tariff controls on imports (particularly the Law of Similars), the Banco do Brasil (the largest state-owned commercial bank), and ABDIB (*Associação Brasileira para o Desenvolvimento das Indústrias de Base*), the non-serial capital goods trade association whose data is used extensively in later chapters.

The rapid industrial expansion of the Kubitschek period was not sustained into the early 1960s as growth faltered and inflation mounted (Baer 1989). Growing economic difficulties and political division helped to prompt a military coup in 1964 in which President João Goulart was overthrown. The military government under General Castelo Branco undertook a substantial reform of Brazil's industrial and trade policy with the objective of re-orienting the economy towards greater integration into the international economy in the belief that the original import substitution model had run its course. The model of industrialization that emerged between 1964 and 1974—sometimes termed 'Post-ISI'—had important implications for the development of the Brazilian non-serial capital goods sector.

In terms of protection, the new régime sought to lower tariffs for a wide variety of industrial products during the period following 1964. However, there was little change in the levels of protection accorded to the non-serial capital goods sector, which had, in any case, been among the least protected in Brazilian industry (Corrêa do Lago *et al.* 1979: 125). Despite this, there were important institutional developments which assisted the development of the sector. In 1964, the *Comissão de Desenvolvimento Indústrial* or CDI was established to intensify the promotion of industry, uniting the various executive groups (one of which was GEIMAPE). The main object of the CDI was to stimulate increased investment within industry (ibid. 125).

In the same year FINAME (*Agência Especial de Financiamento Industrial*) was founded by the Brazilian state as part of the BNDE. The role of FINAME was to offer subsidized credit terms to domestic purchasers of Brazilian-made capital goods. In later years, as following chapters will demonstrate, FINAME would play a crucial role in expanding market opportunities in domestic and, eventually, the foreign markets. This period also saw the establishment of FINEP (*Financiadora de Estudos e Projetos*), an agency which provided financial support for industrial research and development.

At the same time, the multiple exchange rate system underwent substantial reform bringing the rate for the importation of capital goods more into line with that for financial transactions.

As the 1960s progressed, growth began to recover and there was an expansion in the number of enterprises in the sector, particularly those that were subsidiaries of TNCs. From 1968 to 1973 Brazil underwent an unprecedented economic expansion which has frequently been termed the 'Brazilian Economic Miracle'. Throughout this period there was a considerable expansion in the production of non-serial capital goods. However, the sector did not grow as fast as the lead sectors, most particularly consumer durables which, as well as supplying a burgeoning domestic market, were engaged in an impressive drive to expand exports, aided by a programme of mini-devaluations. Protection of the sector remained lower than the industry average and many capital goods without locally produced equivalents entered Brazil without any duties being paid under special import programmes.

However, two crucial stimuli to the sector emerged from developments in government policy. The first was the initiation of large infrastructural projects, particularly in the power-generation sector as the technocratic military government committed itself to modernization. The second was the creation of the FINAME special programme at the end of 1971 which provided longer-term finance for larger-scale equipment for a period of up to eight years. Both these policies can be viewed as important precursors to the more specific policies that emerged to aid the sector following 1973. It is to this period that the discussion now turns.

2.2 Concerted Intervention and Rapid Expansion, 1974–1980

Chapter 1 advanced a number of theoretical arguments supportive of particular forms of state intervention in the capital goods sector of a developing country. Specifically, it was proposed that cases existed for the enhanced protection of the capital goods sector, the development of internal markets through government procurement, support for research and development, regulation of technology transfer, the co-ordination and regulation of the development of new industrial capacity (capacity licensing), and the support of user–producer interaction. During the second half of the 1970s, the Brazilian state engaged in all of these forms of intervention and established a policy environment which proved favourable to the rapid expansion of the non-serial capital goods sector. The remainder of this section describes the development of these policies along with a brief overview of sector performance in this period.

The enhanced support which the capital goods sector received from 1974 onwards was the direct result of the implementation of the Second National Development Plan (PND II). The plan emerged in response to the changed macroeconomic circumstances that followed the OPEC oil price rise in 1973. Faced with a rising import bill for oil—a product that Brazil did not produce at that time—and contracting international export markets, Brazil was faced with growing balance of payments problems and a more severe foreign exchange constraint. Rather than undergoing a phase of stabilization which would have involved fiscal contraction and induced recession, the decision was made to maintain growth and overcome the foreign exchange constraint through a programme of 'deepening' the process of import substitution and a connected series of infrastructural projects. At the same time, attempts were to be made to increase technological self-sufficiency. Any shortfalls on the current account of the balance of payments that emerged in the early stages of this programme would be addressed through increased borrowing on international capital markets.

The process of deepening import substitution gave top priority to the production of intermediate and capital goods (Erber 1986: 228). As such, the non-serial capital goods sector was in an especially favourable position: not only was it itself the object of incentives; so were its principal customers in the process industries and national power and transport utilities. Given the quantity and variety of the new policies that appeared, it is appropriate to break up the discussion into a consideration of separate areas of policy, the first being trade policy.

2.2.1 TRADE POLICY AND THE NON-SERIAL CAPITAL GOODS SECTOR, 1974–1980

As Chapter 1 demonstrated, the strengthening of protection can be theoretically justified as a means of promoting development of an indigenous capital goods sector. However, up until 1974 the non-serial capital goods sector had not in general received especially favourable treatment with respect to trade policy. Indeed, an emphasis was placed on the easy and cheap availability of imported capital goods in order to facilitate efficient and rapid expansion of the consumer durable sectors prioritized under the previous import substitution régime. In many cases, especially where no national similar was available, imported capital goods entered Brazil without payment of duty or at specially reduced rates under special programmes termed *isenções* (exemptions).

The existence of a large number of exemptions led to a substantial divergence between the nominal and realized tariffs. While nominal tariffs (the official tariff rate in percentage terms applying to a particular product line) might remain high, the realized tariff (the actual duty collected as a percentage of the imported product's value) was often much lower as a result of the operation of exemptions. In some cases tariff redundancy developed as realized tariffs fell to zero. From 1974 onwards there was a substantial raising of nominal tariff protection for many non-serial capital goods sectors. At the same time, the number of items exempted from payment of duty fell. These two developments gave rise to a notable increase in realized tariffs as is demonstrated in Table 3. In addition to tariffs, federal and state taxes (IPI and ICM) were levied on the tariff plus the CIF (carriage, insurance, and freight) value

TABLE 3. Nominal and Realized Tariffs for Selected Capital Goods Sub-sectors, 1974–1978

Tariff code	Product group	Nominal tariff (%)		Realized tariff (%)	
		1972	1978	1972	1978
84	Machinery	34.4	41.6	7.2	13.6
85	Electrical equipment	48.5	68.1	12.2	19.5
86	Railway equipment	28.5	34.9	0.3	0.7
89	Shipbuilding	7.8	7.0	0.08	0.1
—	All capital goods	—	—	9.5	13.5
—	All imports	—	—	9.9	8.1

Source: Tyler (1981: 37).

of capital goods imports though the rates of these taxes (roughly between 7 and 10%) did not vary much during the 1970s (Tyler 1981: 38).

More important than the developments mentioned above were changes in the level of non-tariff barriers (NTBs). As later sections will demonstrate, it is the NTBs that came to provide the most powerful protection to the non-serial capital goods sector. The proliferation and intensification of NTB protection of the sector involved a number of measures, many of which were derived from the twin peculiarities of the Brazilian capital goods industry at the time. First was its reliance on orders from the public sector, particularly from large state steel and power enterprises. Second was the fact that the sector was (and continues to be) characterized by lengthy lead times and production cycles which, in an underdeveloped and inflation-sensitive private capital market, have led to the state (principally through FINAME) being an important supplier of credit with which to finance domestic and foreign sales.

The expansion of government procurement of non-serial capital goods was marked during the latter half of the 1970s and was accompanied by two developments with important implications for the rise in NTB protection of the sector. The first was a more rigorous and intensive application of the Law of Similars when the import of capital goods for public sector entities was being considered (Tadini 1993: 6). The Law of Similars has attracted considerable attention in the literature on Brazilian trade and industrialization and it is worth taking the time to examine its meaning and application as there has been a tendency to exaggerate its importance and characterize it as an insuperable barrier to import penetration when the reality has been rather more complex.

The origins of The Law of Similars can be traced to the nineteenth century when measures were introduced to step up protection of domestic industry following independence (Motta et al. 1994: 75). In its simplest form, the Law prohibited or restricted the importation of goods for which there were adequate domestic substitutes. In practice the Law tended to be applied in a way which employed its tests of similarity to assess eligibility for fiscal benefits or duty exemptions rather than its clauses that prohibited imports altogether. The Law was applied in a variety of contexts up until the mid-1970s that affected the non-serial capital goods sector. Principally, capital goods which were to be imported without duty under *insenções* were subject to a test of similarity. Similar tests applied to purchases by or involving public sector entities, CDI projects, or BEFIEX schemes.

The latter schemes were intended to develop export industries and offered reduced or zero rates of duty on imported inputs (drawback). However, the concept of what constituted a similar and thus was prohibited from duty-free import was always a matter of debate and involved a process of consultation between CACEX (the agency administering the law), the relevant trade association (usually ABDIB), and the potential importer. The examination of similarity involved an assessment on several levels of whether any domestic product on offer matched the import. The main criteria examined were technical performance characteristics, price, and delivery times (Tyler 1981: 43). However, in practice, the assessment has always tended to be coloured by the lobbying power and bargaining skills of the various parties involved with the result that the application of the Law has rarely been consistent (see Section 2.3.1). This has meant that the effects of the Law varied through time up until its effective death in 1990. In the case of the PND II in 1974, however, the government, through its pressure on CACEX, was able to impose more restrictive interpretations of the law as far as duty-free imports for CDI and FINAME-financed projects were concerned. At the same time, and very significantly for the non-serial capital goods sector, the Law was extended to cover procurements of capital goods by the public sector (Tyler 1981: 40). This meant that any capital goods imports planned by public enterprises were required to be compared against the domestic alternatives on offer. In addition, government departments and public enterprises were required to submit an annual foreign exchange and import budget to the Ministry of Finance, further restricting the ability of the public sector to import capital goods.

The second major development that affected and raised NTB protection of the sector during this period was the imposition of local content requirements for equipment producers benefiting from CDI fiscal incentives, official financing (FINAME), or orders from publicly financed infrastructure projects. In 1975, the requirement varied between 55 and 82% depending on the particular forms of capital goods involved. However, by 1978 the requirements had been raised and harmonized to 85% and reached 90% by the end of the decade (Motta *et al.* 1994: 26). The growing role of official financing lent great weight to this development.

According to Tyler (1981), the most complex aspect of the NTB protection offered to the sector derived from CDI projects specifically aimed at raising capacity in prioritized sectors which of course included capital goods.

Once a project of investment by the CDI had been approved for an enterprise, it was then able to enjoy a reduction in import duties on imported inputs, provided, of course, that the similarity test had been passed. In addition, the enterprise would be exempt from participation in the import deposit scheme. This scheme, established in 1975, directed that all importers had to place deposits of foreign exchange equal to 100% of the FOB (free on board) value of imports with the *Banco Central* (Central Bank) for one year in an attempt to conserve and control the supply of foreign exchange (Tyler 1981: 40, Oliveira 1993: 11). The enterprise was also able to purchase domestically produced capital goods without payment of the IPI and ICM taxes. Finally, and very significantly, fiscal subsidies were granted for the purchase of domestically produced capital goods along with an accelerated depreciation allowance (Tyler 1981: 41).

Unlike tariff barriers, it is often difficult to measure directly the relative intensity of non-tariff barriers. Given the importance of non-tariff barriers in the protective structure surrounding the non-serial capital goods sectors, the accurate capturing and, if possible, quantification of their intensity would be highly desirable. In practice, however, this is a problematic exercise due to their sometimes deliberate opacity. However, the impact of NTBs through their effect on the overall structure of protection makes itself felt in the value of the effective rate of protection (ERP).The use of ERP analysis enables a broad assessment to be made regarding the impact of trade policy on the intensity of protection enjoyed by a sector. Unlike the nominal rate of protection, which indicates only the extent to which the domestic price of the imported good exceeds what it would have been in the absence of the tariff (i.e. the value of the *ad-valorem* tariff itself), the ERP also considers the effects of tariffs on inputs used by the protected domestic industry and the price-raising effects on inputs and final output facilitated by NTBs.

In essence, the ERP measure provides an indication of the extent to which the structure of protection allows total value added for any particular product produced in a country to exceed that prevalent internationally. The ERP may be calculated by employing either of the formulae below (Weiss 1988: 182).

$$(2.1) \qquad ERP_i = \frac{VADP_i - VAWP_i}{VAWP_i}$$

where $VADP_i$ is value added at domestic prices for product i and $VAWP_i$ is value added at world prices for product i.

$$(2.2) \qquad ERP_i = \frac{t_i - \Sigma a_{ji} t_j}{1 - \Sigma a_{ji}}$$

where t_i and t_j are the tariffs or tariff equivalents for product i and input j respectively and a_{ji} is the number of units of j required per unit of product i under free trade.

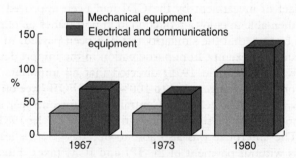

CHART 1. Effective Protection of the Capital Goods Sector, 1967–1980
Source: 1967 data: Fishlow (1975); 1973 data: Tyler (1976); 1980 data: Tyler (1983), all reproduced in Pinheiro and Almeida (1994: 12).

Effective protection will tend to be greater, the higher the degree of tariff and non-tariff protection of final output and the lower the tariff and non-tariff protection on inputs.

In the case of the Brazilian non-serial capital goods sector, the overall effect of the changes in tariff and non-tariff measures in the 1967–80 period was to increase substantially the effective protection offered to the sector as Chart 1 makes clear using the IBGE's (Brazilian Government Statistical Service) 'mechanical equipment' and 'electrical equipment' categories of capital good. Capital goods exports were also subject to incentives during this period. Two lines of credit were provided to enterprises at subsidized interest rates. The first, offered by the *Banco Central*, financed the working capital of export-producing enterprises for up to a year at an interest rate of between 8 and 12%. The second, provided by CACEX, provided long-term suppliers' credit for up to 85% of the FOB value of the exports for a period between five and ten years at an interest rate of between 7 and 8.5% annually (Tyler 1981: 51). This facility was termed FINEX (*Fundo de Financiamento de Exportação*). During this period, the export incentives on offer had to overcome the effects of an overvalued (in the region of 25–35%), though in real terms, relatively stable cruzeiro (ibid. 34).

2.2.2 GOVERNMENT PROCUREMENT, 1974–1980

Perhaps the single most important stimulus to development and expansion of the Brazilian non-serial capital goods sector during this period was the rise in orders from the public sector. Once again, Chapter 1 suggested that a role existed for the state as a procurer of capital goods in that an expansion of public sector orders, in leading to a larger domestic market, could promote economies of scale, increased specialization, and learning. As the previous section illustrated, the sector was highly reliant on such orders during the period. By 1977 the state purchased 100% of the sector's output of electrical

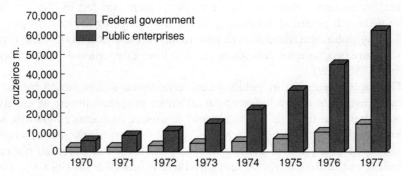

CHART 2. Estimate of Public Sector Demand for Capital Goods, 1970–1977
Source: Corrêa do Lago *et al.* (1979: 232).

energy equipment, 70% of steel equipment production, 100% of railway equipment, and 80% of petrochemical equipment output (Thorstensen 1980).

The biggest source of the increase of demand for non-serial capital goods arose from massive growth in public sector infrastructure projects. These were concentrated in electricity generation and distribution, energy (particularly oil refining, distribution, and petrochemicals), basic industries, and transport (Shapiro 1992: 18). Among the more significant of the projects were the Itaipú and Tucaraí hydro-electric schemes, the third stage of the flat-rolled steel mills expansion programme at CSN, COSIPA, and USIMINAS, the Ferrovia de Aço railway, and the nuclear energy programme (Angra II and III stations) (Tadini 1993: 7).

According to Motta, Knaack de Souza, and Paim (1994: 21) such public sector investments were the decisive factor that lay behind the rapid expansion of the sector during this period. Taken together with the increasingly stringent conditions that attached to the public sector import of capital goods (in particular, the more rigid application of the Law of Similars), the expansion of infrastructural investment had the effect not only of raising sector output but also reducing the ratio of imports to domestic production from 0.7 to 0.5 between 1975 and 1980 (Shapiro 1992: 19). There was also a rise in terms of local content in the key public sector investment projects. For example, this had stood at only 30% during the second stage of the flat-rolled steel expansion programme. By the third stage local content stood at 75% (Tadini 1993: 7). Pre-1975, the local content of turbines, generators, and transformers used in the hydro-electric programme was 60% on average. During the second half of the 1970s this had risen to 90% (ibid. 7). The rapidly rising public sector demand generated during the initial phases of the PNDII plan is illustrated in Chart 2.

From 1977 onwards, rising inflation and an increasingly serious foreign exchange constraint forced a reduction in the announcement of new public sector investments. However, adverse effects were not felt by the sector as there were still plentiful orders originating from ongoing investment projects and many public enterprises were able to sustain and accelerate their capital expenditure programmes through borrowing from international capital markets (Erber 1986: 229).

The rapid expansion in public sector orders was accompanied by an important institutional development. In an effort to spread orders as evenly as possible between firms in the sector and to ensure its balanced growth, special centres were established, known as *Núcleos de Articulação com a Indústria*, which acted as a point of contact between the state and potential domestic suppliers and formed a type of user–producer forum (Tadini 1993: 6). These centres proved crucial in the shaping of the growing capacity that was emerging in the non-serial capital goods sector. Through the co-ordinated allocation of orders and dialogue with the industry, the state was able to determine which firms were able to expand and develop their facilities to produce certain categories of equipment to meet new and expanded demand. In this sense, an informal form of capacity licensing developed. One significant criticism that could be levelled at procurement policy as it developed during this period was that, in an effort to spread orders as widely as possible, the state encouraged an industrial structure that was insufficiently concentrated and firms that were excessively diversified. This is an important theme and will be addressed in more detail in Chapter 6.

2.2.3 GOVERNMENT POLICY AND TECHNOLOGICAL DEVELOPMENT, 1974–1980

The previous chapter highlighted a number of potential roles for the state in supporting technological development in capital goods enterprises. In particular, it was suggested that theoretical justifications could be provided for R&D subsidies and the regulation of technology transfer. During the latter half of the 1970s, the Brazilian state intensified its technology policy in a way that incorporated both of these theoretical propositions into policy reality with the capital goods industry as a special focus.

The foundation of this intensified policy activity was the Second Brazilian Scientific and Technological Development Plan (PBDCT II) which with the accompanying PND II began to operate from 1975 onwards. Increased resources from the federal government enabled FINEP to substantially increase its expenditure on grants for enterprise R&D projects. The capital goods sector benefited especially: most of the new projects measured either in quantity or total value terms were directed at the sector (Corrêa do Lago *et al.* 1979: 444). Technical as well as financial support was made available to enterprises in the non-serial capital goods sector.

The key areas of technological development encouraged were implementation of quality control systems, the expansion of product and process R&D, and the establishment of technological research centres with relevance to

TABLE 4. Quantity and Value of FINEP Projects by Sector, 1973–1977

Sector	Number of projects	Value (1977 cruzeiros 000)
Electrical and electronic equipment	30	123,050
Mechanical and transport equipment	48	244,093
Chemical and petrochemicals	12	59,801
Steel	12	100,092
Non-ferrous metals	8	17,384
Total	110	544,420

Source: Corrêa do Lago et al. (1979: 445).

enterprise activities (ibid. 444). In order to qualify for FINEP support, however, firms had already to possess some local technological capability (Porteous 1986: 89). Some idea of the number of projects, the targeted sectors, and their value is given in Table 4.

In 1978 FINEP reached an accord with FINAME providing subsidized finance at 2–4% per annum for firms engaging in specified levels of R&D. FINEP also concluded agreements with publicly owned mining and steel enterprises, undertaking to support technological development projects whose effects were soon felt in the non-serial capital goods sector (Corrêa do Lago et al. 1979: 412).

The mid to late 1970s also saw the Brazilian state become more active in its regulation of technology transfer agreements between domestic and foreign enterprises. Before technology transfers were able to take place, contracts had to be screened by INPI (*Instituto Nacional de Propriedade Industrial*), a federal agency that supervised industrial patents and intellectual property. According to Erber (1978: 316), the conditions under which technology transfer could take place were tightened and all contracts were required to be disclosed in full. In order for the contract to receive approval, the purchaser of foreign technology had to demonstrate that equivalent technology was not available locally. In addition the potential purchaser had to implement an approved programme of training of its technical staff as well as submit a detailed schedule for the absorption of the new technology (ibid. 317).

2.2.4 FISCAL INCENTIVES, SUBSIDIZED CREDIT, AND SUB-SECTORAL POLICIES, 1974–1980

Section 2.2.1 indicated that fiscal incentives acted as a form of non-tariff protection for capital goods during the 1970s. Such incentives took the form of exemptions of capital goods from the IPI and ICM taxes: essentially this meant that capital goods sales to domestic customers were afforded the same indirect tax treatment as were exports. This measure was introduced under Decree Law 1335 in 1975 (Tyler 1981: 47). In addition to the zero IPI tax rating of capital goods sales, any IPI taxes paid for inputs during production were credited to the enterprise. The effect of these policies was the creation of a *de facto* fiscal subsidy. During 1975 the rate of subsidy was estimated to be 19.4% for electrical energy equipment, 21% for industrial machinery, 23.5% for shipbuilding, and 15.5% for railway and aircraft equipment (ibid. 39).

These fiscal subsidies were not automatically awarded, however. They were subject to approval by both the CDI and the Ministry of Finance and were generally used to support CDI industrial expansion projects. In addition, the Ministry of Finance employed the Decree Law to subsidize the production of particular capital goods. In order to receive subsidies the capital goods were required to be of a sufficient level of 'sophistication' and had to have been produced in Brazil for a relatively short period of time (ibid. 48). Both these criteria tended to favour the emerging non-serial capital goods sector whose products tended to be more technologically complex and of more recent vintage than those of the serial capital goods sector.

An important factor in the expanding domestic sales of the capital goods industry in general and the non-serial sector in particular was the growing role of FINAME (ABDIB 1979). This agency, a division of the development bank BNDE, had been established in the 1960s to provide subsidized credit to buyers and sellers of capital goods. The objective was twofold: to aid the expansion of industrial capacity and the growth of the domestic capital goods sector. Following the introduction of the Special Programme in 1971, the activities of FINAME became increasingly directed at supporting the non-serial capital goods sector. The Special Programme, in providing subsidized buyer and supplier credit lines of between five to ten years, was vital to the internal competitiveness of many enterprises as they could not hope to obtain internationally competitive long-term financing on the domestic capital market. Such credit is vital to the producer of non-serial capital goods as there are long lead times with substantial working capital financing requirements and expensive products that only recoup capital costs after a number of years.

The expansion in FINAME financing operations during the 1970s was impressive. From 7,953 m. cruzeiros in 1973, the total value of approved lendings had risen to 112,580 m. cruzeiros in 1978 at constant 1978 prices (Corrêa do Lago *et al.* 1979: 392). Over the same period, the special programme came to account for about 90% of such approvals (ibid. 398). The rise in credit facilities made available to the sector was accompanied by an initiative to inject additional capital. A subsidiary of the BNDE, EMBRAMEC, was established to take equity stakes in the capital goods industry. By 1978, nine enterprises in the sector had attracted stakes and the capital injected amounted to 27.5% of EMBRAMEC's total disbursements (ibid. 396).

In addition to the policies mentioned above, which were common to the whole of the non-serial capital goods sector, certain measures were taken to support individual sub-sectors. The most notable of these were directed at the shipbuilding and railway equipment industries. The shipbuilding industry had enjoyed special treatment since 1958 when Law 3381 created the *Fundo da Marinha Mercante* or AFRMM (merchant marine fund) and the *Taxa de Renovação da Marinha Mercante* (merchant marine renewal tax). The tax, which was levied on shipments through ports, provided resources for the fund which was aimed at the promotion and expansion of the domestic shipbuilding industry (Borges and Da Silva 1993: 47). GEICON—the executive group for shipbuilding—was established in 1958 and, operating alongside the merchant marine national superintendency SUNAMAN, supervised disbursement of resources from the fund. Following the start of the PND II in 1974, SUNAMAN became a very powerful agency, dispensing grants for shipping lines, financing shipyards, supervising construction, and operating as a liaison between customers and suppliers (Ferraz 1984: 85). During the 1970s SUNAMAN, in conjunction with Petrobrás, the state-owned oil and petrochemical monopoly, and Companhia Vale do Rio Doce, the state-owned mining group, played a critical role in the establishment of the capacity to produce large oil tankers and bulk ore carriers (interviews).

The railway equipment sub-sector was also the object of special initiatives. Up until the PND II, the Brazilian railway equipment industry had produced less sophisticated varieties of equipment—essentially wagons, passenger coaches, and track—and, with one (foreign-owned) exception, did not have the capability to produce more technologically demanding items such as diesel electric locomotives and subway trains. In an effort to upgrade Brazilian industrial capacity in these areas, the *Comissão de Locomotivas* (Locomotives Commission) was founded in 1975 (Corrêa do Lago *et al.* 1979: 410). The Commission co-ordinated the acquisition of locomotives by the publicly owned railways, encouraged domestic capacity expansion, and acted as a point of contact and negotiation between customers and suppliers.

For the non-serial capital goods sector as a whole, the 1970s were a decade of unprecedented expansion. Output and capacity rose in the sector while reliance on imports fell substantially (see Chart 3). By 1980 total output had reached US$ 9,602.5 m. (in US$ 1990 terms), a more than sevenfold increase since 1970 and a level which the sector has yet to surpass. The sector had also begun to achieve some success in export markets. In 1970 total exports stood at US$ 10 m.: by 1980 they had reached US$ 338 m. (US$ current) (ABDIB 1991: 30).

The 1980s and, particularly, the 1990s were to prove much more challenging for the sector as the policy environment underwent substantial changes. It is the reaction of the sector to these changes which, of course, forms the focus of this book. The remainder of this chapter traces developments of policy from 1980 up to the present, examining some of the same areas of policy

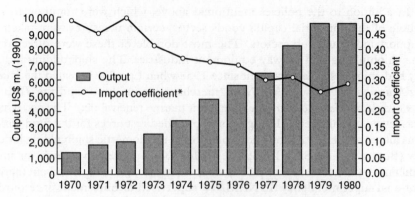

CHART 3. Output of Non-serial Capital Goods and Reliance on Imports, 1970–1980

Note: * Total imports of non-serial capital goods as a proportion of total domestic demand.

Source: Tadini (1993: 8); ABDIB (1991: 29).

employed in the previous section; namely, trade policy, government procurement, and fiscal, credit, and sub-sectoral policies.

2.3 Protection, Contraction, and Liberalization: Government Policy and the Non-serial Capital Goods Sector since 1980

By the beginning of the 1980s it had become apparent that the model of growth contained in the Second National Development Plan could no longer be sustained. Rising debt obligations to international creditors, a deteriorating position on the trade account, and a tightening foreign exchange constraint had characterized the late 1970s. Following the tripling of the oil price in 1979 the current account moved further into deficit. By 1980 the deficit accumulated since 1979 amounted to US$ 23 bn. and external debt rose by a further US$ 10 bn. (Erber and Vermulm 1993: 16). A currency devaluation of 30% in 1979 failed to ease pressure on the trade account. Inflation, too, was becoming an increasingly serious problem and had passed 100% during 1980.

With high international interest rates and increasingly shaky investor confidence, the debt with growth strategy was no longer feasible. Instead the Brazilian authorities were obliged by the circumstances of stabilization to engage in a programme of orthodox adjustment. This involved the operation of a tight monetary policy with high interest rates and other measures to reduce liquidity. At the same time, there was considerable fiscal contraction, concentrated in public salary cuts and sharp reductions in public enterprise investment expenditures (ibid. 17). Accompanying these macroeconomic policies to correct the trade deficit were efforts to restrict imports through higher tariffs and a proliferation of non-tariff barriers. These developments in the early 1980s provide the background to the policy changes that affected the non-serial capital goods sector up to 1987. The general policy environment during this period was of contraction in demand from both the private and, particularly, public sectors accompanied by confused, though generally more restrictive, trade polices and an industrial policy apparatus in almost total disarray.

From about 1987 onwards there has been a distinct change in direction, prompted initially by the move to civilian rule and the respite offered by the return to growth following the adjustment crisis. The policy picture that has emerged has been rather more coherent with determined and generally well-executed attempts to liberalize trade and reduce the role of the state in the economy, although the latter has been accompanied by intensified contractions in public sector capital investment.

The remainder of this section examines this changing policy environment, starting with trade policy in Section 2.3.1. In discussing trade policy, tariff and non-tariff barriers to imports are examined in some detail. In addition, the role of the state in promoting exports is briefly considered. A more thorough treatment is given in Chapter 4. Next, in Section 2.3.2 the evolution of government procurement is examined and the behaviour of private sector fixed capital investment is briefly considered. Finally, Section 2.3.3 discusses the evolution of fiscal subsidies, incentives, and sectoral policies. Thus the remainder of this chapter provides a comprehensive policy overview with the objective of depicting the major shifts in policy that will be argued to have had an impact on sector performance. For the purposes of clear and coherent presentation of the impact of certain policies on specific aspects of firm behaviour (specifically export promotion, quality, and technology policies), it is necessary to leave discussion of the policies until the appropriate chapters on sector performance. This will permit the specificities of these policies to be laid alongside their impacts.

2.3.1 TRADE POLICY AND THE NON-SERIAL CAPITAL GOODS SECTOR, 1980–1994

The evolution of Brazilian trade policy since 1980 with regard to non-serial capital goods is a major research topic in its own right and has received relatively little attention in the Portuguese language literature and none in the English. Given that the next five chapters argue that changes in trade policy have had a substantial impact on sector performance in terms of static and dynamic efficiency, it seems appropriate to discuss its development in some detail. In order to achieve this objective, the remainder of this section is divided into two sub-sections, the first of which examines the evolution of tariff barriers and the effective rate of protection. This section also highlights the political and economic context in which trade liberalization has taken place. The second and final sub-section examines changes in non-tariff barriers (NTBs) over the period.

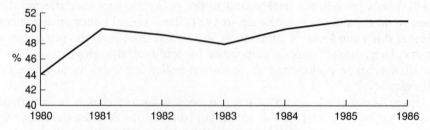

CHART 4. Brazil's Simple Average Tariff Rate, 1980–1986
Source: CTT, reproduced in GATT (1993: 104).

(i) Tariff Barriers

The period since 1980 has witnessed very substantial changes in the intensity of nominal tariff protection afforded to the non-serial capital goods sector. The changes that occurred may be divided into two broad periods, each of which will be examined in turn. The first, which lasted from 1980 to 1987, can be characterized as a period of high tariff protection for the sector as policymakers attempted to stem the flow of imports and correct the trade deficit. The second, which has lasted from 1987 to the end of the study period (1995), may be divided into two sub-periods. The first, which lasted from 1987 to 1990, essentially represents a phase of cautious reform and gradual trade liberalization under President José Sarney's first civilian government. The second, from 1990 to the present, consists of radical trade reform and rapid scaling down of nominal tariff protection afforded to the sector as two interconnected policies—the *Abertura Comercial* (literally 'commercial opening') and MERCOSUL (a free trade area comprising Brazil, Argentina, Paraguay, and Uruguay)—took effect.

Policy-makers' attempts to achieve external equilibrium in the early 1980s led to the retention and, in some cases, the escalation of the high levels of tariff protection afforded to Brazilian industry as a whole (see Chart 4). Considerations of the efficiency of the tariff structure and the effects upon industrial performance were of secondary importance. According to Pinheiro and Almeida (1994: 2) and BNDES (1990*b*), the period between 1981 and 1987 was one in which commercial policy was entirely subordinated to the demands of macroeconomic objectives, in particular the overcoming of the exchange rate and balance of trade crises.

For the non-serial capital goods sector, the trends in nominal tariff protection during this period turn out to be broadly similar. In order to examine the evolution of sector protection with a degree of disaggregation, specific sub-sectors of the non-serial capital goods sector are considered, namely, equipment for the generation and distribution of electrical energy (composed of generators, turbines, transformers, and transmission equipment), mechanical equipment (composed of boilers and metal vessels, mechanical handling

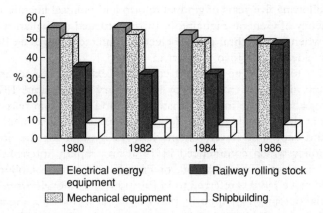

CHART 5. Nominal Average Tariff Protection, Non-serial Capital Goods, 1980–1986

Source: Calculated from *Departamento de Comércio Exterior* (1980–9). Number of tariff lines per sub-sector: electrical 86, mechanical 64, rail 5, ships 7.

equipment, steel-making equipment, and mineral extraction equipment), railway rolling stock, and shipbuilding. The levels of nominal protection afforded to these sectors during the first half of the 1980s are presented in Chart 5.

Thus protection for the sector in nominal terms appeared, with the exception of the shipbuilding industry (for reasons explained in Section 2.3.3), to be both very substantial and stable. However, it is important to bear in mind the limitations of nominal average protection as a measure of protection afforded to any industry. First, and most important, it fails to take into consideration the effect of non-tariff barriers which, as was argued earlier in this chapter (and as will be argued again), played a more substantial role in the protection of the sector. Secondly, being an average measure, the effects of intra-sectoral variations in tariff protection are masked. Compared to some other sectors within the Brazilian industrial economy, tariff dispersion within non-serial capital goods sub-sectors was not especially excessive yet marked variations did exist. For example, in 1980 tariffs within the electrical energy equipment sub-sector ranged from 35.25% for turbines to 59.86% for transformers and electrical transmission equipment while for 1986 the equivalent figures were 34% and 59.94% (calculated from *Departamento de Comércio Exterior* 1980–9).

From 1984 onwards, the Brazilian economy began to recover, following the success of the stabilization programme in achieving a trade surplus and a degree of exchange rate stability. By the end of 1984 the trade surplus had reached US\$ 13 bn. and the growth rate of imports had fallen to virtually zero in real terms. Thus pressure to contain the growth of imports through both tariff and non-tariff measures fell. The more favourable macroeconomic environment emerged at a time when Brazil was facing enormous political change. Following five years of gradual reform and political liberalization under the presidency of General Figueiredo, Brazil returned to civilian rule in January 1985 when an electoral college elected Tancredo Neves as Brazil's first civilian President since João Goulart in 1964.

The move to civilian government caused an extensive reassessment of the development ideologies embraced by the military régime since 1974 and the ultimate rejection of the import substitution model that had reasserted itself by default at the beginning of the decade as Brazil sought to stabilize. These political and economic developments laid the ground for the liberalization of trade policy which commenced in 1988 and rapidly intensified in 1990 following the election by plebiscite of President Fernando Collor de Melo. The period since 1990 is referred to in Portuguese as the '*Abertura Comercial*' (commercial opening), an apposite play on the term *Abertura*, the name given to the earlier period of political liberalization under General Figueiredo.

For the non-serial capital goods sector, an immediate effect of the first cautious phase of the more liberal trade policies implemented by the Sarney government in 1988 was a reduction in nominal tariff protection. Between 1987 and 1989 nominal average tariff protection for electrical energy equipment fell from 53.02% to 41.5%, for mechanical equipment from 46.92% to 41.24%, while for railway rolling stock there was a slight fall from 45.37% to 45%. An exception to this rule was shipbuilding where nominal tariff protection was raised from 7.25% to 32.02%, an anomaly that will be examined in Section 2.3.3 (calculated from *Departamento de Comércio Exterior* 1980–9). Using the broader industrial categories employed by the Brazilian government statistical service (IBGE), a similar trend may be observed. For the category 'mechanical equipment', nominal average protection fell from 49.2% in early 1988 to 44.9% in 1989 (Pinheiro and de Almeida 1994: 6). For the categories 'electrical and communications equipment' and 'transport equipment' the equivalent figures were 65.7% to 50.2% and 74.4% to 47.3% respectively (ibid. 6).

Across industry more generally, the effect of the 1988 reforms was to simplify the tariff system, reduce tariff dispersion, and lower the average tariff on imports of manufactured articles (Tadini 1993: 13). However, by 1989, even once the reforms had been implemented, Brazil's tariffs remained very high by international standards (Oliveira 1993: 13). The following five years would see a rapid transformation of this situation as the effects of the *Abertura Comercial* made themselves felt and Brazil entered negotiations that led to the establishment of MERCOSUL.

Following the coming to power of Fernando Collor de Melo in 1990, Brazil embarked upon a programme of trade liberalization quite unparalleled in its commercial history and certainly much more far-reaching than the earlier phase of trade liberalization associated with the late 1960s 'Post-ISI Model'. In making a decisive break from the protective trade régime, there was a recognition in the new administration that its costs in terms of loss of dynamic efficiency and international competitiveness had become far too high (Fritsch

TABLE 5. Planned Tariff Bands for 1994

Tariff (%)	Type of product
0	Products without national similar. Products where Brazil has no comparative advantage, commodities of little value
5	Products with a pre-existing tariff rate of 5%
10–15	Inputs with previous tariff rates of 0%
20	Most manufactured products (including non-serial capital goods)
30	Chemicals, some foodstuffs, consumer electronics
35	Automobiles, trucks, motorcycles
40	Computer products

Source: Oliveira (1993: 16).

and Franco 1991*b*: 13, 14). Whether or not the new more liberal trade environment has done anything to reduce these costs is, of course, one of the central questions to be addressed in the following chapters. At the same time, Brazil was under pressure from international organizations—especially GATT and the World Bank—to open up its markets to international competition.

In March 1990 laws were passed providing for a timetabled reduction and simplification of the tariff structure, with a targeted date for completion in 1994. By that date, tariffs were supposed to lie within seven bands, depending on the category of good. These bands are illustrated in Table 5.

In reaching these bands, reductions in the level of tariffs were to be very steep across Brazilian industry as a whole, with average tariffs originally scheduled to fall from 32.2% to 14.2% between 1990 and 1994 (Fritsch and Franco 1991*b*: 20).

In fact, the programme of tariff reductions was accelerated in February 1992 (Suzigan 1992*b*: 1), while for capital goods the falls in tariffs were concentrated in the first two years of the timetable. The non-serial capital goods sector faced an especially sharp fall in nominal tariff protection in the three years from 1990 to 1993 (Table 6). In July 1993 the programme of tariff reductions was completed in the sector, ahead of schedule (Tadini 1993: 13, Carvalho and Machado 1994: 25). For the sector as a whole average nominal tariffs had fallen from about 45% immediately prior to the programme to 20% on its conclusion, a dramatic scaling down by any standards (Tadini 1993: 13).

Another factor at work in the scaling down of tariffs across Brazilian industry was the establishment of the MERCOSUL common market, established at the Treaty of Asunción in March 1991 and ratified by Brazil in November of the same year. This provided for the establishment of a trade régime under which goods would be able to circulate freely between member states with a zero internal tariff and without subjection to NTBs (GATT 1993: 79). The target date for the achievement of this objective was 31 December 1994. At

TABLE 6. Nominal Average Tariffs in the Non-serial Capital Goods Sector, 1990–1994 (%)

Sub-sector	1990	1991	1992	1993*	1994*
Electrical energy equipment	35.8	27.4	23.1	18.6	18.2
Mechanical equipment	38.6	29.9	25.6	20.9	19.6
Railway rolling stock	45.6	39.7	34.5	29.5	20.0
Shipbuilding	35.7	29.1	25.3	21.7	18.9
IBGE: Electrical and communications equipment	39.6	34.3	25.9	n/a	21.1
IBGE: Mechanical equipment	39.5	30.4	21.0	n/a	19.7
IBGE: Transport equipment	55.9	42.3	28.6	n/a	25.7

Notes: * 1993 figure pre-July 1993; 1994 figure post-July 1993 and all of 1994.

Source: Non-IBGE categories: IE-UNICAMP et al. (1993b: 49–50). IBGE categories: Pinheiro and Almeida (1994: 6).

the same time, provision was made for the establishment of a common external tariff. The achievement of the zero internal tariff was achieved by the target date, though, in terms of the non-serial capital goods sector, the impact in terms of heightened foreign competition can only be marginal given the virtual absence of the sector in Paraguay and Uruguay and the small Argentinian sector.

In terms of the movement towards a common external tariff, Brazil has not adopted the common external tariff (CET) of 10% on capital goods employed by the other members, keeping instead an average tariff for the sector of around 20% (*Tarifa Aduaneira do Brasil* 1995). As things stand, Brazil has a partial commitment to achieve a 10% average by the year 2000 but there have been few recent signs that it will meet this target. By contrast, Argentina has pursued a more ambitious policy of liberalization of trade in capital goods. In order to facilitate rapid restructuring of domestic industry, the Argentinian authorities, towards the end of 1992, exempted capital goods imports from tariffs. This had the effect of reducing overall protection of the Argentinian sector by 25% (Sirlin 1997). In addition, domestic producers of capital goods were granted drawback of 15% on local sales (ibid.). By March 1995, however, the emergence of fiscal imbalances forced the authorities to rescind this policy and tariffs were raised again to the CET level of 10%.

The stronger commitment to capital goods trade liberalization demonstrated by Argentina has been a source of tension in trade relations with Brazil. The fact that liberalization has been more rapid within Argentina reflects the much smaller scale of its capital goods sector. Brazil, by contrast, has proceeded relatively more cautiously, influenced by the greater importance of its sector within its industrial economy.

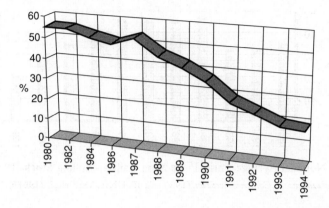

CHART 6. Nominal Average Tariff Protection: Electrical Energy Equipment, 1980–1994

Source: Departamento de Comércio Exterior (1980–9); IE-UNICAMP *et al.* (1993*b*).

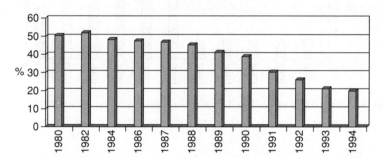

CHART 7. Nominal Average Tariff Protection: Mechanical Equipment, 1980–1994

Source: Departamento de Comércio Exterior (1980–9); IE-UNICAMP *et al.* (1993*b*).

In sum, the Brazilian non-serial capital goods sector has experienced significant changes in the level of nominal tariff protection afforded to it since 1980. As Charts 6 to 9 illustrate, generally high levels of tariffs in the early to mid-1980s have, since 1987, and especially since 1990, been subject to rapid reductions.

(ii) Non-Tariff Barriers

The changes in nominal tariff protection examined in the previous section are only of limited use in understanding the evolution of the overall protective régime faced by the sector since 1980. As the previous section on policy in the late 1970s made clear, much of the protective apparatus in place at the beginning of the last decade took the form of non-tariff barriers. The relative insignificance of tariffs as a means of protection during much of the

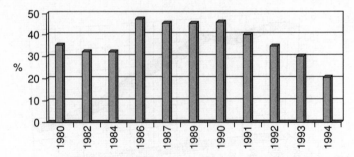

CHART 8. Nominal Average Tariff Protection: Railway Rolling Stock, 1980–1994

Source: *Departamento de Comércio Exterior* (1980–9); IE-UNICAMP *et al.* (1993*b*).

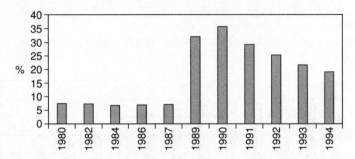

CHART 9. Nominal Average Tariff Protection: Shipbuilding, 1980–1994

Source: *Departamento de Comércio Exterior* (1980–9); IE-UNICAMP *et al.* (1993*b*).

TABLE 7. Realized Average and Nominal Average Tariffs in the
Non-serial Capital Goods Sector, 1980–1989

Sub-sector	1980		1986		1989	
	Nominal	Realized	Nominal	Realized	Nominal	Realized
Electrical energy equipment	55.28	11.06	49.29	8.29	41.5	12.18
Mechanical equipment	50.08	10.95	47.38	7.38	41.24	15.25
Railway rolling stock	35.67	0	47.12	0	45.0	6.01
Shipbuilding	7.62	0.04	7.12	0	53.3	3.33

Source: *Departamento de Comércio Exterior* (1980–9).

1980s is indicated when the realized (i.e. actually collected) average tariff is considered (see Table 7).

The data indicate, that despite high legal nominal tariffs, the actual tariff protection offered to the sector was much lower and in some cases zero. In

TABLE 8. Principal Tariff Exemption Schemes (*Insenções*)
in Force in the 1980s

Scheme no.	Description
16	Shipbuilding construction programme
17	Petrobrás import scheme
18	Federal railway investment scheme
19	Itaipú project scheme
20	Electrobrás exemption scheme

Source: *Comercio Exterior do Brasil: Importações*, various years.

many cases tariff redundancy existed. The reason for these twin phenomena lies with a proliferation of special import régimes (*insenções*) at the beginning of the 1980s which exempted certain imports from the payment of tariffs. The exemptions arose so as to shield certain major importers of non-serial capital goods (particularly public enterprises) from the effects of stepping up NTB and nominal legal tariff protection of the sector. Of course, exemptions of this nature were only available to products without national similars. Some of the major *insenções* are indicated in Table 8.

The result of the arrangements in force over this period was that tariffs took a secondary position in the protection of the non-serial capital goods sector: they only became effective once an import had jumped the barriers of NTB protection and even then were frequently waived under the schemes summarized above. Such protective mechanisms were fairly common throughout Brazilian industry, though for capital goods the NTB barriers (especially those imposed by the Law of Similars) were particularly high (Bonnelli *et al.* 1992: 11).

From 1987 onwards there has been a concerted attempt to reduce the extent of non-tariff protection and increase the significance of tariffs as a means of protection. As a result, there is now much greater transparency attaching to the protective mechanism surrounding the non-serial capital goods sector. The remainder of this sub-section traces the evolution of non-tariff protection since 1980, starting with an examination of non-tariff barriers attaching to public sector procurement of non-serial capital goods.

For the first half of the 1980s, the Brazilian state retained tight procedures with respect to its procurements of imports of non-serial capital goods. Most fundamentally, the Law of Similars was applied to the field of public sector procurement (Fritsch and Franco 1991*c*: 16). The legal principals of the Law were outlined earlier in the chapter and will not be repeated here. However, it is worth re-emphasizing an important point that has already been made with respect to the *de facto* operation of the Law. The implementation of the Law and the assessment of similarity occurred on a case by case basis when the public sector import of non-serial capital goods occurred. The agency in charge of the assessment procedure, CACEX, was itself a part of the public sector, being a division of the state-owned *Banco do Brasil* (not to be confused with the *Banco Central*).

A point which emerged consistently in the course of interviews with industrialists, consultants, and bankers with links to the sector was the discretionary nature of CACEX's decision-making processes during this period. Whether a product about to be imported was considered 'similar' depended on the outcome of negotiations involving the potential customer, CACEX, and, on occasion, industry representatives (usually drawn from ABDIB). The political bargaining power of the particular state enterprise customer in question was frequently a crucial factor in determining the outcome of negotiations. Some state enterprises tended to have more influence than others. Petrobrás, for example, had a reputation for achieving above average success in the securing of import licences for its investment projects. However, this has to be seen in the context of a very high national content in its overall purchasing activity.

The result of the complex negotiating processes that surrounded the Law of Similars, particularly as it applied to public procurement, was to render it a highly opaque form of non-tariff barrier. The opacity of the Law is reinforced by the lack of data concerning the extent to which potential imports were rejected, or accepted, as non-similars. Without doubt, the absence of data is due to the fact that the operation of the Law was, and would appear to remain, a sensitive political and commercial issue.

In 1982, another form of non-tariff barrier aimed at public sector imports was established by the newly created Secretariat for the Control of State Enterprises. The new measure consisted of an annual import quota for each state enterprise (GATT 1993: 141). This was in addition to the government-set global ceiling for public sector purchases of imports established in 1976 which had required the submission by state enterprises of their import plans. This measure was abolished in 1985, however (ibid. 141). In 1986, an effort was made to clarify the position of the public sector with regard to import procurement with the passing of Decree Law 2300. The Law established a special tendering system with which all public entities would have to comply when purchasing. The Decree Law states that preference be granted to Brazilian products when tender bids 'are equivalent in terms of price, contract and delivery time' (ibid. 140).

Thus, the principles embodied in the Law of Similars were restated and the potential for negotiated interpretation retained. This remains the legislative position to this day although the formal apparatus of similarity testing provided by CACEX and the Law itself disappeared following their abolition during the *Abertura Comercial* trade reforms of 1990. Thus, the legislative provision for a non-tariff obstacle to be placed in the path of a potential public sector non-serial capital goods import remains. However, such an obstacle could only come into play in special circumstances and, even if these should apply, its imposition would be highly discretionary.

This conclusion is supported by qualitative evidence gathered in the course of conversations with key sector participants who suggested that the state in the post-1990 period has adopted a much less restrictive approach to the purchase of imports. Another important reform which concerned the public sector's procurement policy accompanied the abolition of the Law of Similars. As was noted earlier in this section, many of the capital goods imports that jumped the barrier of similarity then received exemption from the payment of tariffs under the schemes of *isenções*. In 1990 most of the remaining exemption schemes applying to the public and the private sectors were abolished. Thus the role of (increasingly lower) tariffs has been emphasized while that of the non-tariff barrier of the Law of Similars has been effectively eliminated. Some of the most important changes in public sector procurement non-tariff import controls have occurred in the field of local content requirements. By the early 1980s, the Brazilian state had established a local content requirement of 80–85% of total value added for its purchases of non-serial capital goods. According to Fritsch and Franco (1991*b*: 74), for the non-serial capital goods sector, such public procurement rules 'were the key source of local content requirements'. Furthermore, the authors stress that 'the importance of local content requirements as an import restriction device for capital goods and parts cannot be underestimated' (ibid. 74). Following the trade reforms in 1990 it appeared that this local content requirement had been abolished. However, Decree 123 issued in February 1991 established a new local content requirement at 60% of public sector purchases. Thus the level of the local content requirement has been significantly reduced in the course of the *Abertura Comercial*.

Quite apart from these reforms, to some extent it can be argued that the overall significance of public sector procurement NTBs has been reduced simply because of the fall in public sector relative to private sector demand for non-serial capital goods, a trend that established itself in the early 1980s and accelerated after 1987 (see Section 2.3.2). However, the private like the public sector faced a number of non-tariff restrictions, which during the early part of the 1980s intensified and multiplied and then were subject to reform.

The beginning of the 1980s as indicated previously was a period in which trade policy was determined in large part by macroeconomic considerations, in particular, the need to correct the balance of trade deficit. As part of the effort to reduce the flow of imports, a number of new non-tariff barriers were introduced. The most restrictive of these consisted of outright prohibitions (termed 'temporary suspensions') of the import of specified products. The list of prohibited imports was listed in a special document—*Anexo C*—published by CACEX (Oliveira 1993: 12). Import prohibitions were most widespread for consumer goods, especially those deemed to be frivolous in nature. By

1989, the last year of operation of the temporary suspensions, 36.3% of consumer good tariff lines were affected by this measure. In the case of capital goods the figure had reached 7.5% (Braga and Tyler 1990: 8). In addition to the prohibitions, two other key measures were introduced.

The first was the imposition of an external financing requirement in 1982 for imports of more than US$ 1 m. This measure required enterprises seeking to import expensive capital goods from abroad to obtain financing from outside Brazil, something that became increasingly hard to do in the wake of the debt crisis. The second measure was the introduction of schemes known as *Programas de Importação* (import programmes) under which firms were obliged to negotiate annually their import levels with CACEX (Oliveira 1993: 12). Furthermore, the importation of any product required the acquisition of an import licence which certified that all the above measures had been complied with.

Following the cautious trade liberalization in mid-1988, the dismantling of some of these non-tariff barriers began. The most significant reform was put into effect in July 1988 with the automatic granting of import licences. For most products these were issued provided that the imports did not exceed the totals agreed in the annual import programme. In the case of capital goods, however, the reform was much more radical. Licences would be granted automatically even if they exceeded the specified annual limit (GATT 1993: 99). The reforms of 1990 swept away most of the remaining non-tariff controls on imports. First, the list of 'temporarily suspended' (prohibited) imports was abolished along with the import programmes (Oliveira 1993: 15). Secondly, the external financing requirements for imports were terminated with effect from February 1991 (GATT 1993: 100).

Some of the non-tariff barriers that lay in place during the 1980s resulted from the operation of government industrial policy aimed at the sector's domestic customers, specifically through CDI investment projects and FINAME financing. In the case of the CDI, a number of investment projects had been initiated in the late 1970s in the basic industries sectors of chemicals, petrochemicals, cement, paper, and non-serial capital goods. As was noted in Section 2.2, a number of measures emerged from the operation of CDI investment schemes, principally exemption from IPI and ICM taxes, the provision of an accelerated depreciation allowance for domestically purchased capital goods, and outright fiscal credits.

These measures were supplemented by high local content requirements (usually above 80%) and the operation of the Law of Similars. However, two factors combined to reduce the impact of CDI measures on overall non-tariff protection. The first was the abolition of outright fiscal credits in 1979 (Tyler 1981: 49). The second and the more significant was the decline in resources made available to the CDI following the crisis of 1980–3. Existing projects continued but a brake was put on new developments. As the CDI entered the middle 1980s its resources diminished yet again and the number of projects it could support and thus the extent of the connected fiscal incentives fell. Finally, in 1988 the CDI closed altogether and with it went the protection afforded by the fiscal subsidies.

In the case of FINAME, the state-owned organization that finances domestic capital goods sales, the non-tariff barriers offered by its local content requirements have remained in place through the 1980s and up to the present although the requirements themselves have become less stringent. For most of the 1980s capital goods were only financed if their national content amounted to at least 80%. From 1991, however, this has been reduced to 60%.

In order to overcome the anti-export bias generated by protected (though depressed) domestic markets and the high tariffs attaching to imported inputs, the state developed special export promotion programmes. These will be examined in full detail in Chapter 7 when the export performance of the sector is considered. For the purposes of this section, however, the export-incentive policies will be examined only in terms of their impact on non-tariff barriers. During the 1980s, two major export promotion schemes were in operation: BEFIEX and FINEX. The BEFIEX scheme provided for 90% reductions in tariffs and IPI taxes due on imported machinery (GATT 1993: 162). In certain circumstances these benefits could be obtained even where a national similar existed. In order to benefit from BEFIEX measures, firms had to achieve export targets outlined in a plan signed at the outset of the agreement.

However, firms had to ensure that local content in final exports was at least two-thirds of the total. Thus the BEFIEX measure simultaneously facilitated and controlled the flow of imports. In terms of the non-serial capital goods sector, however, the impact of BEFIEX was not especially significant. The bulk of BEFIEX contracts were concentrated in the automotive, textiles, and clothing industries (ibid. 163), industries which are not intensive users of non-serial capital goods. Following the trade reforms of 1990, the BEFIEX programme came to an end.

Of more direct relevance to the non-serial capital goods sector were the export finance programmes administered by CACEX (the most important being FINEX) which provided pre- and post-shipment lines of credit at reduced interest rates during the 1980s. Again, these schemes stipulated certain levels of local content that would have to be achieved in order for finance to be provided. In the case of long-term FINEX financing—the most significant for the sector—local content requirements followed public sector norms, generally around 80–85%. However, the FINEX scheme suffered from a depletion of resources following the fiscal crisis in the late 1980s (Motta *et al.* 1994: 125) and finally ended in 1990 (Torres *et al.* 1994: 38). The agency that replaced FINEX in 1990—FINAMEX—also provides pre- and post-shipment finance and has established a local content requirement of 60% (GATT 1993: 166).

To conclude, this section has demonstrated the complex and wide-ranging array of non-tariff restrictions that acted to protect the sector in the first half of the 1980s. Since the end of the last decade there has been a considerable scaling down in the number and stringency of non-tariff barriers. More of the responsibility for the protection of the sector has been transferred to tariff measures which themselves have been subject to reduction. As a result, the sector is now less protected that at any time in the last fifteen years. Given the often deliberately opaque character of non-tariff measures, it has been necessary so far to engage in a qualitative discussion: non-tariff measures do not lend themselves easily to quantification (Greenaway and Milner 1993: 16). However, it is possible to devise numerical documentary measures so that the incidence of non-tariff measures can be assessed for any particular import category and then compared over time.

The United Nations Conference on Trade and Development (UNCTAD) has developed a measure of non-tariff incidence which measures the number of non-tariff restrictions per tariff line (individual product type). If any restrictions exist then the non-tariff measure incidence for that tariff line is 100%; if none, the incidence is recorded as 0% (UNCTAD 1994: 43). Simple and trade-weighted averages are then calculated for three-digit product category types using this incidence data for individual tariff lines. For the machinery and equipment sector, the UNCTAD data reveal a fall in the weighted average of non-tariff measure incidence from 36.4% in 1984–7, to 16.2% in 1988–90, and finally to 0% in 1991–3 (UNCTAD 1994: 56). However, these data must be treated with caution: they do not indicate the existence of barriers to trade that remain, such as public procurement minimum content requirements. Perhaps this omission reflects the data availability problems associated with the assessment of non-tariff protection.

(iii) The Effective Rate of Protection

As Section 2.2.1 noted, the effective rate of protection offers a broad measurement of the overall intensity of the protective regime by measuring the extent to which value added domestically for any product group is able to exceed that internationally prevalent. Estimates of the ERP for the Brazilian non-serial capital goods sector in the 1980–94 period are given below in Table 11. Unfortunately, data on the ERP for the particular capital goods subsectors in question (mechanical equipment, electrical energy equipment, railway rolling stock, and shipbuilding) are available only for 1990 onwards. In order to give an indication as to the longer-term evolution of ERP it will also be necessary to rely on estimates for the broader IBGE categories of mechanical and electrical equipment.

The absence of published data on effective protection in the non-serial capital goods sector for some years in the 1980s provides an argument for the calculation and presentation of such data. However, it was decided not to undertake this exercise for a number of reasons. First, the accumulation of data in order to calculate ERPs for the years involved would have been a very lengthy process. Given the time and resource constraints involved, and the principal objectives of the study, the implementation of such data gathering

TABLE 9. Effective Protection of the Non-serial Capital Goods Sector, 1980–1994 (%)

Sector	1980	1985	1990	1991	1992	1993	1994
IBGE: Mechanical equipment	93.3	18.5	—	34.7	24.1	23.1	—
IBGE: Electrical and communications equipment	129.3	108.2	—	44.8	32.0	25.5	—
Mechanical equipment	—	—	44.4	34.6	29.6	24.0	23.2
Electrical energy equipment	—	—	41.1	31.4	26.3	20.8	21.2
Railway rolling stock	—	—	54.9	49.9	48.8	38.0	23.7
Shipbuilding	—	—	40.3	33.7	29.6	25.8	22.3

Source: 1980, 1985: Tyler (1983, 1985); Guimarães (1988), all reproduced in Pinheiro and Almeida (1994: 12). Data for IBGE categories, 1991–3: Hahn (1992) reproduced in Pinheiro and Almeida (1994: 6). Mechanical equipment, electrical energy equipment, railway rolling stock and shipbuilding data, 1990–4: IE-UNICAMP et al. (1993b: 54–6).

would have been hard to justify, especially given the presence of published ERP calculations that provide a good general indication of the main trends. In addition, the desirability of carrying out calculations for the whole of the 1980s was lessened by the fact that the main focus of the research lies in analysing the post-1987 period where, in fact, existing data cover much of the period.

In examining the data for the effective rate of protection in Table 9, it is worth noting that calculations have been undertaken using input coefficients based on an input–output table for the year 1985. Thus the data may be limited to the extent that they reflect the implicit assumption of constant production techniques. With this qualification in mind, it is now appropriate to examine trends in the data along with possible explanations for their main trends.

The data indicate that, for the IBGE categories of capital good, effective protection actually dropped sharply in the mid-1980s before picking up again at the end of the decade. This would appear to run counter to the behaviour of nominal protection experienced by the sectors during this period. From 1980 to 1985 nominal protection for mechanical equipment and electrical and communications equipment actually rose from 56.3% to 62.1% and 99.1% to 100.4% for each category respectively (Pinheiro and Almeida 1994: 6). By 1991 nominal protection for mechanical equipment had fallen to 30.4% while for electrical and communications equipment the equivalent figure was 34.3% (ibid. 6). Two factors may account for these apparently paradoxical movements in effective protection.

The first is that the mid-1980s saw an increase in the number of schemes exempting some imports from the payment of duty, a development discussed in more detail below. Such exemptions would reduce the realized tariff

protection employed in the calculations and, other things being equal, the
observed ERP. However, the very aggregated nature of the IBGE categories
and the effect of the operation of the exemptions programmes may give a
misleading impression of the actual levels of ERP experienced by individual
firms in the sector. As the previous section made clear, in general, exemptions only operated for products where there was no national similar. However, the definition of similars was rather flexible and subject to change on a
case by case basis. This meant that, in any year, for any individual tariff line,
some firms would be highly protected through the decision of the authorities
not to exempt an imported product from the operation of NTBs or the payment of tariffs while others would be less fortunate.

The second possible factor in the decline in ERP from the early to mid-
1980s may lie in the fact that there was increased tariff and non-tariff protection of inputs which, other things being equal, would tend to drive levels of
effective protection downwards. Again, however, there is a danger of over-
looking the differential effects of this measure on different firms. For firms that
had managed to secure tariff or NTB exemptions on their inputs (this was
very common for firms with substantial exports), effective protection may have
actually increased during this period. From the mid-1980s onwards, effective
protection rose for both mechanical and electrical and communications equipment as input tariffs fell and, eventually (from about 1988 onwards), tariff
exemption schemes were abolished.

During the post-1990 period of the *Abertura Comercial*, the levels of effective protection for all capital goods categories under consideration fell very
sharply. The trends in ERP reductions are extremely dramatic with cuts of
the order of 50% for mechanical equipment, electrical energy equipment,
railway rolling stock, and shipbuilding in the period between 1990 and 1994.
These substantial falls in effective protection reflect the operation of a number of factors relating to the liberalization of trade policy. First, as Section
2.3.1 (*i*) illustrated, there were substantial cuts in tariff protection across the
board for the non-serial capital goods sector. Significantly, these cuts were
executed particularly rapidly compared to other industrial sectors (Tadini 1993)
which is likely to have meant that tariff protection on final output fell more
sharply than that on inputs, leading to a pronounced fall in ERP. At the same
time, the 1990–4 period saw the virtual abolition of non-tariff protection of
the sector (discussed in Section 2.3.1 (*ii*)) which accelerated the downward
trend in effective protection for the sector.

2.3.2 GOVERNMENT PROCUREMENT POLICY AND THE NON-SERIAL CAPITAL GOODS SECTOR, 1980–1994

Changes in public sector investment since the beginning of the 1980s and
particularly since 1987 will be argued to have had a greater impact on the
competitive strategy and behaviour of non-serial capital goods firms than any

other single factor. As Section 2.2.2 made clear, the state had played a central role in the emergence of the modern Brazilian non-serial capital goods sector, most particularly through the investment programmes of publicly owned enterprises in the energy, transport, and basic industry fields. By the end of the 1970s, the investment programmes of these enterprises had grown to the extent that they represented the biggest single source of gross fixed capital investment in Brazil (IE-UNICAMP *et al.* 1993*d*: 45). Not only did the purchasing power of the state facilitate the physical expansion of the industry, it also affected the pattern of that expansion (through the *Nucléos de Articulação*) and, as will be made clearer in Chapter 5, its technological trajectory.

Since 1980, however, there have been dramatic changes in the levels of public investment expenditure, particularly on the part of the public enterprises. Between the end of the 1970s and the beginning of the 1990s the share of public sector in total gross domestic fixed capital formation fell from 40% to 12% (ibid. 45) while total gross fixed capital formation itself had fallen by 22.25% in constant 1980 terms (IPEA 1994, 1991: 30–6). The implications of these figures for the non-serial capital goods industry are all too clear. Not only was overall investment declining, but its public sector component was falling even faster. This appears particularly serious for the sector given its heavy reliance on public sector orders which amounted to 60% of total demand in 1980 (ABDIB 1993*a*: 5). Given the significance of these trends and the impact they will be argued to have had on the evolution of static and dynamic efficiency within enterprises, it is important that they be examined in more detail and in a more disaggregated fashion.

To achieve this objective, the remainder of this section is organized as follows. First, the overall pattern of public and private sector investment is examined for the 1980–94 period. Next, the policy background behind the falls in investment—most especially those relating to the public sector—is discussed with particular attention being paid to events after 1987. Thirdly, the investment behaviour of individual public sector enterprises is examined. Those considered include Electrobrás (electrical power utility holding company), Petrobrás (the oil and petrochemical enterprise), the RFFSA railway network, and the steel industry (much of which was in the public sector up until the early 1990s). The choice of enterprises reflects their significance as customers for the particular non-serial capital goods sectors in question; namely electrical energy equipment, mechanical equipment, railway rolling stock, and shipbuilding. Finally, the impact of these developments on the composition of demand faced by the sector is considered.

The overall decline in levels of investment can be ascertained by examining data for gross fixed domestic capital formation presented in Charts 10 and 11. The data reveal that the fall in gross domestic fixed capital formation since 1980 has not been an even or smooth process. Chart 10 indicates a severe decline between 1980 and 1984 followed by a muted resurgence which lasted

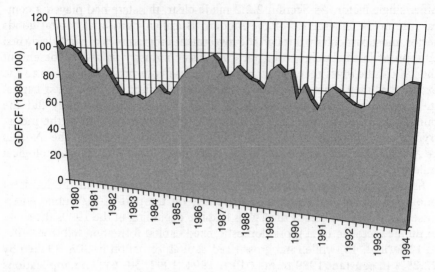

CHART 10. Gross Domestic Fixed Capital Formation, 1980–1994 (1980 = 100)
Source: IPEA (July 1991: 39, July 1994, p. A6).

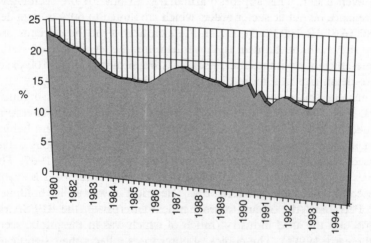

CHART 11. Gross Domestic Fixed Capital Formation as a Percentage of GDP, 1980–1994
Source: IPEA (July 1991: 39, July 1994: 31, A41).

until 1989. However, even at the peak of the recovery, gross domestic fixed capital formation in real terms did not match that in 1980. The beginning of the 1990s saw yet another sharp fall which lasted until the end of 1992. Between 1992 and 1994 a recovery took place, but despite this gross domestic fixed capital formation remains 12% below the level achieved in 1980.

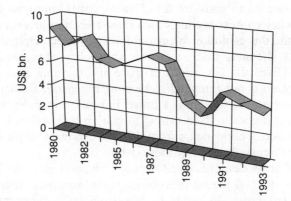

CHART 12. Public Enterprise Investment in Transport, Energy, and Communications Infrastructure, 1980–1993 (constant US$ bn.)

Source: IBRE/FGV data reproduced in CNI (1995: 17).

The decline in the absolute level of gross domestic fixed capital formation was accompanied by its falling share in total GDP. Chart 11 points to this phenomenon. Like the data for absolute levels of gross domestic fixed capital formation, the data for relative share show something of an uneven pattern of long-run decline with recovery observable in the mid to late 1980s and a slight upturn after 1992. The data, in revealing declining overall investment, hint at the pressures experienced by firms in the capital goods sector in general over the past fifteen years. For the non-serial capital goods sector, with its greater reliance on the investments of public enterprises, the situation appears yet more critical.

Chart 12 indicates the extent to which investment in public enterprise infrastructural investment has contracted. Between 1980 and 1993, such investment fell by 43% in real terms. This compares with an overall fall in gross domestic fixed capital formation of 17.78% over the same period. In terms of share of GDP, a similar trend emerges. From 1979 to 1992, the share of public enterprise investment in total GDP fell from 8.5% to 2.2% (ABDIB 1994: 9)—a fall of more than two-thirds—while for gross domestic fixed capital formation, from 1980 to 1992 the decline was milder being from 22.9% to 14.4% (IPEA 1991, 1994: 31–41).

Some interesting trends emerge when the pattern in decline for levels of public enterprise infrastructural investment is examined. As in the case of gross fixed capital formation, the decline has not been even but concentrated into particular periods. There was a rapid fall between 1980 and 1984 followed by a mild recovery. However, following 1987, the decline in investment has been particularly intense. This pattern is mirrored in the more disaggregated data which will shortly be examined concerning the investment behaviour of individual public enterprises.

Before moving on to consider this, however, it is appropriate to examine the general policy context against which these trends in investment emerged. To begin with, the evolution of gross domestic fixed capital formation is set against the changing macroeconomic and policy background of the last fifteen years. Given the limitations of space and the objectives of this book, the account given is not intended to be comprehensive. Rather, in order to provide appropriate background, a broad indication is given as to why the pattern of gross domestic fixed capital formation behaved as it did over the period in question. Following on from this, the evolution of public enterprise investment is discussed in rather more detail.

In terms of gross domestic fixed capital formation as a whole, the initial decline in the 1980–4 period reflects the severe recession attendant on the debt adjustment crisis. In order to reverse Brazil's deteriorating current account position (resulting from worsening trade deficits and increasing debt service payments) and reduce accelerating inflation, the government of General Figueiredo imposed rigorous orthodox monetary and fiscal policies. These policies included high interest rates, cuts in government current expenditures, and large cuts in the investment budgets of publicly owned enterprises (Erber and Vermulm 1993: 17). Following the imposition of these policies, Brazil experienced the most severe contraction in output in its history as an industrialized nation. Inevitably, investment as a whole underwent sharp contraction. In 1983, following the almost complete cessation in international capital flows into Brazil, an accord was signed with the IMF in which commitments were undertaken to maintain the tight fiscal and monetary stances that had been adopted.

From about 1984 onwards there was a hesitant and uneven upturn in industrial production and overall growth, and an improvement in export performance, the latter partially resulting from an IMF-inspired 30% devaluation in 1983. The move back to growth eventually triggered a recovery in gross domestic fixed capital formation. However, by 1990 inflation had mounted and the economy entered a cyclical downturn. The coming to power of Fernando Collor de Melo in 1990 led to an intensification of the downward pressure on investment as a new round of spending cuts was implemented and freezes of liquid assets induced sharp contractions in demand. The recessionary and highly uncertain conditions in this period are reflected in the further contraction in gross domestic fixed capital formation.

Since 1992 the Brazilian economy has returned to growth following the unfreezing of assets, the recovery in international markets, and, since 1994, the successful imposition of an anti-inflationary plan. This period has witnessed a slight upturn in gross domestic capital formation. The failure of gross domestic fixed capital formation to achieve the level it had at the start of the 1980s reflects the severity of the downturns and the unwillingness of industry to invest, given the manifold uncertainty generated by constant changes in monetary, prices, and wages policies as attempts were made to restrain inflation. Some indication of this environment is given when one considers that between 1986 and 1994 there were no fewer than 9 stabilization programmes, 15 wages policies, 54 separate direct price control initiatives, 18 major readjustments of the exchange rate, 11 different indices of inflation, and 5 price and wage freezes (Motta *et al.* 1994: 229). In addition to this, over the same period Brazil launched and retired 6 different currencies.

The development of public enterprise investment policy over the past fifteen years has been intricately tied to the Brazilian state's continuing efforts to stabilize the economy, reduce inflation, and bring the federal deficit under control. During the 1980–4 period of stabilization the first wave of public spending cuts hit public enterprise expenditure especially harshly, forcing the suspension of investment plans and even the halting of work in progress. Following the coming to power of the Collor government in 1990, a further fiscal adjustment attempted to reduce public enterprise expenditure to zero (*Indústria e Produtividade* 1991: 48). In both these instances public enterprise investment expenditure was a primary target. In order to understand why this was so it is necessary to take account of the institutional and political context in which fiscal policy is formulated.

The Brazilian state has long encountered problems in attempting to stem the growth of the fiscal deficit. On the one hand, policy-makers face a narrow tax base in which evasion and opportunities for legitimate tax avoidance are widespread. On the other hand, political and constitutional realities have led to a situation in which the federal government has only limited control over overall expenditures. In large part this results from the requirement of the federal government to transfer substantial resources to the individual state governments every year. The constitution of 1988 further enhanced this obligation and has led to a situation in which many spending decisions by state governments are required to be funded federally. Decision-makers within the states, facing only limited requirements to raise revenue themselves, have no particular incentive to keep spending under control.

In order to address the tendency towards deficit that this has created, the federal government has been obliged to cut expenditures that are under its direct control. The largest single item here is the index-linked wages and salaries of public sector employees. However, this item has been especially resistant to change because of the system of political patronage and the political influence of the employees concerned.

The result of these developments has been that the federal government has been faced with relatively few areas in which expenditure cuts could be made, among which were public enterprise investment expenditures. Thus in periods where fiscal adjustments were required, most particularly in the early 1980s and 1990s, the cuts in investment expenditures tended to be greater on average than cuts as a whole.

However, direct cuts in public expenditure are only a partial explanation for the observed pattern of decline in public enterprise investment expenditures.

Public enterprises, in common with those in the private sector, are also able to finance investment through retained profits or borrowing on capital markets. However, the operation of government policies has adversely affected both of these areas. Profitability of public enterprises in the absence of other measures would have been under pressure given the recessionary environment of the early 1980s and 1990s. However, most especially in the case of the electricity and transport sector, profitability has suffered still further as the prices for these utilities have been subject to price controls as part of the overall effort by the federal government to bring down inflation (IE-UNICAMP/UFRJ et al. 1993d: 46; Motta 1992a: 15). These efforts were intensified after about 1987 with the introduction of numerous stabilization plans and, in the early 1990s, price freezes.

The result of these developments has been the generation of enormous losses and the build-up of debts as prices received for output lagged well behind inflation-induced rises in operating costs. By 1992, for example, the debts of Electrobrás had reached US$ 14 bn., while for steel the figure was US$ 5 bn. and for Petrobrás US$ 3.2 bn. (Motta 1992a: 15). Given this situation, there was considerable pressure within the enterprise to control expenditures, particularly those capital expenditures which could be delayed without an instantly prejudicial effect on day to day performance.

In the early part of the 1980s, public sector enterprises were able to offset the effects of rising losses and avoid a complete collapse in investment by borrowing on capital markets. Until the full impact of the debt crisis hit home state enterprises were able to invest using foreign finance (Folha de São Paulo, 29 May 1994, p. A-3). In fact, such was the need for foreign exchange at this time that a policy of borrowing from abroad was actively encouraged (IE-UNICAMP et al. 1993d: 46).

State enterprises were also active in borrowing from state-owned banks, in particular the BNDES. In terms of the non-serial capital goods sector the most significant borrowings occurred through the BNDES FINAME special programme which provided long-run subsidized finance for purchasers of heavy equipment. From the mid-1980s on, however, these sources of borrowings began to dry up. Following the Mexican moratorium on sovereign debt repayments and widespread defaults and reschedulings throughout Latin America, the flow of foreign funds to Brazilian public enterprises virtually ground to a halt after 1984 (Folha de São Paulo, 29 May 1994, p. A-3). More seriously still, the issue of public enterprise debt became an urgent political priority. As inflation accelerated as growth picked up in the latter half of the 1980s, attempts to control the expansion of public enterprise debt became a key facet of monetary and fiscal policy.

Following deliberations by the National Monetary Council, the Central Bank imposed a number of decrees aimed at limiting public enterprise borrowings. During the 1980s these measures (the most important being Central Bank resolutions numbers 1,135 (16 May 1986), 1,289 (27 Aug. 1987) and 1,464

(26 Feb. 1988)) placed increasingly stringent limits on the amounts the enterprises could borrow, particularly from public sector institutions (Motta 1994: 109). Resolution 1,469 of 21 March 1988 was even more severe, freezing the borrowings of the enterprises at 1987 levels (ABDIB 1989). Finally, resolution 1,718 passed on 29 May 1990 prohibited access of publicly owned enterprises to official (i.e. public sector) sources of financing (ibid. 70). Thus the BNDES FINAME programmes became available only to the private sector.

The impact of this development for public sector investments in non-serial capital goods cannot be underestimated. In 1987, public enterprises accounted for 71.4% of the FINAME special programme disbursements. Following the passage of the resolutions of 1987 and 1988 this was reduced to 45% by the end of 1988 (ABDIB 1988) and by 1991 to 0%. Given the nature of these measures, the onset of recession, and confusion and disorganization within public enterprises, it is hardly surprising that the fall in investment since 1987 has been so steep.

From the point of view of firms in the non-serial capital goods sector, the problems engendered by declining orders from public enterprises in recent years have been compounded by the conditions of contract and payment attaching to such orders as remain. One particularly serious problem, and one which results directly from the weak financial position of public enterprises, is that of late payment. As will be discussed shortly, especially in the case of Eletrobrás, the sums owed have been very substantial indeed. The second problem relates to the contractual difficulties at arriving at agreement over the final price to be paid for heavy equipment with long lead times under conditions of very high inflation. Up to 1993, Brazilian firms supplying the public sector had to tender in local currency. Once this was done, agreed formulas were applied in order to calculate the inflation-adjusted amount to be paid to the enterprise at each stage in the payment schedule. Following the coming to power of President Collor de Melo in 1990, some of the formulas and contracts were subject to 'renegotiation' in the government's favour (*Indústria e Produtividade* 1991: 48) in a policy aimed at reducing the government's financial obligations to the sector. According to the then President of ABDIB, Teófilo Orth, in reality the policy amounted to a 'confiscation' (ibid. 48).

Although the system of *Núcleos de Articulação com a Indústria* (NAI) remained in place, its impact on the development of the capacity of the sector was limited by the dearth of new public sector orders in general and large infrastructural projects in particular. Many large projects commenced under the auspices of the Second National Development Plan were halted with stages left uncompleted. This was particularly true of the hydro-electric power programme. Since 1988, only three large infrastructural projects have been undertaken; the Xingú hydro-electric scheme, the Linha Vermelha motorway project (linking central Rio de Janeiro with Galeão airport and the Petrópolis highway), and the Brasília metro (interviews). Problems in securing investment resources have delayed the progress of the Xingú scheme while work on the Brasília metro has halted for similar reasons with US$ 350 m. already invested and many tunnels and excavations completed (personal visit).

Given the increased relative importance of private sector investment, the non-serial capital goods trade association, ABDIB, has taken its own initiative, launching in 1991 a form of private sector NAI called CADE (*Centro de Articulação com a Demanda Por Bens de Capital*) which may be translated as 'Centre for the Articulation of Demand for Capital Goods' (ABDIB 1993*a*: 3). The centre, based at ABDIB headquarters in São Paulo acts as a point of contact between potential clients and association members (in practice, virtually the entire Brazilian non-serial capital goods sector) and makes information available to firms concerning the availability of orders not only within Brazil itself but also internationally. In turn, CADE supplies potential clients with information concerning available product lines and technologies (ibid. 3). In another development, an organization with close links to ABDIB, the *Companhia Paulista de Desenvolvimento* (Paulista Development Company) has been established with the specific aim of encouraging private sector financial participation in new infrastructural projects planned by the state of São Paulo (interviews). The hope is that these new varieties of project can partially fill the gap left by the decline of federal projects.

Having discussed the pattern of decline in public enterprises as a whole, it is now appropriate to examine the investment behaviour of particular enterprises. Where appropriate, an attempt is made to offer an explanation for the pattern of this behaviour.

Up until February 1995, Brazilian legislation concerning the ownership of electrical power generation and distribution systems required that the vast bulk of capacity be publicly owned. Eletrobrás, the state holding company, was (and remains) the corporate vehicle for the public ownership of the electricity industry. In addition to owning most of the generation capacity directly, Eletrobrás also holds stakes in the smaller, state-government-controlled regional electricity distribution companies (*Financial Times*, 22 Mar. 1995, p. 5). During the 1970s, Eletrobrás carried out a series of major investments in hydroelectric generation projects, the most notable being the Itaipú dam scheme. In the 1980s, however, in common with other public enterprises, there were substantial falls in investment. These are indicated in Chart 13.

Together with the considerations discussed earlier, two major factors stand out as being of particular significance in the electricity industry in explaining the falls in investment. The first was the harmful financial effects induced by a combination of declining electricity prices and heavy debt repayment obligations resulting from previous investment projects (Motta 1992*a*). According to Motta (1992*a*: 14) the effect of declining electricity prices in the face of anti-inflation price controls was of prime significance in explaining the reductions in investment (see Chart 14).

The second factor that must be considered concerns the effects of investment projects initiated in the 1970s that were coming on stream in the 1980s

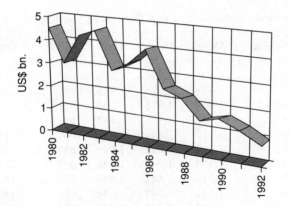

CHART 13. Public Sector Investments in the Electricity Industry, 1980–1993 (constant US$ bn.)

Source: IBRE/FGV data reproduced in CNI (1995: 17).

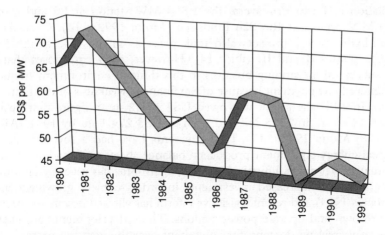

CHART 14. Average Supply Tariff for Eletrobrás, 1980–1991 (constant prices)

Source: Eletrobrás data reproduced in Buslik (1994: 17).

and creating increased generating capacity in the industry (see Table 10). During the 1980s and into the early 1990s this growth in capacity was sufficient to ensure that production exceeded consumption (Buslik 1994: 12), while installed capacity far outstripped demand (ibid. 23). Taken together with the poor financial state of Eletrobrás, the falls in new investment are far from surprising.

The results of this fall in investment for the non-serial capital goods industry made themselves felt in the late 1980s as expansion phases of a number of major hydro-electric projects were cancelled as in the case of the 1,100 MW

TABLE 10. Nominal Installed Electrical-Generating Capacity, 1983–1992 (MW)

Year	Hydro-electric	Diesel	Oil	Coal	Nuclear	Others	Total
1983	33,590	948	1,975	736	—	2	37,251
1984	34,373	978	1,975	736	—	6	38,068
1985	35,538	1,006	1,975	736	657	4	39,916
1986	35,915	1,013	1,975	896	657	11	40,457
1987	38,140	1,015	1,842	1,046	657	11	42,711
1988	39,700	1,201	1,842	1,046	657	30	44,476
1989	43,114	1,173	1,842	1,046	657	113	47,945
1990	44,229	1,110	1,842	1,046	657	172	49,056
1991	45,992	1,131	1,842	1,046	657	184	50,852
1992	46,085	1,210	1,842	1,046	657	—	51,840

Source: Motta et al. (1994, appendix).

installation at Porto Primavera, the 1,800 MW station at Itá and a major 2,500 MW project at Rio São Fransisco (Motta 1992a: 14). Cancellations of non-hydro power projects also took place as in the case of the Angra complex phases II and III (ibid. 14). However, even enterprises that had been successful in winning business in this difficult environment frequently encountered late payment because of the financial weakness of the Eletrobrás system. In 1987 the sector was owed US$ 178.2 m., a figure that declined to US$ 149.5 m. in 1988 but had risen to US$ 274.1 m. by 1991 (ABDIB 1988: 28; Motta 1992b: 17). Late payments have had a severe impact on electrical energy equipment producers' balance sheets and made a challenging situation yet more difficult. However, Eletrobrás has recently announced a programme of increased investments in order to meet growing demand (Eletrobrás 1994) and recent legislative reform has allowed private sector enterprises to own and operate power stations. These developments are likely to create an increasing demand for equipment over the next ten years.

Petrobrás, in contrast to many other state enterprises, has generated a relatively solid financial performance over the years and has built up a reputation for innovation and expertise in engineering which few other Brazilian-owned private or public sector enterprises can match. Petrobrás was formed in 1955, following the decision to nationalize most of the assets of the oil majors that had supplied the market up to that point. The enterprise was given a virtual monopoly over the importation, refining, and distribution of petroleum products although the oil majors retained the right to retail products purchased from Petrobrás.

Following the first major oil price rise in 1973 Petrobrás embarked on a major investment programme aimed at better securing Brazil's oil supply and increasing self-sufficiency in oil extraction, refining, and distribution. The

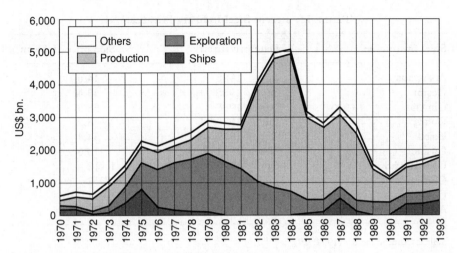

CHART 15. Evolution of Investments: Petrobrás, 1970–1993 (constant US$ bn.)
Source: Petrobrás (1993).

investment programme involved a deep water offshore oil exploration and extraction project, an expansion and modernization of refinery capacity, and the build-up of a fleet of super tankers, some in the 250,000 dwt bracket. The programme of investment expansion provided a substantial market for the Brazilian non-serial goods sector as Petrobrás pursued a policy of very high domestic content which became even more intense in the 1980s (Tadini 1993: 19). Some idea of the extent of expansion in investment can be observed in Chart 15.

As the chart makes clear, in common with other Brazilian public enterprises investments underwent two phases of decline, one in the early 1980s and the other from about 1987 to 1990. The falls reflect constraints on investment common to all Brazilian public enterprises. However, since 1990 investments have risen somewhat as the enterprise's financial position has strengthened and it has been able to raise funds for projects from outside the public sector. One particular investment project stands out as being of significance: that of the expansion and modernization of the tanker fleet. In 1990 sixteen tankers were under construction in an order worth US$ 687 m. while in 1993 a further five ships were ordered, all from Brazilian yards (Petrobrás 1993: 23). FRONAPE, the shipping arm of Petrobrás, currently has the largest fleet of tankers in Latin America with 119 on the register (ibid. 24).

Of all the major customers for Brazilian non-serial capital goods, it has been the steel industry that has undergone the most profound economic and institutional changes over the past fifteen years. Over this period, the industry moved from being predominantly publicly to privately owned as a wave

TABLE 11. Recent Steel Industry Privatizations

Steel firm name	Date privatized		Sale price (US$ m.)
Aparecida	July	1988	14.6
Cosim	Sept.	1988	43.4
Cimetal	Nov.	1988	58.8
Cofavi	July	1989	8.2
Usiba	Oct.	1989	54.4
Cosinor	Nov.	1991	13.6
USIMINAS	Oct.	1991	1,112
CST	July	1992	332
CSN	Apr.	1993	1,057
Açominas	Sept.	1993	597.6

Source: Andrade *et al.* (1994: 89).

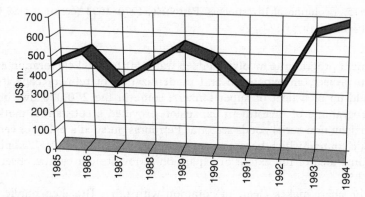

CHART 16. Investments in the Brazilian Steel Industry, 1985–1994 (constant US$ m.)

Source: IBS (1995: 17).

of privatizations occurred from 1988 onwards (see Table 11). Privatizations have been more extensive in the steel industry than in any other single sector.

As Chart 16 demonstrates, investment behaviour in the steel industry differs slightly from the pattern observed in other state enterprises, with fluctuations in the mid-1980s followed by a substantial decline between 1989 and 1991 as the effects of the domestic and international recessions (the Brazilian steel industry exported around 33% of its output at this point (IBS 1995: 16)) made themselves felt. Following on from 1991, however, the newly privatized steel companies have been engaging in investment programmes aimed at modernizing plant and increasing efficiency (Andrade *et al.* 1994: 91–2). Unlike public sector enterprises, the privatized steel companies are able to borrow freely on the open markets as well as gain access to official credits such as those offered by FINAME.

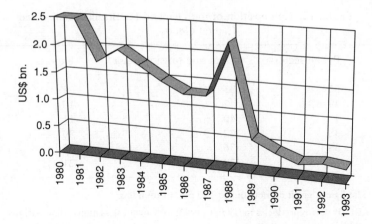

CHART 17. Public Enterprise Investment in Transport Infrastructure, 1980–1993 (constant US$ bn.)

Source: IBRE/FGV data reproduced in CNI (1995: 18).

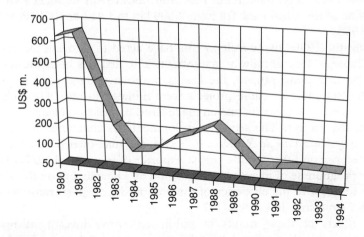

CHART 18. Investments in RFFSA Railway Network, 1980–1994 (constant US$ m.)

Source: RFFSA (1995).

Public investment in transport infrastructure has suffered more than any other sector since 1980 with investments in 1993 little more than 10% of those made fifteen years ago (CNI 1995: 18). Chart 17 makes clear the extent of this decline which has been particularly acute since 1988.

To some extent, investment in the federal railway network (RFFSA) follows this pattern with two major slumps in investment between 1981 and 1984 (which was the most significant) and a second after 1988 (see Chart 18). Route mileage has remained relatively constant as extension plans have been shelved

TABLE 12. Composition of the Demand for Brazilian Non-serial Capital Goods (%)

Year	Public sector	Domestic private sector	Exports	Total
1980	60	31	9	100
1988	49	42	10	100*
1989	49	40	11	100
1990	38	42	20	100
1991	38	36	25	100*
1992	40	39	21	100

Note: * The figures given do not sum to 100 due to rounding.

Source: ABDIB data reproduced in Tadini (1993: 10); own calculations using ABDIB (1993a, 1993b) data.

while, almost incredibly, the extent of electrified line has actually fallen. Between 1980 and 1993, total track miles rose from 29,778 km to 30,214 km while the portion of electrified track fell from 2,600 km to 1,912 km (GEIPOT 1994, 1992, 1985).

During the 1990s two developments have acted to mitigate the extent of this collapse in federal railway investment. The first has been the initiation of the Brasília metro project, the first new urban underground rail system since the Rio and São Paulo projects were initiated in the 1970s. Unfortunately, however, as earlier discussion made clear, financial problems have halted work on the project. The second development has concerned the activities of the *Companhia Vale do Rio Doce* (CVRD), the state-owned mineral extraction enterprise and the world's largest exporter of iron ore which is planning a major programme of investment expansion at Tubarão and on the Ferrovia do Aço to improve the efficiency of mineral product export transport routes (*Revista Ferroviária*, July 1994: 12).

The effects of these trends in public enterprise investment reviewed above have made themselves felt in the composition of demand faced by the sector. As public enterprise investment fell more rapidly than private sector investment, the effect has been to reduce the significance of the state as a component in overall demand faced by the sector as well. This is illustrated in Table 12.

Thus the role of the private sector and of exports has become more significant, although for many years this increasing relative share occurred in a context of declining overall demand. Taken together with the increased exposure to international competition that has occurred since the late 1980s, the effect has been to substantially increase competitive pressure on the sector as it strove to find orders in an increasingly challenging environment. The response of the sector to these conditions forms the focus of Chapters 3 to 6. The remainder of this chapter considers some of the other changes in government policy that have affected the sector since 1980 and most particularly since 1990.

2.3.3 FISCAL SUBSIDIES, SUBSIDIZED CREDIT, AND SECTORAL POLICIES, 1980–1994

During the 1970s, a number of fiscal measures were implemented to encourage the growth of the capital goods sector, the most important of which were outright subsidies, exemptions from the payment of indirect taxes (IPI and ICMS), on inputs, and the zero rating of final output. The granting of these measures was, however, discretionary and usually occurred under the auspices of CDI industrial expansion projects in the basic industries (which were the sector's customers) and the non-serial capital goods industry itself. Two factors acted to reduce the importance of these incentives as the industry entered the early 1980s. The first was that the number of fiscal incentives available to the CDI was reduced quite substantially (Erber and Vermulm 1993: 166). In particular, direct subsidies were removed.

The second factor arose from the fact that the number and value of supported projects fell rapidly as Brazil underwent the fiscal crisis of the early 1980s. Since the early 1980s, the non-serial capital goods sector has been more subject to the imposition of indirect taxation. Unfortunately, data are not available on the precise extent of this increased exposure. The picture is further complicated by the fact that, over the past few years, there have been frequent modifications in the rates of indirect taxes charged, their base of calculation, and the types of equipment granted temporary exemptions (ABDIB 1993c: 11).

According to a survey of major enterprises in the sector, this has meant that long-term planning has been rendered more difficult (ibid. 11) as firms are unable to predict future costs with any degree of accuracy. A further concern expressed within the industry is that the Brazilian indirect tax régime has tended to be less favourable to investments in machinery and equipment than has been the case in some other major industrialized countries. According to data from ABDIB, by 1993 such indirect taxes imposed a tax disadvantage of 32.83% on such investment in Brazil when compared with Germany (ABDIB 1993c: 9).

One important public sector initiative to support the capital goods industry—BNDES FINAME financing—has remained of significance over the past fifteen years and has not suffered the dramatic effects of fiscal contraction to nearly the same extent as public sector investment. The reasons underlying this concern the source of FINAME lending resources which in part originate from interest received on advances but also on a special tax (PIS/PASEP) levied on payrolls (Branco et al. 1992: 1). Resources are thus largely independent of federal spending decisions. FINAME has operated three main financing schemes over the post-1980 period: the automatic, special, and agricultural programmes. Since 1990, it has also administered the

TABLE 13. FINAME Financing Conditions

Programme	Maximum participation share (%)	Maximum annual interest rate (%)	Term (yrs.)
Automatic	40–70	5.5–10.5	1–5
Special	50–60	9.5–10.5	1–8
Agricultural	60–70	8.5–9.5	1–5
FINAMEX	70	Libor + 2	2.5

Source: GATT (1993: 308).

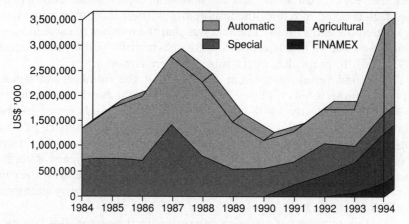

CHART 19. FINAME Disbursements by Programme, 1984–1994
(constant US$ 000)

Source: Calculated from data in BNDES, *Relatórios das Atividades* (1985–94).

FINAMEX export programme whose operation is detailed in Chapter 4. The automatic programme is principally designed for the financing of domestic sales of serial capital goods such as commercial vehicles and machine tools. The special programme with its longer period of finance is designed to meet the needs of the non-serial capital goods sector with its relatively expensive products. The conditions attaching to each of the programmes are outlined in Table 13.

The importance of such finance to the non-serial capital goods sector cannot be underestimated in an economy where high real interest rates have become the norm. For example, in the first quarter of 1995 annual real interest rates stood at 50% (CNI 1995: 23). The evolution of FINAME disbursements is illustrated in Chart 19. The data demonstrate a marked trend in overall disbursements with a steep decline between 1988 and 1990 followed by an upturn. In large part this reflects the impact of growth conditions on the

TABLE 14. BNDES Holdings in Non-serial Capital Goods Firms, 1994
(BNDESPAR Programme)

Enterprise holding	Activity	Holding of voting shares (%)	Total (%)
Aços Villares	Heavy, forged mechanical equipment	26.75	39.26
Dedini	Distillation equipment	0	31.73
Delp	Mechanical equipment	0	4.43
Renk Zanini	Mechanical equipment	1.45	1.45

Source: BNDES (1994a: 56).

investment plans of enterprises and the consequent demand for credit. Given the reduced uptake of credit between 1988 and 1990, the extent to which the BNDES could act to stimulate the market was consequently limited (Branco 1992: 24). Reduced disbursements from the special programme during this period also reflect the impact of the restrictions placed on public enterprise access to official credit from 1987 onwards.

The BNDES has also maintained equity holdings in certain non-serial capital goods enterprises over the past fifteen years under a programme called BNDESPAR, successor to the BNDESMAQ programme. The BNDESPAR programme is designed to enable the injection of capital into troubled, though strategic, enterprises so that restructuring and modernization can take place. Over the past few years the number of enterprises in the sector involved has fallen. By 1994 four enterprises in the sector were part owned by the BNDES, the precise extent to which is indicated in Table 14. Policies directed at the development of individual sub-sectors of the non-serial capital goods industry, which, to some extent had emerged through CDI activity in the 1970s, mostly disappeared in the 1980s following expenditure cuts and the eventual closure of that organization. One sub-sector that did remain subject to a set of special policies and incentives, however, was the shipbuilding industry.

Up until the present, virtually all domestic orders for the sector have originated from the public sector, the largest single customer being Petrobrás. CVRD, the state-owned mineral extraction company, has also been a significant customer most especially in the bulk-carrier sector. Smaller merchant vessels have been purchased by the state-owned Companhia de Navegação Lloyd Brasileira (Lloydbrás), while even for the smallest vessels— the Amazonian riverboats—the state in the form of ENASA has been the dominant customer. The Law of Similars remained the key form of protection for the sector, with relatively low tariffs up until the late 1980s (see Section 4.3.1).

The state has also provided direct finance for the construction of vessels in Brazilian yards through the *Superintendencia Nacional de Marinha Mercante* (SUNAMAN) and later BNDES administered *Fundo de Marinha Mercante* (FMM). The fund draws its resources from a tax—the *Adicional ao Frete para Renovação da Marinha Mercante* (AFRMM)—levied on all imports by sea.

In the early 1980s, funds for the sector were drastically reduced as SUNAMAN's budget was cut from US$ 2.4 bn. to US$1.2 bn. between 1980 and 1983 (Ferraz 1993: 56). Further challenges for the sector resulted from cuts in investment budgets for public enterprises, in particular those of Petrobrás (see above) and CVRD (Borges and De Silva 1993: 48). In the later 1980s, the crisis in the sector along with the impending scaling down of non-tariff barriers prompted a rise in nominal tariffs. As the sector moved further into crisis, a number of measures were taken to improve its competitiveness. From 1990 onwards, tariffs on imported components were sharply reduced and external financing requirements for these items greatly scaled down (Tadini 1993: 21). At the same time, the IPI tax on purchases of domestically produced machines and components was reduced to zero, accelerated depreciation was allowed on investments, and the sector was allowed to import duty-free components up to 30% of the final value of any ship to be exported (ibid. 22).

However, these positive developments were accompanied by a sharp reduction of resources of the FMM, now administered by the BNDES. In part, this originated from the halving of the rate of AFRMM in 1990 (*Portos e Navios*, Jan. 1993: 13) as part of the *Abertura Comercial*. However, the actions of the federal treasury aggravated the problems of the FMM still further as it delayed payments of AFRMM revenues to the fund in an effort to reduce expenditures (ibid. 13). As a result, the sector has been suffering from lack of access to long-term financing of construction, while, in terms of credit to customers, public enterprises have not been permitted to draw on BNDES FINAME firms. As later chapters will demonstrate, these developments have tended to increase the relative significance of export financing and the role of FINAMEX.

Conclusions

The Brazilian non-serial capital goods sector has witnessed considerable changes in government policy in the period since the advent of the Second National Development Plan (PND II) in 1974. The period 1974–80 saw the adoption of a considerably more protectionist trade policy towards the sector encompassing tariff increases and a proliferation of non-tariff barriers. At the same time, the state played a decisive role in the expansion of the sector through its programme of capital good procurement as it pursued a policy of enormous infrastructural investments. Fiscal incentives were also employed as a means of raising capacity in the sector.

The period between 1980 and 1987 witnessed something of a retrench-ment in the state's policy towards the sector. Although structures of protec-tion remained in place—and in some instances were even enhanced—there was something of a fall in public sector investment which translated into a fall in public sector demand for non-serial capital goods. The decline in public sector demand for the sector's output was mainly concentrated into the period between 1980 and 1983; in the three following years public sector procurement rose somewhat. At the same time, the range of fiscal incentives available to the sector under the terms of the CDI and other programmes was greatly reduced. However, the reduction of the role of the state in the affairs of the sector was something of a gradualistic process up until 1987. In the period between 1987 and 1994, however, this picture changed radic-ally with the most dramatic changes in policy environment since the PND II in 1974.

Between 1987 and 1994, the structures of protection that had accom-panied the sector's rapid expansion were sharply pared back with substantial reductions in tariffs being accompanied by a virtual elimination of non-tariff barriers. Given the fact that such barriers constituted the *de facto* primary means of protection afforded to the sector, the importance of this development cannot be understated. At the same time, public sector procurement— which accounted for the bulk of sector demand in the period before 1987— underwent an extremely severe and sustained contraction following a series of fiscal adjustment initiatives in the late 1980s. Public sector demand remained acutely depressed as the fiscal crisis continued into the 1990s. Taken together, the post-1987 policy events constitute an unprecedented compression of the role of the state in the development of the Brazilian non-serial capital goods sector. The next chapter attempts to analyse the impact of these events on the nature of the production process and the consequent changes in productivity performance.

3

Policy Liberalization and the Production Process

Introduction

Chapter 2 demonstrated the profound change in policy environment which the Brazilian non-serial capital goods sector has been faced with since 1987 and most particularly since 1990. Central to the objectives of this book is to determine whether this policy shift has been accompanied by alterations in aspects of sector performance, in particular, those related to changes in static and dynamic efficiency. Perhaps the most widely employed measure of change in efficiency employed in the literature has been that of productivity. To begin the investigation, an examination of alterations in productivity therefore seems appropriate, especially since such changes may indicate underlying shifts in both static and dynamic efficiencies, whose importance has crucial implications for other facets of enterprise behaviour examined in subsequent chapters.

In order to investigate the issue of productivity, this chapter adopts the following approach. First, a general overview is given of output and employment performance in the sector in the period since the start of the 1980s. Besides the obvious connection with the issue of productivity change, this discussion serves to offer some useful background as to the drastic effect of declining demand on the absolute size of the sector over the period. As will become increasingly apparent, it is this marked contraction, and the ability of firms to cope with it, that provides the general context for the emergence of strategies that have resulted in changes in static and dynamic efficiency. Following this, the issue of productivity itself is examined in some detail, the discussion falling into three parts. First, the methodological issues associated with measuring changes in productivity are briefly discussed and their relevance considered for the present investigation with particular reference to the nature of the available data. Following this, data on labour productivity are presented. The data are of three types: output per worker measured in money terms, physical output per worker, and output per hour employed (also in money terms). Data are available not only for the non-serial capital goods sub-sectors in question but also for other industrial activities, thus enabling comparisons to be drawn. Finally, a tentative attempt is made to assess changes in the productivity of capital using output per unit of assets.

Having considered the nature of changes in productivity, the next part of the discussion aims to ascertain the influences underlying them. In this connection, three issues are discussed: namely, alterations in domestic demand (particularly those relating to public sector procurement), trade liberalization, imports, exports and, the Brazilian government's Quality and Productivity Programme (PBQP). Next, the analysis turns to consider the question as to how the changes in productivity were brought about. The key issues examined here include employment levels, capacity utilization, shop-floor organization, investment in new equipment, and outsourcing. In discussing these issues, extensive use is made of data obtained during factory visits, with manufacturing operations described in some detail.

Finally, the chapter concludes by considering the implications of the strategies employed by enterprises to reduce costs and raise productivity with respect to the development of static and dynamic efficiencies. In particular, the discussion seeks to ascertain whether such strategies tended to emphasize innovation in the manufacturing process involving changed techniques and new technologies (dynamic efficiencies) or the control of costs and the removal of 'inefficient' or unused capacity and factors of production with essentially unchanged production techniques (static efficiencies).

3.1 Output and Employment in the Brazilian Non-serial Capital Goods Sector, 1980–1994

The Brazilian non-serial capital goods sector, after experiencing rapid expansion in the 1970s, entered the 1980s in a promising state. By 1980, the total value of output had reached US$ 9602.5 bn. (at 1990 prices) and the sector had come to employ approximately 130,000 people (ABDIB 1991). Much of the capacity then available was of very modern vintage and was sufficiently diversified as to be able to produce a range of non-serial capital goods sufficient to meet around 70% of domestic requirements (calculated from ABDIB 1991). However, 1980 was to prove something of a high-water mark in the fortunes of the sector. The 1980s and 1990s have seen a sharp contraction in sector output and employment to the point where total output in 1994 stood at 53.3% of its 1980 level while numbers employed in the sector had fallen by 60% (calculated from ABDIB 1991, 1994a). This decline in output and employment is much more marked than that within Brazilian industry as a whole, where employment fell by 27% and output (in physical terms) actually rose by 33% between 1980 and 1994 (calculated from IBGE 1981–94).

In examining the development of productivity performance in particular, and changes in static and dynamic efficiencies more generally, it is important to recognize that efforts to effect such changes in the sector, in general, have occurred against a background of contracting demand and, in some cases, serious financial problems among enterprises. However, it is important to note that the pattern of decline has not been constant over time nor has it been uniform across all sub-sectors, the latter being made clear in Section 3.2. For the sector as a whole, the decline in output and employment has been concentrated into two periods, the early to middle 1980s and the late 1980s

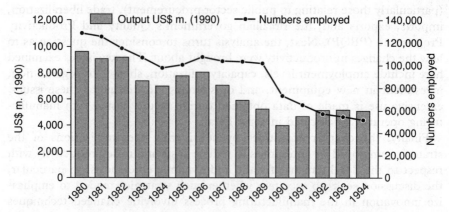

CHART 20. Output and Employment in the Brazilian Non-serial Capital Goods Sector, 1980–1994

Source: Obtained and calculated from ABDIB (1994*a*, 1993*b*, 1991).

to the early 1990s, the latter period coinciding with the key policy changes examined in the current study. These trends are illustrated in Chart 20. The observed variation in output and employment, both over time and inter-sectorally, reflects itself in marked changes in productivity performance. The following sections examine these changes but first the methodological issues associated with the measurement of productivity are considered.

3.2 Productivity Performance and the Brazilian Non-serial Capital Goods Sector: Methodological Issues

The measurement of productivity presents methodological challenges as does the interpretation of its causes and the consequent implications for static and dynamic efficiency connected with any changes that may be detected. Two broad approaches to the measurement of productivity present themselves as possible approaches for the investigation (Weiss 1988). Single factor productivity (SFP) measures attempt to assess the output or value added per unit of a single factor of production. Total factor productivity (TFP) measures attempt to measure the productivity of a composite group of inputs, in most cases labour and capital. Single factor productivity for labour and capital may be written below as follows.

(3.1) $S_l = Y/L$

(3.2) $S_k = Y/K$

where S_l is labour productivity, S_k is capital productivity, Y is output or value added, L is labour input, and K is capital input.

Once single factor productivity has been calculated in this manner for each time period, the next stage consists of calculating percentage changes over time in order to assess single factor productivity growth. Total factor productivity growth over time may be calculated using equation (3.3).

(3.3) $$S_t = Y - p_K - (1 - p)_L$$

where S_t is the percentage growth in TFP; Y, K, and L are the percentage growth in output, capital, and labour respectively; and p is the share of capital in total factor inputs.

The key methodological issue that is involved in the calculation of TFP involves the selection of the correct weights p for the inputs. Perhaps the most difficult aspect of this concerns the weight to be ascribed to capital. This results from a fundamental challenge associated with its measurement. Unlike labour, it can be difficult to measure capital directly in discrete units. Moreover, a question exists as to the 'correct' definition of capital to be employed in the investigation. For example, the definition employed may encompass plant, machinery, or forms of working capital and focus upon factor payments made to capital, value of capital employed, or the quantity of time the capital is employed. The choice of measure is likely to be dependent to a large extent on the availability of suitable data. One commonly employed measure is based upon the number of machine-hours used in production weighted by the base period rentals per machine. This has the advantage that the measurement of capital inputs (hours per machine) allows effective combination and comparison with number of hours employed per unit of labour.

Unfortunately, the data available for capital employed in the Brazilian non-serial capital goods sector do not allow this type of analysis to be undertaken: data for capital input are in the form of total assets employed. In addition, no data were available to allow alternative types of weighting of labour and capital inputs. Given this situation, it was decided not to proceed with an estimation of total factor productivity but rather to concentrate on single factor productivity, focusing primarily on different measurements of labour productivity but also attempting tentatively to estimate a measure of capital productivity. The problems associated with the estimation of TFP are common to many studies. In fact, the majority have tended to focus on labour productivity because of the methodological problems associated with the measurement of capital (Weiss 1988: 228).

Another issue associated with the estimation of productivity relates to the appropriate measure of output employed. Ideally, output should be measured in terms of value added in order that the changes in output considered relate to those generated within the enterprise or sector under consideration alone. Unfortunately, the data available for the Brazilian non-serial capital goods sector relate to gross output alone. Studies undertaken in the early 1980s were able to take advantage of measures of value added in the sector compiled by the IBGE (the Brazilian Government Statistical Service) in its annual industrial survey and five-yearly industrial census. Budget cuts in the mid-1980s meant that 'the latter valuable measure' ceased to be available. However, the problems generated by the absence of value-added measures should not be regarded as overly serious.

The first important point to recognize is that the Brazilian non-serial capital goods industry is notable for its unusually high levels of value added—typically 70% of gross output (interviews)—which in part results from the exceptionally high degree of vertical integration that characterizes enterprises in the sector, a phenomenon explored in detail in Chapter 6. Therefore, measures of gross output in money terms are unlikely to greatly exceed value added. Secondly, some check on the reliability of data for gross output in money terms is provided for some sub-sectors by the availability of IBGE and ABIFER data on physical quantity of output. Finally, qualitative data concerning the relative movements of gross output and value added are available from interviews carried out in the three enterprises and are presented in Section 3.6. This information tends to indicate a fairly constant proportion of value added to gross output over the period up until 1993. Thus changes in gross output for this period seem likely to reflect similar changes in value added. The data suggest, however, that this pattern may be in the process of change with a sudden increase in outsourcing and subcontracting occurring after about 1993. The reasons for this phenomenon are discussed later in the chapter in Section 3.6.

Once data for productivity change have been compiled, the challenge then is to interpret its underlying causes. Nelson (1981) points out that such causes can be very varied. One of the key challenges for any investigation is to account for productivity change which may result from diverse sources. Increases in productivity can reflect improvements in process technology embodied in new machinery, improvements in best-practice technology, increased investment in human capital (through training), decommissioning of inefficient or under-utilized capacity, or removal of inefficient or under-utilized components of the labour force, improvements in the physical layout, and/or organization of the production process, or organizational changes affecting employee/management relations. Given the differing implications of each of these possibilities for static and dynamic efficiency, it will clearly be of prime importance to decompose any observed productivity growth observed in the course of the investigation. This will be achieved through analysing a combination of both sub-sector-level quantitative and firm-level qualitative data.

3.3 Labour Productivity Changes in the Brazilian Non-serial Capital Goods Sector

The period since the early 1980s and especially that since 1988 have seen substantial variations in labour productivity performance within the Brazilian non-serial capital goods sector both temporally and intra-sectorally. Examining data for the sector as a whole based on output in constant dollar terms

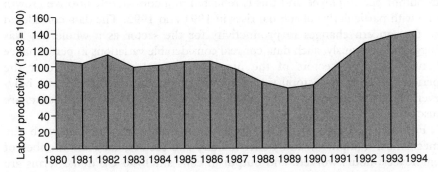

CHART 21. Output per Worker in the Brazilian Non-serial Capital Goods Sector, 1980–1994

Source: Calculated from ABDIB (1991, 1993a, and 1994a). Output per worker figures obtained in calculations are in thousands of 1990 US dollars indexed to 1983 = 100.

TABLE 15. Yearly Percentage Changes in Labour Productivity (Output in 1990 US$ per Employee) in the Brazilian Non-serial Capital Goods Sector, 1982–1994

1982	1983	1984	1985	1986	1987	1988	1989	1990	1991	1992	1993	1994
+9.8	+13.3	+3	+4.3	+0.7	−9.9	−18.8	−9.4	+4.5	+34.2	+22.9	+7.2	+3.5

Source: Calculated from ABDIB (1991, 1993a, 1994a).

per worker employed, the extent of the variation over time becomes clear. Chart 21 demonstrates this pattern.

The data indicate four broad phases in the development of labour productivity change. The period 1980–3 reflects considerable variation in performance where no marked trend is apparent. As will be discussed briefly in the next section, this may reflect the peculiarities of the sector's reaction to the adjustment crisis of the early 1980s. The second phase, 1983 to 1986, reflects a gradual improvement in productivity performance, a trend markedly reversed in the third phase, 1986 to 1989. The fourth and final phase, 1989 to 1994, represents a rapid expansion in output per worker to the extent that the levels achieved by 1994 easily surpass those of any previous year. The trends present in the latter two phases are of particular interest since the period in which they occurred were the scene of the key policy changes of renewed contraction of public infrastructural investment and trade liberalization.

These alterations in productivity performance become yet more apparent when the data are used to calculate year on year labour productivity change. The results of these calculations are illustrated in Table 15. The data reveal modest productivity increases in the middle of the 1980s followed by a marked fall in performance at the end of the decade as growth in output per employee actually became negative. The period 1990–4 has seen a substantial increase in output per employee and this is reflected in a consistently positive growth rate with particularly substantial rises in 1991 and 1992. The data considered so far concern changes in productivity for the sector as a whole. As was suggested previously, such data conceal considerable variations in performance between the sub-sectors of the non-serial capital goods sector over the period. These inter-sectoral variations will be discussed in turn. First, however, the data employed in the calculation of the productivity indicators are discussed in more detail.

For the electrical energy equipment sub-sector, in common with the mechanical equipment and boiler-making sub-sectors, data for number of employees, hours worked, and output in constant 1990 US dollar terms are only available from ABDIB. These data permit the calculation of output per employee and per employee-hour in dollar terms in these sectors from 1983 onwards. Physical output data are supplied by IBGE—the Brazilian Government Statistical Office—and have been combined with ABDIB employment data in index number form to provide an indication of changes in physical output per employee for the electrical energy equipment sub-sector. However, it must be recognized that the samples used in the collection of IBGE and ABDIB data are slightly different and the results of this exercise must be treated with a degree of caution. In the case of the shipbuilding and railway equipment industries, ABDIB data permitting calculation of output per employee and output per employee-hour in dollar terms from 1983 onwards are also available. However, additional data sources for these industries, specifically ABIFER (the railway equipment trade association), IBGE, and the SNICN (national syndicate for the shipbuilding industry) permit the calculation of physical output per employee for these industries from 1981 onwards. In the case of these sub-sectors, the data used to calculate physical output per employee have the advantage that they represent the entire population of firms. To permit ready comparison, all the data for output, employment, and productivity have been converted into index number form. However, at appropriate points in the discussion, indications are provided as to the real magnitudes that underlie the indices.

3.4 Sub-sectoral Changes in Labour Productivity

(i) The Electrical Energy Equipment Sub-sector

Data for productivity performance in the electrical energy equipment sub-sector indicate marked variations since the beginning of the 1980s with a particularly rapid transformation occurring since 1989. These trends reveal themselves in all three of the measures of productivity employed: output per employee (in 1990 US$ terms), output per employee-hour (in 1990 US$ terms), and physical output per employee. The data are presented in Table 16 and Chart 22.

TABLE 16. Labour Productivity Indicators for the Electrical Energy Equipment Sub-sector (1983 = 100)

Year	Output (a)	Physical output (b)	Numbers employed (c)	Employee-hours (d)	Output per employee* (a/c)	Physical output per employee* (b/c)	Output per employee-hour* (a/d)
1981	—	104.4	—	—	—	—	—
1982	—	110	—	—	—	—	—
1983	100	100	100	100	100	100	100
1984	86.3	96.3	88.7	84.9	97.2 (−2.8)	108.6 (+8.6)	101.6 (+1.6)
1985	99.8	111.7	92.4	89.6	108 (−11.1)	120.9 (+11.3)	111.4 (+9.6)
1986	132.5	173.2	100.4	102.2	132 (+22.2)	172.5 (+42.7)	129.6 (+16.3)
1987	135.2	147.5	109.4	111.1	123.6 (−6.4)	134.8 (−21.9)	121.7 (+6.1)
1988	108.5	143.3	114.4	115.6	94.8 (−23.3)	125.3 (−7)	93.9 (−22.8)
1989	88	133.7	106.7	101.8	83.5 (−11.9)	125.3 (0)	86.4 (−8)
1990	74.5	127.2	78.7	98.2	95.3 (+14.1)	161.6 (+30)	75.9 (−12.2)
1991	98.3	92.1	65.5	96.1	150 (+57.4)	140.8 (−12.9)	102.2 (+34.7)
1992	111.5	90.5	59.5	70.4	187.5 (+25)	152.1 (+8)	158.4 (+55)
1993	147.6	127.5	68.1	66.5	216.9 (+15.7)	187.2 (+23.1)	222 (+40.2)
1994	126.5	153.5	56.3	68.9	224.8 (+3.6)	272.6 (+45.6)	183.6 (−17.3)

Note: ★ Figures in brackets indicate yearly percentage changes.

Sources:

(a) Calculated from ABDIB (1994a, 1993a, and 1991). Data are based on annual output measured in constant 1990 US dollars. 1994 figure = US$ 1,666 m.

(b) Calculated from IBGE, *Pesquisa Industrial Mensaal, Produção Física*, various years. Figures are yearly averages.

(c) Calculated from ABDIB (1994a, 1993b, and 1991). 1994 figure = 10,439.

(d) Calculated from ABDIB (1994a and 1991). Figures are yearly averages.

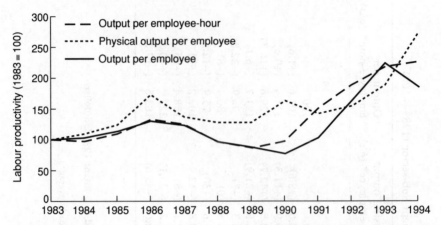

CHART 22. Labour Productivity Indicators in the Electrical Energy Equipment Sub-sector, 1983–1994 (1983 = 100)

Source: Table 16.

Chart 22 and Table 16 reveal broadly similar movements in all three measures of productivity, with variations in output per employee and output per employee-hour being especially closely related. The data demonstrate that the electrical energy equipment sub-sector's pattern of change in productivity was very similar to that of the non-serial capital goods sector as a whole (see Charts 18 and 19). All measures indicate a modest rise in labour productivity in the sub-sector for the period from 1983 to 1986. Between 1986 and 1989 all measures of productivity experience a decline followed by sharp increases between 1989 and 1994. As comparison with data from other sub-sectors will reveal, the increases in labour productivity generated within the electrical energy equipment sub-sector have been the highest within the Brazilian non-serial capital goods sector.

The post-1989 steep rise in labour productivity in the electrical energy equipment sub-sector led to a situation where by 1994, in absolute terms, output per employee in the sub-sector exceeded that of any other at US$ 159,615 (at 1990 prices), with total output standing at US$ 1,666 m. (also at 1990 prices). Throughout the 1983 to 1994 period the data indicate very marked year on year variations in the three measures of productivity. This variability turns out to be a feature common to all of the non-serial capital goods sub-sectors.

(ii) The Mechanical Equipment Sub-sector

The mechanical equipment sub-sector is the largest in output terms after that of electrical energy equipment with a total output in 1994 of US$ 1,319 m. (at 1990 prices). In common with every other sub-sector with the exception of that of electrical energy equipment, real output was actually lower in 1994

TABLE 17. Labour Productivity Indicators for the Mechanical Equipment
Sub-sector (1983 = 100)

Year	Output (a)	Numbers employed (b)	Employee-hours (c)	Output per employee* (a/b)		Output per employee-hour* (a/c)	
1981	—	—	—	—		—	
1982	—	—	—	—		—	
1983	100	100	100	100		100	
1984	104.3	84.3	84.8	121.9	(+21.9)	123	(+23)
1985	123.6	81.6	115.5	151.5	(+24.3)	107	(−13)
1986	123	96.1	114.4	127.9	(−15.6)	107.5	(−0.4)
1987	110.7	90.8	98.9	121.9	(−4.7)	111.2	(+3.4)
1988	105.3	90.9	90.9	115.9	(−7.4)	115.8	(+4.1)
1989	104.8	91.8	98.2	114.1	(−1.6)	106.7	(−7.9)
1990	75.6	74	81	102.2	(−10.4)	93.3	(−12.6)
1991	72.6	63.5	61.4	117.3	(+14.8)	118.2	(+26.7)
1992	70.6	55.7	57.1	126.7	(+8)	123.6	(+4.6)
1993	69.1	51.3	42.3	134.8	(+6.4)	163.4	(+32.2)
1994	74.9	42.9	45.1	167.7	(+24.4)	166.1	(+1.7)

Note: * Figures in brackets indicate yearly percentage changes.

Sources:
(a) Calculated from ABDIB (1994a, 1993a, and 1991). Data are based on annual output measured in constant 1990 US dollars.1994 figure is US$ 1,319 m.
(b) Calculated from ABDIB (1994a, 1993b, and 1991). 1994 figure = 13,936 people employed.
(c) Calculated from ABDIB (1994a and 1991). Figures are yearly averages.

than in the base year of 1983. Despite the differences in output growth, the pattern of labour productivity change within the mechanical equipment sub-sector is very similar to that of the electrical energy equipment sub-sector as Table 17 and Chart 23 demonstrate.

Following a rise in the measures at the start of the period (1983–4), the period 1985 to 1990 witnessed a steady decline in output per employee while output per employee-hour rose only very gradually eventually declining sharply between 1988 and 1990. Between 1990 and 1994 both measures rose sharply to the point that in 1994 both output per employee-hour and output per employee were the highest recorded throughout the period. However, it should be noted that the gains in productivity within the sector since 1990 have been rather more modest than those in the electrical energy equipment sub-sector. Additionally, it is important to recognize that the gains realized since 1990 have to be set against the results of declining productivity in the second half of the 1980s: only since 1993 has output per employee surpassed its 1985 level.

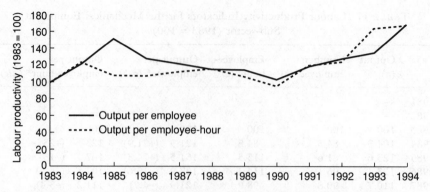

CHART 23. Labour Productivity Indicators in the Mechanical Equipment
Sub-sector, 1983–1994 (1983 = 100)

Source: Table 17.

(*iii*) *The Boiler-Making Sub-sector*

The boiler-making sub-sector by 1994 was the third largest sub-sector (in
real output terms) with an output of US$ 993 m. (at 1990 prices). Output
had fallen from a peak of US$ 2,016 m. (at 1990 prices) in 1986 while employ-
ment had fallen from 24,471 to 10,425 (ABDIB 1993*a*, 1994*a*). Against this
background of considerable contraction, the sector underwent changes in labour
productivity performance not dissimilar to those experienced in the previous
two sectors examined, as Table 18 and Chart 24 demonstrate.

Both indicators of labour productivity decline at very similar rates during
the second half of the 1980s. In common with other sectors, this trend is
markedly reversed from 1990 onwards, with a sharp rise in output per
employee. Interestingly, however, growth in productivity measured in terms
of output per hour, after a sharp increase between 1990 and 1991, appears
to have levelled off and then become negative. Output per employee, by
contrast, increased rapidly up until 1993, although it too experienced an
absolute fall between 1993 and 1994.

(*iv*) *The Railway Equipment Sub-sector*

Between 1983 and 1994, the railway equipment sub-sector experienced the
most dramatic contraction in output of all of the non-serial capital goods sub-
sectors. By 1994, output at 1990 prices had reached 39.5% of its 1983 value
at $316 m. while numbers employed had fallen by over 65% (ABDIB 1994*a*,
1993*a*, 1991). In physical terms (measured in units of rolling stock) the contraction has been even more dramatic with total output falling by almost 90%
between 1983 and 1993 (ABIFER 1993; GEIPOT 1994, 1992, 1985). In
some respects, as subsequent discussion will make clear, the railway equipment industry has been the most seriously affected by the contraction in

TABLE 18. Labour Productivity Indicators for the Boiler-Making
Sub-sector (1983 = 100)

Year	Output (a)	Numbers employed (b)	Employee-hours (c)	Output per employee* (a/b)		Output per employee-hour* (a/c)	
1983	100	100	100	100		100	
1984	101.4	103.9	94.1	97.7	(−2.3)	107.8	(+7.8)
1985	132.5	121.4	128	109.2	(+11.8)	103.5	(−4)
1986	137.6	127	132.9	108.3	(−0.8)	103.5	(0)
1987	101.2	114.7	111.8	88.3	(−18.5)	90.5	(−12.6)
1988	75.9	115.4	118.7	65.8	(−25.5)	63.9	(−41.6)
1989	78.5	117.9	130.5	66.6	(+1.2)	60.2	(−5.8)
1990	46.9	71.9	109.3	65.6	(−1.5)	42.9	(−28.7)
1991	47.5	65.7	67.4	72.3	(+10.2)	70.5	(+64.3)
1992	54.9	51.9	82.2	105.9	(+46.5)	66.8	(−5.2)
1993	62.9	52.1	86.4	128.8	(+21.6)	72.8	(+9)
1994	67.8	54.1	132.9	125.2	(+2.8)	51	(−29.9)

Note: * Figures in brackets indicate yearly percentage changes.

Sources:
(a)   Calculated from ABDIB (1994a, 1993a, and 1991). Data are based on annual output measured in constant 1990 US dollars. 1994 figure = US$ 993 m.
(b)   Calculated from ABDIB (1994a, 1993b, and 1991). 1994 figure is 10,425 people employed.
(c)   Calculated from ABDIB (1994a and 1991). Figures are yearly averages.

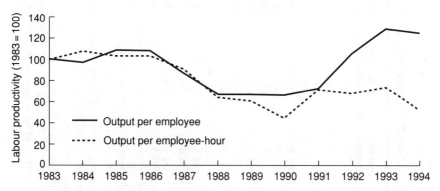

CHART 24. Labour Productivity Indicators in the Boiler-Making Sub-sector, 1983–1994 (1983 = 100)
Source: Table 18.

public investment expenditure. However, the sector, in common with others, has been able to generate increases in output per employee and output per employee-hour since 1990. In the case of output per employee these gains have been quite impressive: in the order of 33.4% between 1990 and 1994 as Table 19 and Chart 25 reveal.

TABLE 19. Labour Productivity Indicators for the Railway Equipment Sub-sector (1983 = 100)

Year	Output (a)	Physical output (b)	Numbers employed (c)	Numbers employed (d)	Employee-hours (e)	Output per employee* (a/c)	Physical output per employee* (b/d)	Output per employee-hour* (a/c)
1981	—	147.1	—	149.8	—	—	98.2	—
1982	—	210.1	—	128.7	—	—	163.2 (+66.2)	—
1983	100	100	100	100	100	100	100 (−38.7)	100
1984	124.5	102.1	95.6	90.6	93.9	130.3 (+30.3)	87.4 (−12.6)	132.6 (+32.6)
1985	154.8	82.8	104.7	104.9	115.6	147.9 (+13.5)	78.9 (−9.7)	134 (+1.1)
1986	108	78.4	114.5	115.2	126.3	94.3 (−36.2)	88.1 (+11.7)	85.5 (−36.2)
1987	109.3	39.7	94.1	111.4	107.7	116.2 (+23.2)	35.6 (−59.6)	101.5 (+18.7)
1988	86.7	25.7	93	94	103.2	93.2 (−19.8)	27.3 (−23.3)	84 (+17.2)
1989	55.9	23.7	90.5	92.3	76.8	61.8 (−33.7)	25.7 (−5.9)	72.8 (−13.3)
1990	31	43.6	72.2	82.4	41.2	43 (−30.4)	52.9 (+105.8)	75.2 (+3.3)
1991	35.5	37.1	59.9	66.9	47.8	59.3 (+37.9)	55.5 (+4.9)	74.3 (−1.2)
1992	45.9	23	56.4	59.2	60.8	81.5 (+37.4)	38.9 (−29.9)	75.5 (+1.6)
1993	37.2	11.1	31	50.3	52.1	120.1 (+47)	22.5 (−42.2)	71.4 (−5.4)
1994	39.5	—	33.8	—	48.3	117.3 (−2.3)	—	81.8 (+14.6)

Note: * Figures in brackets indicate yearly percentage changes.

Sources:

(a) Calculated from ABDIB (1994a, 1993b, and 1991). Figures based on annual output in millions of 1990 US dollars. 1994 value = US$ 316 m.

(b) Calculated from ABIFER (1993); GEIPOT (1994, 1992, and 1985). Figures are based on a unit value weighted index of physical output of locomotives, passenger cars, and freight cars.

(c) Calculated from ABDIB (1994a and 1991). 1994 value = 4,661 people employed.

(d) Calculated from ABIFER (1993). 1993 value = 6,167 people employed.

(e) Calculated from ABDIB (1994a, 1993a, and 1991). Figures are annual averages.

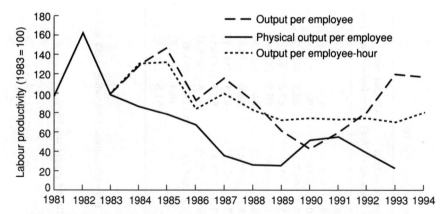

CHART 25. Labour Productivity Indicators in the Railway Equipment Sub-sector, 1983–1994 (1983 = 100)

Source: Table 19.

However, post-1990 rises in output per employee have to be set against earlier declines and a continuing stagnant performance with respect to output per employee-hour. In addition, the period 1990 to 1993 saw a fall in physical output per employee. However, the latter should be interpreted with caution: physical output data on which productivity calculations are made refer only to production of new rolling stock. By 1993, among ABIFER members, 82% of sector output in dollar terms consisted of production of spare parts and the carrying out of repairs and maintenance (ABIFER 1993), a figure reflecting one facet of the sector's response to the lack of new orders. Thus, on this occasion, the physical output per employee measure is likely to understate any gains in productivity that may have been made.

(v) The Shipbuilding Sub-sector

Since the beginning of the 1980s, in common with all other non-serial capital goods sectors bar electrical energy equipment, productivity change within the shipbuilding industry has occurred against a background of declining output and employment. However, the pattern of this decline has been far from constant as Table 20 reveals. Unlike other sectors, there was some recovery in output levels in the late 1980s and early 1990s. Physical output data (calculated on the basis of compensated gross tonnage) indicate marked increases between 1987 and 1989 and 1990 and 1992, while between 1989 and 1992 output (in dollar terms) rose strongly. By 1994, output in 1990 US dollar terms had reached US$ 820 m., some 41.4% of its 1983 value, while employment at 12,093 had halved over the same period.

The data on labour productivity for the shipbuilding sub-sector in Table 20 and Chart 26 indicate substantial growth in output per employee and output per employee-hour between 1988 and 1992 following a period of

TABLE 20. Labour Productivity Indicators for the Shipbuilding Sub-sector (1983 = 100)

Year	Output (a)	Physical output (b)	Numbers employed (c)	Numbers employed (d)	Employee-hours (e)	Output per employee* (a/c)	Physical output per employee* (b/d)	Output per employee-hour* (a/e)
1981	—	157.7	—	131.7	—	—	119.7	—
1982	—	152.1	—	127.8	—	—	119 (−0.6)	—
1983	100	100	100	100	100	100	100 (−16)	100
1984	78.5	102.1	92.7	80.2	95.4	84.6 (−15.4)	127.3 (+27.3)	82.3 (−17.7)
1985	82.1	94.9	85.6	82	94	96 (+13.5)	115.7 (−9.1)	87.3 (6.1)
1986	64.4	87.1	80.1	71.8	75.3	80.5 (−16.1)	121.3 (+4.8)	85.5 (2.1)
1987	49.6	72.4	83.5	78.3	75.2	59.4 (−26.2)	92.5 (−23.7)	66 (−22.8)
1988	42.8	102	79.2	73.6	79.9	54.1 (−8.9)	138.6 (+49.8)	53.6 (−18.8)
1989	34.4	100.7	74.9	68.6	54.5	46 (−15)	145.8 (+5.2)	63.1 (+17.7)
1990	36.7	51.9	49.5	50	42	74.2 (+38)	103.8 (−28.8)	87.4 (+35.5)
1991	59.2	64.5	52.1	50.9	43.6	113.6 (+53.1)	126.7 (+22.1)	135.8 (+55.4)
1992	64	67.6	47.4	49.1	49.8	135.1 (+18.9)	137.7 (+8.7)	128.5 (−5.4)
1993	41.8	—	47.2	—	71.9	88.5 (−34.5)	—	58.1 (−54.8)
1994	41.4	—	50.1	—	80	82.5 (+6.8)	—	51.8 (−10.8)

Note: * Figures in brackets indicate yearly percentage changes.

Sources:

(a) Calculated from ABDIB (1994*a*, 1993*a*, and 1991). Figures based on annual output in millions of 1990 US dollars. 1994 value = US$ 820 m.

(b) Calculated from IBGE, *Pesquisa Industrial Mensal*, various years. Figures are annual averages.

(c) Calculated from ABDIB (1994*a*, 1993*a*, and 1991). 1994 value = 12,093 people employed.

(d) Calculated from SNICN data reproduced in *Portos e Navios*, Rio de Janeiro, 1993. 1992 value = 12,855 people employed.

(e) Calculated from ABDIB (1994*a*, 1993*a*, and 1991). Figures are annual averages.

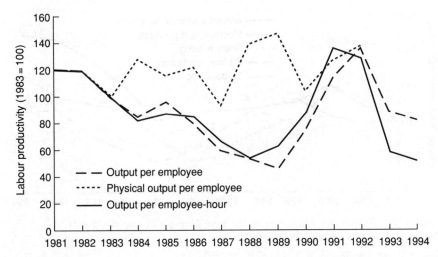

CHART 26. Labour Productivity Indicators in the Shipbuilding Sub-sector, 1983–1994 (1983 = 100)

Source: Table 20.

sustained decline since 1983. The upturn of these measures precedes that occurring in other sub-sectors by approximately two years. However, the period between 1992 and 1994 has seen a dramatic reversal of this trend, in marked contrast to the experience of the other sub-sectors. The data for physical output per employee demonstrate marked variability, although it is possible to observe an upward trend between 1987 and 1992 and a downward one between 1983 and 1987, a pattern broadly matching that of the dollar-based labour productivity data. The reasons underlying this variability are discussed in detail in Sections 3.5 and 3.6.

(vi) Labour Productivity Performance in the Non-serial Capital Goods Sector: A Brief Inter-sub-sectoral Comparison

The data for labour productivity performance in the non-serial capital goods sector reveal marked variations in performance between sub-sectors. In both output per employee and output per employee-hour terms, the electrical energy equipment and mechanical equipment sub-sectors have experienced the most substantial positive changes in labour productivity since 1990 to the extent that the declines in these measures in the second half of the 1980s have been more than offset (Charts 26 and 27).

The result of this has been that output per employee and output per employee-hour achieved at the end of the period were at or near record levels. In the case of boiler making, railway equipment, and shipbuilding, the pattern of productivity change has been broadly similar to declines in the mid to late 1980s followed by sharp rises from 1989 onwards (Charts 27 and 28).

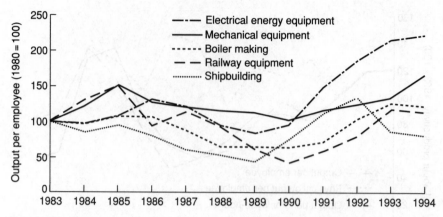

CHART 27. Output per Employee in the Five Non-serial Capital Goods Sub-sectors, 1983–1994 (1983 = 100)

Source: Tables 16–20.

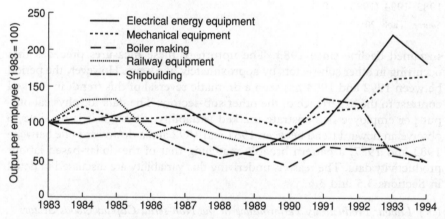

CHART 28. Output per Employee-Hour in the Five Non-serial Capital Goods Sub-sectors, 1983–1994 (1983 = 100)

Source: Tables 16–20.

However, the post-1989 improvements in output per employee have to be set against very substantial declines in the 1980s. In terms of output per employee-hour this has meant that productivity levels still (in 1994) lay below those of 1983, while in output per employee terms, the increases in levels over the base year have been modest (17.3% for railway equipment, 25.2% for boiler making). For shipbuilding, the period actually saw a drop in this measure of 17.5% (Tables 18, 19, and 20).

The strong labour productivity performance of the electrical energy equipment sector in relation to other sectors is also revealed in the data on physical output per person employed (Chart 28). The data indicate that the sector's

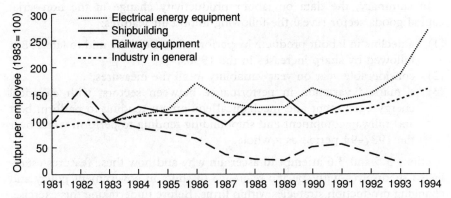

CHART 29. Physical Output per Employee in Three Non-serial Capital Goods Sub-sectors and Industry as a Whole, 1981–1994 (1983 = 100)

Source: Tables 16–20; IBGE, *Pesquisa Industrial Mensal*, various years.

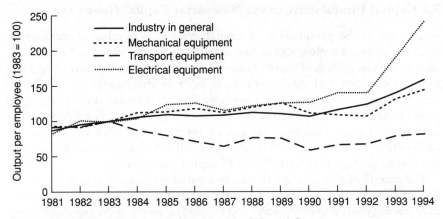

CHART 30. Physical Output per Employee in Selected Sectors, 1981–1994 (1983 = 100)

Source: Calculated from IBGE, *Pesquisa Industrial Mensal*, various years.

performance between 1991 and 1994 comfortably exceeded that of industry as a whole. Comparison with data for other sectors of manufacturing industry demonstrates that the post-1990 productivity gains experienced in the electrical energy equipment sub-sector have been in line with those undergone in the electrical equipment industry as a whole (which of course produces consumer as well as capital goods) (Charts 29 and 30). Chart 29 also indicates the much greater variability in labour productivity performance experienced in the non-serial capital goods sub-sectors compared to that in industry as a whole while, interestingly, the relatively poor productivity performance of the railway equipment industry is mirrored in that of the broader transport equipment sector (Charts 29 and 30).

In summary, the data on labour productivity change in the non-serial capital goods sector reveal the following important features:

(1) a decline in labour productivity performance from the mid to late 1980s followed by sharp increases in the 1990s;
(2) considerable year on year variability in all the measures;
(3) a marked variation in performance between sectors, with electrical energy equipment and mechanical equipment tending to perform best and railway equipment and shipbuilding tending to perform worst over the 1987–94 period as a whole.

Sections 3.5 and 3.6 attempt to ascertain why and how these features established themselves with specific reference to shifts in government policy and changing production strategies within firms. Before undertaking this exercise, however, an attempt is made to examine variations in the productivity of capital.

3.5 Capital Productivity in the Non-serial Capital Goods Sector

Estimation of the productivity of capital involves a number of methodological problems, the most significant of which were discussed in Section 3.2. Ideally, the calculation of capital productivity would be undertaken using some measure of plant and equipment input such as machine-hours employed. Unfortunately, such data are not available for the Brazilian non-serial capital goods sector. However, a broad indication of capital input is available in the form of total assets employed per annum (measured in 1990 US dollars). In conjunction with annual output (also in 1990 US dollars) this can be used to provide an approximate measure of capital productivity.

The results of this exercise should be treated with caution, however, given the breadth of the definition of capital used, incorporating as it does both fixed assets (plant and machinery) and circulating assets, most especially stocks of raw materials, work in progress, and liquid assets. In any economy, the measurement of capital involves practical problems relating to the correct valuation of assets. In the case of the Brazilian economy these problems are especially acute given the high rates of inflation that may affect the valuation of a whole range of assets, most especially liquid assets. Despite these difficulties, the data can be used to provide a useful general indication of variations in capital productivity and the results generated would appear to be consistent with trends in labour productivity. Available data allow estimations of capital productivity to be made for individual sub-sectors from 1986 to 1993 while, for the sector as a whole, the data allow estimations to be made for the period 1980–93. For the non-serial capital goods sector as a whole, the results of this exercise are summarized in Table 21 and Chart 31.

The data demonstrate considerable variation in output per unit of assets over the period since 1980. A sharp fall in the measure between 1981 and

TABLE 21. Capital Productivity for the Brazilian Non-serial
Capital Goods Sector as a Whole

Year	Assets employed (a)	Output (b)	Output per unit of assets (b/a)
1980	122.2	129.8	106.2
1981	106.2	123.2	116
1982	107.5	124.4	115.7
1983	100	100	100
1984	98.7	94.8	96
1985	94.3	105.8	112.2
1986	114.3	109.1	95.5
1987	84.2	95.6	113.5
1988	71	80.2	113
1989	56.5	71.4	121.2
1990	54.3	53.7	98.9
1991	62	63.9	103.1
1992	62.2	69.7	112.1
1993	58.3	70.4	120.8

Sources:
(*a*) ABDIB (1993*a*, 1991). ABDIB data reproduced in Tadini (1993: 10). 1983 = 100.
Index is based on data for total assets measured in 1990 US dollars. 1993 figure is
US$ 4,379 m.
(*b*) ABDIB (1993*a*, 1991). 1983 = 100. Index is based on data for total output measured in
1990 US dollars. 1993 figure is US$ 5,207 m.

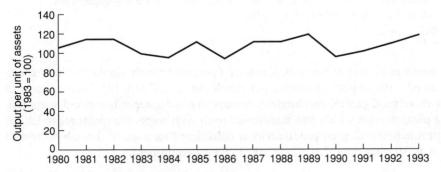

CHART 31. Output per Unit of Assets Employed in the Brazilian Non-serial
Capital Goods Sector, 1980–1993 (1983 = 100)
Source: Table 21.

1984 is followed by a brief rise then a more sustained rise between 1986
and 1989. The latter increase stands in contrast to the fall in output per
employee experienced by the sector in the same period. However, throughout the period 1990 to 1994 there is a sharp reversal in trend with sustained

TABLE 22. Capital Productivity in the Electrical Energy Equipment Sub-sector, 1986–1993

	1986	1987	1988	1989	1990	1991	1992	1993
Output (a)	100	102.1	81.9	66.4	56.2	74.2	84.1	111.4
Assets employed (b)	100	76.4	60.2	47.2	46	48.8	55	57.8
Output per unit of assets employed (a/b)	100	133.6	136	140.7	122.2	152	152.9	192.7

Sources:
(a)   ABDIB (1993a, 1991). 1986 = 100. Index is based on data for total assets measured in 1990 US dollars. 1993 figure is US$ 1,013 m.
(b)   ABDIB (1993a, 1991). 1983 = 100. Index is based on data for total output measured in 1990 US dollars. 1993 figure is US$ 1,944 m.

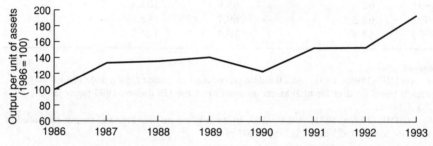

CHART 32. Output per Unit of Assets in the Electrical Energy Equipment Sub-sector, 1986–1993 (1986 = 100)
Source: Table 22.

increases in output per unit of assets, a pattern broadly similar to that experienced with respect to output per employee (see Chart 18). Examination of sub-sectoral capital productivity reveals marked inter-sub-sectoral variation, a phenomenon which also manifested itself with respect to measures of labour productivity. Capital productivity is considered for each of the sub-sectors in turn, starting with that of electrical energy equipment.

(i) Electrical Energy Equipment

The electrical energy equipment sub-sector's performance with respect to the productivity of capital is the strongest among all of the sub-sectors throughout the period, a finding that would appear to be consistent with its record on labour productivity growth. Up until 1990 growth in capital productivity occurred in a context of diminishing output and assets employed. Between 1990 and 1993 this situation has changed with capital productivity improving on the basis of expanding output and (albeit at a slower rate) expanding capital input. These trends are illustrated in Table 22 and Chart 32.

TABLE 23. Capital Productivity in the Mechanical Equipment Sub-sector, 1986–1993

	1986	1987	1988	1989	1990	1991	1992	1993
Output (a)	100	90	85.6	85.2	61.5	59	57.4	56.1
Assets employed (b)	100	70.4	61.5	59.5	49.7	56.9	59.3	50.1
Output per unit of assets employed (a/b)	100	127.8	139.2	143.2	123.7	103.7	96.8	112

Sources:
(a) ABDIB (1993*a*, 1991). 1986 = 100. Index is based on data for total assets measured in 1990 US dollars. 1993 figure is US$ 1,236 m.
(b) ABDIB (1993*a*, 1991). 1983 = 100. Index is based on data for total output measured in 1990 US dollars. 1993 figure is US$ 1,216 m.

The pattern of capital productivity change in the sub-sector differs in some ways from that of labour productivity change, with the period 1986 to 1989 being characterized by sustained increases amounting to 40.7% (Table 19). This contrasts with a 36% reduction in output per employee and a 33.3% reduction in output per employee-hour over the same period (Table 16). However, between 1990 and 1993 changes in output per unit of assets are in the same direction as those of output per employee, output per employee-hour, and physical output per employee with increases of 57.7%, 127.6%, 192.5%, and 15.8% respectively.

(ii) The Mechanical Equipment Sub-sector

Changes in capital productivity in the mechanical equipment sub-sector have taken place against a background of diminishing output and assets employed. Output declined from US$ 2,166 m. in 1986 to US$ 1,216 m. in 1993, while assets employed fell from US$ 2,467 m. to US$ 1,236 m. over the same period (ABDIB 1993*a*, 1991). Up until 1989 the pattern of change in output per unit of assets employed is very similar to that occurring in the electrical energy equipment sub-sector with a 43.2% rise overall (Table 23). However, from 1989 until 1992 there is a steady decline that takes place against a background of an increase in assets employed and further decreases in output. Possible reasons for this phenomenon are discussed in Section 3.6. Only in 1993 does this trend appear to reverse itself with an increase in capital productivity primarily resulting from a cut in assets employed.

Comparison with labour productivity performance for the period 1986–9 reveals contrasts similar to those discussed in the case of the electrical energy equipment sub-sector. Between 1986 and 1989 output per unit of assets in the mechanical equipment sector rose by 43.2% set against a fall of 10.8% for output per employee and 0.7% for output per employee-hour (Table 17). From 1990 onwards both measures of labour productivity rise sharply, the

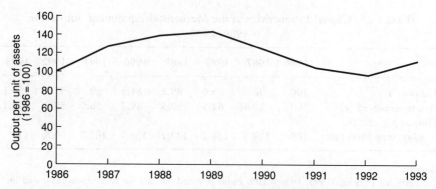

CHART 33. Output per Unit of Assets in the Mechanical Equipment Sub-sector, 1986–1993 (1986 = 100)

Source: Table 23.

capital productivity measure falls, only recovering in 1993, an upturn which occurs rather later than in the electrical energy equipment sub-sector or the non-serial capital goods sector as a whole.

(*iii*) *The Boiler-Making Sub-sector*

As is the case in other sub-sectors, changes in capital productivity in the boiler-making sub-sector have been accompanied by a general tendency for both output and assets employed to fall. Output fell from US\$ 2,016 m. in 1986 to a minimum of US\$ 687 m. in 1990 recovering to US\$ 922 m. in 1993. Assets employed in the same three years stood at totals of US\$ 1,914 m., US\$ 942 m., and US\$ 1,023 m. respectively (ABDIB 1993*a*, 1991).

The pattern of capital productivity change in the boiler-making sub-sector displays similarities to other sub-sectors in that a trend fall between 1986 and 1991 is followed by a renewed upturn (Chart 34). As in the case of the other sectors, assets employed rise at the beginning of the 1990s, a phenomenon which together with stagnant output combines to produce a fall in the productivity of capital. The turning-point is reached in 1991 and is followed by an increase in output per unit of assets employed of 58.5% in the period up to and including 1993 (Table 24). This increase is accompanied by increases in labour productivity measures of 78.1% for output per employee and 3.3% for output per employee-hour (Table 18).

(*iv*) *The Railway Equipment Sub-sector*

Capital productivity performance in the railway equipment industry has followed a somewhat similar pattern to that of labour productivity (in terms of output per employee) with a rise prior to 1988 being followed by a sharp fall which in turn was followed by an upturn from 1990 onwards (Chart 35). However, the recovery in output per unit of assets is much weaker than that

TABLE 24. Capital Productivity in the Boiler-Making Sub-sector, 1986–1993

	1986	1987	1988	1989	1990	1991	1992	1993
Output (a)	100	73.6	55.2	57	34.1	34.5	39.9	45.7
Assets employed (b)	100	78.2	62.6	53.4	49.2	63.9	60.9	53.4
Output per unit of assets employed (a/b)	100	94.1	88.2	106.7	69.3	54	65.5	85.6

Sources:
(a) ABDIB (1993*a*, 1991). 1986 = 100. Index is based on data for total assets measured in 1990 US dollars. 1993 figure is US$ 1,023 m.
(b) ABDIB (1993*a*, 1991). 1983 = 100. Index is based on data for total output measured in 1990 US dollars. 1993 figure is US$ 922 m.

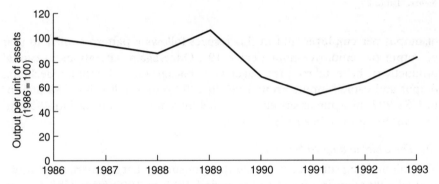

CHART 34. Output per Unit of Assets in the Boiler-Making Sub-sector, 1986–1993 (1986 = 100)
Source: Table 24.

TABLE 25. Capital Productivity in the Railway Equipment Sub-sector, 1986–1993

	1986	1987	1988	1989	1990	1991	1992	1993
Output (a)	100	101.2	80.3	51.8	28.7	32.9	42.5	34.4
Assets employed (b)	100	65.4	39.7	38.1	30.7	33.2	34.2	32.7
Output per unit of assets employed (a/b)	100	154.7	202.3	136	93.5	99.1	124.3	105.2

Sources:
(a) ABDIB (1993*a*, 1991). 1986 = 100. Index is based on data for total assets measured in 1990 US dollars. 1993 figure is US$ 306 m.
(b) ABDIB (1993*a*, 1991). 1983 = 100. Index is based on data for total output measured in 1990 US dollars. 1993 figure is US$ 297 m.

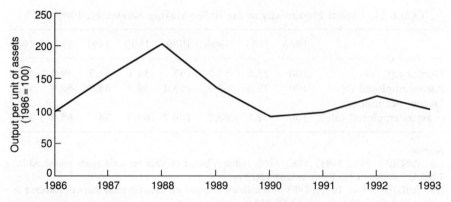

CHART 35. Output per Unit of Assets in the Railway Equipment Sub-sector, 1986–1993 (1986 = 100)

Source: Table 25.

of output per employee and in this respect follows a pattern similar to that of output per employee-hour (Table 19). Once again, alterations in capital productivity have taken place against a background of rapidly declining output and capital input. From 1986 to 1993 output fell from US$ 863 m. to US$ 297 m. while assets employed fell by almost 70% from US$ 936 m. to US$ 306 m. (in 1990 US dollars).

(v) The Shipbuilding Sub-sector

The shipbuilding sub-sector is somewhat unusual in that it experienced a substantial expansion in output in the period 1989 to 1992 from US$ 682 m. to US$ 1,270 m. (ABDIB 1993*a*) at a time when every other sub-sector (bar electrical energy equipment) was encountering marked falls. Growth in output exceeded that of capital input between 1988 and 1992 with the result that there was a sustained rise in output per unit of capital to the value of an accumulated 135.6% (Chart 36 and Table 26). This increase was the greatest among any of the sub-sectors during the period.

Comparison with the labour productivity indicators of output per employee-hour, output per employee, and, to some extent, physical output per employee, reveals a similar pattern of positive growth over the period (Charts 26 and 36). Accompanying the sharp fall in output in 1993, however, there is a sharp reduction in the capital productivity indicator, a trend also clearly evident with respect to the labour productivity indicators.

(vi) Capital Productivity Performance in the Non-serial Capital Goods Sector: A Brief Inter-sub-sectoral Comparison

Between 1986 and 1993 all of the sub-sectors with the exception of boiler making experienced an increase in output per unit of assets. However,

TABLE 26. Capital Productivity in the Shipbuilding Sub-sector, 1986–1993

	1986	1987	1988	1989	1990	1991	1992	1993
Output (a)	100	76.9	66.4	53.4	56.9	91.7	99.3	64.7
Assets employed (b)	100	75.8	78.8	49.9	39.8	57.8	50	53.4
Output per unit of assets employed (a/b)	100	101.5	84.3	107	143	158.7	198.6	121.2

Sources:
(a) ABDIB (1993a, 1991). 1986 = 100. Index is based on data for total assets measured in 1990 US dollars. 1993 figure is US$ 802 m.
(b) ABDIB (1993a, 1991). 1983 = 100. Index is based on data for total output measured in 1990 US dollars. 1993 figure is US$ 828 m.

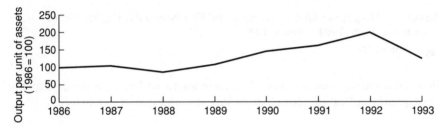

CHART 36. Output per Unit of Assets in the Shipbuilding Sub-sector, 1986–1993 (1986 = 100)

Source: Table 26.

the pattern of change among sectors was neither constant nor uniform. Shipbuilding (up until 1992) and electrical energy equipment experienced the largest and most consistent increases although they were punctuated by falls in 1988 (shipbuilding) and 1990 (electrical energy equipment). In the case of the mechanical equipment, boiler-making, and railway equipment industries, rises at the beginning of the period were followed by marked declines after about 1989 with this trend being reversed after about 1991. However, the recoveries that took place in this latter period were only sufficient to compensate for previous falls with the result that capital productivity levels in these sectors have only improved modestly since the base year and, in the case of boiler making, an absolute decline has been experienced. A comparison of these trends is illustrated in Chart 37.

An examination of both labour and productivity performance in the capital goods sector in recent years raises two important questions. The first (addressed in Section 3.5) concerns the linkage between changes in government policy towards the sector and alterations in its productivity performance, while the second (considered in Section 3.6) relates to the manner in which

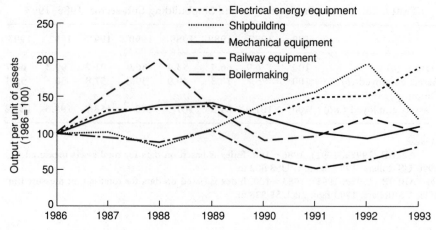

CHART 37. Output per Unit of Assets in the Five Non-serial Capital Goods
Sub-sectors, 1986–1994 (1986 = 100)

Source: Tables 22–6.

these productivity changes have been generated within enterprises and the
consequent implications for changes in static and dynamic efficiency.

3.6 Government Policy and Changes in Productivity Performance

Chapter 2 pointed to two major shifts in government policy that have affected
the sector since 1987. The first has been the greater exposure of the sector to
international competition brought about through the policies of the *Abertura
Comercial*. Starting with modest tariff and non-tariff barrier reductions under
the Sarney government in 1988, the movement towards trade liberalization
intensified in 1990 with the abolition of most of the remaining non-tariff barriers protecting the sector and the implementation of a four-year rolling programme of sharp reductions in tariff levels (BNDES 1993*b*). Over exactly the
same period the sector has been affected by a second significant policy shift
involving a marked retraction in public sector investment expenditure, particularly that relating to infrastructure. As in the case of trade liberalization, there
has been a tendency for this policy to intensify since 1990 following a round
of severe public expenditure cuts imposed during the first phase of the *Plano
Collor* and the continued financial crisis that has beset the federal government.

In this environment of contraction, much of the apparatus of industrial
policy so crucial to the expansion of the sector during the 1970s (most importantly the CDI) has disappeared or been rendered ineffective by lack of funding.
One exception to this is the *Programa da Competitividade Industrial* (PCI) or
Industrial Competitiveness Programme which was established in 1990 with the
aim of assisting enterprises in the transition to the new policy environment

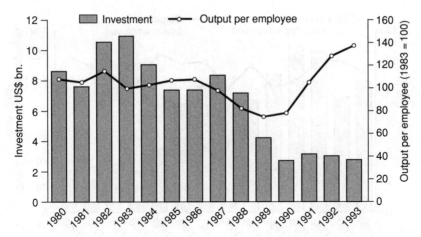

CHART 38. Output per Employee in the Non-serial Capital Goods Sector and Public Sector Enterprise Capital Investment Expenditure, 1980–1993

Source: Investment data comprise investment in electrical energy (CNI 1995) plus investment in petrochemical production facilities and maritime transportation (Petrobrás 1993) plus investment in transport infrastructure (CNI 1995). Output per employee data are obtained from Table 18.

of a reduced role for the state and increased foreign competition. One aspect of this programme is of particular interest in the context of the current chapter: that of the policy initiatives taken to promote increases in productivity in the sector under the auspices of the *Programa Brasileira da Qualidade e Produtividade* (PBQP) or Brazilian Quality and Productivity Programme.

The changes in policy outlined above would appear to be profound, at least in their own terms, representing as they do major breaks with past policy practice and models of industrialization. The purpose of the section which follows is to try to assess the extent to which each has affected the pattern of sectoral and sub-sectoral productivity change discussed in the previous section. In order to do this the impact of each policy is considered in turn, starting with that of public investment reductions (3.6.1), followed by trade liberalization, imports, and exports (3.6.2), and concluding with the Brazilian Quality and Productivity Programme (3.6.3).

3.6.1 PRODUCTIVITY AND CHANGES IN PUBLIC SECTOR INVESTMENT

The evolution of public sector investment policy over the period since the beginning of the 1980s would appear to have had a profound effect on the changing productivity performance of the sector. Comparison between public sector infrastructural investment at an aggregate level and sector-wide labour and capital productivity reveals an interesting and apparently significant relationship (Charts 38 and 39).

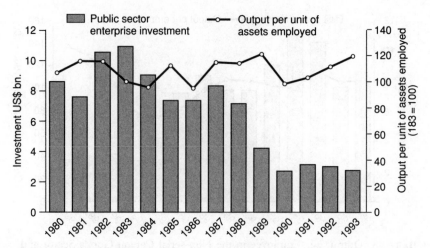

CHART 39. Output per Unit of Assets in the Non-serial Capital Goods Sector and
Public Sector Enterprise Capital Expenditure, 1980–1993

Source: Investment data comprise investment in electrical energy (CNI 1995) plus investment
in petrochemical production facilities and maritime transportation (Petrobrás 1993) plus
investment in transport infrastructure (CNI 1995). Output per unit of assets employed
data are obtained from Table 21.

Prior to the post-1987 rapid declines in public sector infrastructural investment, both capital and labour productivity appear to have fluctuated on a
year to year basis although the trend change in productivity was essentially
static. The period that followed between 1987 and 1990 when the reductions
in public sector investment expenditure got under way in earnest appears
to have been an important period of transition. Both labour and capital productivity appear to have undergone substantial declines during this period.
However, while reductions in expenditure continued and intensified as Brazil
moved into the 1990s, both indicators of productivity reversed their previous
trend and began to exhibit constant growth, a trend that continued up until
the end of the period in 1994. The important point to note is that in the
transition from the essentially static productivity performance of the early to
mid-1980s to the productivity growth of the 1990s, the non-serial capital goods
sector has undergone a substantial shift in the relative importance of public
sector orders, with the domestic private sector and eventually exports becoming of much greater significance (Araújo *et al.* 1991: 76). This is reflected in
Table 27.

A brief consideration of this data would appear to lend support to the hypothesis that the progressive relative reduction of the public sector as the non-
serial capital goods sector's main source of orders has tended to induce greater
efforts to increase efficiency as the sector has been increasingly forced to compete in the more competitive domestic private sector and external markets.

TABLE 27. Composition of the Demand for Brazilian
Non-serial Capital Goods (%)

Year	Public sector	Domestic private sector	Exports	Total
1980	60	31	9	100
1988	49	42	10	100*
1989	49	40	11	100
1990	38	42	20	100
1991	38	36	25	100*
1992	39	40	21	100

Note: * Do not sum to 100 due to rounding.

Source: ABDIB data reproduced in Tadini (1993: 10); own calculations using ABDIB (1993a) data.

This conclusion was lent considerable support in the case of the three enterprises interviewed.

For the three case-study firms, up until 1987, domestic public sector orders had constituted the bulk of demand with reliance on such orders ranging between 60 and 70% of total sales. In the three years prior to 1991, however, the electrical energy equipment enterprise ('Enterprise A') and the mechanical equipment enterprise ('Enterprise B') faced a considerable contraction of public sector orders. Initially, this speared efforts to reduce capacity and shed labour while eventually—especially in the 1991–5 period, the emphasis changed towards strategies aimed at modernizing production facilities and engaging in process innovations. For the shipbuilding enterprise ('Enterprise C'), however, contraction in public sector orders did not commence in earnest before late 1992. At this point, contraction in capacity occurred, although a programme of modernizing innovations had already been put in place through the increased relative reliance of the enterprise on export orders. According to managers of all the enterprises, such modernizing innovations became necessary because of the increasing intensity of competition faced in the domestic private sector and export markets.

However, the posited linkage between changes in public sector demand and productivity change needs further examination because of the influence of two important considerations. The first concerns the effects of the evolution of domestic private sector demand upon performance in the sector while the second concerns the implications of heterogeneous productivity performance in the sub-sectors and the linkage that exists between this and their individual patterns of public sector demand.

The post-1987 period of adjustment for the sector was not only characterized by substantial contraction in public sector investment but was also associated with an extremely sharp reduction in private sector capital forma-tion between 1989 and 1990. This took place during the severe recession that accompanied the *Plano Collor* and was exacerbated by considerable expecta-tional uncertainty among private enterprises together with high interest rates (*Brasil em Exame* 1990: 49). The industries most affected in this manner were paper and cellulose, petrochemicals, and agricultural product process-ing (*Indústria e Produtividade* 1991: 48), all key sources of demand for the mechanical and boiler-making sectors. The intensity of contraction of private sector investment during this period is attributable to the combined effects of a cyclical downturn accompanied by acute fiscal and monetary contrac-tion imposed under the *Plano Collor*. Perhaps the single most contractionary aspect of macroeconomic policy at this time was the freezing of private sector bank balances in an attempt to attain a once and for all reduction in the rate of inflation. An indication of the collapse of private sector demand during this period can be gained by examining the data for FINAME special pro-gramme disbursements (Chart 19) and gross domestic fixed capital forma-tion (Chart 10) in Chapter 2.

With respect to private sector investment, the situation was worsened during the recession of the early 1990s by the financial problems experienced by FINAME as a result of budget cuts. This made it able to finance only 50% of the value of any private sector capital good investment as opposed to 80% in the 1980s (Vermulm 1993: 22).

Thus, it is important to recognize that, although there was a shift between public and private sector demand, this occurred within a context of a very sharp generalized reduction in investment, a situation which forced consider-able restructuring in the sector at the end of the 1980s and the beginning of the 1990s. As Section 3.6 will demonstrate, it was this first wave of restruc-turing, involving as it did a substantial reduction in workforce and capital employed, which to a considerable extent facilitated the productivity gains of 1990 onwards.

Thus, at least for the initial phase of restructuring, it is difficult to separ-ate out the effects of the relative impacts of declining public and domestic sector demand on productivity change within the sector. However, the situ-ation following the 1989–90 recession has been of a rather different charac-ter with a continued subdued level of public sector demand accompanied by an upturn in exports and, especially since 1992, an expansion in domestic private sector demand. This pattern of continued relative decline of public sector demand within the context of an overall expansion of demand has been associated with a second wave of restructuring, which as Section 3.6 will make clear, has tended to emphasize qualitative change in the nature and organ-ization of inputs within the production process rather than their quantitative reduction. Within this second phase, it will become apparent that the demands of private sector clients, often those in export markets, have had a significant impact on the nature and extent of strategies employed to raise productivity.

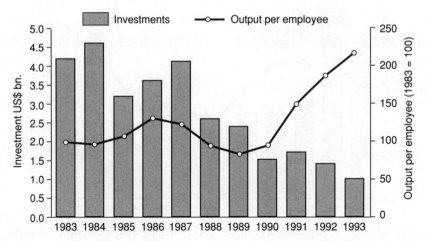

CHART 40. Output per Employee in the Electrical Energy Equipment Sub-sector
and Public Sector Capital Expenditure in the Electricity Sector, 1980–1993

Source: CNI (1995, table 16).

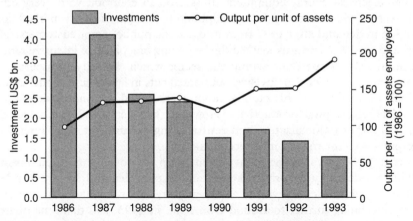

CHART 41. Output per Unit of Assets Employed in the Non-serial Capital
Goods Sector and Public Sector Enterprise Capital Expenditure
in the Electricity Sector, 1986–1993

Source: CNI (1995, table 22).

While a consideration of the relationship between public sector demand
and productivity in the non-serial capital goods sector as a whole illuminates
some significant general trends, it conceals some notable inter-sub-sectoral
variations which have important implications for the current discussion. The
first sub-sector to be examined is that of electrical energy equipment, the
relationship between productivity performance and changes in public sector
investment being illustrated in Chart 40 and 41.

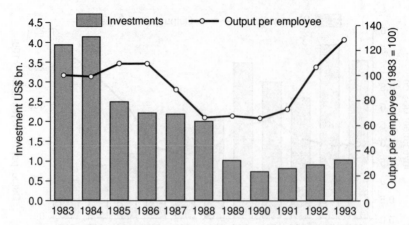

CHART 42. Output per Employee in the Boiler-Making Sub-sector and Petrobrás
Capital Expenditure in Production Facilities, 1983–1993
Source: Petrobrás (1993, table 18).

The electrical energy equipment sub-sector, in common with every other
sub-sector (with the exception of shipbuilding), experienced a marked contraction in demand after 1987 from its domestic public sector customers. The
period from 1987 onwards marked the beginning of a phase of intensive rationalization and restructuring within the sector which, as will be discussed in
more detail in Section 3.6, involved substantial cuts in labour and capital inputs.
Initially, the effects of this rationalization were mixed with improving labour
but declining capital productivity. However, between 1989 and 1990, the
programme of rationalization and restructuring became yet more intense as
the private sector moved into recession.

From 1991 onwards there have been sharp improvements in labour and
capital productivity as private sector and export demand have expanded,
although public sector investment expenditure has remained at a low ebb,
in fact declining further to around US$ 1 bn. in 1993, less than one-quarter
of its 1987 value. For 1994, public sector investment entered a renewed phase
of crisis with a virtual cessation of new investment (ABDIB 1994*a*: 18). Thus
the experience of the electrical energy sub-sector—whose productivity performance has proved the most impressive since 1987—would appear to offer
strong support to the hypothesis outlined earlier in this section, namely, that
improvements in productivity have been associated with a decline in the importance of a public sector as a source of demand.

To some extent, a similar conclusion may be drawn for the boiler-making
sub-sector. In common with other sub-sectors, boiler making experienced a
marked decline in public sector orders from 1987 onwards as is indicated in
Charts 42 and 43 using data for Petrobrás, the sub-sector's largest public
sector client.

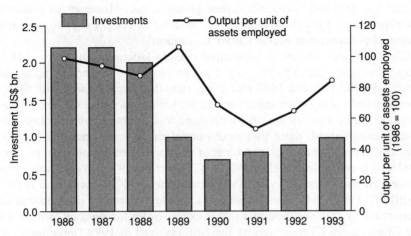

CHART 43. Output per Unit of Assets Employed in the Boiler-Making Sub-sector and Petrobrás Capital Expenditure in Production Facilities, 1986–1993
Source: Petrobrás (1993, table 24).

Declines in public sector investment expenditure from 1987 to 1990 appear to be associated with falls in measures of labour productivity and capital productivity. However, it should also be noted that the years 1989 and 1990 saw dramatic reductions in private sector demand for boiler making as Brazil entered a severe recession. This was especially serious as this sector had historically been rather more reliant on domestic private sector orders than the electrical energy equipment, railway, or shipbuilding industries (ABDIB 1991). Thus not all the pressures that contributed to the measures undertaken that induced rises in productivity (discussed in Section 3.6) emanated solely from reduced public sector investment expenditures.

The period from 1990 onwards saw these trends of falling productivity reversed, at first for labour productivity and eventually for capital productivity. This took place at a time when public sector investment expenditures remained at a very low level. Such growth in demand as has occurred has originated from the domestic private and particularly the export sectors. In the case of the mechanical equipment industry, there has been an upturn in demand from the steel industry as newly privatized enterprises have engaged in programmes of modernization: this is reflected in the data on steel industry investment. Following the resumption of growth in demand, efforts to increase productivity have continued, though, as the next section will make clear, in many cases they have taken on a different character to the 'shock therapy' induced during the 1989–90 recession. In sum, the experiences of the mechanical equipment and boiler-making sectors would appear to support the conclusion that falls in public investment expenditure have, following a period of adjustment, been associated with rises in productivity indicators within the Brazilian non-serial capital goods sector. However, in examining the experience of the shipbuilding, and to some extent the railway equipment sector, this contention seems harder to support.

Charts 26 and 36 reveal substantial rises in labour productivity (149.7% output per employee, 139.7% output per employee-hour) and capital productivity (135.6%) between 1988 and 1992, rises that compare well with those in the electrical energy equipment sub-sector. Unlike the latter sub-sector, however, the period was not one in which there was a contraction in public sector investment. Instead, there was a substantial rise in investment by Petrobrás over the period which took the form of orders for sixteen oil tankers, whose total worth amounted to US$ 687 m. (Petrobrás 1993: 23) and were spread around the main Brazilian yards (Verolme, Caneco, CCN-Mauá, and Ishibrás) (GEIPOT 1992: 164). This substantial increase in domestic demand was supplemented by the capturing of a major export order for eight oil tankers from the Chevron Oil Corporation by the Ishibrás yard in 1990 (interviews).

Within this context, substantial gains in capital and labour productivity were achieved at the start of the 1990s at a time when productivity indicators for other sectors were experiencing marked downturns. However, following completion of the Petrobrás orders at the beginning of 1993 there have been virtually no new orders from Brazilian public enterprises and the sector has been almost entirely dependent on export orders (interviews) although these have not been sufficient to maintain levels of output and improve levels of capacity utilization. The indications at present are that the sector is facing a renewed crisis with productivity indicators displaying marked falls (Charts 26 and 36). This situation would appear to be akin to that faced by other sub-sectors between 1987 and 1990 following the first round of reductions in public sector investment expenditure. Within this context, unless additional orders can be secured, further rounds of rationalization involving quantitative reductions in labour and capital inputs seem likely in order to check the downward trend in productivity, a conclusion supported in the course of interviews at Enterprise C.

In some respects the experience of the railway equipment sub-sector provides an example similar to that of shipbuilding, in that at one stage positive changes in (capital) productivity have been associated with positive variations in public enterprise investment (Charts 44 and 45). However, at least in the 1990s, the evidence is to the contrary with a pattern of productivity change and public investment similar to that of the electrical energy and boiler-making sub-sectors.

Between 1984 and 1988 there was a substantial increase in public sector investment in the railways albeit from a low base when compared to 1980. Interestingly, and in a manner apparently similar to that of shipbuilding, this appears to have been associated with productivity increases. In the case of capital productivity, there was a very substantial increase from 1986 to 1988 while for labour productivity increases (for output per employee and output per employee-hour), increases can be observed between 1983 and 1985 and

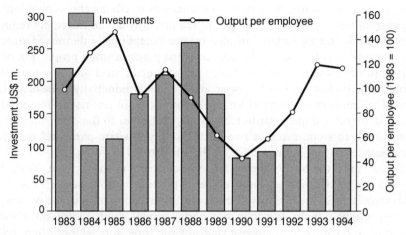

CHART 44. Output per Employee in the Railway Equipment Sub-sector and Federal Railway Capital Expenditure, 1983–1994

Source: RFFSA (1995, table 18).

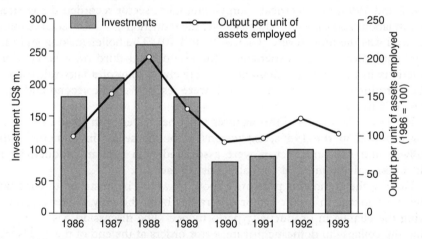

CHART 45. Output per Unit of Assets Employed in the Railway Equipment Sub-sector and Federal Railway Capital Expenditure, 1986–1993

Source: RFFSA (1995, table 25).

1986 and 1987. From 1988 onwards the pattern is rather similar to that of the boiler-making and mechanical equipment sub-sectors, with a sharp decline in public sector investment being associated with declines in all productivity indicators between 1988 and 1990.

Following 1990, there has been an upturn in all measures of productivity despite static and extremely low levels of domestic public sector orders. Once again, 1990 appears to have been a turning-point: output of the sector reached an all-time low in this year and, as will be discussed in Section 3.6, this year was associated with marked reductions in labour and capital inputs, in programmes of rationalization prompted not only by the extremely reduced state of public sector orders but also by the exceptionally depressed state of the domestic private sector (the sub-sector supplied a small proportion of its output of equipment to the domestic private sector steel and petrochemical industries). Following 1990, labour and capital productivity measures have tended to improve as demand for the sector's output has risen. The modest rise in demand is largely attributable to exports, sales to the domestic private sector, and, to some extent a rise in the supply of spare parts and maintenance services to the public sector (ABIFER 1993).

To conclude, the bulk of the evidence would seem to suggest that the declining relative (and absolute) importance of domestic public sector orders has been associated in the majority of cases with a transformation in the productivity performance of the Brazilian non-serial capital goods sector since 1987. There is even evidence to suggest that, for the three sub-sectors where relevant public sector expenditure data are available, the greater the contraction in public sector investment expenditure affecting a non-serial capital goods sub-sector, the greater the rise in its labour and capital productivity. Between 1987 and 1993, the electrical energy equipment sector recorded the greatest rise in labour and capital productivity, yet the reduction in public sector demand it faced was the most severe (Charts 39 and 40). The boiler-making and railway equipment sectors experienced the second and third most severe contractions in public sector demand respectively, a state of affairs mirrored in their productivity performances which were respectively the second and third best (Charts 41–4).

However, the results of this analysis must be treated with some caution as, for a period in the 1980s, expansions in public sector investment in the railway and maritime sectors were associated with rises in productivity in their respective non-serial capital goods sub-sectors.

Despite the arguments presented above, it would be mistaken to conclude that a shrinkage in public sector orders has been the only influence underlying the change in productivity performance. The discussion has suggested that the collapse in domestic private sector orders at the end of the 1980s and the very early 1990s also contributed towards the pressure that induced massive restructuring and rationalization which, as Section 3.6 will demonstrate, underlay much of the improved productivity performance from 1990 onwards. However, the analysis so far has omitted consideration of yet another potentially important influence of the post-1987 period: that of the policy of trade liberalization or *Abertura Comercial*. It is to this that the discussion now turns.

3.6.2 TRADE LIBERALIZATION, IMPORTS, EXPORTS, AND PRODUCTIVITY PERFORMANCE

The Brazilian non-serial capital goods sector, in common with other sectors of Brazilian industry has, since 1987, faced an unprecedented reduction in the protection afforded to it. The programme of trade liberalization that has occurred has emphasized the replacement of non-tariff by tariff barriers which themselves have been progressively reduced in scope. This form of trade liberalization would appear to have especially profound implications for the performance of the non-serial capital goods sector given the historic predominance of non-tariff barriers as the chief instrument of sector protection. Indeed, there would appear to be a clear association between the scaling down of protection in the period since 1987 and an upturn in the various measures of productivity performance. This is most notable in the case of the year 1990 which as well as being the turning-point in the productivity of many of the sub-sectors was also the year in which much of the non-tariff protection, especially that in the form of the Law of Similars, was removed. However, as the previous section noted, the post-1987 period was one in which reductions in public and private sector capital expenditures had a significant impact upon conditions in the sector that would tend to give rise to increases in productivity. What then has been the relative impact of trade liberalization on the observed post-1987 transformation in productivity performance?

In order to address this question fully, it is necessary to examine the impacts not only of the evolution of indicators of trade policy (in the form of average nominal and effective protection) but also of the sector's qualitative perception of the implications of trade liberalization as well the development of imports and exports over the period.

Comparison of data for both nominal and effective protection for the non-serial capital goods sub-sectors, along with their respective indicators of productivity change, reveals an interesting pattern. Reductions in nominal and effective protection have been surprisingly uniform with all bar two (nominal effective protection for shipbuilding at 13% and effective protection for railway equipment at 35%) in the range 20 to 25%. Set against this uniformity there exists a considerable diversity in productivity performance between subsectors, a feature that has already been discussed in some detail.

Charts 46 to 49 indicate that, in general, the reductions in nominal and effective protection have been associated with rises in the productivity indicators, although there would appear to be no connection between the extent of the reductions and the relative size of the productivity changes. In some cases, there have been falls in the productivity indicators, notably in the area of capital productivity. Again, there would appear to no consistent relationship between the extent of variations in protection and the sizes of these falls.

To some extent this analysis, examining as it does the impact of productivity changes over the 1989–94 period, tends to mask positive changes in productivity performance that the changes in trade policy may be argued to have induced. This is because some sectors experienced gains in productivity towards the end of the period after a process of adjustment, although, in absolute terms, levels of productivity remained below those experienced at the start of the period. This is particularly true for capital productivity performance in the mechanical equipment and railway equipment sub-sectors (Charts 33 and 35).

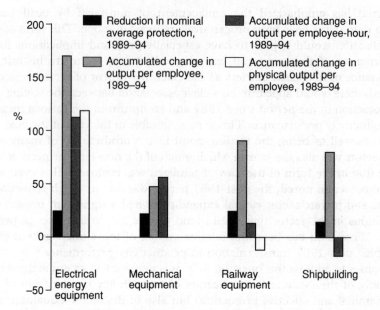

CHART 46. Nominal Average Tariff Reductions and Labour Productivity Changes, 1989–1994

Sources: Tables 16–26, Tables 6 and 7.

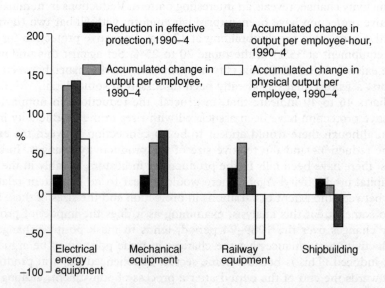

CHART 47. Reductions in Effective Protection and Labour Productivity Changes, 1990–1994

Sources: Tables 16–26, Tables 6 and 7.

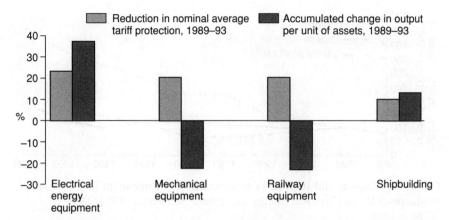

CHART 48. Nominal Average Tariff Reductions and Capital Productivity Changes, 1989–1993

Sources: Tables 16–26, Tables 6 and 7.

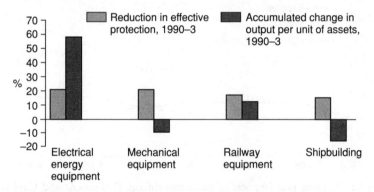

CHART 49. Reductions in Effective Protection and Capital Productivity Changes, 1990–1993

Sources: Tables 16–26, Tables 6 and 7.

The lack of a precise relationship between variations in productivity and protection certainly does not establish that the impact of trade liberalization on productivity performance has itself been weak or unimportant *per se*. However, the disparities would tend to suggest that variations in levels of protection alone cannot explain the observed variations in productivity performance. This conclusion is not altogether surprising since measures of protection do not necessarily indicate the competitive pressure that firms may be experiencing or its nature. The important point to recognize is that reductions in tariffs and, most important of all, reductions in non-tariff barriers can only induce competitive pressures if they generate increases in actual or potential competition through a rise (or the threat of a rise) in imports. At the same time, trade liberalization, inasmuch as it contributes towards

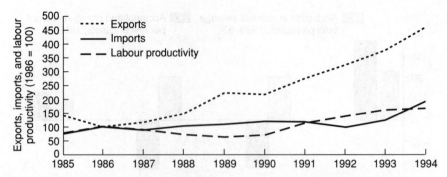

CHART 50. Exports and Imports of Electrical Energy Equipment and Labour
Productivity in the Electrical Energy Equipment Sub-sector, 1985–1994
(1986 = 100)

Source: Table 16; United Nations, *Commodity Trade Statistics*/CEPAL, various years.
Labour productivity data are for output per employee.

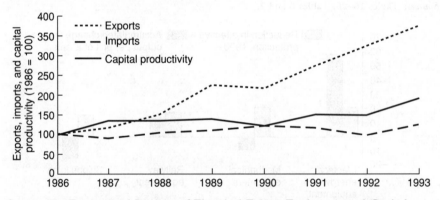

CHART 51. Exports and Imports of Electrical Energy Equipment and Capital
Productivity in the Electrical Energy Equipment Sub-sector, 1986–1993
(1986 = 100)

Source: Table 22; United Nations, *Commodity Trade Statistics*/CEPAL, various years. Capital
productivity data are for output per unit of assets.

increased export intenstity, may also sharpen competitive pressures and thus
give rise to productivity gains (see Chapter 1). Thus it will be necessary to
consider the role of imports and exports in order that the impact of trade
policy change on productivity performance can be more fully ascertained.

For the purposes of the present discussion, it will be necessary to draw on
some of the data found in Chapter 4. Charts 50 to 59 illustrate the relationship between imports, exports, labour and capital productivity for the five
non-serial capital goods sub-sectors.

In examining Charts 50 to 59, it is important to be aware that the trade
and productivity data are drawn from different sources, with productivity data

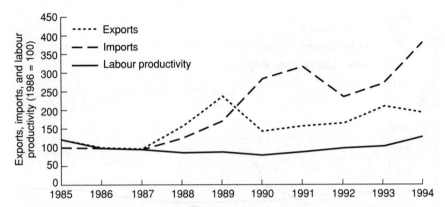

CHART 52. Exports and Imports of Mechanical Equipment and Labour
Productivity in the Mechanical Equipment Sub-sector, 1985–1994 (1986 = 100)

Source: Table 17; United Nations, *Commodity Trade Statistics*/CEPAL, various years.
Labour productivity data are for output per employee.

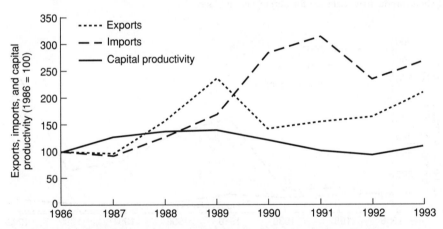

CHART 53. Exports and Imports of Mechanical Equipment and Capital
Productivity in the Mechanical Equipment Sub-sector, 1986–1993 (1986 = 100)

Source: Table 23; United Nations, *Commodity Trade Statistics*/CEPAL, various years. Capital
productivity data are for output per unit of assets.

being obtained from ABDIB and trade data from United Nations sources.
Data from the former source represents the activities of about 80% of all enterprises in the non-serial capital goods sector while the UN data represent
total exports. However, given the predominance of ABDIB members in the
Brazilian non-serial capital goods sector, any discrepancies arising between
the two sets of data are not expected to be too large.

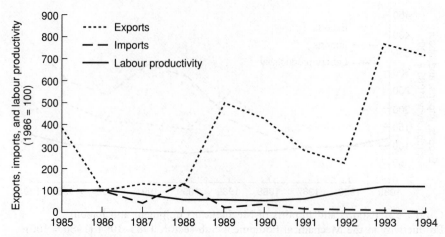

CHART 54. Exports and Imports of Boilers and Labour Productivity in the Boiler-Making Sub-sector, 1985–1994 (1986 = 100)

Source: Table 18; United Nations, *Commodity Trade Statistics*/CEPAL, various years. Labour productivity data are for output per employee.

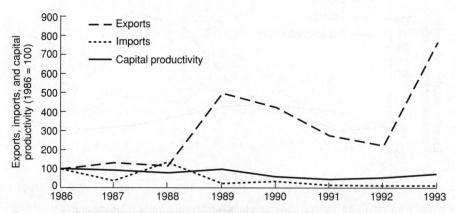

CHART 55. Exports and Imports of Boilers and Capital Productivity in the Boiler-Making Sub-sector, 1986–1993 (1986 = 100)

Source: Table 24; United Nations, *Commodity Trade Statistics*/CEPAL, various years. Capital productivity data are for output per unit of assets.

In general, the data show a positive association between growth in exports and improvements in labour and capital productivity, appearing to suggest that increases in exports help to generate rises in productivity. The relationship between changes in imports and productivity growth is less clear cut, there being something of a positive association for electrical and mechanical equipment and less well-defined relationships for other sectors (Charts 50–9).

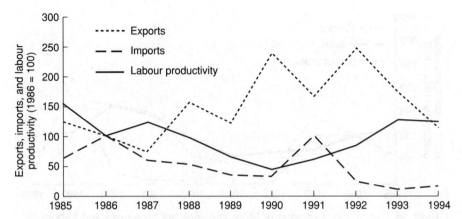

CHART 56. Exports and Imports of Railway Equipment and Labour Productivity in the Railway Equipment Sub-sector, 1985–1994 (1986 = 100)

Source: Table 19; United Nations, *Commodity Trade Statistics*/CEPAL, various years. Labour productivity data are for output per employee.

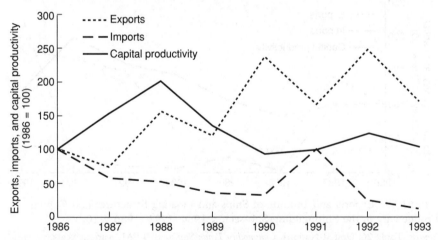

CHART 57. Exports and Imports of Railway Equipment and Capital Productivity in the Railway Equipment Sub-sector, 1986–1993 (1986 = 100)

Source: Table 25; United Nations, *Commodity Trade Statistics*/CEPAL, various years. Capital productivity data are for output per unit of assets.

Thus the data would seem to suggest that the rise in exports appears to be the strongest link between variations in patterns of trade of non-serial capital goods and changes in the productivity performance of the Brazilian non-serial capital goods sector. To the extent that the expansion of exports is attributable to the impact of trade liberalization, then the latter policy

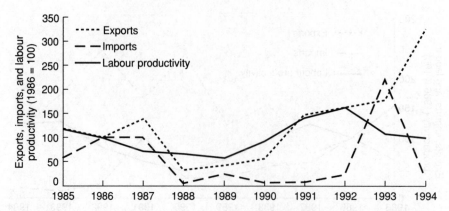

CHART 58. Exports and Imports of Ships and Floating Structures and Labour Productivity in the Shipbuilding Sub-sector, 1985–1994 (1986 = 100)

Source: Table 20; United Nations, *Commodity Trade Statistics*/CEPAL, various years. Labour productivity data are for output per employee.

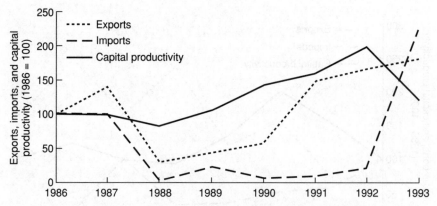

CHART 59. Exports and Imports of Ships and Floating Structures and Capital Productivity in the Shipbuilding Sub-sector, 1986–1993 (1986 = 100)

Source: Table 26; United Nations, *Commodity Trade Statistics*/CEPAL, various years. Capital productivity data are for output per unit of assets.

could be held to have been associated with improvements in productivity. However, as Chapter 4 will suggest, the expansion in exports is not solely attributable to the development of trade liberalization: reductions in public sector demand and the initiation of new forms of export credit are also important explanatory factors.

As previous sections have noted, the productivity performance of the Brazilian non-serial capital goods sector has been somewhat heterogeneous across sub-sectors. Examination of the data reveals interesting linkages between inter-sectoral differences in productivity, import, and export perform-ance. When data on growth in imports and exports for each sector are com-pared with their growth in labour and capital productivity over the 1987–93 period there seems little consistent relationship between the relative success each sub-sector has achieved in raising capital and labour productivity and the relative expansion of exports or imports for each sub-sector. Thus, the electrical energy equipment sector which had the best overall productivity performance out of the five sub-sectors had the second highest growth in exports and the third highest growth in imports, while the railway equipment sector with the poorest productivity performance had the third highest growth of exports and the lowest overall growth in imports. When the data on absolute import and export volumes (taken from Chapter 4) are examined and com-pared with that for productivity growth for the 1987–93 period, an altogether clearer picture emerges.

When the sub-sectors are ranked by average export and import volumes, the ranking generated corresponds almost exactly to the relative success each sub-sector has achieved in raising capital and labour productivity over the period. Thus, the electrical energy and shipbuilding sub-sectors, ranked first and second in terms of productivity performance, achieve the same ranking in terms of their export and import volumes which were the first and second greatest respectively. At the same time, the mechanical equipment sub-sector whose productivity performance was the fourth best among the five sub-sectors held third position in terms of import and export volumes.

In sum, the evidence appears to suggest the following. First, there does appear to be a positive association between growth in exports and gains in productivity, although this relationship is not precise. Secondly, the greater the exposure to international markets, as measured through the absolute volumes of imports and exports, the greater the productivity performance. This would appear to lend support to the theoretical proposition outlined in Chapter 1 that greater exposure to international markets provides greater induce-ments to raise productivity.

Clearly, the role of trade liberalization is of relevance in explaining in-creases in productivity in that it has encouraged increases in imports and, as Chapter 4 will demonstrate, exports as well. However, as has been suggested, trade liberalization can only offer a partial explanation of import and export behaviour. Reductions in domestic public sector demand in part underlay in-creases in export intensity and the maintenance of high export ratios in certain sub-sectors (see Chapter 4). However, it seems likely that trade liberalization had a more critical role to play in explaining the extent of import expansion. To the extent that such import expansion generated incentives to raise pro-ductivity then trade liberalization has been an important policy variable.

The role of increased exposure to international competition in export and import markets was highlighted as an incentive to improve productivity performance for all enterprises interviewed. During interviews at Enterprises

A and *B*, it was established that one of the principal reasons for current investment in productivity-enhancing CNC machinery and the adoption of new modes of shop-floor organization was to counter the increasing challenge generated by imports in the Brazilian domestic market, a challenge that has intensified with the overvaluation of the *real* since July 1994. Such increases in imports were felt, in large part, to be a function of the increased openness of the Brazilian economy to the importation of non-serial capital goods.

However, the role of the export market and the need to achieve competitiveness within it was stated to be of equal if not greater importance in the approval of these investments for both Enterprises *A* and *B*. This point was particularly emphasized in the course of interviews with the shipbuilding enterprise, *C*, whose strategies became very export oriented following the collapse in domestic public sector orders in 1993. This would tend to point to the role of policy-induced reductions in domestic demand which, as Chapter 4 will point out, have forced sector enterprises to export in order to reduce losses and excessive capacity under-utilization.

One further recent impact of trade liberalization has also been connected with renewed investment in the sector. The lowering of tariffs and the abolition of the Law of Similars has enabled enterprises in the sector to import machinery (serial capital goods) with more advanced technologies than available domestically. This is particularly true in the case of computer-controlled lathes and milling machines whose advantages have been felt not only in terms of increased capital productivity but also in terms of greater precision and lower size variability in sub-assembly manufacture (interviews at Enterprise *B*). According to a recent report on the sector (BNDES 1995: 8), such competitiveness and productivity improvements generated by the freer importation of machinery have been widespread. With respect to electronic control systems, the end of the market reserve policy for the micro-electronics and computer sectors has been of particular significance (ibid. 8), enabling enterprises to import the latest CNC control systems (usually embedded in new machinery suites) instead of being forced to rely on less advanced Brazilian equipment and software. The latter was often produced under licence, incorporating an older generation of designs, usually based on 1970s first-generation Japanese integrated circuit technologies (Porteous 1986).

A further implication of trade liberalization—this time for the sector's cost structure—has been the increased availability and lower cost of imported parts and components (Vermulm 1993: 22, Tadini 1993: 13). However, the extent to which the sector is able to reduce costs through sourcing components overseas is somewhat more limited than in the case of the serial capital goods sector. The non-serial capital goods sector by its very nature has a lower requirement for standardized components with smaller sub-assemblies and parts tending to be of varying design and most often being produced on site.

However, there are exceptions to this rule within the sector, most especially within the electrical energy equipment sub-sector where items such as transformers, switch gear, and no-break devices do contain standard components. Between 1987–9 and 1992 the share of imported components and materials as a percentage of total output in the electrical energy equipment sector rose from 1.89% to 4.88% (Strachmann 1993). In the case of Enterprise *A*, many such components (especially semiconductors and even completed circuit boards) are sourced from abroad (usually from the parent company) and reductions in tariffs on such components have assisted in the reduction in costs and a gain in international and domestic competitiveness.

To conclude, the data indicate a clear association between reductions in nominal and effective protection and increases in productivity in the non-serial capital goods sector since the adoption of trade liberalization in 1988. However, despite reasonably homogeneous reductions in such measures of protection across sub-sectors, productivity performance has been very varied across sub-sectors. When variations of export and import performance are compared with alterations in labour and capital productivity, two main trends emerge. The first indicates a positive association between growth of exports and gains in productivity. The second demonstrates an association between exposure to international trade and productivity performance. Sub-sectors with superior productivity performance tend to be those whose respective import and export volumes are greatest. To the extent that alterations in exports and imports are in part a function of trade policy, then such policy appears to have had a positive effect upon productivity change.

Trade liberalization appears to be associated with yet another productivity-augmenting development. The post-1986 liberalization of trade has led to an increase in the relative importance of imported machinery whose superior performance and lower cost (itself partly induced by the effects of trade liberalization) have contributed to observed labour and capital productivity gains. In terms of firms' cost structures, there is some evidence to suggest that trade liberalization has helped to increase cost competitiveness as imported components have become more freely available.

3.6.3 THE BRAZILIAN QUALITY AND PRODUCTIVITY PROGRAMME AND PRODUCTIVITY PERFORMANCE

Although the government of President Collor which came to power in 1990 was committed to removing much of the apparatus of industrial policy, an important policy initiative was launched aimed at enhancing enterprises' ability to compete in the increasingly open economy which would develop as the *Abertura Comercial* proceeded. The Brazilian Quality and Productivity Programme or *Programa Brasileira de Qualidade e Produtividade* (PBQP) was launched on 7 November 1990 to tackle deficiencies in quality and productivity performance throughout industry that were not only threatening future competitiveness but were exerting a current cost estimated to be as much as 40% of industrial GDP (UNIDO 1992: 10). The PBQP comprises five main components which are:

(1)   awareness and motivation building;
(2)   a programme of development and diffusion of modern quality and productivity-related management methods;
(3)   human resource development;
(4)   provision of technical services; and
(5)   institutional support (ibid. 10).

The PBQP comes under the direct control of the President of the Republic. However, unlike previous federal industrial policy organizations, it has no resources available for disbursement itself (Fleury 1995: 79). Instead, the PBQP acts as a co-ordinating agency, facilitating contacts between enterprises, government agencies, universities, and research centres, facilitating the flow of information and ensuring that enterprises are made aware of best quality and productivity practice. In order to provide more specialized assistance to key sectors of Brazilian industry, the PBQP has developed individual sub-sectoral programmes. Shortly after the launch of the main programme, a special programme was launched for the capital goods sector, uniting all the capital goods trade associations and the relevant state agencies.

An assessment of the impact of the PBQP on productivity performance in the non-serial capital goods sector is somewhat difficult to undertake since the programme has predominantly consisted of the diffusion of information and ideas and summit meetings between key industry figures and programme administrators. Given the programme's lack of its own resources, any financial commitments to raise productivity levels have to originate from enterprises themselves. Fleury (1995: 79) concludes that while a consensus and awareness on quality and productivity issues has been built up among participants, the impact of the programme itself on competitiveness has been quite limited, a conclusion supported generally throughout industry where prospects for the buoyancy of the domestic market and the impact of the *Abertura Comercial* are considered much more important (*Indústria e Produtividade*, June 1994: 32). Meyer Starmer (1993b: 1), in similar vein, argues that the main impact of the programme has been on raising consciousness, something that to a great extent would probably have occurred in any case given increased exposure to external competition under the *Abertura Comercial*. Moreover, as the next section will reveal, some of the fundamental structural changes in the sector that permitted productivity growth in the 1990s were under way well before the PBQP rose to prominence.

However, as the sector has recovered, following the recession of 1989–91 there has been an increasing attention paid to qualitative changes in the organization of plant, productivity management techniques, and technological change as exposure to international competitive pressures increased. Many of these developments would appear to fit in with the Japanese manufacturing techniques espoused and diffused by the PBQP. In the course of interviews with the three enterprises, however, the PBQP was never mentioned as an important influence in connection with these techniques which all the enterprises had adopted. For the enterprises in the sector, perhaps the most concrete contribution of the PBQP has been associated legislation introduced in 1991 granting tax exemptions on the purchase of 950 specified items of machinery and equipment and more favourable tax treatment under a new accelerated depreciation régime (UNIDO 1992: 16). This has encouraged the moderate upturn in investment in new and more efficient machinery that has accompanied recovery in the sector.

3.7 Sources of Productivity Change in the Non-serial Capital Goods Sector

Having established the policy background and influences surrounding the alterations in productivity performance in the non-serial capital goods sector, it is now appropriate to consider the manner in which these changes have been brought about. In analysing the strategies that enterprises have employed to raise productivity, it is possible to distinguish two major approaches. The first, termed rationalization, has emphasized the quantitative reduction in labour and capital inputs in an effort to reduce costs, cut losses, and raise productivity in response to adverse demand conditions. To some extent this strategy can be considered reactive in that it was frequently the involuntary consequence of external events, principally domestic market contraction.

The second strategy, that of modernization, has emphasized qualitative rather than quantitative changes in factor inputs very often involving technological change and organizational innovations. This strategy can be considered to be rather more proactive in that it has involved conscious attempts to raise sector productivity in response to perceptions concerning the likely future condition of markets, their patterns of demand and competition. The strategy of modernization has been associated with the post-1991 period of cautious recovery in the sector and in many cases has been aimed at emulating international levels of competitiveness in the face of increased export intensity and the opening up of the domestic market. Each strategy is considered in turn below. In discussing the strategies separately, however, it is important to recognize the fact that they are not mutually exclusive and have frequently been employed simultaneously with quantitative reductions in inputs accompanying organizational and technological change.

3.7.1 RATIONALIZATION AND PRODUCTIVITY CHANGE

Since 1987 every non-serial capital goods sub-sector has experienced a dramatic scaling down in both labour and capital inputs which, for the sector as a whole, amounted to 47.7% for labour and 30.8% for capital (Table 21, Chart 20). To a considerable extent, the evolution of productivity change throughout the period can be understood in terms of this quantitative reduction in these inputs as enterprises sought to reduce costs and stave off losses in the face of reduced demand from the domestic private and particularly public sector. In considering the linkage between this rationalization and productivity change, the discussion is divided into two sections, the first concerning the period 1986 to 1991 which was characterized by dramatic sector contraction and the second concerning the period 1991 to 1994 which may be considered a period of modest recovery.

(i) Rationalization and Recession, 1986–1991

Perhaps the key feature of this first phase of rationalization in the sector was a significant reduction in capital assets employed in the sector. These reductions were made in an attempt to offset losses and to reduce chronic under-utilization of capacity in the face of an average of about 38% capacity lying idle at the beginning of the period (ABDIB 1991). For certain sub-sectors the degree of under-utilization was even more substantial with rates of 55% and 50% for railway equipment and shipbuilding respectively, while for electrical energy equipment, mechanical equipment, and boiler making the figures were 33.5%, 25.8%, and 37.1% respectively (ibid.). The reduction in capacity that took place was in the form of non-replacement of worn-out equipment and the closing of certain areas of particularly under-utilized plant. The evidence of this initial programme of capacity reduction was evident on visits to all plants with certain production areas disused with, in some cases, much machinery removed.

Some of the larger multi-plant enterprises in the sector engaged in the closure of whole production facilities, the most notable example of this being that of Villares in the mechanical equipment sector which shut its oldest plant (and in fact one of Brazil's oldest non-serial capital goods plants) in São Bernardo (Tadini 1993: 14). CBV, one of the largest enterprises in the sector, producing mechanical equipment for the petrochemical sector (principally Petrobrás), reduced the number of its plants from eleven to five while Jaraguá, another producer of mechanical equipment, shut its older plant and continued operations only in its most modern (ibid. 14). In the railway equipment sector, Cobrasma shut its older Osasco plant in São Paulo in response to chronic under-utilization (Revista Ferroviaria, Dec. 1994: 23) while plant closures occurred as locomotive production operations by General Electric do Brasil were merged with those of Villares to form GEVISA.

The data on assets employed in Tables 21 to 26 give some idea of the magnitude of the reduction in capital inputs. However, to repeat the point made in Section 3.2, it is important to recognize that the indicator of capital input used is broad and the data should be treated with a degree of caution. The cuts in capital inputs in the 1986 to 1991 period amounted to 45.8% for the sector as a whole (Table 21). For individual sub-sectors the reductions were 51.2% (electrical energy equipment), 43.1% (mechanical equipment), 36.1% (boiler making), 66.8% (railway equipment), and 42.2% (shipbuilding); rates of reduction which exceeded that of falls in output in all sectors except railway equipment and boiler making. Not surprisingly, output per unit of assets rose in all but the latter two sectors, a situation largely reflecting the automatic capital productivity gains resulting from the removal of capital stock at a faster rate than falls in output. There is also a qualitative aspect to these gains. They also reflect the effects of the removal of more inefficient capacity from the sector as older plants and their associated vintages of capital equipment were withdrawn. Despite these reductions in capital inputs, capacity utilization fell for all but one of the sub-sectors (ABDIB 1994a, 1991).

For the sector as a whole, while reductions in capital input in the period 1986 to 1989 were substantial, labour input fell far less rapidly: in fact by only 5.6% (Chart 20). In the face of more rapidly declining output, the inevitable consequence of this was declining labour productivity in terms of output per employee and output per employee-hour for all sub-sectors (Tables 16–20). However, there was a rise in physical output per employee in the electrical energy equipment, railway equipment, and shipbuilding sectors. The discrepancy between the two is likely to reflect downward price movements experienced during the downturn.

The slower pace of labour force reductions in the period 1986–9 would appear to reflect the initial strategy of rationalization employed by the sector which stressed the relatively costless and rapid removal of spare production capacity (in the form of capital) from the industry through scrapping, depreciation, and non-replacement. Brazilian labour law—for formal employment —imposes relatively high costs on employers seeking to dismiss employees which, combined with a reluctance to lose skilled staff, may have made large reductions in the labour force less desirable in the initial stages of demand reductions, especially as enterprises could have had little inkling of the future duration and intensity of the downturn. However, intensified public sector expenditure cuts combined with drastic reductions in private sector demand in 1990 made further adjustment inevitable as combined losses increased from 2.5% of total output in 1988 to 8.8% in 1990 (calculated from ABDIB 1993a).

The final period of the recession—1989–91—saw very substantial reductions in labour employment in all the sub-sectors of the non-serial capital goods sector as reductions in labour inputs became key features of rationalization in response to rapidly contracting internal demand and output in the years 1989 and 1990. For the electrical energy equipment sub-sector, employment fell by 38.6% while for mechanical equipment, boiler making, railway equipment, and shipbuilding, the figures were 30.8%, 44.4%, 33.8%, and 25.8% respectively. These reductions were mirrored by similar falls in total numbers of employee-hours (Tables 16–20). The falls in labour input exceeded those of output, which by 1991 had begun to level off and rise. Thus the final period of recession witnessed rises in the labour productivity indicators for all sub-sectors. These rises may in large part be viewed as the product of reductions in the labour force to levels compatible with the production of a reduced quantity of output. Productivity gains are automatic as 'excess' labour is removed from the production process and need not necessarily result from technical progress or innovation.

The behaviour of capital productivity over the period 1989–91 is marked by a sharp fall between 1989 and 1990 for all sub-sectors except shipbuilding as previous falls in assets employed reversed themselves but output and capacity utilization continued to fall. The observed increases in capital input are likely to have resulted from the following phenomena. First, and most important, the intensity of the private sector recession combined with the illiquidity of the public sector customers had led to the substantial build-up of stocks of goods which had been ordered but for which customers were unable to pay (*Brasil em Exame* 1990: 48). In the case of the public sector, late payment became a widespread phenomenon. Given the development of these problems, enterprise assets would have risen as output was transferred to stock and involuntary 'credit' extended to late payers. Secondly, asset values are also likely to have risen due to the re-indexation of liquid assets under the Collor plan. Finally, as the next section will make clear, a few enterprises had cautiously begun to invest in additional capital equipment in an attempt to modernize.

Given these considerations, there are reasons to suspect that the observed fall in capital productivity observed during this period may not be connected to poor fixed capital productivity performance so much as to the results of an involuntary increase in working capital.

(ii) Rationalization and Recovery, 1991–1994

During the next phase in the process of rationalization a much greater emphasis has been placed on the reduction of labour input with a fall of 20.6% in total sector employment between 1991 and 1994 (Chart 20). By contrast, between 1991 and 1993 there was only a small fall in overall capital input, of 5.9% (Table 21). For electrical energy equipment, mechanical equipment, boiler making, railway equipment, and shipbuilding, employment fell by 14%, 32.4%, 17.7%, 43.6%, and 3.8% respectively (Tables 16–20). Reductions in employment were universal with all enterprises in the sector engaging in reductions in the size of their labour force (interviews). In the case of Enterprises A and B, reductions in employment were very substantial with reductions of 18,000 to 10,000 and 4,000 to 1,300 respectively (ibid.).

For the electrical energy equipment, mechanical equipment, and shipbuilding sectors, reductions in employment are matched by similar falls in the number of hours worked. However, in the railway equipment sector there was actually a small rise in the number of hours worked while in the case of boiler making this was quite substantial. In the latter two industries the strategy of labour-force reduction would appear to have been to reduce the numbers employed while increasing the average numbers of hours worked per employee, a phenomenon strongly associated with the corporate strategy of downsizing.

In terms of capital inputs, the period 1991 to 1993 saw modest reductions in total assets employed for all sectors except that of electrical energy equipment (Tables 22–6). It is likely that some of this reduction reflects the impact of recovery in the domestic private sector feeding through into reduced stocks. At the same time, 1991 witnessed the unfreezing of public sector payments, thus reducing credits extended by the non-serial capital goods sector as some late payments were released. However, it is important to stress that this period, in the case of some enterprises, represented an important phase of investment in plant reorganization and new plant and equipment. This, in part accounts for the rise in assets employed in the electrical energy sector. In general, the period between 1991 and 1994 was one in which the Brazilian private sector economy recovered, which together with an increase in exports has tended to raise demand for the sector's products.

Set against the effects of earlier and continued reductions in labour and to some extent capital input, it is hardly surprising that productivity indicators have displayed an upward trend in some sectors as a result of these demand increases. Such rises were inevitable given the fact that the factors of production were still very under-utilized at the beginning of the recovery even though previous cuts in capacity had taken place. Once demand rises permitted increases in output, growth in labour and capital productivity could easily take place without technical progress or the use of proactive strategies as excess capacity was utilized. The fact that enterprises continued to reduce their capacity through further cuts in labour employment and relatively stagnant levels of investment simply accelerated the process as excess capacity was eroded through cuts.

In the case of the electrical energy equipment and boiler-making sub-sectors, sharply rising demand was accompanied with rises in labour and capital productivity as the processes described above occurred. Between 1991 and 1994 all productivity indicators (except output per employee-hour in the boiler-making sector) rose as capacity utilization increased from 62.1% to 71.7% and 37.3% to 61.8% for the electrical energy equipment and boiler making sub-sectors respectively (Tables 16–26; ABDIB 1994a). The impressive relative productivity performance of the electrical energy equipment sub-sector would appear to be linked in part to the sharp increases of demand the sub-sector has enjoyed over the period which is reflected in its output and success in raising exports. In the case of the shipbuilding sector a similar trend could be observed between 1990 and 1992 when an upturn in demand accompanied a sharp increase in all productivity indicators and an increase in capacity utilization from 32.1% to 39.6% (Tables 20 and 26; ABDIB 1994a). Subsequently, however, there has been a fall off in productivity performance as demand has slumped.

In the case of the mechanical equipment and railway equipment sub-sectors, however, demand and output have tended to remain static in the period. Notwithstanding this, productivity gains have occurred, from further intensive cuts in capacity. In the mechanical equipment sector large labour productivity gains occurred as total employment fell by over 30% in the face of an increase in output of only 3.2% (Table 17). Between 1991 and 1993 a 12% reduction in assets employed occurred which resulted in a small capital productivity gain. Capacity utilization rose from 64.3% to 72.1% over the 1991 to 1994 period (ABDIB 1994a). Once again, efforts to reduce spare capacity and match overall capacity to demand have had the unsurprising result that productivity has risen. For the railway equipment sector a similar trend may be observed although the increase in capacity utilization is more modest.

In sum, it is possible to understand some of the evolution of productivity performance through the efforts of the sector to match their capacity to produce with demand and thus avoid idleness of factors of production. Continued reductions of capital and labour inputs combined with a post-1990 upturn in demand account for some of the enhanced productivity performance that has occurred. In other cases, increases in productivity have been achieved in the face of stagnant demand with reductions in capacity underutilization occurring mainly through reductions in capacity itself.

3.7.2 MODERNIZATION AND PRODUCTIVITY CHANGE

While many of the reasons underlying the rise in labour and capital productivity since 1990 can be linked to attempts to lower excess capacity by dramatic reductions in labour and capital inputs, it is important to recognize that many enterprises in the sector have supplemented this course of action with more conscious strategies aimed at improving productivity performance through process innovations. Such strategies have also had the aim of positively influencing areas of firm performance closely linked to increases in productivity, the key objectives being reductions in stock levels and throughput time, the economizing of raw material usage, and improvements in quality (Meyer-Starmer 1993a: 23, 26). As the sector has moved into recovery, the relative importance of this modernization approach has increased, especially in larger, more sophisticated enterprises. However, as the discussion will make clear, the extent of modernization has not been even throughout the sector and some enterprises have made far more progress than others.

Efforts to raise productivity in the non-serial capital goods sector are constantly faced with the implications of the sector's principal defining characteristics which comprise the production of heterogeneous, heavy, and high-value items according to order. These characteristics have long made the sector an unpromising environment for the application of traditional Fordist solutions involving increased specialization of labour and capital, the breaking down of tasks into ever simpler operations, and the progressive substitution of automated production lines for manual production processes. However, it is recognized within the Brazilian sector and internationally that price is becoming an increasingly important (if not the most important) factor in achieving international competitiveness, thus increasing the pressure on enterprises to search for process innovations that are capable of delivering the kind of price reductions that have long been associated with Fordist mass production. This is particularly true for sub-sectors of the industry in which the technological frontier is relatively stable and global capacity very high relative to demand. Perhaps the sub-sectors most affected by these pressures are electrical equipment (especially generators) (Strachmann 1993: 10) and shipbuilding (interviews).

The pressure on the sector to reduce prices through raising productivity and reducing costs has become increasingly acute as Brazil has removed barriers to imports and enterprises have been forced to enter the export market to a greater extent in the face of depressed domestic conditions (interviews in Enterprises *A*, *B*, and *C*). This increasing pressure has forced the great majority of enterprises to engage in proactive strategies to raise productivity and lower costs through effecting changes in the nature and organization of inputs. Fortunately, this pressure has emerged at a time when a variety of new non-Fordist approaches to manufacturing management have been gaining ground throughout the world in industry as a whole. These approaches, many of which are Japanese in origin, are rooted in a concept of production known as 'Flexible Specialization' which stresses the benefits to be gained from rapid response to changes in market conditions, the production of a plurality of products based on essentially similar designs in order to meet the needs of niche markets, the production of output directly in response to customer orders rather than for stock, and the tight control and minimization of holdings of work in progress and raw materials (Ferraz *et al.* 1992: 5–11; Besant 1991). Numerous studies concerning the introduction and implementation of flexible specialization have emerged in recent years, some of them concerning Brazil (see e.g. Fleury 1991; Ferraz *et al.* 1992; Tidd 1990; Edquist and Jacobsson 1988).

The advent of new manufacturing strategies linked to efforts to achieve efficient flexible specialization would appear especially propitious for the non-serial capital goods sector given that its characteristics conform very closely with those of an idealized flexibly specialized firm. Not surprisingly, many of the productivity-raising techniques associated with flexible specialization have been adopted within the sector. In discussing the changes in production technique that have been undertaken, the analysis concentrates on the experience of three enterprises, each of which was visited in the course of the fieldwork. The discussion is divided into three parts, the first, entitled 'Organizational Innovation', concerns changes linked with alterations in plant layout, organization of production, and control of stock. The second part, entitled 'Innovations and the Capital Stock and Developments in Training', discusses the impact of new vintages of machinery and their associated technology on productivity levels. The role of the latest computer numerically controlled (CNC) machinery is of particular interest in this context. The role of training is also briefly considered within this section. The third and final part then attempts to provide an indication of the diffusion of these innovations within the sector more generally.

(i) Organizational Innovations

One of the most significant developments within the enterprises studied during the 1990s has been the development and implementation of strategies of internal reorganization of production processes in an effort to raise productivity and quality, reduce costs, and shorten average lead times. By far the most significant of the strategies employed have been those of internal just in time (JIT) and materials resources planning (MRP), the establishment of production cells, and outsourcing. The development of each is now discussed in turn.

(a) *Just in Time and Material Resources Planning* The strategies of just in time and material resources planning represent the key organizational innovations associated with the implementation of flexible specialization within many industries. All strategies aim to induce productivity, cost, and quality gains by accelerating and smoothing the flow of raw materials and part-finished goods through the production process while minimizing the build-up of stocks. Just in time represents the best-known and most widely applied of these strategies. The implementation of JIT requires comprehensive redesign of the production process in order to match incoming raw materials and part-finished goods to production as it takes place. This involves the detailed synchronization of each stage of the production process so that the required supply of these inputs at each stage precisely coincides with the capacity to process them, thus avoiding the possibilities of under-utilized production capacity (idle labour and capital) or the build-up of stocks of unfinished goods as bottlenecks in production develop if capacity at any stage is insufficient relative to the demands placed on it (Schonberger 1986). The achievement of this goal is likely to involve the redesign of individual stages of the production process and efforts to increase the flexibility of capital and labour so that they may be swiftly redeployed to areas of production where bottlenecks threaten to build.

At the same time, in order to reduce lead and throughput times—and to increase the rate of turnover of stock—just in time involves efforts to redesign individual stages in the production processes in order that the time taken for each can be minimized. If successfully implemented, JIT should have the effect of economizing on the use of working capital in terms of stocks of raw materials and part-finished goods, while making more effective use of fixed capital and labour. The potential benefits of the successful application of this strategy are particularly attractive to the non-serial capital goods sector as discontinuities in the production process have frequently meant that periods have developed when particular stages in the production process have lain idle leading to significant under-utilization of labour and capital inputs.

Just-in-time strategies are generally of two varieties, internal and external (Meyer-Starmer 1993a: 6). The first concentrates on the movement of raw materials and part-finished goods through the plant itself—an issue that has just been considered—while the second, in addition, aims to alter relationships with customers and suppliers to ensure that deliveries of inputs coincide precisely with requirements and that production matches the actual rather than anticipated demand from individual customers (in practice this latter feature has always been true for the non-serial capital goods sector).

In establishing a JIT strategy, effective monitoring of flows and requirements of part-finished goods and raw materials is essential if production is to proceed smoothly avoiding the build-up of bottlenecks and overcapacity (Besant 1991). Although such a task could be assigned to production management and carried out manually, the development of inexpensive computing power and customized software makes available the possibility of an automated monitoring system which can be continually consulted in real time and even used to perform forecasting and diagnostic functions. Several such systems have been developed and carry the general label of material resources planning or MRP systems. Systems vary greatly and range from comparatively limited computer warehouse stock-control systems to complex centralized production monitoring systems with widely distributed data acquisition points.

Visits to all three enterprises found evidence of the introduction of varieties of JIT strategy, all of which had been introduced comparatively recently. Perhaps the most elaborate such strategy had been introduced at Enterprise C's shipyard. Within the shipbuilding industry generally there is currently very substantial overcapacity globally, overcapacity that is likely to grow with substantial recent investments in the Chinese and South Korean sectors. Within this context, prices globally in terms of dollars per ton seem likely to continue to fall despite recent increases in demand resulting from the increasing average age of the global merchant fleet and alterations in international maritime regulations which now require the progressive introduction of double-hulled vessels for the carriage of oil and other potentially environmentally hazardous cargoes. With the Brazilian shipbuilding sub-sector increasingly dependent upon export sales and the domestic market exposed to international competition, the pressure on Enterprise C and other Brazilian yards to realize price reductions through enhanced productivity and reduced costs is vital.

Given this background, since 1990 Enterprise C has been progressively introducing a variant of internal just in time and attempting to enhance relationships with its major external supplier for plate steel, the recently privatized CSN. Of all the non-serial capital goods sub-sectors, it is shipbuilding which has the largest physical throughput of raw materials, principally in the form of steel plate. For construction of larger vessels, especially the 150,000 dwt ton oil tankers in which the enterprise has specialized, the management of such material stocks and movements is vital. In order to maximize the use of fixed capital and labour during production, movements of raw material have to be maintained and yet, in order to minimize working capital requirements at each stage of production, it is also important to keep the build-up of stocks to a minimum. In an industry subject to intense price competition, pressure on delivery times, and a stable frontier of product innovation, the effective management of flows of material within the production process can make the difference between profitability and loss.

In response to these requirements, the enterprise has introduced a dedicated materials-flow management system incorporating detailed monitoring of materials requirements and the state of vessel construction at each stage of the production process. Central to the smooth flow of material at the beginning of the production process has been the establishment of a dedicated rail head and receiving area for steel plate which incorporates computer-controlled cutting machinery, enabling the swift processing of the raw material on arrival in accordance with the vessel design. The processed plate is then rapidly transferred to the vessel under construction using a modern heavy lift steerable crane. Further monitoring of materials flow takes place during the construction phase itself. At each stage of construction material flows are monitored and attempts are made to ensure that labour and capital inputs are used to the maximum extent possible, build-up of excessive stocks is avoided, while process time itself is reduced. This applies not only to basic hull construction but also to more technologically sophisticated areas such as pipe fitting and engine construction, the latter taking place on site: an interesting and fairly typical example of the high degree of verticalization in the Brazilian non-serial capital goods industry.

While computers assist in the monitoring of materials flow within and between processes, a formal computerized MRP system has not been introduced: oversight and aspects of detailed production control are in the hands of line management. The lack of a centralized computer system is likely in part to be the result of the physical characteristics of vessel construction in which the non-serial capital good itself becomes the point of production. With its constantly altering physical form, the feasibility of fixed computerized monitoring points is likely to be less than would be the case in a factory-floor environment.

Considerable experience of this form of internal JIT was gained in the course of construction of a series of 150,000 dwt ton crude oil tankers in the early 1990s. According to an engineer in the production division, this provided a rare learning opportunity (in an industry where one-off production of vessels is commonplace) for familiarization with these new techniques under standard and repeated conditions. Significantly, it was stated that productivity gains during this period were 'very substantial'. According to an independent report into the Brazilian shipbuilding industry, commissioned by the International Finance Corporation, labour productivity levels in terms of compensated gross tonnes per employee within Enterprise C are comparable with average levels in Western Europe although still below averages for Japan and South Korea (the world's largest constructors). This represents a considerable closing of the productivity gap since the end of the 1980s. According to the report, one of the main strengths of the yard was its internal materials flow management system which was in line with global best practice.

Although a form of internal JIT is highly developed, a formal system of external JIT has yet to come into operation. However, good relationships with suppliers have been established and no problems were expressed with respect to the responsiveness of the suppliers, the timeliness of deliveries, the build-up of excessive stocks, or sudden shortages. In this respect, Enterprise C would appear to be benefiting from good transport links (which are the exception rather than the rule in Brazil) and supplier efficiency gains: the latter have been particularly rapid in the steel industry (IBS 1995).

The developments in internal JIT outlined above have not been confined to the shipbuilding sector. In the course of the fieldwork, the electrical energy equipment enterprise (Enterprise A's) plant was visited and an inspection of the production facilities and interviews revealed the existence of recently implemented efforts to reorganize the production process to achieve superior productivity performance and reduce throughput times and costs. This has involved enhanced efforts to control stock levels and manage the flow of raw materials and part-finished goods to and through the production process and ensure maximum utilization of labour and capital inputs. The enterprise's plant produces an extremely wide range of made-to-order electrical capital goods including heavy industrial transformers, hydro-electric generators, heavy asynchronous electric motors, turbo generators, no-break devices, and heavy industrial switch gear. Since 1991 major programmes have been introduced aiming at the development of both internal and external just in time through enhancement of relationships between clients and suppliers and between internal production centres within Enterprise A itself (internal company documents). These programmes have aimed not only at increasing productivity, reducing costs and throughput times, but also at raising quality as part of a total quality management (TQM) programme which is itself discussed in the next chapter.

In terms of the management of the production process within the plant there have been substantial efforts made to ensure synchronization between each stage of the production process through a process the enterprise terms 'logistical control'. Every individual stage of production was examined in terms of its relationship to its forward and backward linkages and any particular barriers to the effective utilization of labour and capital, the rapid turnover of raw materials and part-finished goods were examined. Following this, there was considerable reorganization of some areas of the production process. This involved the physical reorganization of some of the plant layout to ensure smoother flows. In many instances this involved simple measures such as the closer physical grouping of related production activities and in some cases the complete refurbishment and reorganization of production facilities as production cells were established (see next section). In addition to physical alterations in plant, there was some alteration of internal management reporting lines in an attempt to enhance informational flows between the various stages of production. In addition, individual production processes were set targets concerning productivity, acceptable tolerances/product quality, and time taken per operation.

In addition to efforts to achieve a form of internal JIT, Enterprise A has also developed a formalized programme of involvement of external JIT with suppliers, known as PAF or programme of supplier partnership (*Programa de Acompanhamento de Fornecedores*), which has been in existence in its present form since 1993 though it originated in 1991 (internal company documents). This programme has sought to build stronger links with suppliers by offering longer-term contracts in exchange for increased supplier flexibility and stricter quality standards. The aim of the programme has been to reduce the costs of holding stocks of raw materials and components by ensuring that they are delivered by suppliers as and when required for actual production. In some cases, suppliers have an on-line computer connection to Enterprise A, enabling constant monitoring of raw material and component holdings within the production process. When these fall below a critical minimum the supplier delivers further supplies without a formal order being raised. Similarly, build-up of such holdings above specified levels results in a cessation of deliveries. At the same time, by raising quality levels of supplies, the PAF seeks to reduce disruptions to production caused through inadequate input quality as well as raising final output quality itself. During the period of operation of the programme, the number of suppliers has been reduced by 65% with consequent reductions in transactions costs.

Although the enterprise does not possess a dedicated centralized MRP computer system, extensive use is made of local area networks (LANs) to monitor and report on the extent of stocks and the performance of particular stages in the production process. Casual observation of the production facilities revealed a much more intensive reliance on information technology for the monitoring of all aspects of corporate activity than was the case in either of the other two enterprises visited.

The next enterprise visited—Enterprise B—is one of the largest enterprises in the mechanical equipment sector, producing a wide range of mechanical handling equipment, cranes, equipment for the steel industry, and turbines. The enterprise is one of the longest established in the sector having commenced operations early this century and occupies an area of 145,000 sq m in greater São Paulo. During interviews with production management it was stressed that the search for productivity increases had been a constant preoccupation, especially since 1990, with much of the motivation for this originating from the need to achieve competitiveness in export markets in the face of rising participation by East Asian, particularly South Korean enterprises. The achievement of productivity increases was viewed to be particularly challenging given the discontinuities associated in the production of highly differentiated products.

Unlike Enterprises A and C, however, Enterprise B has not engaged in the development of a formal internal or external just-in-time strategy but has sought to achieve incremental improvements in its existing internal materials flow procedures. These improvements have also been strongly motivated by the desire to maintain and improve upon standards of quality, established by the enterprise since it was awarded ISO 9000 quality certification.

Perhaps the most notable example of this has been the development of production cells (discussed in Section 3.7.2(i)(b) below), though there has also been some limited reorganization of plant layout. In terms of relations with external suppliers, efforts were being made to improve linkages and lines of communications with these, though the main emphasis is placed on the improvement of quality. In terms of the enhancement of both labour and capital productivity, the installation of new machinery—particularly CNC machine tools—and the development of training programmes are viewed as the most significant influences.

(b) *Production Cells* The development of production cells has been one of the key organizational innovations associated with the movement towards flexible production and the achievement of higher quality and productivity levels throughout many industries. Production cells represent a departure from assembly-line principles of plant organization where operations are carried out sequentially, according to a set pattern, by highly specialized operatives and dedicated machinery. Instead, production cells aim to achieve much greater flexibility of capital and labour in terms of the functions each performs and in so doing match production capacity more readily to material flows, changes in quantity of demand, or changes in the nature of the product produced (Schonberger 1986). This avoids the build-up of idle capacity and also reduces the likelihood of the flow of production being halted by the temporary failure of one item of machinery or the absence of key workers. Labour productivity gains may also result from increases in motivation resulting from the greater variety of tasks undertaken. In performing some of the above functions, production cells are frequently employed in plants pursuing a JIT strategy.

Production cells are generally responsible for a specific aspect of the production process, for example, particular varieties of sub-assembly. Each production cell consists of a team of workers, each of whom is capable of undertaking a variety of production tasks according to requirements. In addition to carrying out labour within the cell, workers also take on much of the responsibility for the organization of production operations (Ferraz et al. 1992: 239). This relative autonomy permits decisions to be taken more rapidly as there is often no need to engage in formal and time-consuming consultations with management before changes can be effected. Capital equipment, like labour, is also likely to be flexible in its function within the production cell. Very often this means the adoption of CNC machine tool suites linked and co-ordinated by computer which are capable of performing a wide variety of production operations (see Section 3.7.2(ii)).

Visits to both Enterprises A and B revealed the existence of production cells. In the case of Enterprise A, the diffusion of production cells within the plant has been very extensive. Production of no-break devices (equipment which smoothes voltage and ensures a continuous power supply) is carried out virtually entirely through the operation of production cells. The assembly of this equipment is a complex operation especially since output is not standardized but must conform to a variety of technical specifications set out by customers. Each individual sub-assembly—for example, circuit board, power transformers, operating panels, and control system—is produced in its own production cell. In some cases cells are actually individual partitioned sections of the shop floor, though in most cases cells are physically separated from each other only by colour-coded markings on the floor.

Each production cell contains strategically placed containers of components to ensure ease and rapidity of access and correct selection. In some cases light manual assembly equipment is supplemented by CNC machinery. Production of sub-assemblies is undertaken by teams of five to ten workers who are conversant with all facets of the operation. Computer monitoring of the progress of the sub-assemblies and the flow of components through the production cells ensures that excess or insufficient supplies of inputs do not develop while communication between cells is encouraged through the provision of communal meeting areas so that problems affecting the progress of work from one cell to another can be discussed and resolved. In addition, a member of management is stationed in close proximity to the cells to facilitate communications with other parts of the organization.

Production cells have also been introduced in the power-generation equipment sector of the plant where key sub-assemblies such as generator coil windings and metal fabrications for generators are produced. In the case of the latter, the physical scope of the operation is on a much greater scale than in transformer or no-break production yet it would appear that the same production-cell techniques have been applied with relative success. In the case of the generator coil winding production facility, considerable effort and money have been expended to reorganize production along production-cell lines. Efficiency and flexibility are deemed to be of particular importance in this facility due to the labour intensity of the production process (attempts at automation were unsuccessful) and the fact that requirements for sizes of coil produced are so heterogeneous. This has resulted in the development of a production cell where considerable attention has been paid to raising the flexibility of the labour force through skill broadening and improving the internal organization of the production process through a reallocation of tool and component disposition.

In all areas, management was keen to stress the success of the movement to production cells and stressed that there was some intention to extend the scope of their operations to those remaining areas of activity where they were not employed.

Whereas in Enterprise *A* the movement towards production cells has been taking place for four or five years, in Enterprise *B* their adoption has been a much more recent phenomenon and has been somewhat more limited in scope. In general, the physical scale of operations is rather more substantial with the bulk of production consisting of the fabrication of large metal sub-assemblies for heavy mechanical equipment. During the visit to the plant, the main orders under construction were for heavy dock cranes for export, a market where price competition has been intense. Considerable attention was being paid to the need to reduce unit labour costs through increases in productivity. In pursuance of this objective, management had recently decided to engage in the limited introduction of production cells. Areas of production already transferred to the production-cell technique were certain steel-plate work fabrications and certain smaller machined components.

In the case of the steel-plate work fabrications, crane-frame sections were being produced in a production-cell environment. Within the cell, multi-skilled production teams were gathered with overall responsibility for completion of their designated sub-assembly. Efforts had been made to improve the physical layout within each cell in order that throughput times could be reduced through decreased average time per operation. At the same time, indications were given suggesting the increasing importance of facilitating effective liaison between individual production cells and other units of production so that quality issues could be discussed, the build-up of bottlenecks avoided, and the flow of components and sub-assemblies smoothed. Perhaps the most comprehensive implementation of the production-cell principle was in the case of smaller component production. Precisely machined components are fundamental requirements for the production of most forms of mechanical handling equipment. In the case of cranes they are required for key moving-part assemblies such as gearboxes, drive systems between motors and cable drums, and mechanical control systems. Given the varying technical requirements of each crane produced and the desire to reduce lead times, many such components are produced on site. In 1994, the enterprise invested over US$ 1 m. in the establishment of a new production cell for the manufacture of such components.

Central to the structure of the new cell is a newly acquired CNC machine tool suite known as a flexible manufacturing system which consists of a series of lathes and milling machines linked by computer control (discussed in more detail in 3.7.2(ii)(*a*)). Together with multi-skilled cell team members and physical reorganization of plant and raw material disposition, the cell is capable of producing a wide range of components whose designs are stored (and easily modified) in computer programs. Management and cell team members stated that they were impressed with the gains in labour productivity, quality, and reductions in machine setting down-time that have resulted from the new investment. Plans were under way to develop further such production cells where feasible in order that additional gains could be realized. This is most likely to happen in some additional areas of component manufacture where production is being undertaken with manual or first-generation numerically controlled machine tools.

In the case of Enterprise C, the shipbuilder, the introduction of formal production cells has yet to take place. In large part, this is as a result of the construction techniques that can be feasibly employed in an industry where the capital good itself is the point of production. However, an opinion was expressed that such techniques may be applied to the production of marine engines in the future, although the current depressed state of orders made this unlikely in the short term.

(c) *Outsourcing* Over the past two years the strategy of outsourcing (*terceirização*) has received considerable attention not only in the Brazilian industrial economics literature but also within the field of industrial sociology (Ramalho 1995). In brief, the strategy of outsourcing seeks to achieve cost savings by subcontracting the performance of certain functions to outside firms and organizations. One of the principal ways in which such savings are achieved is through the new terms that subcontractors are able to impose on employees whose functions have been outsourced. This usually results in lower pay and an inferior level of job security (ibid.). However, from the point of view of the outsourcer, gains may be realized in the form of lower unit costs of labour and improvements in labour or capital productivity, the latter resulting from reduced working capital requirements (Besant 1991). In the Brazilian context, a curious feature of the process of outsourcing has been that much subcontracted activity has physically remained on site. This has had the result that there has been considerable organizational change within plants themselves with, in effect, two or more separate companies operating together in the same location.

During the course of factory visits, the electrical equipment enterprise, A, emerged as having made the furthest progress with outsourcing and appeared to be the enterprise where there was the greatest confidence that its scope would continue to extend. In the two years prior to the plant visit in July 1995, it had outsourced two ancillary functions: cleaning and warehouse operations. In addition to this, the production of certain simple fabrications for generator assemblies had been subcontracted to an engineering company that had begun to operate on site. At the time of the visit, many further aspects of production were scheduled for outsourcing including fabrication of some of the lighter generator assemblies, the production of cabinets for switch gear and no-break devices, and the metal painting and baking shop. The rationale underlying the selection of these items for outsourcing was stated to be the necessity to drive down costs to the minimum for unsophisticated, low value-added aspects of the production process. At the same time, the need was expressed to divert management resources to areas of production where the enterprise possessed a technological edge and there was scope for further product and process innovation.

In the case of the shipbuilder, Enterprise C, the extent of outsourcing has been far less extensive with only catering and cleaning services contracted out. However, for the construction of certain vessels in the recent past, there had been a considerable need to increase temporarily the labour force in order to meet the delivery deadline requirements involved in the production of these 'one-off' craft. This had resulted in the temporary contracting of metal fabrication firms to help meet the orders. However, in the case of the series of five 150,000 ton tankers, such outsourcing did not prove to be necessary as the order proved of long enough duration to justify the expansion of internal capital and labour capacity to meet the increased demands placed on it.

The mechanical equipment enterprise, B, embarked upon a reasonably ambitious programme of outsourcing at the beginning of the 1990s with ancillary functions being subcontracted along with the fabrication of certain metal sub-assemblies and the production of detailed design drawings. However, management expressed dissatisfaction with the quality of much of the output from these operations and was in the process of halting the progress of the outsourcing programme and even reversing it in some instances. After changes in suppliers and the imposition of monitoring systems, it was hoped that the programme could be recommenced.

(ii) Innovation and the Capital Stock and Developments in Training

(a) *Technological Change and Machinery* The development of flexible production techniques within the non-serial capital goods sector is in great part the consequence of technological progress within its serial counterpart. The most significant aspect of this progress has been the emergence of computer-controlled machine tools and their associated software packages. These have permitted the rapid adaptation of machine tools to the production of new designs and the possibility for mass production of heterogeneous products.

With earlier manually controlled machine tools, the production of a differentiated output was impossible without lengthy manual resetting, recalibration, and replacement of cutting heads. The first generation of numerically controlled machine tools simplified and accelerated such setting operations but the programming involved was still comparatively lengthy and an obstacle to true flexibility: operators had to set one parameter at a time and engage in detailed supervision of the machining operation. The real advances in machining technology have emerged with the coupling of computers to numerically controlled machine tools, a technology known as computerized numerical control (CNC). Computer programs can store details of several different kinds of design, each of which can be instantly translated into numerical settings and relayed to the machine tool (Ferraz *et al.* 1992). Current technology allows an enormous number of individual settings to be stored which together with computer-generated interpolation allows constant machining operations as a machine's settings continuously change. This enables the production of complexly shaped pieces and the achievement of extremely fine tolerances. Should specifications for pieces alter or if there are complete design changes, software can be run and the new items produced instantly without the need for complex retooling. Such systems can become yet more powerful and flexible if they are linked to CAD (computer-aided design) packages. Items may be rapidly designed on computer and following this the CAD package can calculate the appropriate machine settings and relay them direct to the CNC control unit for instant production. In some cases individual CNC systems can be computer linked so that a whole manufacturing operation can be correctly and efficiently sequenced as the piece moves from one machine tool to another: this is sometimes referred to as a flexible manufacturing cell (Besant 1991).

Given the obvious attractions of such systems to non-serial capital goods producers, it is not surprising that there has been a considerable expansion in their use over the past five years. In the case of Enterprise A, CNCs are widely distributed throughout the entire production operations from the production of small components to the cutting of large templates for generator stators to computer-controlled plastic injection-moulding equipment. The tool-making workshop is entirely served by CNC equipment. In addition, some of the CNC installations are served by CAD facilities. Much of the CNC equipment has been acquired over the past five years in a US\$ 38 m. investment programme and there are plans to extend its scope in the future. Acquisition of CNC machinery is said to have made a significant contribution towards reducing throughput times, increasing responsiveness to customers, raising quality, and enhancing productivity performance, particularly in production cells. The flexibility of the technology was also stated to have fitted in well with the policy of reducing build-ups of stock and facilitating the smooth flow of production between stages.

CNC machine tools have also been extensively utilized at Enterprise B. Some of the older heavier cutting and grinding equipment has been fitted with CNC control systems to facilitate the more rapid and flexible production of larger sub-assemblies. The enterprise had also recently acquired a Japanese CNC machine tool suite incorporating linked grinding machines and lathes. Instructions could be downloaded from a CAD system enabling a substantial range of smaller components to be produced with exceptional accuracy. This system forms the core of the production cell described in Section 3.7.2(*b*).

The only aspect of production that now lacks numerically controlled machinery is the assembly of large metal structures to form the framework of the cranes and other mechanical handling equipment: that this is the case reflects the inherent unsuitability of this application for CNC machining. This also goes some way to explaining the limited extent of CNC machinery installation at Enterprise C where most fabrication is in the form of welding metal plate. However, the enterprise has invested in a CNC-controlled oxyacetylene gantry cutter for cutting plate to size accurately. This relies on instructions generated by a CAD package.

(b) *Training* Given the changes in working practices and technology associated with increased flexibility in the enterprises studied, it might be expected that significant extra resources and efforts have been given to training in order that skills could be enhanced to match the new requirements. In the course of interviews, representatives of all three enterprises emphasized the central function of training in their modernization strategies.

In all three cases the enterprises possessed formal training centres where employees were given regular brief training courses with the objective of improving the effectiveness of the new patterns of work organization. However, for less skilled assembly operations the bulk of training was conducted on the job, a form of training common in many of the production cells performing less sophisticated production operations. In the case of CNC investments at Enterprises A and B, initial programmes of training were offered by manufacturers of the equipment. However, perhaps one of the key features and advantages of modern generations of CNC equipment is the fact that their training requirements are considerably less than was the case with manual equipment where skilful operation and setting of the machinery required a lengthy apprenticeship. This raises an important point. To some extent, increased flexibility in the workplace is only possible because the skill requirements for individual tasks have been lessened through technological progress and increased productivity of fixed capital equipment. Thus the training programmes that develop are likely to reflect this in imparting a broad range of relatively simple production skills rather than a narrow in-depth knowledge of a particular operation.

Management at Enterprises A and B indicated that they expect to spend an increasing amount on training in the future. In the case of Enterprise A, the increases were due to lead to an expenditure of almost US$ 11 m. in 1995. In the case of Enterprise C, little extra training effort was anticipated in the foreseeable future due to a very reduced expected number of new recruits into the enterprise and the fact that further changes in production techniques were not foreseen.

(iii) *Diffusion of Modernization Strategies in the Non-serial Capital Goods Sector*

Examination of evidence from the case studies set out above reveals a degree of diversity in the intensity of adoption of modernizing innovations among the enterprises interviewed. This inter-enterprise variation would appear to characterize much of the non-serial capital goods sector. Vermulm (1993: 23)

TABLE 28. Usage of Organizational and Technological Innovations in the
Electrical Energy Equipment Sub-sector (%)

Innovation	1987–1989			1992		
	Little or no usage	Medium usage	High usage	Little or no usage	Medium usage	High usage
Micro-electronic-based equipment	88.5	11.5	0	80.8	11.5	7.7
Production cells	72.7	27.3	0	56.5	39.1	4.4
Internal JIT	77.3	22.7	0	86.9	8.7	4.3
External JIT	81.8	13.6	4.5	82.6	8.7	8.7

Notes: The figures refer to the percentage of enterprises in the survey sample engaging in low, medium, or high usage of the innovations where high usage denotes innovations used in over 50% of operations; medium usage denotes innovations used in 11–50% of operations; and little or no usage denotes innovations used in 0–11% of operations.

Source: Strachmann (1993).

points to the co-existence of enterprises engaging in extensive modernization—putting into practice just in time, production cells, and plant upgrading—with others who have merely engaged in 'passive' attempts to raise productivity through factor-input reduction.

The 1993 study into the competitiveness of Brazilian industry revealed the existence of such heterogeneity throughout most of the industrial sectors studied. This pattern held true for the electrical energy equipment sub-sector. A summary of the main findings of the survey is set out in Table 28.

The data reveal the fact that in the majority of cases, the diffusion of the innovations has been quite limited with only a minority of enterprises engaging in intense usage. Thus, on this evidence, the experience of Enterprise *A*—probably the most sophisticated electrical energy equipment enterprise in Brazil—is not likely to be representative of the entire sub-sector. However, it is possible to observe an increase in the diffusion of these innovations over time with the proportion of enterprises engaging in high usage rising.

Interviews carried out within Enterprise *A* suggested that the pace of process innovation had tended to accelerate over the past five years throughout the sector in general and, as the data were collected in 1992, they would almost certainly understate the extent of diffusion of the innovations throughout the sector that had taken place by 1995. However, the data do suggest that the pattern of diffusion is likely to have been less than even.

Survey research carried out in Meyer-Starmer (1993*a*) and Furtado (1994) on modernizing innovations in mechanical equipment and boiler-making enterprises also suggests considerable intra-sectoral variation. Of the nine enterprises surveyed, three were engaged in a programme of comprehensive modernization (Meyer-Starmer 1993a: 54), a strategy incorporating JIT, production cells, MRP, enhanced training, and the greater use of CNCs (ibid. 21–35). In one case—an enterprise producing turbines and paper-making equipment—a more cautious modernization strategy was in place which emphasized investment in CNC machine tools and a formal MRP system (ibid. 52). However, the enterprise had ruled out the introduction of either internal or external JIT. In another case a more modest modernization strategy was under way, while in the remaining four cases there was a complete absence of the implementation of any modernizing strategy, either organizational or technological. Interestingly, the survey revealed no specific tendency for subsidiaries of multinational corporations to engage in more intensive modernization than Brazilian-owned enterprises.

Furtado (1994: 50) examined two enterprises in the mechanical equipment sub-sector in the course of an enquiry into the technological sophistication of Brazilian enterprises. Both had embarked upon programmes of modernization but the character of the modernization was somewhat different in each case. In the first enterprise there had been considerable technological upgrading of the capital stock with extensive use being made of computer numerically controlled machine tools. At the same time, the use of production cells had been greatly extended, with all of light manufacturing operations employing this technique. In the second enterprise, however, the traditional plant layout had been left unchanged while there had been considerable investment in CNC machine tools which had been linked to each other and to a CAD system by central computer to form a DNC (direct numerical control) production system, in many ways the most sophisticated variety. Formal JIT or MRP had not been introduced in either enterprise, however.

In the shipbuilding sector there has also been some diversity in the implementation of modernization programmes. Interviews conducted at Enterprise C revealed a degree of diversity in strategies between the constituent yards of its parent group. Of the yards, Enterprise C had made by far the most progress in implementing an effective form of internal JIT. In the case of another of the group's yards, very little organizational innovation had taken place and the capital stock was of old vintage. These interview findings were backed up in the International Finance Corporation report which identified the yard in question as a relatively poor performer. However, greater organizational innovations were noted in the other major yards examined outside the ownership of Enterprise C's parent group. However, there was still a considerable gap in the scope of modernization between these yards and that of Enterprise C.

Specific data concerning the diffusion of innovations within the railway equipment sub-sector are not available though there is indirect evidence of plant reorganization and materials flow management implementation in the form of recent ISO 9001/2 certification for ABB do Brasil and the Fabrica Nacional de Vagões Vehiculos e Equipamentos S.A. (*Revista Ferroviaria*, Dec.

1994: 36). Such certification, as will be made clear in the next section, requires the attainment of defined standards for stock control and materials flow which can only be achieved through the implementation of efficient MRP systems (which may or may not be centrally computerized) and appropriate plant layout. There is evidence that not all enterprises in the sub-sector are moving towards such modernization, however. Cobrasma and Mafersa (the latter in severe financial difficulty), appear to be reacting to the lack of domestic public sector orders primarily through drastic rationalization involving plant closures and redundancies (ibid. 36, *Revista Ferroviaria*, Jan. 1995: 11).

Conclusions

The Brazilian non-serial capital goods sector has undergone an extremely profound period of restructuring in the face of considerable shifts in government policy since 1987. A reduction in public sector fixed capital formation, later accompanied by a private sector recession, forced attempts at reducing capacity in the sector in an attempt to stem losses through drastic cost cutting.

Following the end of the private sector recession in 1991, the combined impacts of the *Abertura Comercial* and a continuing dearth of public sector orders have maintained pressure on enterprises to increase competitiveness. In a global market where competitiveness is increasingly determined by price, this has resulted in an intensified emphasis on raising factor productivity.

In the majority of cases, the data demonstrate that since about 1990, after a period of adjustment, the sector has managed successfully to respond to this challenge by raising capital and labour productivity. However, the extent of these gains has varied between sub-sectors. To some extent, the evidence suggests that in the period between 1987 and 1993, productivity gains have tended to be greatest in those sub-sectors where reductions in domestic public sector procurement have been greatest. The role of trade liberalization would also appear to have been of key importance, with reductions in nominal and effective protection being associated with improvements in capital and labour productivity across all sub-sectors.

However, the relatively uniform reductions in measures of nominal and effective protection seem unable to help offer an explanation as to inter-subsectoral variations in productivity performance. In this connection, the degree of insertion into the international market (measured by import and export volumes) seems of greater explanatory power, with the data suggesting that increased insertion is associated with superior productivity performance. Interestingly, as will be made clear, sectors associated with high export and import volumes tend to be among the more technologically sophisticated and are more intensely populated with multinational corporations. However, it must be recognized that trade liberalization cannot be regarded as the unique determinant of alterations in such export or import performance. As Chapter 4 explains, private and particularly public sector reductions in demand were also key determining factors. Indeed, the fact that the electrical energy equipment sub-sector faced the greatest proportionate and absolute contraction in public sector demand while producing the consistently highest export volumes cannot be regarded as entirely coincidental.

In trying to account for how this enhanced productivity performance was realized within enterprises, two broad strategies were examined which were termed rationalization and modernization. Rationalization—the removal of excess capacity through factor input reductions—has affected all sub-sectors and was in evidence at all firms visited. Sharp reductions in capital inputs in the late 1980s triggered by falls in public sector procurement of capital goods were soon followed by substantial shrinkage of the labour force as the recession intensified and spread to the private sector. Reduction of the labour force continued right up until 1994 when there was a moderate employment upturn in most sectors.

To some extent, the observed productivity gains of the 1990s can be viewed as the result of this rationalization. In reducing factor-input levels in order to try and more closely match capacity to market demand, the resulting increases in productivity are an arithmetic inevitability and not necessarily the result of a technical advance. Production techniques need not alter and static rather than dynamic efficiency gains result. In this sense the productivity gains may be considered as by-products of a commonly recognized cyclical phenomenon in which capacity is lowered in an industry during the downturn in order to reduce losses. Productivity increases usually result and may accelerate during the initial phase of the upturn as any remaining excess capacity is removed due to increases in demand. In the case of the shipbuilding, boiler-making, and electrical sectors there is evidence that the latter took place. In addition, rational firms are likely to remove their least efficient labour and capital inputs first during the downturn so the average level of productivity was bound to rise. Interviews suggested that this had taken place in the enterprises visited.

While rationalization has been universally applied throughout the non-serial capital goods sector, it has been accompanied, especially over the post-1991 period, with conscious efforts to improve productivity and lower costs through modernization strategies. Such modernization strategies have aimed to change the techniques employed in production through organizational and technological innovations and have been especially associated with the need for enterprises to compete in an increasingly important export market and an increasingly open and competitive domestic market. The techniques employed have been closely linked to the development of Post-Fordist and Post-Taylorist approaches to manufacturing which place a premium on flexibility both in terms of final product and factors of production. Common elements included a just-in-time approach to the holding and movement of stocks, the development of new shop-floor layouts, and the introduction of new generation computer-controlled machine tools. To the extent that changes in production technique were involved, it is clear that there were increases in dynamic efficiency. However, it is important to recognize the relatively low technological (as opposed to organizational) component of the dynamic gains.

In addition, doubt must be cast on the extent to which these gains are evenly distributed throughout the sector as the data suggested that the diffusion of the new production techniques was not universal and that there was a degree of heterogeneity in their precise configuration and intensity of use between individual enterprises. This would suggest that modernization is only able to account for a portion of the overall observed variations in productivity change. However, its impact is likely to rise as diffusion proceeds at an accelerated rate.

In sum, the evidence would suggest that the withdrawal of the state both in terms of its role as a purchaser and a protector has succeeded in raising productivity performance in the Brazilian non-serial capital goods sector. The improvements have occurred as public (and, for a period, private) expenditure cuts induced cuts in the sector's capacity, the increasingly relatively significant domestic private sector market became more exposed to external competition, and firms more intensively participated in the export market. However, the productivity gains have to be seen against a background of huge capacity cuts and a sector still shrunken in relation to its position in 1980.

At the same time, the spread of dynamic efficiencies within the sector has been uneven and perhaps not extensive enough given that rapid improvements in manufacturing technology continue in competitor countries. Perhaps the root of the problem is that while productivity improvements have occurred, these have to be set against years of stagnation in the past and the fact that productivity performance in major competitor countries is accelerating at a higher rate from a higher base. Only 36.4% of respondents in a 1994 PBQP sector survey reported that their productivity levels were up to international standards while none felt that they were superior and 50% reported inferior levels (PBQP 1994: 2). To paraphrase Meyer-Starmer (1995), in terms of productivity, the sector is attempting to chase a train which is rapidly moving into the distance. In this context it seems doubtful whether a mixture of the rationalization and relatively cautious modernization that have taken place up to now will be sufficient to close the productivity gap which has opened up.

4

The External Dimension: Exports, Imports, and Quality

Introduction

The period since 1986 has seen substantial shifts in policy towards the Brazilian non-serial capital goods sector, which, as Chapter 3 revealed, resulted in substantial changes in productivity performance and the organization of production activity within enterprises. Such performance alterations, as the chapter demonstrated, were associated with changes in static and dynamic efficiencies. Part of the impetus underlying the identified alterations in static and dynamic efficiency resulted from the threat posed by increased penetration of imports and the increased importance of the export market.

This chapter attempts to examine the changes that occurred in export performance following the initiation of the policy changes in 1986, while charting any links they may have with the evolving policy of the state and the development of static and dynamic efficiencies within enterprises. Given the very important and interesting theoretical linkages that exist between alterations in policy, exports, and the behaviour of individual enterprises, the primary concern of the discussion is that of export performance and the factors underlying it. However, the behaviour of imports is examined to the extent that it may provide an indication of the competitive pressure that forced enterprises to enhance efficiency and expand exports.

In order to achieve its objectives, this chapter adopts the following approach. First, the chapter briefly reprises the theoretical discussion set out in detail in Chapter 1 concerning the link between reductions in the role of the state, trade liberalization, export performance, and the development of static and dynamic efficiencies within enterprises (Section 4.1). Secondly, the general policy changes to which the sector has been subject are discussed, briefly summarizing the main discussion in Chapter 2, before moving on to consider the changing pattern of explicit export policies employed by the Brazilian state in the period encompassed by the study (Section 4.2). Thirdly, data are presented concerning the import and export performance for the five main categories of non-serial capital goods in the period 1982–94 (Section 4.3). Fourthly, Section 4.4 attempts to assess the relationship between alterations in state policy and changes in the international trade performance of the sector. Finally, Section 4.5 traces the links that may exist between variations in trade performance and the evolution of static and dynamic efficiencies within the sector. In particular, the issues of productivity performance, process innovation, and product innovation are discussed briefly (they are discussed in more detail in

Chapters 3 and 5 respectively) while the process innovation of quality is examined in some detail given the intimate connection that would appear to emerge between quality, import penetration, and export intensity.

4.1 Exports, Imports, Static and Dynamic Efficiencies, and the Role of the State: Some Theoretical Considerations

Chapter 1 demonstrated that the development of a capital goods sector in a less developed country was likely to require the implementation of a number of separate policies by the state, at least some of which would involve the provision of enhanced protection for the sector. In the longer term, however, a considerable volume of literature pointed to the likelihood that such measures of protection would have the effect of constraining the growth of exports from the emergent capital goods sector. The seriousness of this effect was heightened by the possibility that lack of exposure to the export market would result in sub-optimal dynamic and static efficiency gains. The association of a protective régime with poor export performance was held to arise from the fact that it failed to generate sufficient export incentives or to give rise to enterprise competitiveness. Specifically, protective régimes tended to place an implicit tax on exportables (as opposed to importables), thus making the domestic market far more attractive for domestic producers. In the case of the Brazilian non-serial capital goods sector, the relative attractiveness and accessibility of the domestic market to domestic producers was enhanced by very extensive non-tariff barriers and a state procurement policy that explicitly favoured domestic suppliers (Chapter 2).

Simultaneously, such protective measures also tend to increase the price of imported inputs in exported products above international levels, thus further reducing the possibility of effectively competing in the export market. At the same time, protective régimes also tended to be associated with an overvalued exchange rate. In the case of Brazil this was frequently (though not always) an adjunct of the policy of import substitution that guided national economic development up until the mid-1980s. In the long run, Chapter 1 argued that such overvaluations would tend to damage export competitiveness. Export competitiveness was also argued to suffer because of the lack of enterprise experience in competing with foreign rivals in either domestic or foreign markets. Firms faced with the lack of challenge response mechanism generated by participation in such markets were argued to fail to invest in appropriate process or product technologies or to strive to improve existing production techniques, thus further prejudicing their chances of success in the export market and depriving the domestic economy of potential gains in static and dynamic efficiencies.

At the same time, particularly where domestic markets were small relative to minimum efficient scales of production, the dearth of exports engendered by the incentive structure meant that suitably large scales of production could not be achieved and—in accordance with Verdoorn's Law—productivity gains were less than they could have been under a more export-oriented policy régime. Such sub-optimal productivity performance, of course, was likely to further prejudice the likelihood of success in external markets.

Thus, the theoretical literature suggests that protective regimes may act to constrain exports and that this in turn may be associated with sub-optimal static and dynamic efficiency gains. The key policy implication that arises from this literature is that export performance is likely to be enhanced following the implementation of trade liberalization and reduced procurement of non-serial capital goods by the state. In the case of the Brazilian non-serial capital goods sector, of course, the period between 1986 and 1994 witnessed the substantial scaling down of much of the protective structure that had previously surrounded it. Specifically, tariffs were reduced substantially (on average by around 50%) while much of the non-tariff protection of the sector was eliminated. Perhaps the most powerful aspect of the latter development was the rapidly diminishing importance of the domestic public sector market, previously containing many of the *de facto* primary instruments of non-tariff protection of the sector. At the same time, however, the generally overvalued level of the currency and the scaling down of the mechanisms of export promotion had resulted in a declining real effective exchange rate (REER) between 1986 and 1990, although there was a mild recovery between 1990 and 1994 as export finance mechanisms were re-established and the currency underwent limited devaluations. In general, the behaviour of the REER would appear to have unfavourable implications for the expansion of exports. Given this situation, the discussion attempts to establish whether the growth of exports was indeed constrained or altogether eliminated by the decline in the REER despite the export promotional implications of trade liberalization and reduced public sector procurement.

In sum, the remainder of the chapter seeks to ascertain whether the changing policy conditions of 1986–94 were associated with an expansion in non-serial capital goods exports. At the same time, the analysis attempts to establish the causal nature of any identified associations between export expansion and individual policy changes. In addition, the analysis seeks to establish whether any identified expansions were associated with changes in static and dynamic efficiency. Specifically, the chapter attempts to identify whether a relationship exists between export expansion, productivity growth, rationalization, and product and process innovation.

The role of imports is also considered in the discussion. In theoretical terms, *ceteris paribus*, a reduction in the intensity of protection would be expected to lead to an expansion in imports of non-serial capital goods. Whether this theoretical expectation is borne out in reality is an issue examined in Section 4.3. Of greater importance in the context of the current discussion, however, are the implications that observed import behaviour may hold for the competitive performance of the Brazilian non-serial capital goods sector. Specifically, the analysis attempts to establish whether the evolution of imports was such as to encourage enterprises to engage in process innovations and expanded export activities.

4.2 The Evolution of Export Policies Towards the Brazilian Non-serial Capital Goods Sector, 1980–1994

In considering the evolution of policies which might be believed to have affected the export performance of the Brazilian non-serial capital goods sector, it is convenient to distinguish between the roles of implicit and explicit policies. Implicit policies may be described as those which were designed without the explicit aim of generating alterations in export performance but whose effects might have been expected to have had a fundamental impact on it. Explicit policies, by contrast, can be thought of as those which were especially designed to alter export performance in the sector by means of specially targeted policy initiatives.

The evolution of implicit policy initiatives has already been examined in the course of Chapter 2 and discussed in broad terms in the previous section. In the course of the discussion, a number of key policy alterations were identified. First, after a period of high (and slightly increasing) tariff protection in the period from 1980 to 1986, from 1987 onwards tariff levels throughout the entire range of non-serial capital goods exhibited a sustained decline, a trend which rapidly accelerated after 1990. Secondly, after a period of intensified non-tariff protection at the beginning of the 1980s, a number of reforms between 1987 and 1991 largely eliminated the range of non-tariff barriers that Chapter 2 argued had provided the principal form of protection for the sector throughout its development since the advent of the Second National Development Plan. Thirdly, and very significantly, the diminishing role of the Brazilian state as a procurer of non-serial capital goods became a notable trend after 1987 as substantial federal spending cuts restricted public investment expenditures in infrastructure and state enterprises. The reduced relative and absolute size of the state as a customer had the effect of reducing the impact of the range of remaining non-tariff barriers (which themselves were in the process of being removed) as well as progressively depriving the sector of its main source of domestic orders.

Taken together, the evolution of the policies described above might be expected to have provided an environment which would have proved increasingly conducive to the expansion of non-serial capital goods exports. However, these alterations formed only a part of the changing policy environment that the sector faced over the period of the study. Two key policies which have not so far been considered in any detail formed very important components of the evolving pattern of export-related policies, the first implicit in nature and the second explicit.

The role of exchange rates has often been considered of key importance in the determination of export performance in the manufacturing sectors of newly industrializing countries, with the Kiel Institute and NBER (National Bureau of Economic Research) studies standing out as prime examples (Weiss 1988: 222). In fact, devaluations of the nominal exchange rate had provided the centrepiece of the movement away from import substitution and towards export promotion among several Latin American economies in the 1960s (Bulmer-Thomas 1994: 328). Brazil was no exception to this pattern as it pursued a policy of mini-devaluations as part of its pre-1974 'post-ISI strategy'. Such devaluations were designed to stimulate export growth and were in fact associated with such growth between 1968 and 1974. The period between 1980 and 1994 witnessed substantial alterations in exchange rate policy in which the desire to assist the balance of trade through nominal devaluations alternated with periods in which the currency was sharply revalued as an adjunct to the control of inflation. Broadly speaking, the period may be divided into three main phases, the first of which between 1980 and 1982 was associated with a stable and high nominal exchange rate against major currencies (Corrêa 1995: 14). Following the debt-adjustment crisis of the early 1980s, a period of persistent nominal devaluations took place between 1983 and 1987 in an effort to generate a trade surplus and thus provide the foreign exchange required for debt servicing. The period between 1987 and 1994 has witnessed a reversal of this trend as the nominal exchange rate underwent a series of revaluations under the terms of a number of anti-inflationary programmes.

According to Erber and Vermulm (1993: 25), the exchange rate during this period was markedly 'overvalued', a conclusion also shared by Corrêa (1995). In real terms, the appreciation of the exchange rate was considerable: between December 1988 and March 1990 the real exchange rate against a basket of major currencies was estimated to have risen by 43% (Kume et al. 1991 quoted in Corrêa 1995: 25). Following the collapse of the Collor plan in 1991, the nominal and real exchange rates underwent some depreciation, a trend maintained mildly up until 1994. The trend towards real appreciation appears to have returned under the terms of the Plano Real, introduced in July 1994. Between July 1994 and June 1995 the currency had appreciated against the US dollar in real terms by something like 30% (Baer and Paiva 1995: 6).

In an attempt to gauge more accurately the possible effects on the incentives for exporters generated by shifts in exchange rate policy, it is of use to examine the real effective exchange rate (REER). The REER may be defined as 'the nominal rate [of exchange] adjusted for differences between prices of similar goods in domestic and export markets' (Weiss 1988: 221) and may be calculated using equation (4.1) below.

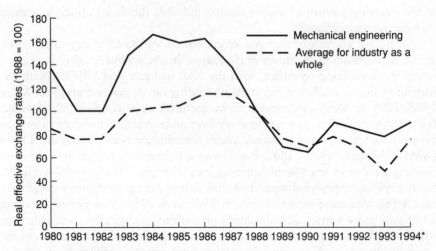

CHART 60. Real Effective Exchange Rates in Industry as a Whole and the Mechanical Engineering Industry, 1980–1994 (1988 = 100)

Note: * 1994 figure is for June 1994.

Source: Corrêa (1995: 17, 21).

(4.1)
$$E = r \cdot \frac{P_x}{P_d}$$

where E is the real effective exchange rate for the manufactures under consideration, r is the nominal rate of exchange in local currency per unit of foreign exchange, P_x is the price received by the exporters of the manufactures in local currency inclusive of subsidies or net of taxes, and P_d is the price of domestic sales of the manufactures inclusive of subsidies or net of taxes (ibid. 221).

An increase in the relative incentive to export (represented by a rise in E) may result from either a nominal devaluation (a rise in r) or as a result of a rise in P_x/P_d, the latter resulting from movements in taxation or subsidization policies that affect the relative prices of exports versus domestic sales. The definition of the REER employed here is a non-standard one in that it focuses on the relative price incentive to export. Thus nominal devaluations, other things being equal, actually lead to an *appreciation* of the REER in that they raise the relative price of exports in local currency terms. Employing this basic definition, Corrêa (1995) provides data on the REER for a number of Brazilian industrial sectors including the IBGE category—'mechanical engineering'—which incorporates the Brazilian non-serial capital goods sector. The data are presented in Chart 60.

For the mechanical engineering sector, the data indicate considerable variations in the REER throughout the 1980–94 period. From 1982 to 1986 there is a marked appreciation in the REER, indicating a strong tendency for the relative incentive to export to increase, a trend running concurrently with that of nominal exchange rate depreciation. From 1987 up until 1990, however, there is a sharp and sustained decline in the REER, a trend accompanied by nominal and real exchange rate appreciation. The recovery in the REER that followed up until June 1994 was only mild and commenced following the nominal depreciation that heralded the end of the Collor plan. Following the introduction of the *Real* in July 1994 there was a marked nominal and real appreciation of the currency against other major trading currencies. Although data for this period are not available, it seems likely given the absence of fiscal changes that the REER has once more depreciated. Thus, on the evidence of the data presented above, the period between 1986 and 1994 was not generally one in which shifts in the REER tended to favour export activity and this was at a time when the role of exports should have been becoming ever more critical given contractions in the domestic public sector markets and the onset of trade liberalization.

The identified movements in the REER would appear to be consistent with the movements in the nominal and real exchange rates mentioned earlier. However, the REER was also affected by changes in another, more explicit, area of export policy: that relating to export finance, subsidies, and taxation. It is to this that the discussion turns next.

Chart 60 demonstrates that while movements in the REER for mechanical engineering were broadly in line with that of industry as a whole over the period, there was a marked tendency for the levels of REER for the former to consistently exceed that of the latter. Such a difference arises from the fact that the application of taxes and subsidies has always tended to be constructed so as to favour the export of capital goods relative to many other industrial products. Of course, the absolute extent to which such taxation and subsidization policy provided an incentive to export has been subject to considerable variation, with a marked tendency towards a less favourable policy environment since 1987. Prior to 1987, Brazilian exporters of capital goods enjoyed a considerable range of tax exemptions and fiscal benefits as part of a programme to encourage exports. Such measures were especially necessary given the need to overcome the disincentives to export generated by an effectively closed domestic market and expanding domestic private and public sector demand. The key policies of export promotion employed during this period were numerous and are discussed below.

First, a programme of income tax exemption was made available to firms which generated operational and taxable profits on export activities. The subsidy rate per unit of goods exported was estimated to be 0.004472% by the year of termination of the scheme in 1987 (GATT 1993: 158). Secondly, duty and indirect tax concessions were available under the terms of two schemes established by the Brazilian state well before the advent of the Second National Development Plan. The Drawback scheme, established in 1964, granted exemption from payment of import duties and other indirect taxes on imported inputs for export-intensive industries, provided that the free on board (FOB) value of import content was 40% lower than the total value of the exported product (ibid. 160). Unlike other export-incentive schemes that were operational in the period up until 1987, Drawback remains in operation though its relative impact has diminished in the face of the reduced import duties ushered in by the *Abertura Comercial*.

The second of the two schemes—BEFIEX—was established in 1972 and operated continuously up until its abolition in March 1990. Under the terms of BEFIEX, enterprises in the sector committed themselves to the achievement of specified export targets. Provided these targets were achieved, enterprises were able to gain considerable fiscal and duty benefits, including a 50% cut in the rate of import duties and IPI (industrial products tax) on imports, accelerated depreciation, and income tax reductions on profits (ibid. 162). Of the non-serial capital goods sub-sectors, electrical energy equipment tended to be the biggest beneficiary of this programme. Perhaps the highest profile of all of the export promotion schemes in operation during the first half of the, 1980s was the export finance programme known as the *Fundo de Financiamento da Exportação* or FINEX. This programme was established in 1966 and was administered by the foreign commerce department (CACEX) of the *Banco do Brasil*, the state-owned commercial bank (Motta *et al*. 1994: 121).

The FINEX programme provided pre-shipment working capital finance for exports at subsidized interest rates, the rate of subsidy varying between 5 and 7½%. Such forms of credit lines were—and remain—vital to the international competitiveness of Brazilian non-serial capital goods exporters because of the combination of relatively long lead times intrinsic to the production process and the very high prevailing real domestic interest rates. The interest rate subsidy was funded from federal government revenues and ultimately proved extremely vulnerable to the renewed fiscal constraint that emerged following the National Monetary Council rulings of 1987. By 1988, FINEX operations had been greatly reduced in scope by reductions in budget allocations, while in October 1990 they ceased altogether (ibid. 122; GATT 1993: 166).

In addition to the pre-shipment credit lines, the Brazilian state also made available post-shipment subsidized finance packages to importers of Brazilian non-serial capital goods under a series of programmes associated with FINEX and administered by CACEX. The programmes allowed the post-shipment financing of capital goods exports over long periods of time, with the limits set at eight years for high-value capital goods such as turbines (GATT 1993: 166). Unfortunately, these programmes also suffered from the post-1987 fiscal cuts, with a freezing of the programmes in February 1989 followed by their formal abolition in 1990 (Motta *et al*. 1994; GATT 1993: 165). Thus by the autumn of 1990, the comprehensive system of pre- and post-shipment financing and fiscal incentives that had developed had been virtually entirely dismantled after three years of sharp contraction, with only the Drawback programme remaining in place. From 1991 onwards, however, the Brazilian state has attempted to restore some of its explicit export programmes with a renewed emphasis on the promotion of non-serial capital goods exports.

At the beginning of 1991, a new export credit facility known as FINAMEX commenced operations, being organized by and under the control of the BNDES (the national development bank). Unlike previous export finance schemes, FINAMEX was not reliant on central federal funds, being financed instead by the activities of the BNDES (interviews). This greater independence from the fiscal policies of the state was to prove essential in providing the basis for the substantial expansion in FINAMEX activities that took place between 1991 and 1994 and that has continued subsequently. In addition—and in contrast to FINEX—FINAMEX was designed exclusively for promotion of capital goods exports with a particular emphasis on the export of non-serial capital goods (interviews). The FINAMEX programme offers low levels of interest rates which are unattainable in the Brazilian private capital market where generally tight monetary policies and inflation risk premiums have pushed up real interest rates to very high levels. In essence, FINAMEX aims to provide export finance on terms which compare favourably with those available to enterprises based in other industrial economies. Presently, FINAMEX offers two forms of export finance package: a pre-shipment and a post-shipment line of credit (BNDES 1996).

The FINAMEX pre-shipment line of credit, in operation since early 1991, offers the financing of working capital over long production cycles (typically 180 days), which is especially suited to production conditions prevalent in the non-serial capital goods sector (Motta et al. 1994: 125). Interest rates are set at 2% above the London Inter-Bank Offered Rate (Libor) with financing provided for up to 70% of the export value (GATT 1993: 166). The FINAMEX post-shipment line of credit began operations in September 1991 and provides credits to importers of Brazilian capital goods of up to 85% of the total value of the equipment with maturity terms of up to 96 months. Interest rates for this programme are variable but have stood at roughly 4% above Libor for much of the programme's period of operation (ibid. 166; interviews). Because of legal restrictions, post-shipment credit facilities are only available to finance exports to signatories of the International Conference on Reciprocal Credit (CRC). Unfortunately, the USA, Canada, much of Western Europe, and South East Asia are not signatories, thus depriving Brazilian firms of access to FINAMEX post-shipment credit to these important markets. Many of FINAMEX's activities in the field of post-shipment credit have been concentrated within Latin American markets, particularly with members of the Latin American Integration Association, with the two single most important markets being Mexico and Argentina (interviews).

The expansion of FINAMEX activity was very rapid between 1991 and 1994, a feature that is discussed in more detail in Section 4.4. According to the Head of Operations of FINAMEX, the take-up rate of FINAMEX financing has been of the order of 85%, with non-serial capital goods exports representing the vast bulk of total finance disbursements. This situation may be contrasted with FINAMEX's domestic counterpart, FINAME, where the take-up rate tended to be around 50% and non-serial capital goods tended to be relatively less important in terms of overall disbursements. In June 1991, a new export financing package called PROEX was established by the federal government, the programme being administered by the *Banco do Brasil* and financed out of central government funds (Motta *et al.* 1994: 126; GATT 1993: 166–7). PROEX offers both pre- and post-export financing facilities, with interest rates pegged to Libor. Financing may be either direct or may take the form of compensation paid to enterprises for the difference between the interest rate they pay commercially and the Central Bank's Libor-pegged reference rate, a form of finance known as interest rate equalization. The importance of PROEX for the non-serial capital goods sector has only been limited, with approximately 85% of exports being financed through FINAMEX. The reasons for the smaller role of PROEX result from a number of factors.

First, obtaining finance from PROEX is administratively more complicated, with disbursements being approved on a case by case basis by the treasury and themselves subject to the vicissitudes of fiscal policy (Motta *et al.* 1994: 126). In addition, FINAMEX was specifically established with the aim of promoting capital goods exports and benefits from a specialized staff with extensive knowledge of the capital goods sector, whereas PROEX is a general programme where sector experience has been less extensive (interviews). Finally, enterprises participating in FINAMEX programmes have been unable to benefit from PROEX facilities because of rules prohibiting the simultaneous use of both credit facilities (GATT 1993: 167).

4.3 The Evolution of Brazilian Exports and Imports of Non-serial Capital Goods, 1981–1994

The period since 1981 has seen substantial and far-reaching changes in the export performance of the Brazilian non-serial capital goods sector. The most outstanding feature of these alterations has been a marked increase in total exports to the point where they had virtually doubled in real terms between 1981 and 1994 (Table 32). Set against the fact that total output in the non-serial capital goods sector had by 1994 yet to regain the level achieved at the start of the 1980s, it becomes evident that the relative importance of exports to the sector has markedly increased. Among ABDIB members, the period

1988–91 alone saw the share of exports in total sales rise from 10% to 25% (Tadini 1993: 10).

As Section 4.4 will argue, the expansion of the role of exports has in some cases been associated with profound changes in enterprise behaviour which in turn have ushered in important alterations in static and dynamic efficiency. At the same time, there has been a shift in the geographic concentration of exports, with a growing emphasis on the markets of Latin America and a diminished role for the markets of OECD countries. The period also witnessed a number of changes in patterns of non-serial capital goods imports, with a marked tendency for import expansion following the dismantling of the mechanisms of protection at the end of the 1980s and the beginning of the 1990s.

The movements in export and imports discussed above may only be described as general tendencies, however, and mask considerable temporal, sub-sectoral, and inter-enterprise variations. In order to fully understand the processes underlying the evolution of the sector's trade performance, it will be essential to examine these variations in some detail. The remainder of this section therefore considers alterations in exports and imports for each of the five non-serial capital goods sub-sectors. Following this, the changing composition of export markets is considered. Finally, the issue of inter-enterprise variations in export performance is examined, paying particular attention to the question of the extent to which the expansion in export activity is a diffuse or a concentrated phenomenon within particular sub-sectors.

4.3.1 EXPORTS AND IMPORTS OF NON-SERIAL CAPITAL GOODS: GENERAL TENDENCIES AND SUB-SECTORAL VARIATIONS

Table 29 and Chart 61 illustrate the extent to which trade in non-serial capital goods has undergone substantial changes in the period between 1981 and 1994. Total exports of non-serial capital goods tended to fall in real terms between 1981 and 1986, although the precise manner in which they did so is partially obscured by the absence of data for the years 1983 and 1984. Between 1986 and 1994, however, there was a dramatic expansion in exports: in real terms exports more than tripled. The pace of expansion of exports over this period was not even, however, with exports rising more slowly in the 1986 to 1990 period (by 49.2%) than they did between 1990 and 1994 when the increase was of the order of 111.8%. The evolution of non-serial capital good imports presents a number of contrasts when compared to the pattern described above. Although there is a tendency for total imports to fall between 1981 and 1985 (a pattern which matches the behaviour of exports), the period between 1985 and 1991 is characterized by a degree of stability with no discernible tendency for total non-serial capital goods imports to rise or fall.

TABLE 29. Total Exports and Imports of Non-serial Capital Goods, 1981–1994

	1981	1982	1985	1986	1987	1988	1989	1990	1991	1992	1993	1994
Exports	581.3	507.7	468.3	365.1	438.2	410.1	594.2	544.7	713.4	798.9	913.7	1,156.1
Imports	1,097.1	952.3	713.6	902.6	735.6	834.7	759.7	887.6	905	722	1,079	1,275.5
Balance	−515.8	−444.6	−245.3	−537.5	−297.4	−424.6	−165.5	−342.9	−191.6	+76.9	−165.3	−119.4

Note: Figures are in millions of constant 1990 US dollars.

Source: United Nations, *Commodity Trade Statistics*, various years; CEPAL (1993). Deflator used is based on import and export prices, Brazil, World Bank (1994), *World Tables*, and the US wholesale price index, IMF (1995), *International Financial Statistics*.

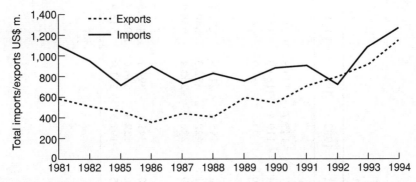

CHART 61. Total Exports and Imports of Non-serial Capital Goods, 1981–1994 (constant prices (US$ m. 1990))

Source: Table 29.

That this should be the case seems remarkable given the fluctuations in domestic demand discussed earlier and will be discussed further in Section 4.4. From 1991 to 1994, however, there was a rapid rise in imports of the order of 40%. The effect of these movements in exports and imports was, from 1986 onwards, to close rapidly the large trade deficit for non-serial capital goods that had developed in the early part of the 1980s. By 1992, Brazil had achieved a trade surplus in non-serial capital goods although a mild deficit recurred in the two following years.

The electrical energy equipment sub-sector has consistently generated more exports than any of the other non-serial capital goods sub-sectors with total exports approaching US$ 485 m. in 1994 (Table 30). In common with the pattern for total non-serial capital goods exports presented in Table 29 above, exports of electrical energy equipment have experienced rapid expansion since 1986 with a particularly rapid increase after 1990. Despite the improving export performance of the sub-sector, data in Table 30 and Chart 62 reveal a persistent and eventually widening trade deficit in electrical energy equipment. This, of course, is intimately connected with the expansion in imports of such equipment which took place between 1985 and 1994 with a particularly large increase between 1992 and 1994. The overall trade gap for electrical energy equipment is largely accounted for by deficits resulting from trade in electrical switch gear and control equipment. For imports and exports of generators and rotating electric plant, a combination of rapidly expanding exports and stagnating imports led to a reduction of deficits and the eventual development of trade surpluses in the 1990s (Table 30). The reasons underlying this superior performance are connected with the development of export specialization in the heavy generator, motor, and turbine sectors and are discussed in more detail in Section 4.3.3 and Chapter 5.

TABLE 30. Exports and Imports of Electrical Energy Equipment

	1981	1982	1985	1986	1987	1988	1989	1990	1991	1992	1993	1994
Generators and rotating electric plant												
Exports	26.2	14.9	48	51.7	62.1	88.5	120	115.7	157.8	145.7	174.8	212.7
Imports	177.3	151.1	126.1	214.1	193.1	262.9	205.2	215.9	214.2	110.4	184.3	187.7
Balance	−151.1	−136.2	−78.1	−162.4	−13.1	−174.4	−85.2	−100.2	−56.4	35.3	−9.5	25
Transformers, switch gear, and control equipment												
Exports	114.4	89.6	99.8	53	59.4	67	115.9	113.6	132.8	195.4	219.9	271.1
Imports	523.6	555.4	284	318.8	281.5	286	381.1	435.1	411.8	422	482.3	840
Balance	−409.2	−465.8	−184.2	−265.8	−222.1	−219	−265.2	−321.5	−279	−226.6	−262.4	−568.9
Total												
Exports	140.6	104.5	147.8	104.7	121.5	155.5	235.9	229.3	290.6	341.1	394.7	483.8
Imports	700.9	706.5	410.1	532.9	474.6	548.9	586.3	651	626	532.4	666.6	1,027.7
Balance	−560.3	−602	−262.3	−428.2	−353	−393.4	−350.4	−421.7	−335.4	−191.3	−271.9	−543.9

Note: Figures are in millions of constant 1990 US dollars.

Source: As for Table 29.

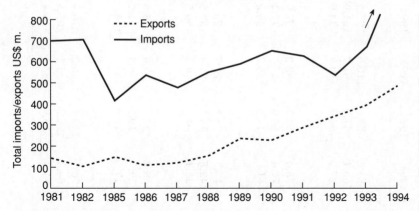

CHART 62. Exports and Imports of Electrical Energy Equipment, 1981–1994 (constant prices (US$ m. 1990))

Note: Figure for 1994 is $1,027.7 m.

Source: Table 30.

In general, exports of mechanical equipment have exhibited a broadly similar pattern of behaviour to that of the non-serial capital goods sector as a whole in that declines up to 1986 were followed by rapid expansion. However, the pattern of export growth in the 1986–94 period appears rather uneven with a rapid fall between 1989 and 1990 followed by a renewed expansion (Table 31 and Chart 63). This uneven path is in large part attributable to exceptionally high exports of pulp and paper-making equipment in 1989. While the mechanical handling equipment product category has remained the most significant in terms of exports, there was also rapid growth in the exports of other equipment produced by the sector, particularly after 1990. This is especially true in the case of construction and mining machinery (Table 31). Despite the size of the Brazilian steel equipment industry and its numerous producers, the sector's exports have remained relatively modest with exports worth only $26 m. in 1994. However, this figure represents a doubling of exports in relation to 1989.

The behaviour of mechanical equipment imports divides into two distinct phases. The first, beginning in 1981 and terminating in 1985, witnessed a sharp decline while the second, from 1985 onwards, saw a steady level of imports up until 1987 followed by a generally sustained rise (Table 31 and Chart 63). Increases in imports were particularly pronounced in the mechanical handling equipment and pulp and paper machinery product areas. The overall rises in imports were not sufficient, however, to fully offset the growth in exports with the result that Brazil continued to run the trade surplus in mechanical equipment that had originated in the mid-1980s. However, the data indicate that the trade surplus tended to narrow considerably, particularly after 1990.

TABLE 31. Exports and Imports of Mechanical Equipment

	1981	1982	1985	1986	1987	1988	1989	1990	1991	1992	1993	1994
Mechanical handling equipment												
Exports	64.1	45.1	48.6	39.1	42.7	57.7	78.6	80.1	83.4	88.4	110.6	97.5
Imports	106	115.7	40.1	30.1	25.8	35.2	42.1	51.6	66.1	51.7	91.7	121.9
Balance	−41.9	−70.6	+8.5	+9	+16.9	+22.5	+36.5	+28.5	+17.3	+36.7	+18.9	−24.9
Pulp and paper machinery												
Exports	67.9	36	72.3	57.9	60.8	97.5	168.6	65.4	78.4	53.7	82.2	57.9
Imports	32.9	13.1	11.3	17.4	13.1	20.7	34.3	82.7	77.4	64.4	47	72.1
Balance	+35	+22.9	+61	+40.5	+47.7	+76.3	+134.3	−17.7	+1	−10.3	+35.2	−14.2
Steel-making equipment, rolling mills												
Exports	—	—	10.7	11.3	—	—	13.5	15.2	17.7	28.1	27.7	26
Imports	—	—	4.5	10.4	—	—	17.9	17.1	42.8	29.1	75.9	85.5
Balance	—	—	6.2	+0.9	—	—	−4.4	−1.9	−25.1	−1	−48.2	−59.5
Construction and mining machinery												
Exports	108.1	85.2	10.7	11.1	12.8	15.7	11.4	10.4	8.9	38	35.4	55.5
Imports	120.2	74.8	4.5	6.1	12.3	13	14.9	17.7	25.9	10.1	6.4	11.5
Balance	−12.1	11.2	6.2	5	0.5	2.7	−3.5	−7.3	−17	+27.9	+29	+44
Total*												
Exports	240.1	166.3	131.6	108.1	106.3	170.9	258.6	155.9	170.7	180.1	228.2	210.9
Imports	259.1	203.6	55.9	53.6	51.2	68.9	91.3	152	169.4	126.2	145.1	205.5
Balance	−19	−37.3	75.7	+55.1	+55.1	+102	+167.3	+3.9	+1.3	+53.9	+83.1	+5.4

Notes: Figures are in millions of constant 1990 US dollars.

* Excludes steel-making equipment and rolling mills.

Source: As for Table 29.

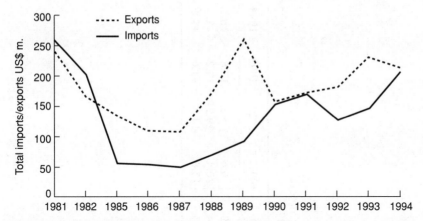

CHART 63. Total Exports and Imports of Mechanical Equipment,* 1981–1994 (constant prices (US$ m. 1990))

Note: * Excludes steel-making equipment and rolling mills.

Source: Table 31.

The boiler making sub-sector has not traditionally been a major particip-ant in export markets being instead very focused on supplying the Brazilian market. This situation is reflected in Table 32 and Chart 64 where exports in 1994 stood at a total of only $16.5 m. Despite the low absolute volume of exports, it is worth noting that the sector substantially increased its export activities, albeit from a very low base. From 1986 to 1994 exports rose approx-imately sixfold, from $2.3 m. to $16.5 m. Imports of boilers tended to be greater and subject to more extensive fluctuation than was the case with exports. Table 32 and Chart 64 reveal a substantial rise in imports in the mid-1980s, which given the very low levels of exports led to the development of consid-erable trade deficits in this product area in this period. By contrast with other sectors, the period from 1988 onwards witnessed a considerable contraction in imports to the point where the trade deficit had been eliminated and converted into a surplus by 1993.

In common with imports of boilers, exports of railway vehicles and equip-ment have also been subject to considerable fluctuation, although it is pos-sible to discern three major trends. Between 1982 and 1987, there was a substantial fall in exports of the order of 67%. Between 1987 and 1992, how-ever, and despite fluctuations, exports rose rapidly to reach US$ 62.7 m., more than double the 1987 figure (Table 33 and Chart 65). From 1992 to 1994, however, there was a rapid decline in which exports more than halved, a development accompanying a period of crisis and restructuring within the sub-sector. Imports of railway vehicles also underwent considerable variations in the 1981–94 period with peaks in 1986 and 1991, the latter being followed by a precipitous fall. The result of the combined volatile export and import

TABLE 32. Exports and Imports of Boilers, 1981–1994

	1981	1982	1985	1986	1987	1988	1989	1990	1991	1992	1993	1994
Exports	9.2	6.7	8.8	2.3	3	2.8	11.4	9.9	6.6	5.3	17.8	16.5
Imports	37.6	5.9	136.3	128.4	52.5	172.3	27.1	49.4	20.4	19.9	13.2	8.6
Balance	−28.4	+0.8	−127.7	−126.1	−49.5	−169.5	−15.7	−39.5	−13.8	−14.6	+4.6	+7.4

Note: Figures are in millions of constant 1990 US dollars.

Source: As for Table 29.

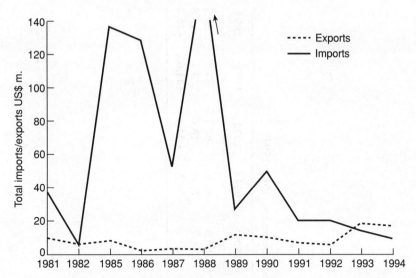

CHART 64. Total Exports and Imports of Boilers, 1981–1994 (constant prices (US$ m. 1990))

Note: → 1988 value is $ 172.3 m.

Source: Table 31.

trends has been to create large swings in the trade balance with alternating surpluses and deficits.

In contrast to the railway equipment sub-sector, export and import trends in the shipbuilding sub-sector are markedly well defined. In the case of exports, the period between 1981 and 1988 was generally one in which total exports tended to decline in real terms. Between 1988 and 1994, however, and in common with all other sectors bar railway equipment, there was a very substantial rise in exports, the increase being slightly more than tenfold (Table 34 and Chart 66). The magnitude of the increase is of special significance given the fact that the sub-sector has historically tended to be much more export intensive than others in the non-serial capital goods sector. By 1994 the shipbuilding sub-sector was second only to the electrical energy equipment sub-sector in terms of the total export sales generated. Imports of ships and floating structures tended to remain subdued throughout much of the period in question although there was a period of increased imports in the mid to late 1980s and a one-off increase in 1993, the latter resulting from the operation of a Petrobrás investment programme. Given the situation described above, Brazil has tended to run substantial trade surpluses in ships and floating structures throughout much of the 1981–94 period.

TABLE 33. Exports and Imports of Railway Vehicles and Equipment, 1981–1994

	1981	1982	1985	1986	1987	1988	1989	1990	1991	1992	1993	1994
Exports	41.8	57.6	31.6	25.4	18.9	39.9	30.9	60.4	42.5	62.7	43.7	29.3
Imports	49	18.6	48.9	76.8	45.1	40.6	27.4	26.7	77.8	18.6	9.1	13.8
Balance	−7.2	+39	−17.3	−51.4	−26.2	−0.7	+3.5	+33.7	−35.3	+44.1	+34.6	+15.5

Note: Figures are in millions of constant 1990 US dollars.

Source: As for Table 29.

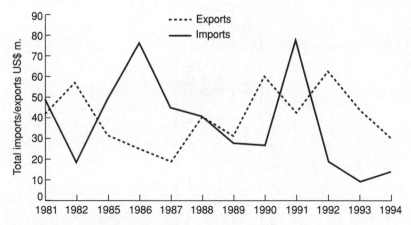

CHART 65. Total Exports and Imports of Railway Vehicles and Equipment, 1981–1994 (constant prices (US$ m. 1990))

Source: Table 33.

4.3.2 MERCOSUL AND THE CHANGING COMPOSITION OF EXPORT MARKETS

The rise in exports of non-serial capital goods has been accompanied by marked changes in the regional composition of export markets. Historically, Brazilian exports of non-serial capital goods tended to be concentrated in the markets of the developed economies, particularly those of North America (Torres *et al.* 1994: 46). However, the post-1986 period of export expansion has witnessed a substantial reorientation of exports towards the markets of Latin America for all sectors except shipbuilding and railway equipment. Significantly, in the majority of cases, the most rapidly growing sector of the Latin American export market in terms of sales has been the MERCOSUL free trade area, a regional entity encompassing Argentina, Uruguay, and Paraguay.

Charts 67 and 68 show the extent to which the general trends discussed above are reflected in the case of the electrical energy equipment sub-sector. The shift towards the Latin American market—particularly that of MER-COSUL—was very pronounced over the period in question. Accompanying this trend was a distinct reduction in the relative importance of the European and North American markets. In country terms, this changing pattern is reflected in the diminishing importance of the USA, Italy, and Germany as overseas markets and the increasing role of Argentina, Chile, and Mexico (United Nations 1986, 1994).

The changing patterns of export destination for electrical energy equipment are repeated for the mechanical equipment sub-sector with a very substantial shift from the markets of North to South America (Charts 69 and 70).

TABLE 34. Exports and Imports of Ships and Floating Structures, 1981–1994

	1981	1982	1985	1986	1987	1988	1989	1990	1991	1992	1993	1994
Exports	149.6	172.6	148.5	126.9	178.5	41	57.4	74	185.3	209.7	229.3	415.6
Imports	50.5	17.7	62.4	110.3	112.2	4	27.6	8.5	11.4	24.9	245	19.9
Balance	+99.1	+154.9	+86.1	+16.6	+66.3	+37	+29.8	+65.5	+173.9	+184.8	-15.7	+395.7

Note: Figures are in millions of constant 1990 US dollars.

Source: As for Table 29.

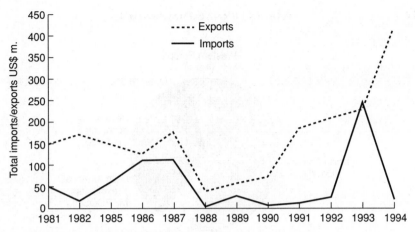

CHART 66. Total Exports and Imports of Ships and Floating Structures, 1981–1994 (constant prices (US$ m. 1990))

Source: Table 34.

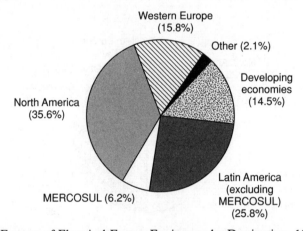

CHART 67. Exports of Electrical Energy Equipment by Destination, 1986

Source: United Nations, *Commodity Trade Statistics: Brazil* (1986 and 1994).

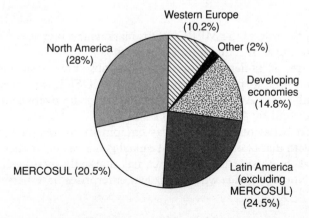

CHART 68. Exports of Electrical Energy Equipment by Destination, 1994

Source: United Nations (1986, 1994).

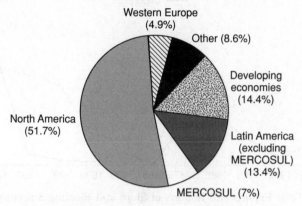

CHART 69. Exports of Mechanical Equipment by Destination, 1986
Source: United Nations (1986, 1994).

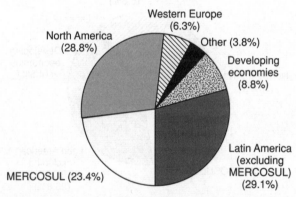

CHART 70. Exports of Mechanical Equipment by Destination, 1994
Source: United Nations (1986, 1994).

Once again, the role of the MERCOSUL markets has increased substantially in relation to those of Latin America as a whole.

In the case of boilers, the relative and absolute expansion of Latin American markets, in particular those of MERCOSUL, has been very pronounced with Latin American economies forming the overwhelming source of export demand by 1994 (Charts 71 and 72).

The export behaviour of the railway equipment sub-sector is notable for its contrast with that of other non-serial capital goods sectors in that the importance of markets outside Latin America has markedly increased, notably in the case of North America where Brazilian enterprises have been attempting

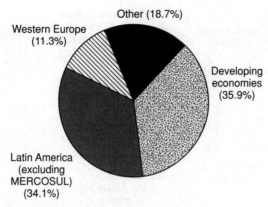

CHART 71. Exports of Boilers by Destination, 1986

Source: United Nations (1986, 1994).

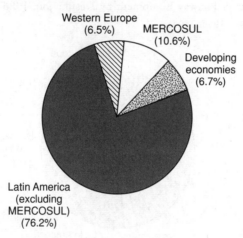

CHART 72. Exports of Boilers by Destination, 1994

Source: United Nations (1986, 1994).

to develop an export niche in freight and passenger vehicles (Charts 73 and 74; *Revista Ferroviaria*, Dec. 1994). The significance of this trend for overall geographical export patterns of the Brazilian non-serial capital goods sector is only limited, however, due to the relatively subdued export performance of the sub-sector by comparison with others.

Although UN commodity statistics trade data exist for the shipbuilding sub-sector, their usefulness is very limited due to the fact that only countries of registration—usually Liberia or the Cayman Islands—are indicated rather than the countries in which ownership resides. However, it is possible to make some comments as to the final destination of vessels based upon interviews

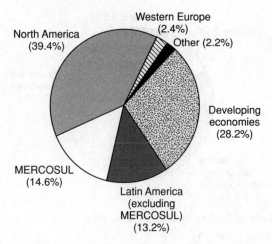

CHART 73. Exports of Railway Equipment by Destination, 1986
Source: United Nations (1986, 1994).

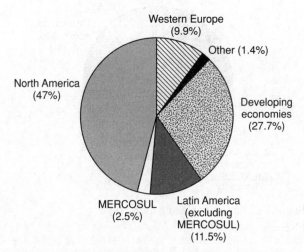

CHART 74. Exports of Railway Equipment by Destination, 1994
Source: United Nations (1986, 1994).

conducted at Enterprise *C*. Throughout the period in question, much of the export activity of the Brazilian shipbuilding sub-sector has tended to be concentrated outside the Latin American market, the latter being, in world shipping terms, comparatively small. Most of the export sales realized have been made to European, Japanese, and American shipping lines which placed major orders for oil tankers and bulk carriers. Managers stressed that the Brazilian shipbuilding sub-sector was likely to maintain this pattern of regional focus for the foreseeable future.

Significantly, of all goods traded among MERCOSUL member countries, trade in capital goods and vehicles grew most rapidly between the mid-1980s and 1994 (Yeats 1996). For Yeats (1996), intensified trade in these products indicates that the creation of MERCOSUL has served to divert rather than create trade (ibid.). According to Yeats this is because the MERCOSUL economies have failed to demonstrate an ability to export these goods competitively elsewhere. Following Yeats's logic, therefore, the Brazilian capital goods sector diverted its export efforts to Argentina, Paraguay, and Uruguay, rather than face more competitive markets outside MERCOSUL. Thus, the sector took advantage of privileged market access to the other MERCOSUL countries while benefiting from the fact that the competitive challenge posed by capital goods manufacturers in these economies was minimal. Viewed in this sense, MERCOSUL may have served to slow the pace of efficiency gains within the Brazilian non-serial capital goods sector. This interpretation of the consequences of MERCOSUL has received wide attention. However, at least in terms of the Brazilian non-serial capital goods sector, it possesses significant flaws.

First, as the discussion has already noted, two of the sub-sectors, shipbuilding and railway equipment, did not become any more reliant on MERCOSUL markets between 1986 and 1994. Where greater relative reliance on the MERCOSUL market did occur, as in the case of electrical energy and mechanical equipment, this has to be seen against a background of greatly expanded export activity in which export volumes to non-MERCOSUL countries actually increased. Finally, and very importantly, up until 1995, the sector's largest MERCOSUL market, Argentina, operated an exceptionally liberal import régime for capital goods. Between 1992 and 1995 Argentinean tariffs were actually set at zero on all imports of capital goods, irrespective of their country of origin. Despite the highly open nature of the Argentinean market, Brazilian producers of non-serial capital goods managed to increase sales and market penetration. This would not have occurred had the sector been fundamentally uncompetitive.

4.3.3 EXPORT SPECIALIZATION AND INTER-ENTERPRISE VARIATIONS IN EXPORT PERFORMANCE

The expansion of non-serial capital goods exports discussed above was the result of a general movement towards a greater reliance on exports within the sector. However, it should be recognized that some enterprises played a greater role in the overall expansion than others as they embarked upon a strategy akin to export specialization. For the capital goods sector as a whole, BNDES (1994b) and Torres, de Carvalho, and Torres Filho (1994), reveal that between 1986 and 1992 much of the growth in exports was accounted for by the larger enterprises in the sector. In 1986 the 21 enterprises whose annual exports exceeded US$ 10 m. accounted for 83% of the total exports that would have been eligible for financing under FINAMEX rules (ibid.)

with there being a total of 82 exporting enterprises altogether. By 1992 the number of enterprises exporting more than US\$ 10 m. worth of equipment had expanded to a total of 34, out of a total of 147 exporting enterprises, and collectively accounted for 84% of total exports (ibid.). Thus, the expansion in exports was dominated by a relative minority of enterprises, though as time went on the absolute size of that minority expanded considerably as did the total number of enterprises participating in the export market.

According to the head of operations at FINAMEX, in the specific case of the non-serial capital goods sector, virtually all enterprises within the sector increased the absolute level of their export sales (interviews). However, within the non-serial capital goods sector, there existed a degree of unevenness of absolute export expansion among enterprises, although this was not as great as that in the capital goods industry as a whole, where the size of enterprises (and thus total export potential) tended to be much less uniform (ibid.). The latter feature arises from the co-existence, in the capital goods sector as a whole, of large non-serial and serial capital goods producers with extremely small serial capital goods producers, such as toolmakers and small power-tool manufacturers with only very limited export revenues.

Such unevenness as can be detected in the inter-enterprise export performance of the non-serial capital goods sector arises primarily from the characteristics of two of the largest sub-sectors in export terms; those of electrical energy equipment and shipbuilding. As Section 4.3.1 revealed, the greatest absolute expansion in exports between the mid-1980s and 1994 was generated by the electrical energy equipment sub-sector. By 1994 this accounted for 42% of total non-serial capital goods exports (calculated from United Nations 1994), with the share of sales in total sub-sector output rising from 3.7% to 16.1% between 1987–9 and 1992, according the 1993 competitiveness study (Strachmann 1993). Within the sub-sector, exporting activity has tended to be concentrated among the major foreign-owned enterprises, most particularly ABB, Siemens, General Electric, Mecânica Pesada, and Merlin Gerin (ibid.; interviews). As Chapter 5 will reveal, there was a considerable emphasis on specialization in the area of hydro-generators and heavy transformers, the vast bulk of which were exported following the domestic market contractions of the late 1980s.

To some extent this picture is reproduced in the mechanical equipment sub-sector although the degree of export concentration is rather less pronounced with a general shift towards greater export intensity in a sub-sector which has remained inherently more atomized than that of electrical energy equipment (interviews). However, Bardella, Usiminas Mecânica, Buhler, and Sulzer were all particularly active (and largely successful) in seeking new export markets from the late 1980s onwards (interviews). In the case of Enterprise B, the degree of export concentration was particularly marked, with 70% of total sales being accounted for by the export market, in marked contrast to 1986 when approximately 90% of sales were made to the domestic public sector (interviews). Enterprise *B*'s key export products were concentrated in the mechanical handling equipment product area with which the enterprise has successfully penetrated Latin American and US markets. Export growth in steel-making equipment was more restrained.

In the case of the boiler-making sub-sector, Section 4.3.1 noted that exports had tended to remain at a markedly low absolute level, although there was something of an expansion between 1993 and 1994. In keeping with the sector's inherently atomized nature (see Chapter 6), there has been little of the degree of export concentration witnessed in other sectors (interviews). Within the railway equipment sub-sector, export activity has been fairly evenly spread between the railway vehicle producers, with GEVISA, Cobrasma, Convap, Mafersa, and Iochpe-Maxion all engaging in exports and the largest single market being North America (*Revista Ferroviaria*, Jan. 1995, Dec. 1995; ABIFER 1993).

Within the shipbuilding sub-sector the pattern is somewhat different, a state of affairs strongly linked to the heterogeneity of the shipyards highlighted in the previous chapter. Of the shipyards capable of producing ocean-going vessels and floating structures, exports have been dominated by CCN-Mauá, Verolme, and Ishibrás (the two latter enterprises merged in 1994), whose production facilities are the only ones in Brazil capable of producing the higher tonnage, higher value-added vessels that have constituted the bulk of export demand (interviews).

Thus, while the expansion of exports has been virtually a global phenomenon within the non-serial capital goods sector, the pace at which some enterprises have succeeded in raising their exports has been greater than that for others. The relatively more concentrated industrial structures of the electrical energy and shipbuilding sub-sectors, along with their greater absolute contribution to export growth and larger share of total non-serial capital goods exports, have meant inevitably that enterprises in these sub-sectors have contributed disproportionately to non-serial capital goods export expansion as a whole. Significantly, these sub-sectors were characterized by higher participation rates by transnational corporations (TNCs) than was the case in the other three sub-sectors. Not surprisingly, the available—though far from comprehensive— evidence tends to suggest that TNC subsidiaries in the non-serial capital goods sector tended to be more export intensive than their Brazilian-owned coun- terparts. Examining data for the 1986–92 period, a BNDES report (BNDES 1994*b*) found that TNC subsidiaries were responsible for 70% of overall exports of capital goods while representing only 35% of the total number of enter- prises. Fritsch and Franco (1991*a*: 132–3) note that majority-owned foreign affiliates of US capital goods enterprises showed a significantly higher pro- pensity to export than their Brazilian-owned non-serial capital goods enter- prises, with an export propensity of 25.36% in the former case and 13% in the latter. However, these data should be treated with caution as they refer to 1985 and thus predate the expansion in exports. Moreover, the data concentrate on US subsidiaries alone, whose presence in the sector is far less significant than that of European or Japanese-based corporations.

4.4 Accounting for Movements in the Export and Import of Non-serial Capital Goods: The Role of Government Policy

The shifts in patterns of exports and imports of non-serial capital goods identified in Section 4.3 had a number of distinct features. First, exports, after falling in total value up until 1986, began a rapid rise towards the end of the decade before accelerating further in the period 1991 to 1994. Underlying this increase were particularly large absolute rises in the exports of electrical energy equipment and ships and floating structures. Imports, after a period of falling up until the mid-1980s, remained roughly constant up until about 1990 and subsequently rose rapidly in the period up until 1994, with particularly rapid increases occurring for imports of electrical energy equipment. In trying to understand the evolution of these patterns of import and export performance it is necessary to take account of a number of important influences. In order to best present the relative role of these, the discussion divides into two sections, the first covering the period 1986–91 and the second the period 1991–4.

(i) Exports, Imports, and the Role of Policy, 1986–1991

The dramatic reductions in public sector orders for non-serial capital goods that commenced in 1987 proved to be a prime stimulus in initiating the move towards the greater export intensity and export expansion that have characterized the sector between the mid-1980s and 1994. Chapter 2 demonstrated the severity of the contractions and noted that they were especially concentrated in the 1987–91 period. That enterprises commenced their export expansion during the same period of time is no coincidence. Enterprises in the sector, faced with a dearth of public sector orders and domestic private sector markets increasingly open to, and penetrated by, external competition (see below), increasingly turned to the export market in an effort to raise levels of capacity utilization and reverse the growing tendency towards the accumulation of losses and debt. Thus enterprises effectively were attempting to employ the export market as a substitute for an increasingly precarious position in the domestic public sector market and reduced market share in the relatively more buoyant private sector market.

That this motivation in large part underlay the expansion of exports in the first part of the period, that is, between 1987 and 1991, is amply supported by the evidence. All the enterprises interviewed essentially viewed their relatively greater export intensity as having been primarily initiated by the declines in their core public sector markets in the late 1980s. For Enterprise C, the necessity to export was amplified by the fact that domestic private sector demand for its core products—large bulk carriers and oil tankers—was virtually non-existent. For Enterprises *A* and *B*, the continued inflow of imports, despite a slowdown in domestic private sector demand during the initial phase of trade liberalization, meant that domestic private sector market share was tending to come under pressure, thus providing an additional stimulus for exports. In addition, during the late 1980s, traditional export markets—especially the USA and Germany—were enjoying a phase of steady growth, providing opportunities not then available within the Brazilian domestic market. The influences underlying the expansion in exports of the interviewed enterprises would appear to be common to most if not all of the enterprises in the non-serial capital goods sector.

According to the director of operations at FINAMEX, the overwhelming motive among non-serial capital goods enterprises to expand their exporting activities arose from the decline of the public sector market at the end of the 1980s. During the initial stages of the export expansion between 1986 and 1990, the director described enterprise export strategies as being essentially 'reactive' as they were forced to turn to the export market as conditions in the domestic market rapidly deteriorated, principally as a result of the decline in public sector non-serial capital goods procurement, but also because of the growing penetration of the domestic market by imported goods. This conclusion was broadly supported in the course of interviews with a leading sector consultant, and the director of the economics department at ABDIB. The sense in which enterprises were forced to export as a result of the fall in public sector procurement is highlighted in a number of Brazilian sources. *Indústria e Produtividade* (Mar. 1991: 49) ascribes the increased reliance on exports directly to the fall in public enterprise orders, a point repeated in *Brasil em Exame* (1993: 69; 1990: 50) and in broad terms by Tadini (1993). That the decline in public sector orders was the prime influence underlying the initial expansion in exports is further underlined when the rather unfavourable nature of the other policies which might have been expected to have affected the export performance of enterprises is considered.

Section 4.2 highlighted the way in which, between 1987 and 1990, the policy apparatus of export promotion and finance was progressively dismantled to the point where it had effectively ceased to exist by the autumn of 1990. Simultaneously, the real effective exchange rate for the capital goods sector was moving in an unfavourable direction, partly as a result of the dismantling of the regime of export subsidies but also through the albeit discontinuous trend towards the real and nominal appreciation of the various currencies brought in under the terms of stabilization plans. The combination of circumstances that these developments brought about was anything but favourable to the expansion of non-serial capital goods exports. According to Walter V. Kalm, the director of the mechanical equipment enterprise, Voith, by 1990 the lack of access to competitive export finance during this period combined with exchange rate overvaluation had put a serious obstacle in the way of further export expansion in the sector (*Brasil em Exame* 1990:

50), a conclusion reiterated elsewhere in the sector (*Indústria e Produtividade*, Mar. 1991: 49; Motta *et al.* 1994). Thus the expansion of exports in the sector during the initial phase of export growth had to overcome exchange rate and export finance regimes that were essentially unfavourable. Despite the difficulties in exporting faced under these circumstances, enterprises had little choice but to export given the scale of the compression of demand in the domestic market.

In the discussion above, part of the reduction of domestic demand faced by enterprises was attributed to the effects of increased import penetration. Section 4.3 noted the fairly stable, mildly rising trend of overall non-serial capital goods imports during the period between 1985 and 1991. Given the fact that overall domestic demand for non-serial capital goods after an initial rise then commenced a precipitous fall (see Chapter 2), this trend seems somewhat surprising and certainly implies increased market share for imported non-serial capital goods at the expense of their domestically produced counterparts. In accounting for this development two factors stand out as being of particular importance.

First, the initial stages of the *Abertura Comercial in* 1987 and 1988 had been concentrated in the area of liberalizing the import of capital goods in an effort to permit modernization of the manufacturing sector as a whole in advance of wider trade liberalization (GATT 1993; interviews). During the initial phases of the Collor administration's intensified trade liberalization, the non-serial capital goods sector once again experienced some of the sharpest reductions in protective measures of all industrial sectors. Secondly, as has already been mentioned, the period was one in which there was a considerable tendency towards the nominal and real overvaluation of the currencies which gave imports—already more accessible through lower tariff and non-tariff barriers —an added price advantage.

Taken together these trends led to a situation in which imports were able to remain at sustained and mildly increasing levels (Vermulm 1993: 21–2), even though Brazilian non-serial capital goods demand as a whole was diminishing. The extent to which imports were able to maintain their level in a contracting market during this period was also assisted by the fact that the Brazilian non-serial capital goods sector's modernization programme was in its early stages, a factor likely to impede the relative competitiveness of the sector in domestic markets in the context of a situation already made unfavourable through exchange rate overvaluation.

(ii) Exports, Imports, and the Role of Policy, 1991–1994

To some extent, the expansion of exports up until 1991 could be regarded as a recession-induced phenomenon brought on by contracting domestic public and eventually private sector markets. Viewed in this manner, the export market becomes a substitute for the domestic one or to quote Erber and Vermulm (1993), a form of 'vent for sales'. As such, the expansion could hardly be viewed as unique in the history of the Brazilian non-serial capital goods sector. During a previous phase of public investment contraction at the end of the 1970s, there was a marked expansion in sector exports as enterprises sought alternative markets (Teubal 1984: 854). Growth in exports eventually tailed off, however, as private sector growth and some public enterprise investment expenditure returned in the two years immediately prior to the debt-adjustment crisis of 1983.

Following the emergence of Brazil from recession in 1992 and its return to vigorous growth in the following two years, however, the pace of export expansion actually increased despite renewed domestic private sector investment expenditures (see Chart 10; Chapter 3). Given the extent of the expansion of non-serial capital goods exports and the domestic economic circumstances in which they occurred, it would be hard to term more recent increases in exports as being 'recession induced'. Instead, it will be argued that the expansion of exports in the 1991 to 1994 period was the result of the operation of a special set of circumstances in which the state played a decisive role.

When Brazil commenced an upturn in economic activity towards the end of 1992, it did so in the context of a policy environment radically different to that which had accompanied previous cyclical recoveries in the post-1950 period. Most fundamentally, the *Abertura Comercial* had opened up domestic markets to levels of external competition unparalleled since the adoption of import substitution strategies in the 1950s. The non-serial capital goods sector was also, of course, faced with this new structural reality as the privileged protected position it had enjoyed since the advent of the Second National Development Plan vanished. Thus although the domestic private sector market was expanding, not least as manufacturing industry re-equipped itself to meet the challenge of the *Abertura Comercial* (CNI 1991), the extent of competition faced there by the Brazilian non-serial capital goods sector was much greater than in previous upturns (Tadini 1993).

This reality is reflected in the data for total imports, the expansion of which proceeded at a faster rate between 1990 and 1994 than did domestic production of non-serial capital goods, the figures being 35% and 22% respectively (ABDIB 1994a; United Nations, various years). The increased openness to imports also, of course, benefited Brazilian non-serial capital goods enterprises to the extent that imported machinery, components, and raw materials could be more readily and cheaply secured, lending the sector an increasingly necessary lower cost base with which to compete in domestic external markets (Tadini 1993).

However, at the same time, public sector procurement of non-serial capital goods remained at a depressed level, depriving enterprises of access to their traditional core market. In addition, the public sector market itself became far more exposed to external competition following the abolition of a number of non-tariff barriers in 1990 and 1991 (see Chapter 2). In sum, despite the overall growth in the domestic market, the ability of the Brazilian non-serial capital goods sector to increase sales there, and thus reduce capacity under-utilization, chronic indebtedness, and losses, was more limited than it might have been in the absence of trade liberalization. Faced with these circumstances, the focus on export markets was maintained.

The factors discussed above certainly form part of the explanation for the maintenance of export expansion that emerged in the course of interviews with managers in the sector. In all cases the mangers viewed the post-1992 recovery as having had a positive effect upon domestic sales, with Enterprise A appearing to have benefited most. However, the continuing weakness of public sector demand combined with the perceived fragility of the private sector recovery had persuaded enterprises to remain strongly involved in the export market. In the case of Enterprise B, the view was expressed that the enterprise would have wished to increase its involvement in the domestic market (which accounted for only 30% of sales in 1994/5) but this was felt to have been unworkable, principally because of the continued subdued level of public sector demand and increased competition in the domestic market. Managers at Enterprise C expressed the view that the export market would remain of overwhelming significance because the domestic market—dominated by the public sector—remained so depressed.

The director of operations at FINAMEX stressed that the continued expansion of exports could, at least to some extent, be attributed to the factors of increased competition in domestic markets and the continuing dearth of public sector orders. However such an explanation can only be viewed as partial and most certainly is not satisfactory in accounting for the fact that export expansion tended to accelerate in the 1991 to 1994 period. Four other key developments turn out to have been decisive in determining the magnitude of export expansion that characterized the 1991 to 1994 period: the resumption of export finance packages, the entry of Brazil into MERCOSUL, a mild upturn in the real effective exchange rate, and lastly, the development of exporting as a proactive strategy amongst enterprises.

As Section 4.2 made clear, 1991 saw the commencement of operations of FINAMEX, an agency of the national development bank BNDES, specially aimed at boosting the export performance of the capital goods sector through a programme of pre- and post-shipment finance. The period between 1991 and 1994 saw a very large increase in disbursements of finance from under US$ 100 m. in 1991 to US$ 300 m. in 1993 to well over US$ 500 m. in 1994. By mid-1995 total annual disbursements were on course to form an annual total of around US$ 1 bn. (interviews). According to FINAMEX sources, 85% of exports of non-serial capital goods were financed through the programme's facilities while at least some of the remainder accessed the facilities of the PROEX scheme also established in 1991.

All enterprises interviewed stressed the importance of these facilities in intensifying their export activities and stated that in their absence the high prevailing levels of Brazilian interest rates would have severely jeopardized their export performance. In addition, the efficiency and swiftness of operation of the programme and its quasi-commercial status were seen as extremely positive competitive attributes and a significant improvement over previous programmes. The importance of the FINAMEX programme is also stressed by Motta, Knaack de Souza, and Paim (1994), Tadini (1993), Fabio Erber (interviews), and ABDIB officials (interviews).

The operation of the FINAMEX programme, as well as assisting the acceleration of exports after 1991, has, to some extent, also affected the destination of those exports. While pre-shipment credit facilities are available for most nations, post-shipment lines of credit are only available to destinations which are signatories of the Convention on Reciprocal Credit (CRC). Most CRC signatories are located in Latin America, the major export markets being Mexico, Argentina, Chile, and Peru (Motta et al. 1994, annex). The availability of competitive pre- and post-shipment lines of credit to these nations in part explains the relative shift to Latin American markets noted in Section 4.3.2. There are, however, other important explanations.

First, Brazil's entry into MERCOSUL in 1990 meant that tariffs facing Brazilian non-serial capital goods in Argentina, Uruguay, and Paraguay were progressively reduced between 1990 and 1995 at a time when there was considerable growth in these markets, not least in Argentina where the most rapid expansion in over twenty years was being experienced (*Financial Times*, 25 Mar. 1996).

Secondly, Mexico—another key Brazilian market—was also undergoing an import-intensive economic expansion which lasted until the peso crisis of 1994 (ibid.). At the same time, ABDIB in conjunction with ECLAC had established a body called CADE with the specific aim of increasing exports of non-serial capital goods to other Latin American economies and achieved a degree of success in identifying export opportunities and establishing contacts (interviews). However, not all sub-sectors benefited from the expansion of Latin American opportunities. The railway equipment sub-sector increased its commitment to the North American market in the face of widespread public sector capital expenditure reduction programmes in Latin America, while the shipbuilding sub-sector was constrained by the fact that the majority of export opportunities lay outside the South American continent (interviews). The latter feature has contributed to the problems facing the sub-sector in that it has been denied FINAMEX post-shipment finance as it has attempted to step up exports to the rest of the world. Managers at Enterprise *C* expressed the view that it was important to open up adequate very long-term (up to fifteen years) post-shipment financing if the sub-sector were to maintain its competitiveness in international markets.

The third explanation underlying the accelerated expansion of exports is connected with movements of the real effective exchange rate (REER). Chart 60 illustrates that after a period of precipitous decline up to 1990, the REER tended to stabilize and even mildly appreciate, a tendency in part brought about by a trend towards nominal devaluations. Following the introduction of the *real* in July 1994, however, there was a considerable nominal and real appreciation of the currency which appears likely to have resulted in a lowering of the REER. In the course of interviews in 1995, considerable concern was expressed as to the eventual impact of this development on export performance. At the time of writing, the value of the *real* has developed into an extremely contentious issue in government–industry relations. The expansion of export activity undertaken by the Brazilian non-serial capital goods sector, especially from 1991 onwards, should not, however, be conceived exclusively as the inevitable outcome of the play of policy alterations on enterprises characterized as reactive rather than strategic or proactive institutions. To some extent—and this particularly applies to the larger foreign-owned enterprises —the expansion of export activities formed part of a longer-term strategy to increase participation in global markets, a strategy which, though informed by contemporary policy changes, was to some degree independent of them.

As Sections 4.3.3 and 4.3.1 noted, the expansion of exports tended to be greatest in the electrical energy equipment and shipbuilding sub-sectors where enterprises tended to be larger on average and more likely to be of non-Brazilian ownership. According to Fritsch and Franco (1991*a*: 132) such enterprises were always better suited to the expansion of exports than their smaller domestic counterparts because of their ability to specialize within the context of a global corporation. At the same time, such enterprises benefit from superior access to international markets made possible by their affiliation to a global organization, while problems of access to export finance are circumvented by internal resource flows within the corporation. In sum, according to Fritsch and Franco, such firms are 'sensitive to the discontinuities in government investment programmes, but their more active involvement in world markets compared to national firms, which relates to the global strategies of their parents, partly offsets the instability of domestic demand' (ibid. 132).

Thus, the larger foreign-owned non-serial capital goods enterprises would, while being able to respond rapidly to a positive shift in export incentives, also be more likely to be committed to a long-run strategy of integration into global markets in the first place. As Chapter 5 makes clear, there is ample evidence that such enterprises have engaged in a programme of specialization within the context of a global manufacturing strategy, while the export data make clear the relative success such enterprises have experienced in expanding exports through the exceptional performance of the electrical energy equipment and shipbuilding sub-sectors. By contrast, the mechanical equipment and boiler-making sub-sectors (which on the whole are constituted by smaller, less specialized, Brazilian-owned enterprises) have tended to be relatively less export intensive to begin with and have achieved lesser success in expanding their exports.

Despite this, it must be recognized that some Brazilian-owned enterprises in these sectors have achieved considerable export success through the development of deliberate, as opposed to reactive, export strategies. In the case of Enterprise *B*, for example, insertion into the export market which began as a necessity is now viewed as a core component of long-term corporate strategy and managers talk of the need to become a major 'global player' in the industry in an effort to diminish long-run reliance on the Brazilian market and thus diversify risk. The enterprise has adopted a form of export specialization with a particular emphasis on sales of dock cranes and specialized mechanical handling equipment. Similar tendencies can be noted in other major Brazilian-owned enterprises in the mechanical equipment sub-sector such as Villares and D-Z Equipamentos (interviews).

4.5 Exports, Imports, and the Development of Static and Dynamic Efficiencies within the Brazilian Non-serial Capital Goods Sector: A Summary of Findings and the Role of Quality

The increasing participation of Brazilian enterprises in the export market and the increasing role of imports in the post-1986 period have not, of course, been unconnected to changes in modes of enterprise operation. These in turn have affected the development of static and dynamic efficiencies within the non-serial capital goods sector. For the remainder of this section, the discussion focuses on the links between the development of static and dynamic efficiencies and the role of exports and imports. In undertaking this task, the following approach is adopted. First, the linkages established in Chapters 3 and 5 are briefly summarized. Their inclusion in this section, although involving a degree of repetition, is necessary for reasons of completeness and coherence of argument. Secondly, the issue of quality is discussed in some detail, as it has profoundly affected the internal organization and production strategies of firms and is directly linked to the enhanced emphasis on exports and the increased penetration of imports that were discussed earlier in this chapter.

The increased scale of exports and imports of non-serial capital goods that developed between 1986 and 1994 affected the development of static and dynamic efficiency through a number of channels. First, as Chapter 3 noted, increasing import penetration between 1986 and 1990 and its acceleration in the 1990–4 period was one of the key influences in propelling efforts to achieve increases in cost competitiveness through increases in productivity. At the same time, further incentives for such improvements were generated as firms attempted to expand sales in export markets. Data were presented which demonstrated a positive association between increases in import penetration, export growth, and labour and capital productivity growth, with the relationship between export expansion and productivity gain being particularly strong. At the same time, the data also indicated that those sub-sectors associated with greater export and import volumes tended to perform best in labour and capital productivity terms. Directly underlying the productivity growth were strategies which attempted to raise static and dynamic efficiency, the former by matching capacity more closely to demand through capacity reductions (rationalization) and the latter through changes in the organization of production and the introduction of new process technologies (modernization).

However, the discussion stressed that the influence of trade liberalization and export expansion, although significant, could not by themselves account for productivity growth or its immediate technical determinants. Most importantly, substantial reductions in public sector demand in the 1987–91 period were a crucial influence in forcing the capacity cuts (rationalization) that underlay the later upturns in productivity as demand expanded. Although exports accounted for some of the increases in demand that resulted in superior capacity utilization and gains in static efficiency and productivity (a manifestation of Verdoorn's Law), a significant portion was attributed to the eventual upturn of the domestic private sector market, itself a largely cyclical phenomenon.

At the same time, while strategies of modernization involving efforts to raise dynamic efficiency were largely ascribed to actual or impending insertion into the international market (whether through increasing import penetration or export expansion), other influences were identified, most significantly the replacement of older vintages of capital stock after a prolonged period of under-investment within the sector, a phenomenon held to be inevitable if production were to continue under any circumstances.

The development of dynamic efficiencies may also be achieved, of course, through product innovation. As Chapter 5 makes clear, the impact of increased insertion into international markets did not generally have the effect of increasing enterprise technological dynamism or self-reliance in the field of product innovation. The only exceptions to this rule were certain specialized export product lines in the electrical energy equipment sub-sector where multinational corporations had encouraged the development of local research and development facilities within their Brazilian subsidiaries.

In general, however, enterprises largely remained reliant on imported basic designs, a tendency reinforced by the risk averseness of foreign buyers and the importance of internationally known brand-names in securing export sales. At the same time, the switch in regional focus of exports away from the more technologically demanding markets of North America and Europe tended to compound a tendency towards relative technological conservatism. Managers remained more convinced of the virtues of competing on cost than on product innovation in the increasingly competitive Brazilian and external markets. According to the director of operations at FINAMEX, the strategy of exporting relatively low-priced equipment employing intermediate product technology has proved very effective at gaining market share in the new export markets of Latin America.

Perhaps the most easily identifiable impact of the expansion of exports and the increasing penetration of imports in terms of dynamic efficiency has been the effect on the pursuit of quality in the production of non-serial capital goods. The achievement of high levels of quality in the production of non-serial capital goods has always been of primary importance given the safety-critical nature of many of the production processes in which the equipment operates and the need for high levels of reliability in competitive manufacturing environments. In the past ten years, however, the issue of quality within the international non-serial capital goods industry has been elevated to a new importance with the introduction of a series of internationally recognized quality standards, the most well known of which is the International Standards Organization 9000 certificate (ISO 9000).

In the period since 1990, customers for non-serial capital goods around the world have increasingly come to demand quality certification of equipment as a precondition for purchase. By 1995, it had become virtually impossible to export non-serial capital goods without having achieved a quality certification of some form (interviews). In practice, this usually meant the possession of a ISO 9000 certificate but, depending on the market, other forms of certification might be acceptable, including the British Standards Institute's BS 5750 or the German Standards Institute's equivalent. At the same time, the Brazilian state's *Programa Brasileira de Qualidade e Produtividade* had managed to raise the profile of quality issues, although, as Meyer-Starmer (1993*b*) points out, this was largely inevitable given the insertion of the sector into the international market.

The Brazilian non-serial capital goods sector was increasingly faced with this reality as its dependence on exports increased and domestic customers then faced with quality-assured imports increasingly began to demand the same standards from Brazilian suppliers. According to Meyer-Starmer (1995: 144), *Brasil em Exame* (Aug. 1994: 9), and all managers and consultants interviewed, this has forced Brazilian enterprises to rapidly pursue quality improvements and ISO certification. Within the non-serial capital goods sector, there has been an extremely sharp increase in the number of enterprises possessing the ISO 9000 certificate. By 1993, 15 enterprises in the sector had obtained the ISO 9000 certificate (information supplied by ABDIB) from a total of zero in 1990, while by 1995 around 51, or 63% of ABDIB members, had obtained, or were in the process of obtaining, certification (BNDES 1995). Interestingly, the extent of certification in the serial capital goods sector was much lower with only 1.7% of enterprises in the machine-tools product area in possession of ISO 9000 by 1995 (ibid.). The increase in ISO certification was not, however, a phenomenon confined to the non-serial capital goods sector. According to data supplied by the Brazilian Quality Committee (ABNT), 370 Brazilian industrial enterprises had obtained certification in 1994 compared with only 18 in 1990.

Visits to all three enterprises allowed a view to be taken as to the impact of the process of quality certification on the internal organization of production and the consequent impact on dynamic efficiency. Enterprises *A*, *B*, and *C* had all received certification in the three years prior to the plant visits in August 1995. In the case of Enterprises *A* and *B*, quality certification was obtained through ISO 9000, while in the case of Enterprise *C*, the BS 5750 and the American Bureau of Shipping standards certificates had been obtained, with the process of ISO certification under way.

In all three cases, the pursuit of quality certification involved a lengthy process of reorganization of production along total quality principles, with frequent audits being employed to assess the progress towards the achievement of quality objectives. In all cases, quality control departments had been greatly expanded and management had pursued the achievement of total quality vigorously. The reorganization of production required by the adoption of total quality principles involved, in many instances, shop-floor reorganization of plant layout and some production processes, in programmes which accompanied parallel efforts to introduce just-in-time manufacturing principles.

The objective of such changes, from a quality perspective, were to enhance the ease with which production quality could be monitored by line management and to increase team working and production cells wherever possible, enabling workers to collectively monitor production and engage in collective problem-solving and incremental quality improvement. At all stages in the production process, quality manuals were employed providing specifications against which production activities and work in progress could be measured. According to the quality assurance manager at Enterprise *A*, the pursuit of total quality could be viewed as a process involving two components, the first being the physical and organizational reordering of production activity and the second being the rigorous codification and enforcement of quality standards at each stage in production. In all three cases, it was emphasized that the pursuit of improved levels of quality was very strongly associated with efforts to raise productivity through modernization strategies. The pursuit of modernization strategies and total quality were viewed as complementary if not inseparable objectives.

Despite the advent of ISO 9000 and international certification, it should be recognized that the pursuit of quality within the sector was not entirely lacking before 1990. Many enterprises had developed their own internal quality control programmes before being forced to adopt ISO in the face of increased exposure to foreign competition within and outside Brazil. This was particularly true of the larger Brazilian and foreign-owned enterprises (interviews). However, such strategies did not normally embrace the substantial plant reorganization and rigorous audit procedures entailed by ISO certification (interviews). In addition, it is also interesting to note that Petrobrás operated its own system of quality assessment for its purchases of non-serial capital goods, though the relative impact of this declined as the enterprise's investment programme withered.

While the spread of ISO 9000 certification offers one measure of the spread of quality among enterprises in the sector, other indicators are available which give some indication of how well Brazilian-based enterprises compare against international best practice. Meyer-Starmer (1995) provides some interesting quantitative evidence obtained from a FESBRASIL survey into quality practices in the Brazilian capital goods sector. Between 1990 and 1993, according to this study, the parts needing reworking fell from 30% of the total to between 12 and 20%. However, the world-class manufacturing standard in 1993 lay at only 2% (ibid. 145). Similarly, rejects per million among the survey sample of Brazilian capital goods firms fell from 23–28,000 to 11–15,000 per million against a world-class manufacturing standard of only 200 per million. Finally, warranty and repair costs as a percentage of gross sales fell from 2.7% to 2.2% compared with an international best practice standard of 0.1%.

Thus, although significant quality improvements appear to have occurred, the fact remained that, by 1993, standards still seemed to lag a long way behind international best practice. However, the development of a 'culture of quality' appears to be making rapid inroads into the operations of the sector, thus making it likely that deficiencies with regard to international best practice are likely to be reduced.

Conclusions

In the course of the post-1986 period, the Brazilian non-serial capital goods sector in general proved successful in managing to raise its levels of exports, faced as it was with a combination of reduced domestic public sector demand and increased import penetration in domestic markets, the latter in large part the consequence of trade liberalization. As the sector progressed into the 1990s, continued import pressure in domestic markets, in association with the development of formalized export strategies, an improvement in export finance facilities, and enhanced export market conditions, resulted in an acceleration of exports to record levels, with the transnational corporation-dominated sub-sectors performing particularly well.

The improvement in export performance combined with increased domestic exposure to imports added to the momentum for modernization and rationalization in the sector that had started with the collapse in public sector demand in the 1987–90 period. In particular, the increased international insertion of the sector helped to accelerate the adoption of strategies aimed at increasing dynamic efficiencies in the field of process innovation, with the development of total quality approaches becoming widespread. The role of product innovation, by contrast, was distinctly marginalized as enterprises pursued export strategies based primarily on cost and quality rather than technological innovation.

5

Technological Development and Policy Liberalization

Introduction

In Chapter 1 it was argued that the single most important justification for the development of an indigenous capital goods sector within an LDC emerges from the potential it has to generate and diffuse technological progress throughout the economy through product innovation. Chapter 1 pointed to a number of possible roles for the state that arise in connection with this central justification. Principally, a role for the state was identified in terms of providing direct financial and institutional support for indigenous research and development. Secondly, it was suggested that advantages might stem from governmental regulation of the process of technology transfer between foreign and indigenous enterprises in the sector. Thirdly, an argument was advanced for enhanced tariff and non-tariff protection of the domestic sector. Finally, it was suggested that a role for the state existed in terms of promoting techno-logical progress through the support of user–producer linkages.

However, another literature was identified which pointed to the frequently limited amounts of learning and technological change which have occurred in those LDC capital goods sectors subject to explicit technology policies and protection. Such literature pointed to the potential benefits of increased exposure to international and domestic competition on indigenous techno-logical development in the capital goods sector as market sizes are increased and firms are subjected to the challenge–response mechanism of intensified competition.

The period since 1987 has seen a considerable scaling down of the extent of the Brazilian state's policy of technological support towards the sector, invol-ving a reduced scope for many of the explicit interventions mentioned above. This, of course, has been associated with a more general reduction of the role of the state both in terms of its role as a source of demand and as an agent of protection. In this context, and given the objectives of the current book, it is clearly of interest to determine the impact of this policy shift on the pattern of technological development in the sector. The results of such an exercise would enable an assessment to be made regarding the relative valid-ity of the two sets of literature highlighted above. In order to achieve these objectives, this chapter adopts the following approach.

First, Section 5.1 discusses the alterations in technology policy that have taken place in the post-1987 period. In particular, the roles of government agencies are considered with respect to their direct financial support of research and development and regulation of technology transfer. Additionally, the nature and scope of the 'new' industrial technology policy embodied in the *Programa de Competitividade Indústrial* (PCI) is discussed. Secondly, in Section 5.2 the pattern of technological development and acquisition in the Brazilian non-serial capital goods sector is examined for the post-1987 period and compared and contrasted with that of earlier periods. In examining the technological behaviour of the sector, a number of key issues are discussed, including the evolution of corporate R&D spending, the existence and growth of R&D departments, the role of technology transfer and licensing agreements, the extent of self-sufficiency in basic and detailed designs, the nature of user–producer linkages, and the availability of suitably trained personnel. The discussion draws on a number of secondary sources as well as interviews conducted within the three enterprises visited and with outside specialists. Next, in Section 5.3, an attempt is made to evaluate the relative impact of post-1987 changes in policy on patterns of technological development and acquisition in the sector. The chapter concludes with a consideration of the implications of the observed trends in technological performance for the evolution of dynamic efficiencies within the sector.

5.1 Changes in Technology Policy and the Non-serial Capital Goods Sector

(i) *Expansion, 1950–1980*

Prior to 1960, Brazil's programme of import substitution industrialization had incorporated virtually no explicit technology policies (Adler 1987: 154). The state did not attempt to regulate the manner of technological acquisition (which in practice had been strongly focused on the licensing of foreign technologies) or explicitly support the development of indigenous technologies. From 1960 onwards, however, the state began to reverse its historically *laissez-faire* approach and a number of explicit policies began to emerge, their size and scope increasing sharply after 1968 and once more accelerating under the terms of the Second National Development Plan (PND II) of 1974 (ibid. 156; Dahlman and Frischtak 1993: 419). The motivations underlying the Brazilian state's increased emphasis on indigenous technological capability during this period are complex. Some of the more important imperatives included the necessity to reinvigorate and deepen the process of industrialization following the crisis of primary ISI in the early 1960s, the need to raise the technological self-sufficiency of the military–industrial complex in the face of similar Argentinian efforts, and finally the necessity of reducing the considerable drains on the current account engendered by the payment of technology licensing fees.

For the Brazilian non-serial capital goods sector, as Chapter 2 demonstrated, the late 1960s and the 1970s were a period of considerable expansion, propelled by increased public sector investment and protection of the domestic market. In themselves, these policy shifts may be viewed as implicitly supportive of technological development in the sector: an expanding domestic market enables the risks of research and development to be spread over further units of output, while increased protection of the sector, in reducing the immediate threat of external competition, may provide an opportunity for a period of learning and internally generated technological progress. In addition to these developments, the sector also became subject to more explicit technology policies arising out of the policy initiatives described above. The two most important policies to emerge concerned the funding of R&D and the regulation of technology transfer agreements. Such policies were and continue to be implemented by two key agencies—FINEP and INPI—which were founded in 1965 and 1971 respectively (IE/UNICAMP *et al.* 1993*a*: 31; Adler 1987: 158).

FINEP (*Financiadora de Estudos e Projetos* or Finance Agency for Studies and Projects) was established in order to encourage private sector indigenous research and development within the industrial sector. FINEP's principal mode of technological assistance consists of the provision of long-term finance at advantageous interest rates. In order to qualify for such funding, enterprises are required to submit a technological development plan and, in addition, to provide a specified proportion of the total project costs themselves. According to the 1993 Competitiveness Study, this form of state assistance for technological development has been dominant since the inception of explicit technological policies (IE/UNICAMP *et al.* 1993*a*: 28). In the period up until 1990, FINEP activities tended to be focused on the generation of new technologies within enterprises rather than diffusion or adaptation of existing ones.

During the 1970s the capital goods sector in general, and the non-serial capital goods sector in particular, attracted a substantial proportion of FINEP's total disbursements. According to Ferraz, Rush, and Miles (1992: 69), 44.3% of FINEP's activities were directed at the mechanical engineering and metallurgical sectors between 1970 and 1978. The non-serial capital goods sector benefited from a number of significant and financially substantial initiatives during this period which included a programme of technological upgrading in the travelling crane sector, a proposal for the establishment of a hydraulics laboratory for the development of hydro-turbines, the installation of a quality control laboratory for the railway equipment sub-sector, and a managed programme of technology transfer for the shipbuilding sub-sector (Corrêa do Lago *et al.* 1979: 446).

The INPI (*Instituto Nacional de Propriedade Industrial* or National Institute of Industrial Intellectual Property) was founded in order to regulate the process of technology transfer between Brazilian and foreign industrial enterprises. As Sections 5.2 and 5.3 will reveal, enterprises in the non-serial capital goods sector, in common with much of Brazilian industry, were and remain heavily dependent on foreign technologies obtained under licence for basic product design. As early as the 1950s, concern was expressed regarding the adverse balance of payments consequences of licensing fees and royalty payments given the consequent scale of technology transfer. By 1962 this preoccupation had led to the establishment of a 5% maximum royalty rate and compulsory registration for all technology transfer agreements (Dahlman and Frischtak 1993: 429). The establishment of INPI in 1970 represented a broadening of the state's concern with the impact of technology transfer. In addition to traditional considerations of foreign exchange outflows, the state became concerned as to the long-run effects of technology transfer on indigenous technological capability. In particular, it was felt that many technology transfer agreements had led to limited learning within enterprises, the stifling of in-house technological effort, and the transfer of outmoded technologies. In order to combat these tendencies INPI required that all new technology transfer agreements satisfied a number of specific requirements.

The first of the requirements specified that any new technologies transferred should not already be available domestically. Secondly, licensees of the technology were required to demonstrate that they had established appropriate systems, schedules, and training procedures in order that the transferred technology could be thoroughly mastered before the expiry of the transfer contract. Thirdly, any new technology transfer agreement would have to be consistent with the objectives of raising product quality and permitting the further deepening of import substitution. Fourthly, new limits were placed on the size of royalties which enterprises were permitted to pay licensers while, finally, restrictive clauses—most particularly those which placed limitations on exports—could no longer form part of technology transfer agreements (ibid. 429–30; Erber 1978: 316–17).

The intensification of explicit technology policies directed at the sector manifested itself in the foundation of specialized research and development institutions by the state. Perhaps the most important of these was the IPT (*Instituto de Pesquisa Tecnológico* or Institute of Technological Research) which is based in São Paulo and has one laboratory dedicated to research into capital goods technologies (Adler 1987: 183). The IPT conducted extensive research into power plant technologies and—very significantly for the mechanical equipment and boiler-making sub-sectors—it also played a role in the development of the technologies for producing alcohol-based fuels. In addition, the large state-owned energy and basic industry enterprises founded their own R&D institutes during this period (BNDES 1988: 88) which were to play a role in the development of indigenous technological capabilities in certain specialized areas of the non-serial capital goods sector (see Sections 5.2 and 5.3). Eletrobrás, Companhia Vale do Rio Doce, and Petrobrás all established such facilities, with that of Petrobrás being particularly celebrated within Brazil for its achievements in deep-water oil exploration and production technology.

In addition to the provision of specialized research and development facilities, the state, from the late 1960s onwards, began to make efforts to strengthen linkages between the university system, the research funding councils (CNPq and CAPES), and industry, both as a means of directly facilitating technological development and of providing appropriately trained personnel for innovative functions (Adler 1987: 158–62). The budgets of CAPES and CNPq were both enlarged and there was an expansion in the funding of scientific and technological research at university level and an increase in training of engineers at doctoral level, frequently through the provision of scholarships to study in the USA and Europe.

(ii) Retrenchment, 1980–1987 and Crisis, 1988–1994

The period from 1980 onwards, most especially that since 1987, has been marked by a scaling back of the Brazilian state's support for technological development within the non-serial capital goods sector and a change in the very nature of technology policy itself. The sharp decline in state involvement in the sector's technological development has occurred in every area of policy with the result that, by 1993, despite numerous policy proposal initiatives, little de facto remained of the policy apparatus established in the 1960s and 1970s. Only since March 1994, following the implementation of new legislation and an expanding industrial economy, has this long-run tendency towards a reduced role for the state in the field of technology appeared to reverse itself. Despite this very recent change, the cumulative effect of years of public expenditure reductions and the impact of the Abertura Comercial have meant that by 1995 the sector was facing a more laissez-faire technology policy régime than at any time since the 1950s.

The origins of this long-run crisis may be traced back to the beginning of the 1980s when the debt-adjustment crisis imposed widespread public spending cuts with science and technology policy appropriations being particularly badly hit. Although there was a modest recovery in expenditures in the mid-1980s, further budgetary crises in 1988 and 1990 led to renewed and unprecedented reductions, pushing public funding of technological development in 1991 to lower real levels than at any time since the beginning of the 1970s (Motta 1994: 44). These trends are illustrated in Chart 75 using data for the national science and technology development fund, a fund used mainly to finance FINEP activities. Although data are not available for the period 1991 to 1994, it appears that there was only a modest recovery in expenditures up until 1994 (Correio Braziliense, 11 Dec. 1994, p. 14) though there are signs of a substantial increase from 1994 onwards (ibid. 14; Motta 1994: 42).

In order to trace the evolution of technology policy towards the sector more accurately during the post-1980 period, the remainder of this section examines the operations of each of the established technology policies in turn, starting with that of FINEP, INPI, and the research institutes. In doing so,

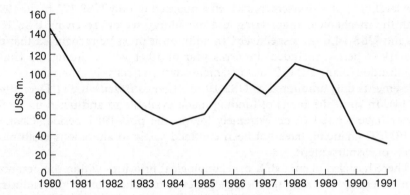

CHART 75. Federal Government Funding for The National Science and
Technology Development Fund, 1980–1991

Source: Motta (1994: 44).

the development of the more recent policy initiatives incorporated in the
Industrial Competitiveness Programme of 1990 and Law 8661 of 1994 is
considered. Finally, the 'implicit' technology policies generated by the post-
1988 *Abertura Comercial* and reductions in public sector investment expenditures are briefly reviewed.

Over the period 1980 to 1994 there have been considerable variations
in the level of FINEP activity and changes in the nature of the varieties of
technological development it supports. From 1980 to 1985, there were size-
able reductions in disbursement of FINEP funds across the board resulting
from the twin phenomena of budgetary cutbacks (Chart 75) and an unwillingness of enterprises to undertake research and development given depressed
and uncertain market conditions. Very significantly for the non-serial capital
goods sector, this period saw a sharp reduction in the portion of FINEP R&D
funding directed towards it. From 1970 to 1978, the metallurgy and mechanical engineering sectors (incorporating the non-serial capital goods sector)
accounted for 44.3% of total disbursements. By contrast, funding for these
sectors had fallen to 19.7% of the total between 1985 and 1987 (Ferraz *et al.*
1992: 69). This proportional reduction in part reflects a shift in sectoral priorities with a sharp increase in the funding of research in the chemical and
electronic sectors (ibid. 69).

From 1987 up until 1994 there were particularly sharp reductions in
FINEP disbursements reflecting renewed budgetary cuts (ibid. 68) and the
effects of recession on private sector investment in technological development.
Against this background the proportion of funding destined for the non-serial
capital goods sector has continued to fall with a reduction in the proportion
of funds allocated to the metallurgical and mechanical engineering sectors from
19.7% of the total in 1985–7 to 17% in 1993 (ibid. 69; IEI-UFRJ, Oct. 1994:
63). These proportional reductions have to be seen in the context of a very

low level of total disbursements which amounted to only US$ 175 m. in 1993, with the mechanical engineering and metallurgy sectors receiving US$ 15.3 m. and US$ 14.6 m. respectively. In addition it must be recognized that the post-1987 period included the crisis year of 1991 when, during the Collor stabilization plan, FINEP disbursements were effectively frozen: total disbursements only amounted to US$ 10 m. (*Correio Braziliense*, 11 Dec. 1994, p. 14). In sum, the totals of funding made available to and taken up by the sector have tended to be extremely low in the post-1987 period. Changes in FINEP financing have not been confined solely to alterations in absolute levels of disbursement.

There has also been a shift in technological priorities within the organization reflecting the new technology policy established under the Industrial Competitiveness Programme or PCI. The PCI, launched in August 1990, incorporated a technology policy component entitled the technology capability programme or TCP (UNIDO 1992: 16). This had the aim of raising both the overall level of R&D effort as well as the proportion accounted for by industry (ibid. 17). However, according to the 1993 competitiveness study, the programme was to try also to effect a qualitative shift in the nature of R&D undertaken, emphasizing the effective absorption and diffusion of innovations rather than their indigenous development from scratch (ibid. 30). The emphasis was thus to shift innovative activity into less risky areas and increase the possibility of short-term returns. However, the continued funding crisis at FINEP made a full implementation of this policy—involving substantial planned expenditure increases—impossible (Furtado 1994: 93). In terms of the non-serial capital goods sector, it is unlikely that a full application of this policy would have made much difference to its patterns of technological acquisition and development in any case, given its relatively low levels of indigenous technological generation and heavy reliance on foreign basic designs.

In March 1994 the Brazilian state's technological policy at last appeared to have begun its emergence from the crisis which had periodically affected it since 1980. The passing of Law 8661 introduced a series of tax incentives and increased funding designed to bolster technological development within industry. The fiscal incentives included tax deductions of up to 8% against R&D expenditures, the zero rating of machinery and equipment destined for R&D purposes, and accelerated depreciation allowable against R&D activity (Motta 1994: 42). At the same time the resources made available to FINEP were substantially increased, allowing an increase in disbursements of up to US$ 700 m. in 1994 (*Correio Braziliense*, 11 Dec. 1994, p. 14). At the same time, and of particular significance to the sector, FINAME announced that it would increase its level of participation in the finance of capital goods sales from firms who met certain targets for R&D expenditure (IEI-UFRJ, Dec. 1994: 67). Given the high level of prevailing interest rates and the importance of competitive finance as a means of winning domestic market share, the significance of this measure is likely to be substantial.

Throughout the 1980 to 1994 period, and even following the post-1987 fiscal crisis, INPI remained active in regulating the process of technology transfer between foreign and domestic enterprises in the non-serial capital goods sector. The *modus operandi* of INPI remained substantially unchanged in that it continued to regulate technology transfer on the basis of taxing royalty payments and scrutinizing contracts according to long-established criteria (see Section 5.1(i)). However, there is evidence to suggest that INPI's role as a proactive promoter of technology through the close supervision of technology transfer contracts became increasingly subordinated to its revenue-raising function. According to Franco (1990: 20), in the immediate period up until 1990 there was little evidence to suggest that INPI's operations had given rise to increased domestic technological effort, even if this was limited to learning and adaptation on the basis of foreign designs, a conclusion supported by the 1993 competitiveness survey (ibid. 35). Little attention seems to have been paid (whether by enterprises or INPI itself) to INPI stipulations concerning joint work with R&D institutes, user–producer linkages, and joint programmes with FINEP aimed at spreading the effects of imported technology (ibid. 31).

To an extent, this conclusion would appear to be supported in the light of interviews conducted within enterprises where the operation of INPI did not arise as having been a major influence in the determination of learning patterns on the basis of imported designs. More speculatively, there may be reasons to suspect that the recent operational patterns of INPI have inhibited the acquisition of the most modern vintages of technology by the sector. These arise from the transactions costs and patent stipulations attaching to INPI-approved technology transfer contracts.

The time and resource costs involved in the submission of contract applications are likely to act as a deterrent to the frequent signing of new contracts with different technology suppliers (Franco 1990: 20). This may go some way towards explaining why enterprises in the non-serial capital good sector have tended to remain attached to particular suppliers of technology in long-run partnership agreements, a feature discussed in more detail in Section 5.3. In addition, until the 1995–6 reform of intellectual and commercial property rights legislation in Brazil, foreign enterprises proved reluctant to transfer certain technologies to Brazil, fearing that existing legislation inadequately safeguarded their patent rights. In particular, certain INPI clauses stated that technology licensees would, after a specified period, become the exclusive owners of that technology within Brazil. In many cases this situation has resulted in the transfer of older generation rather than state of the art technologies (interviews). The research institutes and departments established during the 1960s and 1970s have continued to function during the post-1980 period. However, budgetary cuts, particularly those from 1987 onwards, have put great limits on the extent to which they were able to generate and transfer technology to the sector. This was especially true of the research departments of some major state-owned enterprises who were struggling with major reductions in their investment resources. According to Motta (1994: 40), with a very few notable exceptions—Eletrobrás, Petrobrás, and CVRD—state enterprises have ceased to engage in technological development and rarely support private sector initiatives aimed at seeking support for the development or absorption of new technologies. Thus a major source of state support for technological development within the sector has been subject to severe limitations and the potential for user–producer linkages has consequently diminished. Even in the case of the more technologically active enterprises mentioned above, resources targeted for R&D have come under the same pressure as investments whose fall was documented in Chapter 2.

Over the 1980 to 1994 period, the Brazilian state retained through CNPq and CAPES its capacity to fund directly university research and training in areas of technology of relevance to the sector. However, these organizations, like other federally funded entities, suffered budget reductions which intensified in the late 1980s and early 1990s. Despite the proclaimed desire of successive governments to enhance the links between universities, their funding councils, and the private sector, the strength of the links so far remains comparatively weak. According to Meyer-Starmer (1993b: 3–4), efforts to improve them are likely to encounter significant problems, specifically the highly variable quality of many universities and departments, the relative lack of incentive for universities to enter into relationships with private sector enterprises given their relatively solvent financial state, and a scepticism within universities as to the possible effects on scientific freedom of collaboration with the private sector.

In discussing alterations in technology policy that the sector has faced, it is important to recognize that many of the most significant changes have occurred as a result of more general policy shifts elsewhere which themselves were not explicitly aimed at effecting change in sector technological development. Through the twin policies of trade liberalization and public sector fixed capital formation reductions, the Brazilian state has effected changes in incentives to innovate in the non-serial capital goods sector. Perhaps the single greatest implicit shift in policy has been the post-1988 liberalization of capital goods imports discussed in Chapter 2.

Prior to 1987 the sector was heavily protected through the use of high tariffs and extensive non-tariff barriers, the latter most especially in the form of the law of similars. Such a policy had significant technological implications in that in many instances the exposure of the sector to competing technologies embodied in imported capital goods was very limited. The only exceptions to this pattern occurred in those instances where importers had succeeded in obtaining exemptions and in most cases this meant that the import had been demonstrated not to comprise a similar. Thus the Brazilian non-serial capital goods sector in most cases was the object of an infant industry régime of protection, which Chapter 1 argued might be expected to provide

conditions favourable to the enhancement of indigenous technological capability and learning.

From 1988 onwards, and especially since 1990, the mechanisms of protection enjoyed by the sector have been systematically dismantled or reduced
in scope to the point where the sector is more exposed to international
competition than at any time since the advent of the Second National
Development Plan in 1974. As Chapter 4 demonstrated, this policy shift has
been associated with a substantial increase in imports of non-serial capital
goods to the point that Brazil began to run a trade deficit in these goods
from 1993. At the same time, the exposure to international competition has
intensified through the increased export intensity of the sector, especially in
mechanical equipment and shipbuilding. Taken together, these trends might
be expected to have had a profound effect on the sector's methods of technological development and acquisition as enterprises were increasingly forced
to compete with products of the most recent technological vintage in both
domestic and external markets.

Running in parallel with the policy of reducing the scale and scope of
protection in the post-1987 period was the profound reduction in the role
of the state as a procurer of non-serial capital goods. This in itself may be
viewed as a major shift in implicit technological policy in that the state has
ceased to provide expanding markets for the sector's output. Such expanding
markets—especially if they are open only to domestic producers—provide the
scope for extended production runs and specialization within the sector, both
of which make more feasible the pursuit of relatively more risky (and less
adaptive) research and development. In the absence of such expansion—and
given the added effects of the 1989–91 private sector recession—it might be
expected that the post-1987 period has been associated with a downgrading
of research and development effort. Moreover, the reduction of the role of
the state as a source of demand for non-serial capital goods might be expected
to have impaired the technological benefits arising from user–producer interaction which have undoubtedly occurred in the past, especially in the cases
of the more technologically sophisticated public sector enterprises such as
Petrobrás.

To sum up, there have been major shifts in both the explicit and implicit
technology policy faced by the sector since 1987. Reductions in explicit
technological support for the sector have been accompanied by compression of the domestic market (especially its public sector component) and
an increased exposure to international competition. Taken together from a
theoretical perspective, these tendencies would appear to have conflicting implications for technological effort in the sector. While reductions in domestic
market size and explicit technology policies would appear to have deleterious
implications, this has to be balanced against the possibility of enhanced technological effort resulting from the potential of increased exports, a greater
exposure to international competition, and the challenge-response mechanism

these may contain. The remainder of this chapter seeks to establish the manner in which patterns of technological development may have changed in the course of the post-1987 period and any linkage to policy shifts that may exist. Finally, in the light of this discussion, the consequent implications for theory are considered.

5.2 Technological Development and Acquisition in the Non-serial Capital Goods Sector: Historical Patterns and Post-1987 Developments

The development and acquisition of technology in the Brazilian non-serial capital goods sector has been, and continues to be, a complex, multifaceted process involving a number of distinct issues and areas of technological activity. In order that these can be fully addressed, it seems appropriate to sub-divide the discussion into a few key sections, each concerned with a particular aspect of the process. Within each section, evidence is drawn from a variety of secondary sources in addition to case-study material obtained in the course of enterprise interviews. To begin the discussion, the issue of research and development within enterprises is examined, concentrating on the division between basic and adaptive designs and innovation. Secondly, the role of technology transfer in the sector's technological development is considered, with indications given as to the areas of technology in which it is most prevalent and to its diffusion across the sector. Thirdly and finally, the role of Brazilian research and development institutions is discussed along with the evolution of user–producer linkages and human capital formation in the sector.

5.2.1 RESEARCH AND DEVELOPMENT IN THE NON-SERIAL CAPITAL GOODS SECTOR

In analysing the evolution of research and development (R&D) in the Brazilian non-serial capital goods sector, it is important to be aware of the breadth of technological activity that R&D encompasses. Following Felix (1978), research and development programmes may take on a number of forms ranging from fundamental scientific research (with highly uncertain returns) to low-risk adaptive development work based on known principles, technologies, or even specific designs. In practice, since its inception, the overwhelming bulk of R&D efforts in the sector have been of the latter variety.

Early studies of the sector, for example, Cruz (1983) and Erber (1978, 1982), all pointed to very similar modes of technological development and acquisition. For inherently less sophisticated technologies based on long-established principles of mechanical engineering, Brazilian enterprises had, through a combination of incremental learning and reverse engineering, been able to acquire a comprehensive basic and detailed design and production capability.

For more sophisticated varieties of equipment, however, particularly those in which the technological frontier was moving and not static, there was a heavy reliance on transfer of technologies from overseas. Very often this would take the form of the importation of basic designs which, in consultation with licensers, were then adapted to suit local production and market conditions. In the case of subsidiaries of transnational corporations (TNCs), technology transfer occurred internally with basic designs originating in the corporations' R&D facilities, themselves located (in the vast majority of cases) outside Brazil (Erber 1978). In both Brazilian and TNC-owned enterprises, such R&D as occurred was focused on facilitating the necessary adaptations and revolved around such activities as reworking engineering drawings, retooling plant and equipment to enable production of the new equipment, or simply engaging in 'passive' learning resulting from an increased familiarity with a particular technology.

Such limited R&D efforts were synonymous with the rapid expansion of the sector up until the early 1980s and perhaps were to be expected given the relative youth of many of its enterprises. Under conditions of a rapid expansion in demand for increasingly sophisticated non-serial capital goods, there was insufficient time and in-house technological capability for enterprises to engage in the more risky fundamental research and development necessary to bridge the gulf between existing and desired technological capacities. According to Erber (1986: 233), this created the conditions under which technology increasingly came to be imported and led to the development of the adaptive technological capability outlined above. Perhaps more significantly, Erber goes on to suggest that the development of an adaptive R&D capability in the sector, focusing on the development of detailed designs and the introduction of innovations, could not be expected eventually to lead to the development of basic design capabilities from which true innovations would stem. To paraphrase Erber (1986), this arises from discontinuities in knowledge between the technologies underlying the basic design on the one hand and the detailed design and manufacturing on the other (ibid. 234). While the latter technologies are likely to require readily available mechanical engineering and manufacturing skills, the former are likely to demand the undertaking of more fundamental scientific research.

While adaptive research and development may permit a rapid move into the production of sophisticated capital goods, there are a number of dangers associated with the development of such a limited R&D capability. From a neo-Schumpeterian perspective, such limited R&D does not afford the opportunities that new technological paradigms may offer to develop new and rapidly expanding markets. In addition, the technological dependency literature points to long-run financial costs and sub-optimal technological trajectories which may arise in the course of limited R&D. Finally, the ability of the capital goods sector to generate technological externalities will be constrained the more limited in scope are its technological efforts. This may be true particularly if its ability to transfer technology is restricted by licensing conditions imposed by foreign technology suppliers.

TABLE 35. Self-Sufficiency and Domestic Design Content for Selected
Non-serial Capital Goods, 1974–1985

Item	Self-sufficiency index* pre-1974 (%)	Domestic design content pre-1974 (%)	Self-sufficiency index* 1985 (%)	Domestic design content 1985 (%)
Turbines	60		>90	
Generators	60		>90	
Transformers	60		>90	
Floodgate/dam equipment	>90		>90	
Substations	60		>90	
Pylons and power lines	100		100	
Cables	100		100	
Compressors	65	0	95	80
Boilers	85	0	95	80
Columns	85	0	95	80
Pressure vessels	85	0	95	100
Tanks	95	100	95	100
Furnaces	85	50	95	80
Agitators	85	50	95	80
Mixers	85	50	95	80
Control panels	85	100	95	100
Power control instrumentation	50	0	50	20
Valves	65	70	50	80

Note: * Denotes proportion of Brazilian market supplied by domestic producers.
Source: Tadini (1986: 9).

As Brazil's non-serial capital goods sector moved into the 1980s, the phase of expansion it had enjoyed since the advent of the Second National Development Plan was clearly at an end. The 1980s saw very little physical expansion of the sector or addition of new production facilities. Given the enormous expansion of capacity in the 1970s, the sector was able to supply a comprehensive range of basic and sophisticated non-serial capital goods to the point where Brazil was practically self-sufficient in most key items (Table 35). Against this background, and faced with stagnant or declining domestic demand, the sector entered a stage of development that could increasingly be characterized as one of maturity. Given the sector's growing age and diversity by the mid-1980s, it might be expected that there would have been an accompanying rise in its technological capability, perhaps even extending to basic rather than adaptive R&D. To some extent this expectation is borne out by the evidence presented in Table 35 in that the data indicate a notable rise in national design content between 1974 and 1985.

However, it is important to note that this rise is primarily attributable to an increase in domestic adaptation of basic foreign designs over the period. Tadini (1986: 12) stresses that, particularly for the more complex varieties of non-serial capital equipment, imported basic designs continued to be of great significance throughout the period. Only in the cases of simpler items—specifically the boiler-making sub-sector's tanks and pressure vessels—was a full basic and detailed design capability achieved (Table 40). This conclusion is supported by extensive research undertaken by the national development bank, BNDES, in its influential report published in 1988. For the sector as a whole in the mid to late 1980s, the report established that substantial 'technological dependence' continued to exist, especially in the case of more complex forms of equipment (BNDES 1988: 82). In many cases, such reliance on foreign basic designs took place within the context of internal TNC technology transfer.

Parenthetically, as Section 5.2.2 will later demonstrate, TNCs have tended to operate in the more technologically demanding areas of the sector (Cruz and Da Silva 1990: 54). For less sophisticated equipment or in the case of equipment characterized by a stable technological frontier, Brazilian-owned enterprises were able, by the mid-1980s, to engage in the full design process from basic conception to detailed engineering drawings to production (BNDES 1988: 82). In some cases, this full design capability permitted incremental technological improvements to take place as enterprises became increasingly familiar with the production of basic and detailed designs (ibid. 82). Perhaps the most accomplished enterprise in this respect was the formerly state-owned railway equipment group, MAFERSA. In some cases, local subsidiaries of TNCs had developed teams capable of producing basic product designs (ibid. 83), although these teams often drew on the results of innovative activity produced in R&D centres outside of Brazil.

To sum up, the period up to 1987 can be characterized as one in which Brazilian and TNC subsidiary enterprises successfully entered the production of a wide range of non-serial capital goods. However, the rapid expansion of production took place against a background of reliance on foreign basic designs, a reliance that barely diminished as the sector matured. Research and development effort remained concentrated in the adaptation of basic designs to suit local production and market conditions. However, as the remainder of this section will demonstrate, despite the substantial shifts in policy after 1987, there is little evidence to suggest that this pattern of technological development and acquisition has altered.

As Chapters 4 and 6 made clear, the late 1980s and early 1990s constituted a period of substantial contraction for the sector after a phase of tentative expansion in the mid-1980s. For industry as a whole—which also faced substantial cuts in demand over this period—the effects of this background on research and development effort were broadly negative with reduced expenditure on innovative activity (Suzigan 1992a: 31). This situation was held to be especially serious given the fact that there appeared to be a growing technological lag between enterprises operating in Brazil and their foreign counterparts. According to Suzigan, this was as true in the capital goods sector as it was in others (ibid. 31) and was in part associated with an extremely low level of R&D spending in relation to turnover.

The continuing relatively low priority accorded to internally generated research and development in the post-1987 period is reflected in the *Confederação Nacional de Indústria* technology survey in 1991. The survey revealed that in the mechanical engineering and electrical equipment subsectors, in terms of the ordering of technological strategies, investment in internal technological development of products was surpassed in importance by rationalization, quality control, and training (for the mechanical engineering sector) and purchase of foreign technology, rationalization, quality control, and training (for the electrical equipment sector) (CNI 1991: 24). Thus internally generated product innovation appears to have been subordinated to process innovation and the reliance on foreign technological sources. In similar vein, Cruz and Da Silva in their 1990 survey of technological capacity in the capital goods sector as a whole found relatively low levels of research and development effort. From a sample of 344 enterprises, 23.2% engaged in no research and development expenditures whatsoever. Of the remainder, 44% spent less than 2% of turnover on R&D while 26% allocated between 2 and 5% for this purpose. Only 6.8% of respondents spent more than 5% of their turnover on R&D effort. A survey of patenting activity from the same sample revealed that only 33.5% of enterprises had secured patents in the five years prior to 1990 (ibid. 82).

For the non-serial capital goods sector as a whole, the established patterns of technological acquisition and development discussed earlier remained in place. TNC subsidiaries remained broadly reliant on basic innovatory capacities established outside Brazil. At the same time, Brazilian-owned enterprises' capacity to generate basic product designs independently remained very limited. According to Fritsch and Franco (1991a), such enterprises 'do not generally possess the technology for equipment design in the whole product range, and often resort to licensing. Still, they have developed capabilities for adaptation and construction, which, from the technological point of view, are the less demanding stages of the production process' (ibid. 132). According to Erber (interview, 28 June 1995), the post-1987 period has been one in which sector enterprises have scaled back product innovations to the minimum level consistent with remaining viable competitors in their respective markets. For Erber, non-serial capital goods enterprises can be thought of as operating within certain specified technological parameters, the lower limit consisting of a threshold of the minimum technological skills necessary for the engagement in the production of a particular capital good. Upper limits

TABLE 36. Sources of Technologies Acquired in the Electrical Energy Equipment Sub-sector, 1991/1992

Technology type	No. of designs obtained from domestic sources	No. of designs obtained from foreign sources
Third-party technological consultancy	1	3
Basic designs	1	4
Detailed designs	1	1
Viability studies	2	0
Measurement studies	8	1

Source: Strachmann (1993: 100).

will be defined by the most advanced technologies in use within the sector as a whole internationally. Movement towards the upper limits will involve greater resource costs and quite possibly enhanced risks as the size and scope of internal R&D or technology licensing have to expand.

In the majority of cases, however, enterprises faced with depressed domestic demand, a reduction in explicit forms of state support for R&D, and continuing uncertainty have opted for technological strategies within the lower range of the parameters. The continued unwillingness of enterprises to engage in more risky and extensive forms of R&D—particularly those which might have afforded an enhanced basic design capability—is also stressed by Motta (interview).

At a more disaggregated level, there is much evidence to suggest that such innovative activity as had developed prior to 1987 came under renewed pressure in the subsequent period. In the electrical energy equipment sub-sector, for a sample of 19 enterprises the 1993 competitiveness survey revealed a fall in R&D as a percentage of turnover from 0.94% in 1987/9 to 0.89% in 1992 (Strachmann 1993: 100–5). By contrast, the proportion of resources allocated to practical preparation for production of new designs rose: resources devoted to engineering departments rose from 1.8% of turnover in 1987/9 to 2.03% in 1992 (ibid. 100–5). Within the sub-sector, the capacity to engage in more fundamental R&D remained extremely limited with some enterprises engaging in no formal innovative activity at all: the only aspects of technological modernization engaged in were limited to process innovations such as the installation of CNC machinery and production cells discussed in Chapter 6 (ibid. 61). Such innovative activity as occurred remained concentrated in adaptive R&D of the type long practised by the non-serial capital goods sector as a whole. Some indication of this situation is given in Table 36.

The data reveal a continuing reliance on foreign sources for basic designs with only the more routine and less technologically intensive activities of viability and measurement studies being sourced primarily within Brazil. Within the sub-sector as a whole, the only substantial domestic innovative capacity exists in the heavy power transformer product lines and, to a lesser extent, in the hydro-generator categories (ibid. 61).

In the case of the hydro-generator sector, much of the domestic technological capacity is possessed by Enterprise *A* whose basic design facilities were visited in the course of the fieldwork. Enterprise *A*'s decision to develop a basic design and research and development capacity within Brazil for hydro-electric generators arose from the heavy state investments in hydro-electric power projects in the 1970s. During this period, the enterprise constructed a special facility designed for the construction of exceptionally large hydro-electric generators for such projects as the Itaipú and Xingú dams. Following the reduction in domestic orders, in the mid to late 1980s, production was maintained at the site through reliance on export orders. Indeed, during this period, Brazil became the parent company of Enterprise *A*'s single manufacturing facility for large capacity hydro-electric generators.

Given the decision to concentrate the manufacture of these items within Brazil, a successful attempt was made to establish full local research and development, design, and testing facilities. In trying to develop such local capabilities, Enterprise *A* was able to draw on existing technological capabilities within other parts of the organization and effect a full internal technological transfer. At the same time, there was considerable capital investment in a computer-aided design (CAD) suite, increasing the ease with which basic designs could be rapidly converted into detailed engineering drawings. A subsidiary of Enterprise *A* also established a basic design capability in the heavy transformer section after an initial programme of technology transfer. The subsidiary possesses the largest transformer production facility in Latin America and has the greatest output capacity of any transformer enterprise in the region.

The case of Enterprise *A* would appear to demonstrate that under certain circumstances—most particularly when there is a degree of specialization and concentration of production—a full local research and development capability can be established even where the enterprise is a TNC subsidiary. However, as Section 5.2.2 makes clear, hydro-generators and transformers are just two of many products manufactured by the enterprise. For most of these product areas—for example, no-break devices—there is effectively no local basic design or R&D capability. Looking at the electrical energy equipment sub-sector more generally, Section 5.2.2 reveals a heavy reliance on foreign basic designs across the product ranges but particularly in the turbine, generator, and switch gear sectors.

The mechanical equipment sub-sector is technologically very heterogeneous, incorporating products of greatly varying sophistication. Patterns of technological development and acquisition, however, remain much as they were before

1987. In less sophisticated product areas—for example, simple mechanical handling equipment, basic travelling cranes, compressors—enterprises have long possessed the capability to produce designs from scratch without engaging in internal R&D or resorting to licensing (interviews). In other more sophisticated areas of the sub-sector, access to foreign technology remains vital to ensuring continued production. One of the areas of the sector in which the latter tendency has been most apparent—though with interesting exceptions —is that of oil exploration and production equipment (Tadini 1993: 18).

In the course of successful attempts since the mid-1980s to explore and drill for oil on the Brazilian continental shelf in the Campos Basin, Petrobrás, in association with a number of the sub-sector's enterprises, developed new technologies appropriate to drilling in the exceptionally deep waters of the area (often exceeding 400 m). New designs for automatic drill bit and shaft exchangers, maintenance equipment, and valves had to be developed due to the depths involved and the consequent inaccessibility by divers. Brazil's technological achievements in deep-water oil exploration and production are well recognized within the industry and illustrate the potential for successful technological collaboration between the sector and major state enterprises.

However, despite the development of basic research and development capabilities in certain specialized areas, it should be recognized that the majority of less specialized, non-deep-water oil production and exploration equipment produced in Brazil relies on foreign basic designs (ibid. 18), a situation examined in the next section. However, the manufacturing and detailed design capabilities of enterprises in this area are well established and the rates of self-sufficiency are high.

Within the steel industry equipment area of the mechanical equipment sub-sector, the process of technological acquisition and development has tended to follow a similar pattern to that in other areas of the non-serial capital goods sector with limited basic but advanced adaptive technological capabilities. In terms of the technologically more demanding equipment, for example, blast furnaces, and rolling mills, production capacity has been established that remains reliant on foreign basic designs (ibid. 20). Development of more extensive R&D capability within the steel equipment sector was impeded in the late 1980s by reductions in investment programmes by the then state-owned Siderbrás holding company. In the course of a visit to Enterprise *B*—one of the largest suppliers of equipment to the steel and mining industries—a similar pattern of technological innovation and self-reliance was revealed.

Enterprise *B* produces a wide range of equipment for these industries, ranging from travelling cranes to reclaimers, continuous casting mills, hot and cold strip rolling mills, and cold steel laminators (interviews). For much of this equipment, the technologies involved are relatively sophisticated and there is considerable competition in the global market on the basis of the cost efficiency and output quality of the machinery. Given this situation, the enterprise has chosen to engage in extensive licensing, a process described in the next section. In terms of internal technological development, Enterprise *B* has managed to achieve a well-developed adaptive innovatory capability in which it has established close links with technology licensers. Interviews revealed, however, that the pursuit of more extensive design and research and development capabilities had come under considerable pressure in the period between 1987 and 1995. The period witnessed no overall growth in internal R&D effort and cutbacks in certain areas. The latter was true particularly in the case of steel industry equipment where a substantial contraction of domestic demand took place from the mid-1980s onwards.

As Chapter 4 revealed, the export market has become increasingly significant for Enterprise *B*, accounting for approximately 70% of demand in 1995. However, exports have tended to be concentrated in the crane sector whose technological requirements tend to be less stringent than is the case for steel plant equipment. However, the view was expressed that a degree of continued product innovation was vital in order to maintain market share in both domestic and foreign markets in the enterprise's key product lines. The key issue regarding the introduction of product innovations concerned the source of the technology rather than the need to acquire it. Interviews with management revealed an unwillingness to engage in more extensive internal 'basic' research and development until there was a more extensive recovery in the domestic market. Market conditions in the period up to and including 1995 were felt to be too uncertain to justify large internal investments in riskier forms of R&D. As a consequence, the view was expressed that the enterprise would continue to rely on technology licensing in more sophisticated product areas. Specialized design teams employing CAD equipment would continue to produce detailed engineering drawings of equipment, where necessary adapting licensed technology for the production of more sophisticated goods or their components.

The railway equipment industry has been faced with acute levels of overcapacity and low levels of demand since 1987. These phenomena have particularly affected the more technologically sophisticated components of the sector's output, namely locomotives and subway trains (*Revista Ferroviaria*, Dec. 1994: 23–31). Despite the substantial changes in demand, it needs to be recognized that the sector's pattern of technological development and acquisition has remained largely unchanged, with continuing heavy reliance on basic designs obtained from overseas. In the case of locomotive production, the extent of technology transfer has tended to be even greater with detailed designs being transferred (see Section 5.2.2). Internal technological development has remained of distinctly secondary importance with only one enterprise— MAFERSA—generating all of its technology internally (ABDIB 1994*a*: 47). Since privatization in 1991, this enterprise has been faced with an acute financial crisis forcing a contraction in its activities (*Revista Ferroviária*, Jan. 1995).

The shipbuilding and boiler-making sub-sectors have long been the relatively least technologically sophisticated in the non-serial capital goods sector. The sectors may be viewed as technologically less intensive because, for the most part, the technological frontier for the products produced is stable and product design and fabrication follow long-established, well-understood, technological principles. The bulk of manufacturing processes in these sectors is reliant on traditional and fairly labour-intensive steel-plate fabrication.

For the boiler-making sector, Table 35 revealed that, by 1985, high levels of domestic design content had been achieved in the key product areas, namely, boilers, tanks, distillation columns, and pressure vessels. By 1993, according to Tadini (1993: 20), domestic design capability in these product areas was virtually total, encompassing all aspects of the design process. Only certain aspects of the process control systems associated with the boiler-making sub-sector's output have continued to lie outside the sub-sector's innovatory capability (see Section 5.2.2) Significantly, the proportion of Brazilian-owned firms in this sub-sector has tended to be particularly high, amounting to 11 out of the top 15 by sales in 1986 (Fritsch and Franco 1991a: 127). However, given the stable technological frontier in these equipment areas, technological self-reliance need not imply or require active R&D effort and innovation. Indeed, it seems likely that the necessary technological capability to design and produce these products can be obtained in the course of incremental learning efforts: the technologies involved are not characterized by discontinuities in knowledge and consequent substantial divisions between know-how and know-why.

The shipbuilding sub-sector has been subject to profound changes in structure and ownership in the post-1987 period as Chapter 6 will demonstrate. By 1994, the most important enterprises in the sector, those with the capacity to build large ocean-going vessels—EMAQ, Indústrias Verolme Ishibrás (IVI), CCN-Mauá, and CANECO—were all Brazilian owned. However, up until 1993, Verolme and Ishibrás were both separate subsidiaries of transnational corporations, the parent companies being respectively Verolme Verenidge Scheepwerken of Holland and Ishikawajima of Japan (ABDIB 1994a: 29, 41). The development of technological capability in the sector has been conditioned by historical patterns of ownership as well as the varied technological demands associated with the production of different types of vessel. For the more sophisticated, higher value-added varieties of vessel, for example, certain of the large oil tankers and oil exploration platforms, designs have usually been developed by overseas naval architects in consultation with the parent companies. For smaller, less sophisticated vessels, such as medium grain carriers and certain coastal vessels, designs have been produced domestically. According to Tadini (1993: 22), the absence of a domestic design capability for some of the larger vessel categories constitutes the principal technological limitation of the sub-sector.

In the course of a visit to Enterprise *C*, an opportunity was afforded to study the recent patterns of technological acquisition and development. The yard had long possessed the ability to develop designs for certain categories of vessels and had a dedicated ship-design department on site with drawing office and CAD suite. The design facilities are concentrated around the production of hull designs. Both basic and detailed design functions are undertaken. For more specialized and technologically demanding areas of vessel construction—for example, propulsion and control systems or equipment for tank pumping and equalization—there has long been a reliance on foreign designs, a situation discussed in more detail in Section 5.2.2. The design of certain vessels, most especially the larger oil tankers and oil platforms, has also tended to draw heavily on foreign basic designs, though there has been local design input in adapting and interpreting these for manufacture. In this context, and with the increased importance of certain imported basic designs, the continued maintenance of a design office was viewed as essential in facilitating their efficient adaptation to local production conditions and individual client requirements.

Prior to 1993, Enterprise C possessed a dedicated, though relatively small, research and development department. Following a programme of corporate restructuring, the department was abolished as part of a programme of rationalization. According to the chiefs of the production division and quality control departments, research and development activity has fallen to 'practically zero'. Although this development was perceived as unfortunate, it was felt that any long-term unfavourable effects could be offset through increased technology transfer from abroad. More generally, the view was expressed that with respect to the shipyard's core activities—hull construction and fitting out of vessels—the movement of the technological frontier was relatively slow if not altogether static. This was held to account for the increased emphasis on process, rather than product innovation, an emphasis that was likely to increase given international overcapacity, the extensive use of sector subsidies outside Brazil, and the consequent need to maintain price competitiveness.

However, it must also be recognized that the enterprise has been attempting to establish a speciality in the production of oil storage platforms, vessels which are more technologically demanding than bulk carriers or tankers. Oil storage platforms consist of an array of storage tanks linked by complex pipework and pumping systems. In order to remain stable in open seas while rapidly discharging and taking on cargo, such platforms require efficient control and pumping systems capable of monitoring weight distribution and effecting rapid inter-tank transfers should the need arise. During the visit, the enterprise was in the course of constructing one such vessel and was bidding for the construction of similar vessels for Petrobrás.

The production of such higher value-added vessels has also become increasingly attractive for many European yards in the face of intense price competition for less sophisticated vessels (*Financial Times*, 22 Feb. 1996). In the case of Enterprise C, the increased importance of these vessels as a proportion of total production, taken together with the greater reliance on foreign technology in their construction, seems likely to reduce the relative significance of internal design capability and R&D.

5.2.2 TECHNOLOGY TRANSFER FROM ABROAD IN THE NON-SERIAL CAPITAL GOODS SECTOR

The corollary of generally low levels of research and development effort within the non-serial capital goods sector has been a continuing reliance on technology transfer from companies and organizations outside Brazil. Section 5.2.1 argued that this relative lack of technological self-reliance was a feature that established itself at the inception of the sector and remained a major feature throughout the 1980s and into the 1990s. The remainder of this section examines the process of technology transfer from abroad in the post-1987 period and attempts to identify its nature, the technological areas in which it has been most concentrated, and the extent to which technology transfer in the period has altered in character and extent from that of previous periods. According to Erber (interviews), three long-standing features of the process of foreign technology transfer to the sector continue to remain in place. First, technology transfers from overseas have continued to be dominated by transnational corporations which have facilitated transfers either through licensing or internal transfer to subsidiaries. Secondly, the relationships which are built up in the course of the transfers have tended to be characterized by substantial stability both in terms of duration and in terms of the licensers and licensees involved, a characteristic that is held to be a critical determinant of the long-run success of technology transfers. The stability of technology transfer relationships highlighted by Erber is a feature that is also stressed in the 1988 BNDES sector study (p. 82). Thirdly, in the post-1987 period, technology transfer to the sector has tended to take the form of licensing or internal transfers of designs rather than imports of technology embodied in capital goods, transfers of skilled personnel, or reverse engineering. In the majority of cases, as the previous section noted, the designs involved have tended to be 'basic', that is, designs which incorporate the main technological principles and concepts of the product to be produced.

By contrast, detailed designs have tended to be produced within Brazilian enterprises and consist of the detailed engineering drawings necessary to prepare and adapt the basic design for production (Fritsch and Franco 1991a: 126). Evidence from individual sub-sectors points to a pattern of technology transfer similar to that described above. In the case of the electrical energy equipment sub-sector, transfer of technology from abroad remains the dominant means of acquisition of the more advanced technologies employed in the sector's products. Some indication of the extent of technological dependence in the sector can be obtained by a consideration of the data in Table 37.

The data indicate that a substantial number of technology licensing agreements have been signed between domestically owned enterprises in the sector and foreign corporations. One important feature of the sub-sector is the

TABLE 37. Technology Licensing Agreements in the Electrical Energy Equipment Sub-sector

Enterprise	Nationality of controlling interest	Equipment produced	Technology licensers for equipment produced
ASEA Brown Boveri Ltd.	Sweden/Switzerland	Hydro-generators, turbines, generators, substations, transformers	Parent company's own technology
Coesma Ansaldo S.A.	Italy	Turbines, generators, transformers	Parent company's own technology
General Electric do Brasil S.A.	USA	Switch gear, transformers, voltage stabilizers, interrupters	Parent company's own technology
Inepar S.A.	Brazil	Control panels, power capacitors, protection relays	Goldstar (Korea), Reliable (USA), GE/Fanuc (USA), General Electric (USA)
Mecânica Pesada S.A.	France	Hydraulic turbines, servo motors, gas turbines (also equipment supplied to steel and petrochemical industries)	GEC/Alsthom (UK/France)—parent companies
Merlin Gerin S.A. (formerly Inebrasa)	France	Transformers, switch gear	Parent company's own technology
Pirelli Cabos S.A.	Italy	Power cables	Parent company's own technology
Sade-Vigesa S.A.	Brazil	Hydraulic turbines, generators, Power lines and pylons, Power station equipment in general	Dominion Engineering (Canada), General Electric (Canada), Cooper (USA)
Siemens do Brasil S.A.	Germany	Hydro-generators, generators, switch gear, transformers	Parent company's own technology
Toshiba do Brasil S.A.	Japan	Generators, transformers, control panels, substations, frequency inverters	Parent company's own technology
TUSA Ltd.	Germany (Siemens)	Transformers	Parent company's own technology
Villares S.A.	Brazil	Turbines, generators	General Electric (USA), GEC/Alsthom (UK/France)
Voith S.A.	Germany	Hydraulic turbines (this enterprise also produces machinery for the pulp and paper sector)	Parent company's own technology, Heidenheim An Der Brenz GmBH (Germany)

Source: ABDIB (1994a: 1–71); Strachmann (1993); Perez (1993); BNDES (1988); interviews. The data, with the exception of Merlin Gerin, refer

very high degree of TNC participation and product specialization compared with the mechanical equipment, boiler-making, railway equipment, and ship-building sub-sectors.

The high rate of TNC participation reflects the relatively more sophisticated technologies employed in the sub-sector and the associated barriers to entry. Significantly, technology transfer licensing agreements are far less numerous in the case of those enterprises which are of predominantly foreign capital: in the majority of these cases technology is transferred to Brazil from the parent companies' basic design facilities located abroad. However, as Section 5.2.1 noted, after a phase of technology transfer, TNCs have undertaken extensive local R&D work in certain cases, most particularly in hydro-generators and transformers.

Having established the general significance of foreign technology transfer in the electrical energy equipment sub-sector, it is important to note that it has been especially concentrated in certain product areas. Perhaps most significantly, the post-1987 period has seen a strong continuing reliance on the acquisition of foreign basic designs in the hydro-turbine sector. The development of efficient turbines (be they gas, water, or jet) depends on extensive testing and experience with different blade arrays and configurations and can be a very expensive process (*Financial Times*, 23 July 1996). This is especially true in newer turbine applications such as combined cycle thermal power plants. The heavy sunk costs and experience necessary to generate a full capability in basic turbine designs have precluded Brazilian enterprises from achieving self-sufficiency in this product area. Assistance in the establishment of such a basic design capability might have arisen through the establishment of a hydro-dynamics laboratory by FINEP or Eletrobrás. However, budgetary problems at these organizations have led to the suspension of this project (Strachmann 1993: 59).

Against this background, the two major Brazilian-owned producers of hydro-turbines—Villares and Sade-Vigesa—remain primarily reliant on foreign basic designs under licence, while ABB, Voith, Coesma-Ansaldo, and Mecânica Pesada, as TNC subsidiaries, rely on their parent companies' technology. Technology transfer in the turbine and generator sectors is not restricted to the transfer of basic designs which then form the basis for local production. Some of the more technologically challenging components of this equipment, most specifically the control systems, are reliant on technology transfer embodied in imported components. In the case of hydraulic turbines, all speed regulators continue to be imported while the same is true for certain generator exciter components.

In the case of switch gear and electrical control systems, there is very little local innovatory capability, with designs being obtained from outside Brazil (Strachmann 1993: 61). In large part the significance of technology transfer in this product area can be viewed as the result of the increased importance of micro-electronic monitoring and control systems as older generation electro-mechanical technologies have been phased out (interviews). In the case of

Enterprise *A*, some of the more technologically complex micro-electronic control systems incorporating heavier electrical equipment are not even manufactured within Brazil, being imported instead from the parent company's home country. Therefore, such technology transfer as occurs is extremely limited in scope: the technology is embodied in imported components with very little if any opportunity to engage in learning or adaptive innovation.

For some varieties of electrical control system, even the detailed designs have been obtained from the parent company's facilities abroad: local input is restricted to assembly. The only exception to this pattern is that of Merlin Gerin, a subsidiary of the French Groupe Schneider, where components as well as finished products are produced on site. The enterprise has developed a speciality in the production of 800 kV switch gear (it is the world's largest producer of this class of equipment) for use in conjunction with large scale hydro-generation schemes. There has been considerable local adaptation of French basic designs for use at high voltages.

According to Strachmann (1993: 59), the process of technology transfer between TNC and subsidiary in this instance has been unusually bi-directional with considerable user–producer linkages developing between the French suppliers of the basic technologies and their Brazilian subsidiary-based clients who have engaged in a substantial programme of adaptive innovation. Once again, the development of local technological capabilities within the context of technological transfer seems to have been most successful where local market requirements have exhibited peculiarities which have required individual rather than generic solutions.

The mechanical equipment sub-sector displays a far greater proportion of Brazilian-owned enterprises than does the electrical energy equipment subsector. Significantly, this is associated with a far more extensive reliance on technology licensing as a means of technology transfer than is the case in the electrical energy equipment sub-sector (Table 38).

An examination of the licensing-dominated pattern of technology transfer in this sector reveals interesting conclusions regarding the instances in which licensing occurs and the problems that are associated with it. The signing of technology licensing agreements has tended to be most prevalent in the more technologically advanced areas of the sector's production. One area where technology transfer through licensing has been most intense in the post-1987 period has been that of oil production and exploration equipment.

Despite the exceptions outlined in the previous section, the majority of oil production and exploration equipment produced in Brazil—specifically blow-out preventers, Christmas tree valves, well-head control equipment, exploration platforms, and drilling heads—continues to be based on basic designs obtained from abroad under licence (Tadini 1993: 18, Perez 1993: 92). Many of these technology transfer contacts have been of substantial duration and originate from the mid-1980s when Petrobrás embarked upon an expanded programme of exploration, most particularly in offshore areas (Perez 1993:

Table 38. Technology Licensing Agreements in the Mechanical Equipment Sub-sector

Enterprise	Nationality of controlling interest	Equipment produced	Technology licensers for equipment produced
ABB Vetco Gray Brasil Ltd.	Sweden, Switzerland, USA	Well-head equipment/Christmas tree valves	Parent company's own technology
AKZ S.A.	Brazil	Compressors, centrifuges	Nuovo Pigone (Italy), Machine Impianti (Italy), Peabody Eng. Co. (USA)
Bardella S.A.	Brazil	Mechanical handling equipment, casting equipment, rolling mills, hydraulic turbines, hydraulic presses, unloaders, mining equipment	SMS Schloemann (Germany), Stemag AG (Germany), Mitsubishi Heavy Industries (Japan), Mitsul Milke Machinery (Germany), Concast Standart AG (Germany)
Brasflex Tubos S.A.	Brazil	Flexible tubes	Coflexip S.A. (Brazil), Flexibrás Tubos (Brazil)
Buhler S.A.	Switzerland	Mechanical handling equipment	Parent company's own technology
CBV Indústria Mecânica S.A.	Brazil	Valves, connectors, Christmas tree valves, well-heads for oil exploration and production	FMC Petroleum Equipment Group (USA), Smith Tools (UK), Otis Engineering (USA)
Christensen Roder Ltd.	Brazil	Oil drilling equipment, drill bits	Hughes Tool Company (USA)
Combustol Ltd.	Brazil	Furnaces	Stein Heurtey (USA), Ajax Magnethermic (USA), Ipsen Industries (USA)
Detector Electronics do Brasil Ltd.	USA	Heat detection and control equipment, air quality monitoring equipment	Parent company's technology, Fenwal Safety Systems Inc. (USA)
DZ S.A. Engenharia, Equipamento e Sistemas	Brazil	Steel and metallurgical plant equipment, mechanical handling equipment	Ikio, Kobokuru (Japan), Wheeler (Canada), Biotim (Belgium), and many others
Engemaq S.A.	Brazil	Drilling and mining equipment	Houston Engineers (USA), Tampográfica (Argentina)

TABLE 38. (cont'd)

Enterprise	Nationality of controlling interest	Equipment produced	Technology licensers for equipment produced
IMS S.A.	Brazil	Valves, pneumatic actuators	Wesclock Corporation (USA)
Irmãos Geremia Ltd.	Brazil	Pumps, submersible pumps	Own technology
Kvaerner Pulping Tecnologia Para Celulose Ltd.	Norway	Equipment for cellulose production	Parent company's own technology, Carthage Machine Co. (USA), Hudson Products Inc. (USA)
MFX do Brasil Ltd.	Not known (non-Brazilian control)	Pneumatic, hydraulic and electrical control systems for deep-water oil production and exploration equipment	Parent company's own technology
PWR Mission Indústria Mecânica Ltd.	Brazil	Pumps, oil drilling equipment, diverse components	Amri (USA), A Camco Company (USA), Stockham Valves (USA), Hydril
Sulzer Brasil S.A.	Switzerland	Pumps and compressors	Parent company's own technology, Howden Compressors Ltd., Teikoku Manufacturing Co. Ltd. (Japan)
TBM Ltd.	Brazil	Steel-making equipment, casting equipment, cement plants, petrochemical processing equipment	Blake & Pendleton (USA), Boxmag Rapid Ltd. (UK), Goodmann Co. (USA), Thomas Broadbent & Sons UK and many others
Usiminas Mecânica S.A.	Brazil (part of Usiminas steel group)	Steel-making equipment, casting equipment, cement plant equipment, petrochemical processing equipment, equipment for pulp and paper plants	Usiminas (Brazil) Air Industrie Environnement (France), Hydro Vevey S.A., (Switzerland), Hitachi (Japan), Pragoinvest CKD (Czech Republic) and many others

Source: ABDIB (1994a: 1–71); Fritsch and Franco (1991a: 127–8); interviews. All enterprises referred to are ABDIB members.

92–3). In some instances (for example, the case of Irmãos Geremia Ltd.), licensing eventually led to technological self-sufficiency, particularly where deep-water technologies were involved and local conditions demanded a greater degree of adaptation. However, such self-sufficiency remains the exception rather than the rule and licensing remains the dominant means of techno-logy acquisition in the oil exploration and production equipment area.

Licensing also remains of primary importance in the steel equipment pro-duct area. According to Tadini (1993: 20), internationally, the steel equip-ment industry has witnessed a dramatic increase in concentration in the period since the mid-1980s. This has occurred against a background of a consider-able increase in the importance of product innovation in the sector. Taken together, these trends have led to the concentration of technological know-how and know-why in increasingly few hands. The Brazilian steel-making equip-ment sector is predominantly comprised of domestically owned enterprises which have long relied on imported basic designs obtained under licence, usually from Japanese, German, or US enterprises (interviews). Thus TBM, Bardella, and USIMEC, the largest Brazilian producers of steel-making equipment, have established relationships with specialist technology suppliers such as Blake & Pendleton (USA), Boxmag Rapid Ltd. (UK), Goodmann Co. (USA), Thomas Broadbent & Sons (UK), Air Industrie Environnement (France), SMS Schoelmann (Germany), Concast A.G. (Germany), and Hitachi (Japan) (Table 38).

In the case of Enterprise B, licensing of technology has been most pre-valent in the technologically demanding cold carbon steel-rolling mill and continuous casting mill machinery product areas where licences have long been held. During interviews, considerable importance was attached to the stability of these relationships and the importance of the 'brand-name' of the technology supplier as a means of achieving and sustaining market share. However, one disadvantage of licensing relationships as they have developed in the steel equipment sub-sector has been the imposition of export restric-tions by licensers. According to Tadini (1993: 20), the development of such restrictions has been the direct result of increasing concentration and tech-nological rivalry among leading technology suppliers.

Within the technologically less sophisticated travelling-crane product area, Enterprise B has also made extensive use of technology licensing, having estab-lished a long-term relationship with a major foreign technology supplier. These technologies have been intensively employed in the dock-crane product area, most especially in the hydraulic and electrical operating systems. Unlike steel-making equipment, however, licensing arrangements in this product area have not entailed export restrictions.

The railway equipment sub-sector is another in which technology transfer through licensing has remained the dominant form of technology acquisition (Table 39). This has been particularly true in the locomotive area where both basic and detailed designs have been transferred under long-term licensing

TABLE 39. Technology Licensing Agreements in the Railway Equipment Sub-sector

Enterprise	Nationality of controlling interest	Equipment produced	Technology provider for equipment produced
Cobrasma S.A.	Brazil	Railway vehicles and equipment, Cobrasma also produces Vessels for the steel and petrochemical industries	Babcock & Wilson Co. (USA and Canada), Bombardier Eurorail S.A. (Belgium)
GEVISA S.A.	Brazil (minority GE US holding)	Railway locomotives, heavy electric motors and generators	General Electric (USA), Villares (Brazil), Yaskawa (Japan)
MAFERSA S.A.	Brazil	Railway vehicles, Subway cars and Equipment	Own technology

Source: ABDIB (1994*a*: 1–71); interviews. All enterprises referred to are ABDIB members.

agreements between General Electric of the USA and Equipamentos Villares (later GEVISA) of Brazil for the production of heavy diesel electric locomotives (Perez 1993: 90–3). The pattern of technological reliance on overseas enterprises for both basic and detailed equipment designs in this product area seems likely to continue following the signing of a licensing agreement between Mecânica Pesada and General Motors of the USA in 1994 (*Revista Ferroviaria*, Dec. 1994: 31).

Reliance on technology licensing has also been a long-standing feature of the subway train sector: detailed designs for the Rio and São Paulo metro rolling stock were obtained from the Budd Company, USA and Bombardier of Canada. Even in the less sophisticated wagon sector there has also been a degree of technological licensing: a recent US order for 125 vehicles from Cobrasma involved the development of a technological partnership with Alcan of Canada (*Revista Ferroviaria*, Dec. 1994: 23). Technology licensing has also been significant in the components sector: one of the largest producers of running gear—Iochope Maxion—has long-standing technology licensing agreements in place with the Griffin Wheel Company (USA) and American Steel Foundries (USA) for the production of bogies.

The role of technological transfer from abroad in the boiler-making subsector has tended to be reduced by the relatively high degree of technological self-sufficiency in the sector, a characteristic discussed in Section 5.2.1.

Significantly, the participation of Brazilian-owned enterprises in this sector is very substantial. Despite generally high technological self-reliance, there are product areas of the sector where licensing has been and remains of significance (Table 40). Predictably, such areas tend to be those which involve a higher degree of technological sophistication than the plate work and metal fabrication processes which constitute the bulk of the sector's productive activities. The main technologies transferred are concentrated in the flow control systems that govern production processes using pressure vessels and tanks and in the nuclear power product area. With respect to the latter area, it should be noted that budgetary problems and energy policy shifts have put a virtual halt to Brazil's civilian programme (Motta *et al*. 1994). The extent of future technology transfer in the nuclear power sector is therefore not likely to be great.

The shipbuilding sub-sector has been subject to long-standing technology transfer in two particular areas: that of large vessel design and that of propulsion systems (Table 41). With respect to the former, basic designs have been prepared by outside agencies for oil tankers and oil storage, exploration, and production platforms. Interestingly, as Section 5.2.3 will make clear, not all designs have originated outside Brazil; some have been developed by specialist domestic naval architecture practices. In the case of propulsion systems, reliance on basic and detailed designs acquired under licence from foreign corporations has been total. Following the merger between Ishibrás, Verolme, and EMAQ, Ishibrás has become the primary manufacturer of heavy marine diesel and oil-fired engines in Brazil, drawing on long-standing licensing arrangements with Sulzer, Wärtsila, and Daihatsu.

5.2.3 DOMESTIC TECHNOLOGY TRANSFER, USER–PRODUCER LINKAGES, AND TRAINING

Although the process of technology transfer to the non-serial capital goods sector has been primarily dominated by foreign enterprises, it is important to note that in particular areas domestic organizations have been able to play a role. The IPT laboratory in São Paulo continued to function in the post-1987 period, although its primary role as a developer of technologies in the PROALCOOL (alcohol fuel from sugar) programme became of increasingly less significance as the programme experienced cutbacks in the 1990s. The role of FINEP in the post-1987 period, has been considerably diminished due to budget cutbacks and a reluctance by enterprises to borrow funds when faced with unfavourable market conditions. The reduction of FINEP programmes in the sector (there was only one by 1993—BNDES 1993*a*) has inevitably reduced contacts that the organization attempted to initiate between enterprises and university-based research institutes. The reduction of the role of the state as a facilitator of technology transfer in the sector does not necessarily suggest that domestic technology transfers have experienced a similar decline. There is evidence to suggest that specialist private sector technology development and consultancy enterprises may be at least partially

TABLE 40. Technology Licensing Agreements in the Boiler-Making Sub-sector

Enterprise	Nationality of controlling interest	Equipment produced	Technology provider for equipment produced
Brastubo S.A.	Brazil	Steel tubes, general boiler making	Own technology
CBC S.A.	Japan	Tanks, ventilators, brewery equipment, incinerators, pressure vessels, filters	ABB (US division) and Mitsubishi Heavy Industries Ltd. (Japan)—for electrical control systems
CBI-LIX Industrial Ltd.	Brazil/USA (joint venture between Constr. Lix de Cunha and Chicago Bridge and Iron Co.)	Tanks, pressure vessels, columns, silos	Own technology
Codistil S.A. Dedini	Brazil	Sugar, brewery, chemical, and food processing equipment	Paques B.V. (Holland), Huppmann GmbH (Germany), Hunt Manufacturing Inc. (USA) and many others
Confab Industrial S.A.	Brazil	Tanks, pressure vessels, columns, silos, heat exchangers, furnaces	Petrochem (USA), Kraftwerk Union (Germany) and others
Conforja S.A.	Brazil	Steel structures, plate work fabrications	Own technology
Convap Mecânica e Estrutura Metálica S.A.	Brazil	Silos, tanks, ducts, water treatment plants; Convap also produces railway wagons	Own technology
Delp Engenharia Mecânica S.A.	Brazil	Silos, furnaces, water treatment equipment, metal fabrications	Own technology
EBSE S.A.	Brazil	Silos, tanks, ducts, distillation towers	Own technology

TABLE 40. (cont'd)

Enterprise	Nationality of controlling interest	Equipment produced	Technology provider for equipment produced
Filsan Ltd.	USA	Pumps, filters, water treatment equipment	FMC Corporation (USA) (parent company), Nippon Steel (Japan) Skimovex B.V. (Holland) and many others
Jaraguá S.A.	Brazil	Valves, pumps, condensers, furnaces, heat exchangers, many others	Carthage Machine Co. (USA), Glitsch Inc. (USA), Hudson Products Inc. (USA), ESP-Electric Submersible Systems (USA)
Nordon Indústrias Metalúrgicas S.A.	France	Silos, tanks, distillation towers, Brewery, pharmaceutical and chemical industry equipment	Parent company's own technology, Ballestra S.P.A. (Italy), Kobe Steel (Japan), Petrolite (USA) and others
Nuclebrás Equipamentos Pesados S.A.	Brazil	Boiler-making components for nuclear industry (pressure vessels, heat exchangers); tanks, condensers, and pressure vessels for conventional power stations and petrochemical industry	Siemens (Germany), Kraftwerk Union (Germany), Man-Ghh (Germany), Voest Alpine (Germany)
Pérsico Pizzamiglio S.A.	Brazil	Tubes, boilers, heat exchangers	Own technology

Source: ABDIB (1994a: 1–71); Fritsch and Franco (1991a: 127–8); interviews. All enterprises referred to are ABDIB members.

TABLE 41. Technology Licensing Agreements in the Shipbuilding Sub-sector

Enterprise	Nationality of controlling interest	Equipment produced	Technology provider for equipment produced
CCN-Mauá	Brazil	Ships (up to 120,000 dwt), offshore platforms	Own design technology for smaller vessels, CEC Ltd. (Brazil), PRINASA designs (Brazil), Helistone Ltd.
EMAQ-Verolme*	Brazil/Holland	Ships, floating structures, oil platforms, boiler-making products, EMAQ also has the capability to produce heavy diesel engines and locomotives	PROJEMAR (designs and engineering studies) (Brazil), EISA S.A. (Brazil), SADE (Brazil)
Ishibrás*	Brazil/Japan	Ships, floating structures, heavy diesel engines	Sulzer Bros. Ltd. (Switzerland), Daihatsu Diesel Manufacturing Co. Ltd. (Japan), Wärtsila AB (Finland)—all for engine and propulsion systems

Notes: * Post-1994 changes in ownership have led to the formation of the IVI group under Brazilian ownership, merging both enterprises. EMAQ left the group in mid-1995.

Source: ABDIB (1994*a*: 1–71); interviews. All enterprises referred to are ABDIB members.

filling the gaps left by the state. Although very rarely mentioned in the literature concerning technology transfer in the Brazilian capital goods sector, such enterprises have developed to provide the sector with a range of basic and detailed designs along with training of key personnel. According to the trade association ABDIB, there are five key enterprises operating in the field of the non-serial capital goods sector, namely Jaakko Pöyry, Logos Engenharia, Montreal Engenharia, Promon Engenharia, and Tekhnites. Although these enterprises have a basic capability in plant design and some forms of machinery, some are still dependent in certain technologically demanding areas on imported basic designs (ABDIB 1994*a*).

In the shipbuilding sub-sector, two naval architecture practices—PROJEMAR and PRINASA—supply CCN-Mauá and EMAQ-Verolme with designs for small and medium vessels (Table 41). In the course of enterprise visits, none of the enterprises claimed to have employed the services of any such consultant engineering practices and thus no information was available concerning their role. Investigation into the operation of these organizations and the contribution that they make to the development of indigenous technological capability is likely to prove a fruitful area for future research.

Chapter 1 argued that the state could play a direct role in the fostering and propagation of user–producer linkages in order that innovations could arise from information flows between producers of non-serial capital goods and their clients. In the 1970s, the state partially fulfilled this role through the operation of the *Nucléos de Articulação de Demanda*. However, the scaling down and virtual cessation of large infrastructural projects in the post-1987 period have virtually put a halt to this aspect of state-supported user–producer interaction. The only systematic form of such interaction which continued beyond 1987 has been that involving Petrobrás, CVRD, and Eletrobrás. As Section 5.2.1 demonstrated, interaction between these technologically sophisticated enterprises and enterprises in the non-serial capital goods sector have on occasion led to genuine basic product innovation in specialized areas, for example, in heavy switch gear and deep-water drilling equipment. However, such fruitful interactions would appear to remain the exception rather than the rule, with public investment expenditure reduction reducing their scope. In terms of private sector user–producer interactions, the evidence would suggest that these have tended to remain very limited in extent.

In the course of interviews, all enterprises stated that participation with clients in the arrival at final designs formed an important part of their design activity. However, this would appear to be inevitable given the custom-made character of many non-serial capital goods. Detailed designs are altered to suit clients but the underlying technologies (usually obtained under licence) are not subject to alteration as a result of client feedbacks. In large part, this may be viewed as the inevitable result of the division between possession of basic and detailed design capabilities, know-why, and know-how. In one case, the role of the enterprise in any such user–producer linkage was viewed as secondary to that of the relationship between clients and the technology licensers. According to one manager, clients were broadly aware of the technologies required, knew of the licensers of those technologies, and through them arranged to have the equipment built to order in Brazil using recommended licensees. In this case, the role of the Brazilian manufacturer has altered from that of technological intermediary and detailed designer to that of contractor: the potential for user–producer interaction is thus reduced further.

The availability of trained personnel capable of carrying out research and development work in the sector was not perceived in the course of the interviews as placing a limitation on innovatory effort. All enterprises expressed

the view that skill shortages in R&D areas were not acute and that any con-
ceivable shortfall could be addressed with a programme of in-house training.
However, this view must be seen in the context of generally low levels of in-
house research and development where little innovatory demand is placed on
local personnel. More generally, there would appear to be a relative lack of
university engineering research institutes, while research activity and training
within these has tended to be of sporadic and, occasionally, low quality. Within
the Brazilian higher education system as a whole there is concern at the
general quality of postgraduate training and, more particularly, the generally
weak character of university–industry relations (Meyer-Starmer 1993b). In the
long run, these are bound to act as fundamental constraints on the achievement of a more dynamic basic research and development capability within
non-serial capital goods sector enterprises.

5.3 The Impact of Policy Shifts upon Patterns of Technology Acquisition and Development: Some Conclusions

The previous section pointed to the remarkable persistence of patterns of technological acquisition, development, and dependence for product innovation
in the Brazilian non-serial capital goods sector throughout its development,
both prior to and during the post-1987 policy shifts. The relative constancy
of patterns of technological behaviour lies in marked contrast to the changes
in plant organization and process innovation identified in Chapter 3. The conclusion that domestic product innovation—particularly in more sophisticated
product areas—remained at a low level (and indeed came under pressure),
while technological dependence remained high, would appear to support the
proposition that the reductions in explicit and implicit forms of technology
policy have adversely affected the development of indigenous technological
capability in the sector. This would appear to be consistent with the literature supportive of technological intervention in the sector which pointed to
the adverse consequences of reduced interventions.

At the same time, the challenge-response mechanisms induced by increased
exposure to international competition and reduced intervention appear not
to have resulted in enhanced product innovation effort among enterprises.
Only in the case of process innovation do these mechanisms appear to have
had a discernible positive association with technological progress in the sector (see Chapter 3). Given these preliminary conclusions, it is tempting to
draw the inference that the withdrawal of the state underpins the sector's continuing relative lack of internal technological dynamism and, by implication,
its return could engender (or, counter-factually, could have engendered) a
reversal of this situation. This conclusion, is, to some extent, supported by
interview evidence gathered during the fieldwork.

In the course of interviews with enterprises, the reduction of the role
of the state was certainly perceived as a strong influence on low innovative

activity within the sector. The most commonly raised opinion was that the reduction in government procurement had, through inducing a degree of enterprise financial precariousness, reduced the willingness of management to engage in riskier and more costly forms of research and development. More generally, the macroeconomic instability and high inflation of the 1987–94 period were felt to have provided a uniquely unsuitable background for long-term investment in general and basic R&D in particular. Faced with increasing competition in domestic and overseas markets in the period since 1990, management repeatedly stressed the overwhelming importance of cost reductions, productivity gains, and process innovations rather than any potential held by expanded product innovation, a viewpoint common to much of the sector (Dantas 1993). In terms of technology licensing, the stability of relationships with licensers was felt to be a vital ingredient in the long-run ability to produce complex non-serial capital goods.

However, the view was expressed that the choice of technologies and the ability to switch between licensers had been somewhat restricted by the operational practices of INPI which had tended to raise transactions costs and lengthen the time involved in the approval of new licences. Another factor which was felt to have acted as a continuing impediment to the expansion of in-house technological activity was the reduced level of FINEP funding, a feeling reflected generally across the sector (Tadini 1993: 25). In particular, the financing of hydro-electric technological developments was felt to be an area in desperate need of greater governmental research funding, given that Brazil has achieved something of a comparative advantage in the production of certain categories of equipment (interviews).

Another area of policy with the potential for a damaging effect upon the sector's innovative capability appears to be that of increased freedom of entry of capital goods components following in the wake of the *Abertura Comercial* and the end of the information technology market reserve policy. All enterprises expressed the view that they would be making increasing use of imported complex components, particularly those incorporating control systems and electronic components. The problem with such technology transfer lies in the fact that the embodied nature of the technology may make the potential for learning, adaptive, or basic innovation even less than would be the case with licensing or internal TNC transfer.

Thus, there are reasons to suspect that the impact of policy shifts on the sector's technological dynamism and self-sufficiency have tended to be negative and, by implication, counter-factually, that an enhanced role for the state might have prevented these developments. Such a conclusion needs, however, to be qualified by a consideration of the structural context within which both explicit and implicit technology polices have operated. To an extent, it will be argued, observed patterns of technological acquisition and development have been determined by the sector's historical structural and institutional characteristics, characteristics which, for a variety of reasons, have proved themselves in some cases to be largely unaffected by changes in the external policy environment.

One of the principal structural characteristics which has characterized the sector from its inception has been the high levels of TNC participation through the operation of their subsidiaries in Brazil. In itself this characteristic might be expected to impart a bias towards the development and acquisition of technology outside Brazil. Additionally, it is important to note that TNCs tend to participate in the technologically more challenging areas of sector activity, most particularly in electrical energy equipment and control systems. Such areas demand a more continuous focus on product innovation than do others where Brazilian enterprises are comparatively of greater significance as producers. Given this structural background, a continuing degree of technological dependence and low internal innovation are likely to persist despite policy alterations. This argument, however, rests on the assumption that Brazilian TNC subsidiaries do not and will not engage in innovative activity.

The previous two sections demonstrated that, while this has been broadly true (especially for basic designs), there are notable exceptions. In the case of Enterprise *A*, for example, the unusual patterns of local demand resulting from large hydro-electric power projects led to the development of local specialized design and production capabilities for certain categories of equipment. These capabilities were then successfully employed for the export market once public expenditure cuts reduced domestic demand. This would seem to suggest that, under particular circumstances, the implementation of certain policies by the state is able to influence the extent of local R&D effort in TNC subsidiaries.

One of the most serious structural obstacles to greater technological self-reliance lies in the excessive product diversity maintained by many of the sector's enterprises. This is particularly true among Brazilian-owned enterprises, most especially in the mechanical engineering sub-sector (Fritsch and Franco 1991*a*: 132). Continued product diversification among enterprises has resulted in a situation where, in many product areas, there is excessively low concentration in the domestic market by comparison with other industrial nations. For example, Brazil has six producers of hydro-turbines compared with one in the USA, two in Germany, and three in Japan (Araújo *et al.* 1991: 76). In steel-making equipment, the lack of concentration is also remarkable with seven Brazilian producers of rolling mills compared with three in the USA, Germany, and Japan and one in France, while in blast furnaces Brazil has four manufacturers compared with one each in the USA and France, three in Germany, and four in Japan (ibid. 76).

The development of such lack of concentration and excessive diversification was a function of the policies which accompanied the sector's expansion in the 1970s. As industrial sectors were sequentially developed under the terms of the PND II, enterprises were encouraged to extend the range of products produced by the *Nucléos de Articulação de Demanda* in order that technological competence could by diffused through the sector and a degree of competition introduced to a heavily protected market. During this period, enterprises such as Enterprise *B* signed many licensing agreements and developed the capability to produce a very broad range of products. Excessive product diversification is a feature which continued through the 1980s and has remained in place up until the conclusion of the study period (1995). During the latter period, the persistence of diversification appears to have been linked to attempts by enterprises to spread risks, maximize capacity utilization, and maintain relatively constant turnover faced with volatile international markets and depressed domestic demand for particular products (see Chapter 6).

The problem with such diversification is that it tends to inhibit the process of learning and development of know-why that might be expected to be obtained from greater specialization and familiarity with particular products (ibid. 76; Baark 1991). Significantly, according to Baark (1991), it is only through such specialization that enterprises can achieve full technological mastery and eventually leadership. Thus, the opportunities offered by greater specialization appear to be being systematically forgone in an industrial structure conditioned by the sector's historical development and propagated by risk aversion among enterprises. It seems unlikely that a resumption of high levels of protection and public investment or explicit support for technological development alone would have any far-reaching effects on existing patterns of diversification in the sector: more explicit sector policies emphasizing specialization and rationalization would have to be implemented before this structural constraint to greater technological reliance could be overcome.

A third major structural constraint to the more intensive pursuit of product innovation and the achievement of greater technological self-sufficiency in the sector is connected to customer demands in domestic and, particularly, foreign markets. In the course of all the interviews conducted, the brand-name and reputation of the technologies embodied in the sector's products were considered to be vital components in securing sales. For Brazilian enterprises, the licensing of technologies is seen not only as a means of securing technological competence but as a form of marketing strategy (interviews). The growing importance of export markets—where the reputation of Brazilian enterprises is less well known than domestically—has, if anything, enhanced this marketing aspect of technology transfer. In both Enterprises *B* and *C*, market demands for established technologies from established suppliers were viewed as a significant obstacles to the achievement of further technological self-reliance.

The fourth constraint faced by the non-serial capital goods sector in any attempt it may make to engage in a more self-reliant pattern of technological acquisition is that of what might be loosely termed Brazil's 'technological infrastructure'. Numerous studies (e.g. Furtado 1994; Kirschner 1993;

Matesco 1994*a*; BNDES 1990*a*) have pointed to the very low levels of innovative effort that characterize much of Brazilian industry. The absence of intensive technological activity has led some to talk of the absence of an 'innovative culture' within Brazil. The absence of such domestic activity on a general scale provides the context in which the non-serial capital goods sub-sector proceeds in its patterns of technological acquisition. The domestic demon-stration effect of low innovative effort within industry as a whole and the non-serial capital goods sector in particular may have the effect of culturally conditioning managers in the sector towards less ambitious patterns of tech-nological development. In other words, there is a degree of cultural inertia which may need to be overcome if enterprises are to become technologically more self-reliant. More concretely, the absence of such generalized domestic innovative activity imperils the development of technological linkages be they user–producer or supplier–producer. The absence of domestic technological interaction makes it all the more likely that enterprises will turn abroad for their technological requirements.

At the same time, the potential for the engagement in more ambitious basic design in conjunction with Brazilian universities is hampered by the poor state of industry–university relations and the variable quality of higher education institutions highlighted in Sections 5.1 and 5.2.3. Taken together with the reductions in public funding for research institutes and the low level of user–producer interaction, the Brazilian non-serial capital goods sector would appear to be suffering from the absence of key components in what Nelson (1993) terms a 'National System of Innovation'. According to Nelson, the existence of such a system is vital for the effective generation of innovative effort and the efficient diffusion of its benefits throughout the rest of the economy.

Conclusions

Despite the maturity of the non-serial capital goods sector and the major shifts in policy it has encountered since the mid-1980s, patterns of technological development and acquisition for product innovations have remained essenti-ally unchanged. While enterprises possess the capability to engage in adaptive innovation and the development of basic designs for production, they have yet to achieve technological self-sufficiency in basic designs, particularly in more advanced and technologically challenging areas. In many cases, enter-prises remain in a state of technological dependence from which they show few, if any, signs of emerging. Thus, the post-1987 withdrawal of the state appears to have been associated with a reinforcement of long-standing pat-terns of technological behaviour in product innovation. Only in the case of process innovation does there appear to have been a substantial break with previous patterns of sector technological development (see Chapter 3).

There remains doubt, however, whether a maintenance of the role of the state in its old form would have necessarily engendered a reversal of the

historical pattern of technological acquisition and development for product innovations. Some of the influences underlying the sector's continuing
technological dependence stem from structural features which have become
deep rooted. Only through addressing these fundamental characteristics could
any future policy régime achieve success in generating enhanced internal
dynamism in product innovation.

The implementation of such a policy would, of course, require recognition
among policy-makers and sector participants that long-run weaknesses stem
from the sector's established patterns of technology acquisition. While this
view is sometimes expressed, especially within government, the majority of
enterprises in the sector would appear to be less preoccupied with changing
their traditional patterns of technology acquisition than with achieving short-
run cost competitiveness in order to ensure short- to medium-run survival
in increasingly competitive international and domestic markets. Perhaps this
behaviour is not surprising given the legacy of caution and financial constraint
engendered by the relatively recent and extraordinarily severe collapse in
traditional markets and, consequently, in the fortunes of some enterprises.
Whether the continuing relatively low priority afforded to product innovation
and technological self-reliance represents a sustainable or desirable strategic
option remains open to doubt, however.

Chapter 1 argued that the most important justification for the development
of a capital goods sector arose from the potential it possessed to generate and
diffuse innovations throughout an economy. It is clear that, in its present form,
the sector is only partially matching up to this potential. In particular, some
of the more dynamic long-run efficiencies that might result from internal technological development are being forgone. Principally, the potential to enter
new markets and technological paradigms appears to be being bypassed in
the sector's continued adherence to traditional patterns of technological
acquisition. At the same time, the continuing viability of the sector depends
in large part on the continued willingness of TNCs and technology licensers to
transfer technology. As the sector increasingly turns away from the domestic
market, it seems likely that this may decline, particularly in the case of the
granting of licences to Brazilian-owned enterprises.

6

Concentration, Diversification, and Financial Performance

Introduction

As Chapter 1 demonstrated, much recent theoretical work on the role of the capital goods sector in developing economies has pointed to the importance of achieving long-run dynamic comparative advantage through specialization and economies of scale within the context of an increasingly concentrated and global market. In particular, it is argued that full technological self-reliance for basic products can only be achieved on the basis of enhanced specialization and the opportunities for enhanced learning that this affords. However, the development of the Brazilian non-serial capital goods sector was associated with the emergence of an unusual pattern of industrial structure which was characterized by very low degrees of concentration, high levels of product diversification, and technological dependence among enterprises. Theoretical literature critical of the role of the state, in particular that emerging from the theoretical critique of import substitution industrialization, would point to these developments as being the natural consequences of prolonged protection of the sector and associated attempts by the state to induce domestic, in the absence of foreign, competition through implicit or explicit forms of capacity licensing.

Given this theoretical and empirical background it will clearly be of interest to determine whether the post-1987 withdrawal of the state—principally through its roles as an agent of protection and as a procurer—has resulted in a less diversified, more concentrated sector of the type that is held to be more appropriate for the long-run development of dynamic efficiency gains. In order to achieve this objective, this chapter adopts the following approach. First, patterns of concentration and diversification are identified for the pre-1987 period and contrasted against those that have occurred subsequently. Secondly, an attempt is made to assess the relative importance of the changing role of the state in any identified alterations. Having analysed the key issues of diversification and concentration, the final part of the chapter examines the changing financial performance of the sector over the post-1987 period. In undertaking this exercise, a brief attempt is made to identify the relationship between 'bottom-line' financial performance indicators and the development of enterprise rationalization, product, and process innovation.

6.1 Concentration and Diversification in the Non-serial Capital Goods Sector: Historical Patterns and Post-1987 Developments

(i) *International Trends*

In the fifteen years leading up to 1994, worldwide patterns of diversification and concentration in the non-serial capital goods sector have undergone a profound transformation in response to two pronounced trends. The first trend may be characterized as the tendency for growth in worldwide fixed capital formation to slow down in relation to levels achieved in the 1960s and 1970s, thus placing severe constraints on the extent to which the market for non-serial capital goods could grow. The second trend emerges from the increasing technological threshold required for entry into production of many forms of complex capital good (Tadini 1993: 2). Taken together these trends have had the effect of placing a premium on competitive strategies which focus on horizontal integration and specialization as firms merge in the face of reduced demand and attempt to focus on particular product groups in order to master increasingly specialized, costly, and complex technologies.

On a global scale, there has been a considerable increase in concentration and specialization, especially in North America and Europe, among the larger enterprises in the non-serial capital goods sector. The most substantial episodes of this restructuring have involved joint ventures, mergers, and rationalization of product ranges and have led to the combination of GEC (UK) and Alsthom (France) to form GEC-Alsthom in the electrical energy equipment and railway equipment sub-sectors, ASEA (Sweden) and Brown Boveri (Switzerland) to form ABB in the electrical energy equipment sub-sector, ABB (Sweden/Switzerland) and Combustion Engineering (USA) in the boiler-making sub-sector, and AEG (Germany) and Daimler Benz (Germany) in the electrical energy equipment sub-sectors (Tadini 1993: 2; *Financial Times*, 16 May 1995). Over the same period, the two largest North American producers of electrical energy equipment, General Electric (USA) and Westinghouse (USA) were involved in significant concentration and specialization in which Westinghouse purchased General Electric's electrical energy transmission business while both enterprises began to specialize in the production of higher technology value-added products such as electronic power control systems, turbine systems, and nuclear power plant equipment. More recently, ABB purchased the bulk of the electrical generation and transmission businesses of Westinghouse.

In the mechanical equipment sub-sector, there was a considerable increase in concentration among major enterprises as mergers occurred and some enterprises left the market. Thus Demag (Germany) acquired Standard Messo (Germany) in the steel equipment sub-sector, while Thyssen (Germany) and GHH (Germany) pooled some activities in the same sector and Krupp (Germany), Nippon Steel (Japan), and Sumitomo (Japan) greatly reduced their presence in the market (Tadini 1993: 3). In the rolling-mill sector of the market, Mesta (USA) left the market entirely leaving SMS Schloemann (Germany) the dominant producer and supplier of technology (interviews; ABDIB 1994a: 5).

The railway equipment sub-sector has also seen considerable increases in concentration internationally as a number of significant mergers have taken place, the most notable being between GEC of the UK and Alsthom of France, the purchase of BREL in the UK by ABB of Switzerland/Sweden, and the consolidation of the German railway equipment industry under Daimler Benz and Siemens. The shipbuilding industry has also become increasingly characterized by concentrated market structures, especially in the larger vessel categories where many European and North American yards closed in the 1980s and where an increasing proportion of output (around 70% in 1994) is accounted for by major yards in Japan and South Korea (*Financial Times*, 22 Feb. 1996), the most significant being those of Daewoo, Hyundai, Mitsubishi Heavy Industries, and Ishikawajima. The global trend towards concentration and specialization in the non-serial capital goods sector shows little sign of slowing down, with the 1995 purchase of Babcock Power Engineering (UK) by Mitsubishi Heavy Industries (Japan) in the boiler-making sub-sector and the 1996 purchase of Trafalgar House (UK) by Kvaerner Group (Norway) in the shipbuilding and mechanical equipment sub-sectors.

(ii) Trends within Brazil

While there has been a strong tendency towards concentration and specialization in the sector internationally, in the case of Brazil the trend has tended to be rather more muted. Taken together with the Brazilian sector's historically low levels of concentration and high levels of enterprise product diversification, this has led to a situation in which the sector's industrial structure remains far more atomized than that of the sectors of most other major industrial economies. The remainder of this section portrays the emergence of this development in more detail, while Section 6.1(iii) considers the factors that underlie it, in particular those related to the role of the state.

The portrayal of changes in concentration would ideally be carried out using concentration ratios based on market share and sales for individual enterprise. Unfortunately, following the demise of the official Industrial Census, such data are not available for the Brazilian non-serial capital goods sector, thus preventing the calculation of formal concentration ratios. However, a very approximate indication of the degree of concentration in the sector can be obtained by examining the number of producers present in particular product lines. Taken together with similar data for other major industrial economies, an idea can be gained as to the extent to which the Brazilian patterns of concentration may differ significantly from those of other nations.

The presence of a large number of firms competing in each particular non-serial capital goods product line has been a long-standing structural

TABLE 42. Number of Manufacturers of Selected Non-serial Capital Goods in Brazil and Principal Industrial Economies, 1978

Equipment description	No. of manufacturers in Brazil	No. of foreign manufacturers
Hydro-electric generators	4	Germany: 2, France: 2, Japan: 4, Switzerland: 1, Canada: 1, UK: 1, USA: 3
Turbines	4	Germany: 2, Switzerland: 1, Japan: 3, Sweden: 2, Italy: 1, USA: 1
Rolling mills	7	USA: 3, Germany: 3, Italy: 1, France: 1, UK: 1, Japan: 3
Blast furnaces	4	USA: 1, Germany: 3, UK: 1, France: 1, Japan: 4
Sintering plant	2	USA: 2, Japan: 2, Germany: 3, Austria: 1, France: 1, UK: 1
Continuous casting equipment	4	USA: 2, Germany: 2, France: 2, Japan: 4, Italy: 1, UK: 2
Other steel-making equipment	4	USA: 3, Germany: 3, Japan: 3, UK: 1, France: 1, Austria: 1
Heavy mechanical presses	5	USA: 2, Germany: 2, Italy: 1

Source: Motta, T. F. (1978), quoted in Corrêa do Lago et al. (1979: 277).

feature of the Brazilian sector, dating back to the phase of rapid expansion in the 1970s. According to Corrêa do Lago, Lopes de Almeida, and de Lima (1979: 276), the later 1970s were characterized by an 'excess' of producers in many of the product types encompassed by the sector which led to a marked 'pulverization' of the market for many non-serial capital goods. The degree of market atomization was indeed remarkable during this period, especially when comparisons are drawn with other major non-serial capital good producing nations, as Table 42 reveals.

As the sector moved into the 1980s, the conditions of rapid market growth that had been associated with the 1970s quickly evaporated. Interestingly, however, the impact of this major change in external environment appeared to have little impact on the development of market structure which continued to be characterized by a relatively high level of producers for most of the sector's major products.

If anything, by the mid-1980s, the data suggest an intensification of the tendency towards relative market atomization that Motta and Corrêa do Lago, Lopes de Almeida, and de Lima identify for the 1970s. Table 43 points to this conclusion using the years 1978 and 1986 as points of comparison.

TABLE 43. Number of Brazilian Producers of Selected Non-serial
Capital Goods, 1978–1986

Equipment type	No. of producers, 1978	No. of producers, 1986
Hydro-electric generators	4	4
Turbines	4	5
Rolling mills	7	5
Blast furnaces	4	3
Sintering plant	2	3
Continuous casting equipment	4	4
Mine transport systems	7*	13
Dryers for mine use	4*	8
Diesel electric locomotives	1	2
Large ships and floating structures	6	6

Note: * Data refer to 1976.

Source: Motta, T. F. (1978), quoted in Corrêa do Lago *et al.* (1979: 277); Fritsch and Franco (1991: 130–1); interviews.

The period between 1987 and 1994 was, of course, associated with major changes in the external policy environment, which comprised principally the application of progressive trade liberalization combined with substantial reductions in public sector fixed capital investment. Given these changes, it might be expected that the more competitive and internationally exposed environment they brought about would tend to give rise to conditions under which patterns of concentration in the Brazilian sector would increasingly come to resemble those prevalent internationally. The evidence tends to suggest, however, that such alterations may have been somewhat limited in scope and concentrated within certain sub-sectors. Table 44 gives an indication as to the nature of the changes experienced within the sector over the period.

Table 44 indicates that, in the case of the major product types (i.e. turbines, generators, blast furnaces, and steel rolling mills) produced by the electrical energy equipment and mechanical equipment sub-sectors, there was no change in the number of producers operating within Brazil. In fact, all the firms that had participated in these product areas in 1986 continued to do so in 1994. The lack of movement towards concentration in these markets within Brazil combined with continuing concentration internationally has had the effect that, in international terms, the structure of the Brazilian sector has become relatively even more atomized. According to Tadini (1993) and Araújo, Corrêa, and Gatilho (1991), this conclusion remains valid, in the vast majority of cases for the Brazilian non-serial capital goods sector as a whole, a view widely shared by sector managers and academic specialists within Brazil (Fritsch and Franco 1991*a*; interviews).

TABLE 44. Number of Producers in Brazil of Selected Non-serial Capital Goods, 1986–1994, and Number of Foreign Producers, 1994

Equipment type	No. of producers in Brazil, 1986	No. of producers in Brazil, 1994	No. of foreign producers, 1994
Hydro-electric generators	4	4	USA: 3, Japan: 4, France: 2, Germany: 2, Sweden: 1
Turbines	5	5	USA: 1, Japan: 3, France: 1, Canada: 1, Sweden: 1, Germany: 1
Blast furnaces	3	4	USA: 1, France: 1, Germany: 2, Japan: 4
Rolling mills	5	6*	Japan: 3, Others: 3*
Continuous casting equipment	4	4	n/a
Sintering plant	3	3	n/a
Diesel electric locomotives	2	1	USA: 2, UK: 1, Germany: 2, France: 1
Large ships and floating structures	6	2	S. Korea: 3+, Japan: 4+, UK: 4

Note: * Data are for 1993.

Source: ABDIB (1994a); Tadini (1993); Fritsch and Franco (1991a: 130–1); Araújo *et al.* (1991: 77); interviews.

However, there would appear to be exceptions to this relatively static pattern of industrial structure within the Brazilian non-serial capital goods sector. Within the electrical energy and mechanical equipment sub-sectors, there was limited merger activity at the end of the 1980s, although the enterprises involved were not among the more significant in their respective sub-sectors. Within the electrical energy equipment sub-sector, the subsidiaries of ASEA and Brown Boveri merged as a result of the creation of the ABB group worldwide. Within the power transmission tower and line product category, there was a dramatic increase in concentration as the ABB group purchased SBE—*Sociedade Brasileira de Electrificação*—and two further Brazilian-owned enterprises—Itel and Lorenzetti—left the industry (Tadini 1993: 14; interviews). Within the mechanical equipment sub-sector, two enterprises producing plant for the steel, chemical, and pulp and paper industries—Metalúrgica Dedini and Zanini Equipamentos—merged in 1992 to form DZ Engenharia, Equipamentos e Sistemas (BNDES 1995: 17–20) while Equipetrol acquired another oil equipment producer, Conforja, in the early 1990s (Tadini 1993: 14).

In the boiler-making sub-sector Grupo Lix da Cunha acquired the Brazilian subsidiary of the Chicago Bridge and Iron Co. to form CBI-LIX in which there was still some US equity participation. However, the merger activity described above can only be described as limited in scope and concentration, as measured by number of participants in the electrical energy equipment, mechanical equipment, and boiler-making sub-sectors, which has remained virtually unchanged in the period between 1986 and 1994. This relatively unchanging picture is not, however, repeated in the railway equipment or shipbuilding sub-sectors where restructuring has been pronounced in the post-1987 period.

The shipbuilding sub-sector has experienced extensive merger activity and changes in ownership since the end of the 1980s. As subsequent discussion will reveal, such merger activity was prompted by a chronic shortage of orders and very high rates of capacity under-utilization. In 1993 the two largest shipyards in the sub-sector—Ishibrás and Verolme—were merged to form a new group known as Indústrias Verolme-Ishibrás (IVI). Interestingly, these yards are the most modern in Brazil, having been established under the Kubitschek administration's sectoral plan in 1958 and allocated the production of the largest category of vessels such as bulk carriers and oil tankers (Ferraz 1984: 114; Pessanha 1996: 6). Up until 1993, Ishibrás was majority owned by Japanese capital, with Ishikawajima group holding a 98% equity stake. Similarly, Verolme was largely owned by foreign capital, in this case the Dutch shipbuilding group Verolme Scheepwerken. Shortly before the merger with Ishibrás, Verolme group merged with another smaller yard, EMAQ, to form a group under Brazilian control with the entrepreneur Nelson Tanure as majority shareholder. Following the merger of Ishibrás with Verolme-EMAQ, the equity stake of Ishikawajima was reduced from 98% to 20%, leaving Nelson Tanure as majority shareholder in the newly formed IVI group (*Jornal do Brasil Online*, 8 Feb. 1996).

By the end of 1994 the original six enterprises capable of producing larger ocean-going vessels had been reduced to just three: CCN-Mauá, Caneco, and IVI. However, continuing problems of operational efficiency at EMAQ led to difficulties with its integration into the IVI group, difficulties that were exacerbated by the fact that EMAQ did not have the capability to produce the largest vessel categories that had become the focus of IVI's product range under a strategy of increased specialization. Consequently, the EMAQ holding was divested in 1994.

The railway equipment sub-sector has also experienced a substantial restructuring, most especially in the more technologically demanding product area of locomotives. Prior to 1993 there were three producers of diesel and diesel-electric locomotives within Brazil (Brazil does not produce other forms of locomotive, with the exception of subway and commuter train power cars)—General Electric do Brasil, Villares, and EMAQ. General Electric do Brasil produced locomotives based on its parent company's designs, while Villares and EMAQ made use of designs obtained under licence from General Motors (Perez 1993: 90). In 1993 there was a substantial increase in market concentration with the merger of the locomotive building subsidiaries of General Electric and Villares to form a new group known as GEVISA, jointly owned by two former enterprises with a minority stake from Grupo Safra (BNDES 1995). GEVISA abandoned General Motors technology, instead relying solely on General Electric designs. At the same time, EMAQ abandoned locomotive production altogether as part of its merger agreement with Verolme (ABIFER 1993: 13). As a result of these developments, only one diesel/diesel electric locomotive producer remained in Brazil by 1994. However, in December 1994, General Motors announced that it was intending to return to the Brazilian market so that it could compete with GEVISA for a substantial CVRD order. Under the terms of General Motors' re-entry, the GEC-Alsthom subsidiary, Mecânica Pesada, would produce its designs for very high-powered SD-70 180 ton 4,000 hp diesel-electric locomotives under licence (*Revista Ferroviaria*, Dec. 1994: 31).

The restructuring of locomotive production has not, however, been accompanied by similar trends in other railway equipment product areas. For example, in subway train and passenger coach production, Brazil has five competing producers including the recently privatized MAFERSA (ABIFER 1993), a number unchanged since 1986 and far greater than that prevailing in the UK, France, Germany, the USA, or Japan. A similar lack of concentration may be observed in the wagon and components product areas (ibid.).

The maintenance of relatively high observed levels of atomization and diversification within the non-serial capital goods sector as a whole need not necessarily preclude the formation of formal or informal collusive pacts among enterprises. Such arrangements might come into operation in order to avoid what the sector might perceive as 'excessive' levels of competition. However, in the course of the fieldwork, no evidence was discovered which might point to the existence of such arrangements, with management stressing the 'very competitive' nature of the domestic market. In keeping with this conclusion, none of the literature concerning the sector suggests that any such collusive arrangements are in place. However, it should be realized that the absence of evidence concerning collusion does not provide conclusive proof that any such arrangements are entirely absent. If any collusive arrangements were in place, then it would seem likely that enterprises within the sector would try to suppress any relevant evidence.

(iii) Accounting for Patterns of Concentration in the Brazilian Non-serial Capital Goods Sector

The persistence of the low levels of market concentration highlighted in much of the discussion so far, emerges from the continuation of a long-running tendency among most enterprises to pursue strategies of diversification rather than specialization coupled with the fact that relatively few enterprises have left or entered the industry. The extent of diversification, however, varies between enterprises and turns out to be strongly influenced by the role of the state and the nationality of the controlling interest.

While many non-serial capital-goods-producing enterprises outside Brazil have tended towards greater specialization and control of the market through product-line rationalization and aggressive programmes of horizontal integration (General Electric and ABB are excellent cases in point), within Brazil such specialization has been eschewed in favour of maintaining a market presence in many product areas. Occasionally, such product diversification has involved enterprises in producing product lines that are technologically unrelated to each other. The extent of product diversification tends to be greatest in Brazilian rather than foreign-owned enterprises. This differential pattern of diversification is revealed in Fritsch and Franco using data collected by Malcher for 1986 (Malcher 1987: 130–1). The data reveal a marked tendency for Brazilian-owned enterprises to operate in a greater number of product areas than their foreign counterparts. This turned out to be especially true for enterprises in the mechanical equipment and boiler-making sub-sectors where not only did Brazilian enterprises tend to produce a greater range of equipment than their foreign counterparts but they also supplied a greater range of industries.

Examination of similar data for 1994 supplied by ABDIB reveals exactly the same pattern (ABDIB 1994a). If anything, the extent of product diversification among domestically owned enterprises would appear to have increased: this would especially appear to be true for the largest such enterprises in this category namely Bardella, Usiminas Mecânica, D-Z Equipamentos, Cobrasma, CBV, Jaraguá, and Confab. The extent of product diversification is truly remarkable in some cases. For example, Usiminas Mecânica supplied at least ten different industry types in 1994, up from around four in 1986. The number of product areas in which the enterprise participated was at least fifteen encompassing such diverse products as road bridges, rail wagon repairs, electrostatic precipitators, blast furnaces, chemical tanks, jetways for aircraft access, and continuous casting machines (ABDIB 1994a).

The extensive diversification practised by Brazilian-owned enterprises can be contrasted with the greater relative degree of specialization favoured by their foreign-owned counterparts within Brazil. Using 1986 and 1994 as points of comparison, it becomes apparent that foreign-owned enterprises tend to supply fewer industry types, and fewer lines of product within each industry category (Malcher 1987: 130–1; ABDIB 1994a). Moreover, the data reveal little or no tendency for this pattern to change between the two years. Approximately three-quarters of foreign-owned enterprises supplied only one or two different industries in 1986 and 1994 whereas for domestically owned enterprises the figure is much lower, standing at approximately one-fifth. There is also a strong tendency for foreign-owned enterprises to engage in higher product specialization within the product ranges supplied to each industry, a feature which would appear to have been as marked in 1994 as it was in 1986 (ibid.).

Significantly, the tendency towards higher product specialization among foreign-owned enterprises appears to be closely linked to their tendency to participate in the more technologically demanding areas of capital goods production. Foreign-owned enterprises have long been particularly active in the production of electrical energy equipment, control systems, and complex chemical and petrochemical plant production equipment (BNDES 1988; Tadini 1993). Within these product areas, foreign enterprises have tended to specialize. Thus Siemens, for example, has concentrated on the production of heavy hydro-electric generators and transformers, ABB on generators and power transmission equipment, Pirelli on power cables, and Sulzer on fluid pumps, centrifuges, and compressors (ABDIB 1994a; interviews). There remain exceptions, however, to this general rule. Mecânica Pesada and CBC, under French and Japanese ownership respectively, operate in more product areas and supply more industry categories than virtually any Brazilian-owned enterprise with the exceptions of Usiminas Mecânica and D-Z Equipamentos, producing electrical in addition to mechanical equipment (ibid.).

The predominance and persistence of strategies of product diversification within the Brazilian non-serial capital goods sector and the associated low concentration and high pulverization of domestic markets may be viewed in part as arising from the legacy of government policies associated with the original development of the sector and in part from the reaction of enterprises to subsequent reductions in public sector demand and increased openness of the market to external competition. The Second National Development Plan, outlined in Chapter 2, aimed to increase dramatically domestic capacity to produce non-serial capital goods in order to meet burgeoning demand resulting from state expenditures on infrastructure and basic industries within a context of enhanced protection for the sector (Corrêa do Lago et al. 1979: 375–417). In particular, the Plan sought to encourage the entry of Brazilian capital into the sector and to increase the number of enterprises within each market segment in order that a degree of competition and technological 'spread' could be encouraged. The development of the Nucléos de Articulação provided a formal institutional framework within which this process could be undertaken, a framework that remained in place until the mid-1980s.

As the Plan proceeded, new waves of infrastructural projects were initiated, ranging from expanded downstream petrochemical production by Petrobrás to the hydro-electric installations at Itaipú and Xingú and to the sugar-cane alcohol fuel programme (PROALCOOL). As each wave of projects began construction, the state developed fiscal and credit initiatives to encourage the entry of Brazilian producers (particularly those primarily domestically owned) into the production of the new varieties of equipment required of each project. Sensitive to the changing patterns of public sector demand and incentives, enterprises were by the late 1970s and early 1980s expanding their activities into ever greater numbers of product areas with the result that diversification became a marked feature of the sector (Fritsch and Franco 1991a: 132).

Some of the more successful and rapidly expanding enterprises of the period—for example Bardella and Usiminas Mecânica—were notable for the facility they displayed in moving into new product areas, albeit with extensive reliance on imported designs and technical assistance. Domestically owned enterprises also tended to eschew internal technological development in favour of purchasing technology under licence from overseas (see Chapter 5). According to Fritsch and Franco (1991: 132) such a strategy was a 'corollary' of that of extensive diversification: in rejecting technological self-reliance, enterprises hoped to achieve economies of scope and reductions in R&D expenditure.

The behaviour of foreign-owned enterprises during this period differs somewhat from that of domestically owned ones in that the intensity of diversification (with some exceptions) tended to be less. According to Fritsch and Franco (1991: 132), this feature reflected two trends which tended to be more prevalent among such enterprises. First, the tendency towards a greater emphasis on specialization which such enterprises displayed is held to be closely linked to the execution of similar strategies employed by their parent companies on a global scale, a feature discussed in the previous sub-section and one which became of increasing significance towards the end of the 1980s and into the early 1990s (Tadini 1993). Secondly, the pursuit of a relatively narrower, more specialized product range by foreign subsidiaries may have been more feasible for such enterprises because of their lesser relative reliance on the Brazilian domestic market, in particular, that generated by the investment policies of the state. Given the fluctuations and changing pattern of the latter market, multinational subsidiaries with their greater access to international markets would not have needed to diversify to the same extent in order that production capacity could remain adequately utilized.

Thus for the period up until 1987, a combination of the legacy of previous public investment policies and patterns of technological acquisition had brought about a situation in which high diversification and the associated feature of low market concentration had become established characteristics of the Brazilian non-serial capital goods sector and were especially marked where domestic enterprises were concerned. The post-1987 policy changes involving trade liberalization and reductions in public sector capital expenditure might have been expected to have had some impact on this established pattern. Specifically, reductions in public sector demand (which represented between 60 and 70% of demand for Brazilian non-serial capital goods in the mid-1980s), along with increased exposure to international competition, might have been expected to have led to extensive restructuring within the sector as the impetus towards diversification implicit in the Second National Development Plan faded away and the pressure of international competition forced rationalization of product lines and horizontal integration in an effort to achieve competitiveness through greater economies of scale.

However, as the previous section demonstrated, the shift in policy experienced by the sector has not in general—as Hirschman or Baark (Hirschmann

1968; Baark 1991) might have predicted and desired—resulted in a more concentrated sector in line with international norms. The reasons underlying this relatively static picture reflect three main factors, specifically structural inertia among enterprises, risk aversion in the face of changes in policy, and the unwillingness of the state for the most part to facilitate sector restructuring through a relaxation of anti-trust legislation or the implementation of capacity-scrapping programmes.

Chapter 5 demonstrated the continuing reliance of most enterprises within the sector on foreign sources for their technology supplies. The argument was made that the withdrawal of explicit state support for technological development and the uncertain condition of the domestic market since 1987 have tended to encourage the maintenance of technological dependence throughout much of the sector. In addition, the lack of a culture of innovation and a poor record of investment in human capital were seen as factors contributing towards the low levels of technological self-reliance. Given the continued depressed levels of technological capability within many enterprises, the option of altering competitive strategies to those that centred on the development of product specialization and long-run dynamic comparative advantages based on technological advance seems extremely limited. This seems especially true for the most diversified enterprises such as Bardella and Dedini-Zanini. Given the inherited characteristics of such enterprises, therefore, the continued pursuit of strategies that emphasize economies of scope rather than economies of specialization might well appear more appropriate and rational to managers faced with growing competition in domestic and foreign markets, a conclusion that was supported in the course of interviews at ABDIB and with sector consultants.

Of course, as Fritsch and Franco (1991a: 132) accurately point out, such diversification is the corollary of technological dependence: to some extent, many enterprises within the sector would appear to be locked into a path of development in which excessive diversification and technological dependence mutually condition and propagate each other. This structural characteristic would appear to be especially marked in the case in the mechanical equipment and boiler-making sub-sectors where product diversification is strongly associated with frequent resort to technology licensing from overseas (see Tables 38 and 40; Chapter 6).

The pursuit of strategies of risk aversion has also had more direct implications for perceived desirability of maintaining a diversified product range, particularly among domestically owned enterprises in the sector. The desire to spread risk by possessing the capability to produce a wide range of products was given impetus by the implementation of the Second National Development Plan in which firms diversified in response to continued changes in public sector demand. In the post-1987 period, the primary role of the state as a customer has been supplanted by that of the domestic private sector market. The latter market has, of course, experienced numerous fluctuations in both overall demand and its product composition since 1987. In addition, whatever predictability attached to patterns of public sector demand prior to the mid-1980s through the operation of the *Nucléos* has been forgone by their demise. The uncertainty generated by this development has been so great that the sector through ABDIB and with UNIDO support has established its own *Nucléo* in 1993 known as CADE (ABDIB 1994*a*), the development of which was in its infancy at the end of the study period.

Given this situation, it is hardly surprising that firms that have tended to remain relatively more dependent on the domestic market, most particularly domestically owned enterprises, have tended to maintain diversified product ranges as a hedge against fluctuations in the pattern of demand. In the course of interviews with Enterprise *B*, the importance of such risk spreading was emphasized strongly. The larger, foreign-owned subsidiaries have, however, been able to maintain relatively lower levels of product diversification because of their access to export markets through their parent companies and the fact that they often perform a specialist function within the overall multinational organization. A prime examples of this is provided by Enterprise *A*, which is the parent group's main worldwide source for hydro-generators (interviews). Significantly, as Chapter 4 indicated, the specialized multinational subsidiaries have had the most impressive export performance among all Brazilian non-serial capital goods producers.

The maintenance of historical patterns of diversification among enterprises forms only part of the explanation for the continued high degree of pulverization and low degree of concentration existing within most markets for non-serial capital goods. The period since 1986 has seen remarkable little merger activity (considering the apparent potential that exists) and entry and exit both to and from the sector and within its individual market segments has been very limited. The absence of the entry of new firms into the sector would seem hardly surprising given the depressed market conditions that pertained up until 1992 and the uneven recovery that occurred subsequently. However, the fact that hardly any firms have left the sector appears remarkable given the severity of the contraction in the period 1989–91. A number of explanations present themselves to account for the relative lack of restructuring. First, in the period 1986–94, merger activity was subject to often substantial legal constraints associated with the implementation of anti-trust legislation (interviews). Such legislation has tended to be formulated with the objective less of achieving microeconomic efficiency (for example, the achievement of efficient scales of production) than with the prevention of the development of market structures conducive to 'abusive' pricing within the context of a protected economy.

In addition to the force of the general legislation, in the case of the non-serial capital goods sector the state retained its role as a capacity licenser. The state had established this role in the 1970s (Suzigan and Villela 1997) but later proved unwilling to contemplate a wholesale restructuring of the sector involving a wave of mergers (interviews). The lack of firm exit from the sector would appear more difficult to explain though a number of possibilities present themselves. First, as Chapter 4 demonstrated, many firms were able to address their mounting losses (the latter detailed in the next section) by drastic cuts in labour and capital inputs which may have precluded closure. Secondly, Tadini (1993) suggests that many firms adopted a defensive wait and see attitude in the depths of recession, believing that any subsequent recovery would bring about a dramatic improvement in financial performance.

Given the heavy sunk (and functionally specific) capital stock prevalent in much of the sector, such an explanation seems persuasive if one assumes that variable costs could continue to be covered. At the same time, the state did not encourage the exit of firms or removal of excess capacity through capacity-scrapping programmes, for reasons which may have had as much to do with political constraints as with lack of resources. Finally, the national development bank, BNDES, injected capital into some particularly indebted enterprises under the terms of its BNDESPAR programme (BNDES, *Relatório Anual*, various years).

Despite the retention of patterns of diversification and concentration in much of the capital goods sector, the previous section revealed that two sub-sectors, namely, shipbuilding and railway equipment (specifically the locomotive building component), did undergo marked changes in the period between 1986 and 1994. In the case of the shipbuilding sub-sector, significant mergers in 1994 greatly increased concentration in the large vessel and floating structure market segment with the creation of the IVI group under the control of Nelson Tanure. In the locomotive market segment, the number of producers was reduced to one with the formation of GEVISA. The reasons for this relatively greater move towards concentration and specialization are intimately linked to the role of the state both as a customer and as an industrial regulator. In both cases, the sub-sectors had long been characterized by capacity utilization that was far below the average for the non-serial capital goods sector as a whole (see Chart 76). The cumulative effect of such capacity under-utilization and loss making had been to render both the railway equipment and shipbuilding sectors extremely vulnerable to further reductions in demand. By the early 1990s the compression of public sector orders, particularly from Petrobrás, CVRD, and RFFSA resulted in record capacity under-utilization and substantial losses for both sub-sectors (see Chart 76). After a brief recovery, there was yet another decline in public sector orders in 1993.

For the shipbuilding sub-sector, 1993 represented a crisis year in which no further public sector orders were received and the prospects for export orders seemed very bleak (interviews). Following representations by management and unions within the sector, the state, in the form of the SUNAMAN agency and the Sectoral Chamber for Shipbuilding (a management–union–state forum created under the Collor administration), announced the creation of

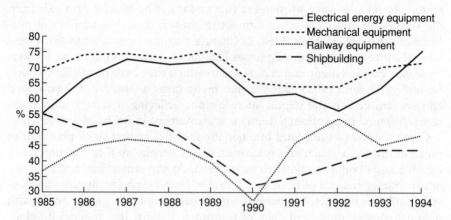

CHART 76. Capacity Utilization in Selected Sub-sectors of the Brazilian Non-serial Capital Goods Sector, 1985–1994

Source: ABDIB, *Relatório Anual*, various years.

a strategic plan for the industry with a promise of increased orders and employment safeguards. Although the latter did not materialize, the state did prove willing to countenance a restructuring of the sector in order to remove excess capacity and stem its ever increasing losses.

Under these circumstances the creation of IVI was permitted and the programme of mergers described in the previous section proceeded. Under the terms of the merger, Ishibrás and Verolme established an efficient division of labour between their yards, with the largest tonnage vessels being produced at the merged enterprise's Rio de Janeiro yard and slightly smaller vessels being constructed along the coast at the former Verolme yard at Angra dos Reis. Engine production was concentrated at the Ishibrás yard in Rio de Janeiro. In a similar vein, the collapse in public sector locomotive orders in conjunction with the entry of EMAQ into the IVI group precipitated a situation in which the state was forced to accept the creation of GEVISA: the dearth of orders, chronic capacity under-utilization (only one locomotive was produced in the whole of 1992 and 1993 (ABIFER 1993)), and losses left it little alternative. Thus, increasing concentration appears to have been most pronounced where a point of crisis had been reached within particular sectors and mergers were accepted as an alternative to enterprise failure.

6.2 Financial Performance in the Brazilian Non-serial Capital Goods Sector

Although the Brazilian non-serial capital goods sector has undergone a number of performance changes in response to policy shifts in the period since 1986, so far the only ones that have been analysed in this book have been technological capability, productivity, and export performance. For many managers and shareholders within the sector, the latter performance criteria have only been of significance inasmuch as they constitute pointers towards a number of ultimate objectives, those objectives being the avoidance of insolvency, the reduction of debt, and an increase in rates of return on capital (interviews). An examination of these measures would therefore appear to be in order to see whether the changes described in the previous chapters have been associated with an improvement in 'bottom-line' financial performance.

At the same time, data on financial performance allow a picture to be built up of the financial constraints under which enterprises have been operating. In particular, the build-up of losses in the early part of the period and initial reductions in liquidity help to explain why short-run strategies of rationalization rather than modernization predominated in the sector's adjustment and why technological self-reliance remained at a low level.

Four indicators of financial performance are available with which to examine the Brazilian non-serial capital goods sector. The first, return on equity, shows total annual net profits as a percentage of total equity capital for each sub-sector. The second, net profits (losses), measures profits or losses occurring in each financial year, expressed in constant 1990 US dollars. The third, the liquidity ratio, provides an indication of the relationship between liquid assets and short- and long-run liabilities and is obtained by dividing working capital plus other realizable assets by short- and long-term liabilities. The higher the value of the ratio, the more liquid is the total sub-sectoral financial position. The indebtedness ratio is calculated by dividing total liabilities by total assets. The smaller the value of the ratio, the relatively less is the burden of debt for the sub-sector.

For the electrical energy equipment sub-sector, Chart 78 reveals a marked deterioration of profitability in the period up to 1992, with the sector recording losses for 1990 and 1991. This was followed by a substantial recovery in the two subsequent years which saw a rapid restoration of profitability. Despite the move into losses for 1990 and 1991, the sub-sector has been among the most consistently and highly profitable of all the sub-sectors, something that is confirmed if calculations of return on equity are performed (see Chart 77). For reasons of graphical clarity, the data on the railway equipment sector are included in a separate chart (Chart 77b).

Like other sub-sectors with the exception of the railway equipment sub-sector, the electrical energy equipment sub-sector has experienced a reasonably consistent fall in indebtedness between 1988 and 1993 (Chart 78). At the same time, the liquidity ratio tended to rise over the period, following a fall in the years prior to 1988. Thus, in sum, the financial strength of enterprises in the sub-sector tended to improve in the course of the period under consideration, despite losses in the early part of the 1990s as the public sector spending freeze and the domestic recession reduced domestic demand substantially.

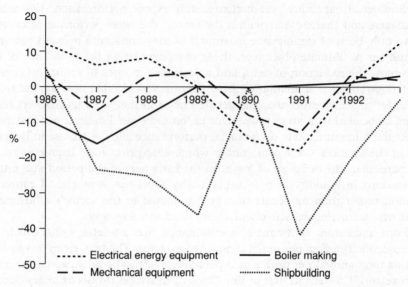

CHART 77. Return on Equity in the Brazilian Non-serial Capital Goods Sector, 1986–1993 (1986 = 100)

Source: ABDIB, *Relatório Anual*, various years.

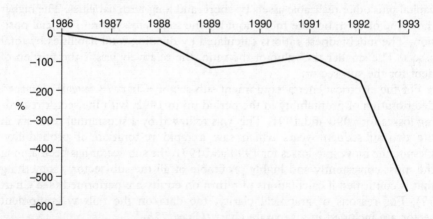

CHART 77*b*. Return on Equity in the Railway Equipment Sub-sector, 1986–1993 (1986 = 100)

Source: ABDIB, *Relatório Anual*, various years.

For the mechanical equipment sub-sector, levels of profitability have tended to be lower than for the electrical energy equipment sector (though often higher in terms of return on equity). Like the electrical energy equipment sector, there was a sharp fall into loss as the recession was experienced at the beginning of the 1990s although there was a subsequent recovery (Chart 79). In

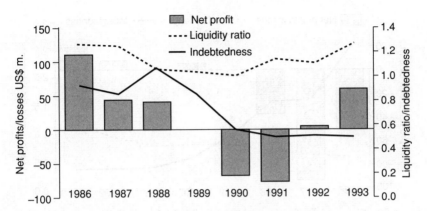

CHART 78. Financial Performance in the Electrical Energy Equipment
Sub-sector, 1986–1993

Note: 1989 figure is $0.

Source: ABDIB, *Relatório Anual*, various years.

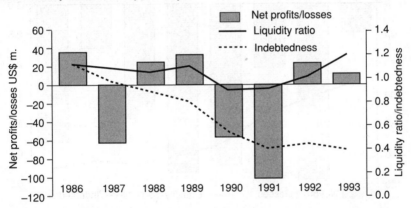

CHART 79. Financial Performance in the Mechanical Equipment Sub-sector,
1986–1993

Source: ABDIB, *Relatório Anual*, various years.

common with other sub-sectors there was a distinct trend for indebtedness
to fall and, after 1990, for liquidity to improve.

The boiler-making sector experienced consistent losses up until 1990 and
even subsequently, the profit performance having been comparatively poor
set against that of other sub-sectors. However, the sector experienced a trend
improvement in profitability performance as its losses were reduced year by
year (Chart 80). In common with other sub-sectors, there is a marked tendency for indebtedness to fall and for the liquidity position to improve.

The railway equipment and shipbuilding sub-sectors were in a particularly
precarious financial state throughout the post-1987 period and experienced

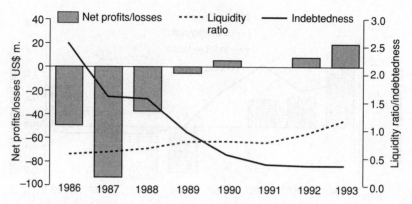

CHART 80. Financial Performance in the Boiler-Making Sub-sector, 1986–1993
Note: 1991 figure is $0.

Source: ABDIB, *Relatório Anual*, various years.

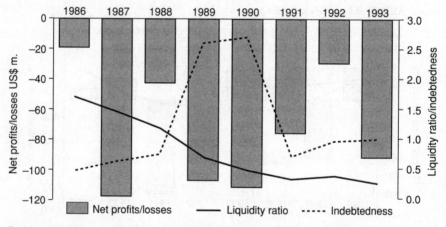

CHART 81. Financial Performance in the Railway Equipment Sub-sector, 1986–1993

Source: ABDIB, *Relatório Anual*, various years.

very substantial under-utilization of capacity. The poor financial state of these sectors is illustrated in Charts 81 and 82.

For the railway equipment sub-sector, the data indicate the absence of profits throughout the period and, uniquely, a tendency for the liquidity ratio to deteriorate consistently, pointing to the sector's growing difficulty in meeting its financial obligations. For the railway sector, the rise in loss making hit chronic proportions as indicated by the data for return on equity in Chart 77b.

The shipbuilding sub-sector is also characterized by extensive periods of loss making, although a period of recovery would appear to be under way

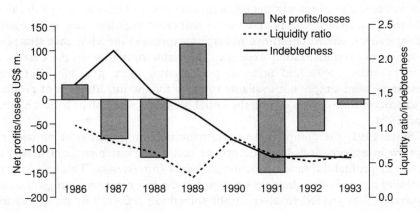

CHART 82. Financial Performance in the Shipbuilding Sub-sector, 1986–1993
Source: ABDIB, *Relatório Anual*, various years.

from 1991 onwards, though losses were still being made in 1993. In common with most other sectors, indebtedness appears to have fallen consistently over the period while there was a moderate improvement in the liquidity ratio from 1989 onwards. Because data are only available up to 1993 they do not fully indicate the impact of the crisis that hit the industry towards the end of 1993 when the industry temporarily faced an empty order book and a phase of mergers commenced. In fact, the crisis brought about intensified losses and increasing indebtedness throughout the sector. In the case of the IVI group, debts have mounted considerably, including US$ 280 m. owed to Ishikawajima Heavy Industries, US$ 15 m. owed to *Banque Nationale de Paris*, R$ 10.9 m. owed to *Banco do Brasil*, and a loan package from the Union Bank of Switzerland (*Jornal do Brasil Online*, 8 Feb. 1996). By early 1996 IVI was in the position of having to sell fixed assets (principally office property) in order to pay instalments on the debt (ibid.).

Thus, in general, the period between 1986 and 1993 saw an improvement in financial performance for most of the non-serial capital goods sector, at least as measured by the liquidity and the indebtedness ratios. After a sharp fall at the beginning of the 1990s, profitability began to improve. Despite this generally 'optimistic' picture, the shipbuilding and railway equipment sectors showed few signs of increasing financial health with increasing indebtedness and liquidity problems. Having made a brief assessment of the financial performance of enterprises, the question then arises as to the light the measures employed can throw on the issues of static and dynamic efficiency.

The rapidly deteriorating financial position of enterprises in the late 1980s, triggered for the most part by the decline in public sector orders, made it imperative that enterprises adjust in a manner whereby increasing losses could be stemmed and indebtedness reduced. Given this context of financial fragility, it hardly seems surprising that enterprises' initial reactions made themselves felt in the shape of rationalization, with capacity and inputs being substantially reduced. Indeed, this point arose on numerous occasions during the course of interviews, where enterprise managers expressed the view that strategies emphasizing rationalization were the only viable option given the deterioration in order books and financial performance more generally. Financial resources were simply not available to allow for the introduction of product and process innovations during the initial period of adjustment between 1987 and 1991.

Since 1991, the completion of rationalization programmes along with an upturn in exports and domestic private sector markets have contributed to a rise in profitability and reduction in losses (interviews). This rise in profitability has provided the context in which the less reactive strategy of modernization has tended to assert itself, something reflected in the increasing efforts made towards process innovation which were noted in Chapter 3.

Conclusions

Evidence arising from an examination of patterns of concentration, diversification, and financial performance in the Brazilian non-serial capital goods sector over the period encompassed by the post-1987 policy shifts points to a mixed picture in terms of static and dynamic efficiency gains. In the case of issues of concentration and diversification, the legacy of the state policies pursued in the 1970s and early 1980s, combined with institutional inertia, risk aversion, and an unwillingness by the state to facilitate or contemplate sectoral consolidation have in general resulted in the maintenance of a very diversified and pulverized non-serial capital goods sector. The retention of such an industrial structure at a time of increased international specialization and technological intensity within the global non-serial capital sector would appear to place a grave obstacle to the achievement of long-run dynamic efficiencies and the development of comparative advantages inside the Brazilian sector.

In terms of financial performance, most sub-sectors appear to have improved profitability, reduced debt, and enhanced their liquidity. However, the improvements came in the wake of substantial loss making and increases in indebtedness in the period up until 1991. The more recent improvements in the financial performance of enterprises would appear to be providing the context in which enterprises are switching the emphasis of their strategies away from rationalization towards modernization.

7

Conclusions

The discussion so far has aimed to assess the effects of progressive reductions in the role of the state on the development of an advanced industrial sector in an important emerging market economy. Specifically, an attempt has been made to establish the impacts of rapid market liberalization on the competitive performance of the Brazilian non-serial capital goods sector through the examination of alterations in static and dynamic efficiency. In doing so, it was hoped that some light could be shed on the theoretical issue of whether a withdrawal of the state would be likely to induce benefits or losses in terms of such efficiencies.

This chapter draws together the key conclusions from earlier chapters in an attempt to address this key question. In addition, however, the discussion examines a number of important practical issues with direct relevance to investors and policy-makers in an emerging market setting. First, a number of policy conclusions are derived regarding possible future roles for the state in the development of the Brazilian non-serial capital goods sector. Secondly, a number of lessons are drawn from the specific case of the sector which have broader relevance for the formulation of industrial policy, not only within Latin America but in other emerging market regions. Finally, the future prospects for the Brazilian capital goods sector are considered, taking into account the potential roles of MERCOSUL, hemispheric integration, and foreign direct investment.

7.1 Liberalization and Industrial Performance: Some Theoretical Implications

The Brazilian non-serial capital goods sector, whose initial growth and expansion took place within the context of enhanced protection and rapid increases in infrastructural investment under the terms of the Second National Development Plan, began to face a very different set of policy circumstances from 1987 onwards as long-established mechanisms of support and protection were rapidly stripped away. The combined impacts of trade liberalization, reductions in fiscal incentives for technological development and public sector procurement brought about a situation, which by the end of the study period (1995), meant that the sector was far more exposed to the forces of international competition than at any time since the early 1970s. To a very great extent, the 1987–94 period marked the ending of the Brazilian state's supremacy as a guiding influence in the development of the sector. Incentive structures generated by the operation of the public sector came to be supplanted by those emerging from increasingly competitive private foreign and domestic markets.

In the course of the investigation, the evidence uncovered tended to suggest a reasonably clearly defined set of conclusions in respect of the impact of the changing role of the state on the performance of the Brazilian non-serial capital goods sector. In terms of the development of static efficiencies, Chapter 3 suggested that considerable alterations had occurred and that a definite linkage existed between this and the progressive withdrawal of the state after 1987. Specifically, rapid contractions in public sector procurement of capital goods between 1987 and 1991 forced enterprises throughout the sector to engage in a programme of cutting capital and labour inputs to match the lower levels of demand prevalent under the new policy régime. Gains in static efficiency arose as more intensive use was made of each unit of factor input following a period in which there was substantial under-utilization of such inputs. Such capacity contractions were held to account for some of the gains in labour and capital productivity that arose following an upturn in the domestic private sector and the export market as levels of capacity utilization rose and inputs were used more intensively. The data even suggested that sub-sectors of the non-serial capital goods sector that had experienced the most severe contractions in public sector demand and were most involved in the export markets eventually developed the most rapid gains in capital and labour productivity.

However, the influence of contractions in public sector demand was not the only factor of importance in the determination of such increases in intensity of factor usage. Chapter 3 also suggested that the sharp private sector recession between 1989 and 1991 could be viewed as an important determining factor, as could the influence of progressive trade liberalization. The latter, in conjunction with the collapse of traditional domestic public sector markets, forced enterprises to become more reliant on exports while making the domestic market in general increasingly open and competitive. These influences maintained the pressure on enterprises to match capacity to demand and avoid the emergence of underemployed inputs. Thus, in general, reductions in inputs and increases in output per unit of input (productivity) were maintained once the domestic private sector market recovered and exports accelerated.

The issue of quality provides, in part, another manifestation of the increasing efforts on behalf of enterprises to raise static efficiencies through the better implementation of existing production techniques. Chapter 4 identified a strong linkage between the increased reliance on exports among enterprises in the sector and the heightened importance of quality issues in the production process. In terms of quality, the role of the state was seen to have been of importance in that reductions in public procurement and increased import penetration (resulting from the impact of trade liberalization) forced enterprises to become more export oriented and thus more subject to the increasingly stringent quality demands of international markets. At the same time, the state had been actively encouraging a greater focus on quality throughout the sector through the operation of the Brazilian Quality and Productivity Programme (PBQP). To the extent that improvements in quality reflected the superior operation of constant production techniques, then it is clear that static efficiency gains resulted. However, evidence from the case studies and additional secondary evidence suggested that much of the improvement in quality performance throughout the sector occurred in the context of substantial reorganization of plant and production processes. This was particularly true for enterprises who were pursuing, or had achieved, formal quality certification. Thus, the dynamic component of increasingly good quality performance was likely to be substantial.

The evolution of other forms of dynamic efficiency within the Brazilian non-serial capital goods sector, following the withdrawal of the state, formed the major focus of the investigation. The evidence revealed in the course of the analysis pointed to the existence of two contrasting pictures as far as improvements in dynamic efficiencies were concerned. In terms of process innovation, Chapter 3 highlighted the extent to which enterprises within the sector had engaged in modernization and reorganization of their production processes. Identified changes in production techniques indicated that enterprises were making efforts to move towards flexible specialization, a relatively new concept in manufacturing which has come to represent something of an international industry standard. In some cases just-in-time techniques had been introduced on the shop floor along with production cells, changes in shop-floor layout, and suites of numerically controlled machine tools.

The progressive introduction of flexible specialization as the key principle governing the production of non-serial capital goods was seen to be associated with and linked to improvements in productivity in the sector, particularly in the period following 1990 which was associated with a rise in exports and a recovery in the domestic private sector market. Evidence presented in Chapters 3 and 5 indicated that, to some extent, the strategy of modernizing the production process through the use of flexible specialization tended to supersede that of the absolute reduction in factor inputs which had predominated in the period up until 1990. The role of the state in promoting the observed process innovations was held to arise from the desire of enterprises to raise productivity, reduce unit costs, and improve quality in the light of increased exposure to international competition. This latter was brought about through the influence of trade liberalization and the increasing reliance of the sector on export markets given the reductions in domestic public sector demand. However, it was noted that the spread of new production techniques among enterprises in the sector was by no means universal or homogeneous, although the trend towards their increased adoption was unmistakable. At the same time, it is important to note that the dynamic gains arising from the introduction of modernizing process innovations had as much to do with reorganization of plant and equipment as with technological upgrading such as new machinery and enhanced training. To some extent, the character of the observed process innovations suggests more of an organizational and conceptual revolution among enterprises than a strictly technological one.

The relatively significant dynamic changes observed in the field of process innovation, are not mirrored in that of product innovation, where a tendency towards relatively static patterns of technological development and acquisition was noted. In particular, the majority of enterprises within the sector remained highly reliant on basic designs and research and development originating outside Brazil. Product technologies tended to be transferred to enterprises based in Brazil either through licensing agreements or in the course of intra-transnational corporation transfer of designs and personnel. In the majority of cases, technological inputs within the sector were restricted to the adaptation of externally generated basic designs for local production. At the same time, research and development effort within most enterprises remained at very low levels and, in some cases, even this restricted activity appeared to be under threat as competitive pressures mounted on management to reduce costs.

Overall, the observed patterns of such technological behaviour throughout the period of the withdrawal of the state appeared to differ little from those which had preceded them. As such, the Brazilian non-serial capital goods sector remains highly technologically dependent. Despite this general pattern, a few examples were uncovered where Brazilian subsidiaries of transnational corporations were engaging in their own research, development, and basic design activity as part of an overall strategy of regional and divisional specialization. However, such technological intensity remains the exception rather than the rule.

In accounting for the lack of dynamism in technological development and acquisition revealed by the sector, a number of explanations were highlighted, all of which related to the role of the state either prior or subsequent to its post-1987 withdrawal. Most significantly, the reductions in public sector expenditures on non-serial capital goods had eliminated a stable revenue base from which to finance more costly or risky innovative activity. At the same time, the increased insertion of the sector into the international market following trade liberalization and the collapse of public sector demand had made the sector increasingly reliant on markets where well-known technology brand-names were of increasing importance in securing sales. In addition, the virtual demise of government funding for technological innovation had provided a further disincentive to pursue more technologically ambitious strategies.

Despite all of these considerations, doubt was expressed as to whether a resumption in direct funding for technological development, increased protection, or a recovery in public sector procurement would necessarily alter the patterns of technological development and acquisition which, in fact, had become deeply rooted in the sector prior to the reform period. The analysis suggested that long-established structural impediments were preventing the development of greater technological self-reliance. In particular, high levels of product diversification, the absence of well-developed user–producer linkages, and relatively poor university–industry relationships provided obstacles to the sector's achievement of greater technological mastery of product design and innovation. The analysis suggested that these issues would need to be addressed in the framing of any future policy to promote the development of the sector. As things stand, the Brazilian non-serial capital goods sector's relative inability to generate anything but a fraction of the product technologies it employs would appear to present great cause for concern, given that its theoretical *raison d'être* supposedly lies in its inherent ability to generate and diffuse dynamic efficiency gains. It is clear that dynamic efficiencies connected with product innovation and technological self-reliance have not been associated with the sort of increases that may be observed in the case of process innovations. As such, the effect of shifting policy on dynamic gains would appear to be somewhat lop-sided.

In sum, the withdrawal of the state in the period since 1987 does appear to have resulted in some notable changes in the performance characteristics of the Brazilian non-serial capital goods sector. However, such performance changes have tended to reflect an increasing strategic priority among enterprises aimed at achieving cost competitiveness and high levels of quality rather than upgrading the inherent technological sophistication of the products themselves or the enterprise's capacity to develop and design them. The strategies employed would therefore appear rather conservative, especially in the light of their relatively low technological content either from a process or product innovation perspective. Dantas (1993), in the context of the Brazilian mechanical engineering industry as a whole, aptly terms this strategic ethos one of 'defensive modernization' (translated from the Portuguese). To what extent does this generally adopted pattern of response to the retraction of the state accord with the theoretical perspectives as to the role of the state outlined in Chapter 1?

Many aspects of the behaviour of the Brazilian non-serial capital goods sector in the course of the withdrawal of the state would appear to be reflected in the predictions derived from different theoretical perspectives in earlier chapters. The neoliberal and neoclassical literature advocating a withdrawal of the state as a procurer of non-serial capital goods, as a granter of fiscal subsidies, and as an agent of protection suggested that productivity, quality, and technological sophistication would tend to benefit as the role of the state diminished and the sector became increasingly inserted into the international market. In part, the evidence revealed in this study lends support to this conclusion.

Following the collapse in public sector demand and the progressive removal of trade barriers, enterprises responded with a mixture of capacity cuts and, eventually, reorganization of production processes in order to stem losses and respond to the challenge of an increasingly competitive environment. At the same time there was a substantial increase in the export activities of enterprises and a concurrent augmentation of efforts within the sector to improve levels of quality. All in all, the evidence suggests that the sector delivered a combination of productivity growth, reductions in unused capacity, a rise in quality, and a substantial acceleration in export growth. Such a combination of performance improvements would appear to fit in extremely well with the predictions implicit in the neoliberal and some of the neoclassical literature. As market signals replace those of the state, enterprises respond and attempt to optimize in the new environment, resulting in static and some dynamic gains.

Equally, however, the alterations in sector performance highlighted above would appear to be consistent with Contemporary Structuralist accounts of the impacts engendered by increased exposure to export markets for certain formerly heavily protected industrial sectors in South Korea. In such cases, the relative incentive to export was increased through a degree of trade liberalization and export promotion measures. The role of the state, however, remained fairly strong and certainly did not correspond to the dramatic retraction experienced in Brazil.

Despite the positive performance aspects described above, from the perspective of certain theoretical viewpoints, concern would arise that, in engaging in such short-run optimization, the Brazilian non-serial capital goods sector was failing fully to realize all of its potentially achievable dynamic efficiency gains. For such theorists, the full achievement of dynamic gains is only held to be feasible, given an alternative policy environment in which the state plays a more significant role. Indeed, from the perspective of Contemporary Structuralist and some neoclassical viewpoints, the major deficiency in both the theoretical foundations and policy recommendations of the neoliberal approach is its relegation if not negation of the importance, potential, and possibilities of the generation of long-run dynamic efficiencies and comparative advantages in the process of industrialization.

For the former groups of economists, the non-serial capital goods sector constitutes a vital repository of skills, technologies, and positive externalities that are likely to suffer if the operation of markets alone provides signals and incentives. Although recognizing that exposure to international competition and a reduction in the state's purview is capable of inducing certain categories of efficiency improvement, concern remains that, without sufficient state involvement in certain areas, technological capability, self-reliance, and the long-run dynamic efficiencies which they convey are likely, at least in part, to be forgone.

To the extent that the experience of the Brazilian non-serial capital goods sector in the post-1987 period demonstrates the persistence of low levels of technological self-reliance, particularly with respect to basic designs, then the view of more pro-interventionist economists is upheld. Crucially, however, such economists would have to recognize that technological dynamism in the area of product innovation failed to flourish even in the period preceding the withdrawal of the state. While the removal of the state from many aspects of the sector's activity may have exacerbated its condition of technological stagnation and inertia, it is evident that these policy shifts alone cannot fully explain the phenomenon. By the same token, it seems highly unlikely that a restoration of the *ancien régime* of policy would succeed in significantly enhancing its performance in this area.

Overall, therefore, the evidence uncovered in the course of the book suggests that the withdrawal of the state from the Brazilian non-serial capital goods sector presented certain costs and benefits, the significance of which depends on the particular theoretical viewpoint adopted. For neoliberals and some neoclassical economists, the primacy of short-run optimization in their theoretical outlook would allow the impact of the state's withdrawal on the Brazilian non-serial capital goods sector to be classified as essentially favourable. For economists of a more pro-interventionist perspective, the achievement of greater static efficiencies and limited dynamic efficiencies (the latter arising from process innovations) must be seen in the context of continuing weakness with regard to product innovation.

Despite the predictive successes displayed by the theoretical literature discussed above, it will be clear that both mainstream anti- and pro-interventionist accounts suffer from significant weaknesses. While the anti-interventionist literature accurately predicts certain facets of sector behaviour, it fails adequately to address or predict the phenomenon of technological inertia with regard to product innovation, surely a crucial issue with respect to a developing country's capital goods sector. In large part, this may be due to the secondary role that technology plays in a literature where short-run optimization remains a benchmark of industrial performance. Much of the literature more supportive of state intervention recognizes the importance of dynamic efficiencies in the development of the capital goods sector, yet does not appear to be able to offer a full explanation as to the long-run technological stagnation of the sector, especially in the field of product innovation. The absence of such an explanation is especially disturbing given the sector's supposedly crucial role as a generator and diffuser of technological progress. However, the theoretical work of some Contemporary Structuralist and neo-Schumpetarian writers would appear to lend itself to a more fruitful approach to the understanding of the problems of the sector and the manner of its behaviour over the period of the study.

Contemporary Structuralists and neo-Schumpeterians such as Lall (1994), Amsden (1989), and Perez and Soete (1988) are very conscious that interventions, to be successful, need to pay regard to the institutional and structural characteristics of the industrial sectors to which policy is to apply. By the same token, a full understanding of the impacts of changing interventions on industrial sectors is only realizable when recognition is made of the particular institutional and structural circumstances of the sector. In the case of the Brazilian non-serial capital goods sector, previous chapters underlined the basic structural features which tended to condition the continuing weaknesses of the sector, particularly with regard to product innovation. In brief, these were the existence of excessive product diversification, the emergence of a culture of risk aversion among enterprises, continuing market uncertainty, and the lack of a national system of innovation. Only through addressing these features, it was argued, could the Brazilian non-serial capital goods sector have achieved its full potential to deliver long-run dynamic efficiency gains.

The tackling of these deeper-rooted structural features was not addressed in the course of the post-1987 policy reforms, nor would it be with a return to the older policy régime. To the extent that the problems and performance of the Brazilian non-serial capital goods sector partly reflect these institutional and structural weaknesses, the theoretical approach offered by the Contemporary Structuralists seems especially appropriate. However, it should be stressed that the Contemporary Structuralist approach offers more of a methodological approach to the understanding of particular circumstances than a set of invariant theoretical predictions. Over the period of the study, the Brazilian non-serial capital goods sector has come to face a series of very challenging conditions brought about by far-reaching policy reforms. The sector, which once formed the commanding heights of a developmentalist military régime's industrial economy, has made the transition to participation in an international competitive environment where market signals have supplanted the guiding hand of the state. To some extent, the sector has emerged the stronger, having substantially increased its levels of productive efficiency and having integrated itself into international markets to an extent which would have been inconceivable in the mid-1970s. This is an especially impressive achievement given the severity of the conditions faced by the sector and the sharpness of the policy transformation. However, long-standing structural weaknesses remain, not the least of which is a general systemic inability to become more technologically self-reliant.

7.2 Policy Implications

(i) Implications for the Brazilian Non-serial Capital Goods Sector

Now that the policy environment has stabilized to some extent, the sector is able to look forward to the future with a little more certainty. In doing so, however, it is important that participants within the industry and policy-makers remain focused on the key strategic issues facing the sector. In particular, in the light of a growing international trend towards specialization and technological intensity, it seems unlikely that the sector's traditional pattern of diversification and technological dependency will prove sustainable given that it is more exposed than ever to international competitive pressures. At some stage in the future it seems inevitable that the sector will be forced to undergo a phase of consolidation with greater emphasis on specialization, if it is to emulate the competitive strategies of any of its international counterparts.

At the same time, it seems likely that traditional patterns of technological acquisition will have to be reviewed, if the sector is to build market share through anything other than price competitiveness. In some areas of non-serial capital goods production such as turbines, even the maintenance of low prices is unlikely to provide a guarantee of maintenance of market share. The gaining of international market share through technological edge is likely to require a greater emphasis on technological self-reliance as licensers of technology will be unwilling to countenance the transfer of their most up to date technologies to potential or actual competitors. Taken together, the related needs to achieve greater specialization and technological self-reliance constitute an enormous challenge for the Brazilian non-serial capital goods sector, but is one which it must face if its long-term viability and role in the development process is to be maintained. The meeting of this challenge is likely to require more than the individual efforts of enterprises. For a number of reasons outlined previously, many of the obstacles to such a reform are systemic in nature and are likely to require the application of careful and selective state interventions.

Perhaps the most critical role for the state lies not in the arena of traditional, sector-specific interventions but in the provision of more generic policies that enhance competitiveness. Such policies provide a favourable background for the development of efficient industrial capacity while leaving micro-level resource allocation decisions predominantly in the hands of the private sector. The enhancement of competitiveness in the Brazilian non-serial capital goods sector will require more effective and comprehensive involvement of the state in a number of key areas. First, the state will need to assume some of the costs and organizational burden involved in strengthening linkages between firms and research institutes. In the course of this book, it has been frequently noted that an important systemic explanation for technological conservatism and dependence on foreign designs lies in the weak institutional linkages which enterprises have with both domestic users and producers of technology. Through the proliferation and strengthening of these links, Brazil would move further towards the possession of a viable National System of Innovation, a development which would greatly enhance domestic technological capabilities and render possible changes in technological strategy among enterprises. There are already signs that policy may be moving in this direction. Following the passage of Law 8661 in 1993, special financial incentives are provided for enterprises which conduct R&D in association with research institutes (Matesco and Hasenclever 1996). The Law also makes specific provision for a series of incentives aimed at the promotion of intra-enterprise R&D.

The provision of incentives of the nature described above will not be sufficient, however, to ensure that technological dynamism thrives within the sector. Investment in technology, like any other investment, is a risky activity and is particularly vulnerable to shifts in medium- to long-run expectations concerning future levels of demand. The experience of the 1980s demonstrated that macro-economic instability strongly contributed to under-investment and technological conservatism in the sector, particularly in relation to product innovation. Consequently, over the next few years, it is important that such instability is minimized and a smooth growth path adopted. However, despite the early achievements of the Real Plan, strong tendencies towards fiscal and external disequilibria remain. These, in turn, have promoted something of a stop–go approach to economic management. This source of instability will have to be removed in order that more favourable conditions for investment are created.

The need to create a more specialized Brazilian non-serial capital goods sector has been highlighted frequently in the course of this book. Again, the state will have a role to play in any process of industrial restructuring that emerges. During the years of ISI, the state tended to look unfavourably on any tendency towards increased concentration in the sector. This was because, in the partial absence of foreign competition, heightened domestic competition was seen as an appropriate means of maintaining downward pressure on prices. With the advent of the *Abertura Comercial*, however, this long-held position is in need of urgent reform. Faced with intensified international competition and the need to achieve the economies of scale implicit in specialization, the state will need to adopt a more accommodative approach to mergers and acquisitions. Indeed, there are already signs that this is happening, given the sharp rise in merger activity across the entire industrial sector between 1994 and 1998.

The insertion of the sector into the international economy has, as Chapter 4 indicated, led to an increased emphasis on the export market for enterprises within the sector. Given the continuing shrinkage of public sector fixed capital investment and increased import penetration of the domestic market, this is a trend which is likely to continue. The state, through the operation of FINAMEX and other export finance programmes, has already proved willing to support the export activities of the sector.

However, there is a recognition within the sector, and Brazilian industry as a whole, that more needs to be done to overcome a number of specific competitive disadvantages in the export market. These disadvantages, collectively labelled the *Custo Brasil* (Brazil Cost), largely consist of unfavourable tax treatment for exports and the inadequacy of infrastructure for their shipment. In particular, there has been concern at the impact of the state government imposed value-added tax (the ICMS), employers' social security contributions, and the cost and efficiency of port facilities. Once again, the state appears to be making some progress in these areas. The process of port privatization has begun with major investments and efficiency gains promised. At the same time, the federal government has recently succeeded in having ICMS exemption granted to industrial exports.

(ii) Implications for Trade and Industrial Policy in Other Emerging Market Countries

The experience of the Brazilian non-serial capital goods sector under trade and market liberalization contains some important lessons for the pursuit of trade and industrial policy in other emerging market countries. Most importantly, the analysis of the sector's response to changes in the policy environment indicates that the impacts of trade and market liberalization are by no means always unambiguously favourable. This conclusion is broadly similar to that reached by a number of other studies examining liberalization episodes other than that of Brazil (see Chapter 1).

More specifically, the experience of the Brazilian non-serial capital goods sector points to the importance of distinguishing between static and dynamic effects when evaluating the impact of liberalization. In particular, the sector's reactions tend to suggest that there may be substantial gains in static efficiency as excess capacity is removed and existing production processes optimized. However, the pursuit of critically important, but less observable, dynamic efficiencies may be underemphasized in the course of this process.

This conclusion has particular significance for policy-makers as it is by no means unique to the Brazilian capital goods sector. A number of studies examining different sectors and countries have produced broadly similar results (see e.g. Katz 1996; Unger 1994). The bulk of evidence to date suggests that policy-makers need to be aware of the differential impacts of liberalization on individual components of corporate strategy.

The core challenge facing all emerging-market advanced industrial sectors undergoing structural transformation is to simultaneously achieve global competitiveness while contributing to the process of national development. The preceding chapters demonstrated that such an objective may be hard to achieve if policies of liberalization are unaccompanied by measures that seek to support the development of longer-run dynamic efficiencies. The key question, of course, concerns the nature of appropriate policies. The experience of the Brazilian capital goods sector in the pre-liberalization era suggested that traditional interventionist approaches are likely to give rise to only limited learning and dynamic gains. Such a conclusion is strongly reminiscent of the findings of a number of other country and sectoral studies of which Katz (1987) and Fransman (1986) are prime examples.

In essence, traditional interventionist approaches failed for two reasons. First, the stifling of market competition through enhanced protectionism blunted the challenge-response mechanism which, under a more liberal regime, might have been expected to stimulate innovative efforts. Secondly, traditional approaches failed to develop institutional structures, incentives, and linkages which would have supported to a greater extent the adoption of more

ambitious technological strategies at enterprise level. The absence of such
structures also ensured that the fruits of technological progress emerging from
advanced industrial sectors were not adequately diffused throughout the rest
of the economy.

The new policy context of accelerated liberalization and the shrinkage of the
state renders inevitable the abandonment of the old model of intervention.
As the market supplants the guiding hand of the state, incentives generated
by enhanced levels of competition are forcing enterprises to reconfigure their
competitive strategies. In doing so, this book has argued, enterprises are more
likely to focus on the pursuit of strategies which are predominantly short
run in orientation. In other words, without additional policy input, the new
liberal model threatens to replicate the sins of the past, threatening the long-
run viability of the industrial sector. In order to counter this threat, policy-
makers will need to develop incentive and institutional structures supportive
of longer-run optimization.

The most urgent policy requirement in the new competitive environment
consists of the need to develop a better institutional context for the pursuit
of longer-run technological strategies among enterprises. One of the defining
characteristics of less developed economies is the weakness of inter- and
intra-industry technological linkages and technology transfer networks con-
necting enterprises with public and private sector research institutes. The absence
of such structures leads to the emergence of national innovative capacities
that are both weakened and disarticulated. This, in turn, greatly increases the
chances that enterprises will resort to foreign technologies where the development of domestic alternatives might have been both economically feasible
and favourable to the development process.

The development of domestic technology transfer networks, and the institutions that act as their nodes, offers the means by which domestic innovative effort can be both increased and its fruits more effectively captured in the
economy at large. The provision of such networks would need to be supplemented by measures targeted at individual enterprises. Such measures would
aim at increasing the attractiveness at innovation through, for example, the
provision of financial incentives or favourable tax treatment. In particular,
tax policy in many emerging market economies needs to become a lot more
favourable towards long-term investment, especially where R&D expenditure
is concerned.

However, such incentives and institutional frameworks are only likely to
be effective in achieving their objectives provided that appropriate skills are
available. In many emerging market economies, Brazil included, the shortage of such human capital has provided a substantial obstacle in the path of
technological self-reliance. The challenge facing policy-makers is therefore
to improve the quality of human capital at all levels. This will involve a much
greater emphasis on the development of applied science and substantial skill
upgrading of manufacturing personnel. The importance of such investment

is now being recognized within most industrialized emerging market economies. The increasing complexity of technologies and production processes means that the rapid development of human capital, ignored for so long, can now no longer be viewed as a luxury.

The pursuit of longer-run corporate strategies emphasizing greater national technological self-reliance should not be taken to imply that technological autarchy is an appropriate long-run objective. Instead, efforts to induce greater technological self-reliance should be selective and concentrate on sectors in which developed comparative advantages already exist or in which readily exploitable market opportunities are at hand. These criteria are, of course, employed by the private sector which, in any case, should have the final say over which technologies are to be developed. However, the fact that imports of foreign technologies will remain indispensable should not obscure the necessity to continually improve domestic technological capabilities. In this context, efforts should be made to maximize the learning that takes place as a result of such technology transfers. This can be achieved through a combination of measures to encourage intra-enterprise R&D and the screening of technology transfer contracts. The screening process employed should try to ensure that contracts involve elements of 'know-why' as well as 'know-how' transfer. In addition, contracts should be scrutinized to ensure that the learning effects of any transfer are able to spread beyond the recipient enterprise.

The final crucial element in any policy complex designed to promote the pursuit of dynamic efficiencies is that of long-term credit. In Brazil, as in many other emerging economies, higher risk premia and thinner capital markets have often resulted in market interest rates greatly exceeding those in developed industrialized countries. This persistence of this situation partially underlies the history of technological under-investment highlighted in the course of this book. Given this situation, efforts need to be made to bring down interest rates to internationally prevailing levels. This would bring the cost of capital faced by emerging market enterprises into line with that of their advanced economy competitors. In the long run this can best be achieved through structural reform aimed at reducing macroeconomic uncertainty and deepening capital markers. Pursuit of the first objective would also have the favourable effect of reducing uncertainty regarding long-run market demand. In the shorter run, however, the state may be able to play a useful role in supplying capital to enterprises at lower than market rates. This would facilitate both the finance of long-run investment, especially in R&D, as well as the provision of lines of credit to customers of complex, high-value products.

7.3 Future Prospects for the Brazilian Non-serial Capital Goods Sector

Despite its structural weaknesses, the Brazilian non-serial capital goods sector can face the future with a degree of optimism. Over the ten years between

1996 and 2006 total domestic market demand is expected to rise with over US$ 15 bn. of infrastructural investments scheduled to take place (ABDIB 1996). This rise in demand is primarily the result of the privatization of much of the energy and communications sectors. Freed from the spending constraints imposed under public ownership, newly privatized enterprises are acting urgently to address the legacy of years of under-investment. Underlying all of the new investment is the realization within Brazilian business that the nature of the economic environment has changed. In particular, the domestic market can no longer be viewed in isolation. Rather, it must be viewed as part of a larger regional entity: MERCOSUL. In addition, the prospect of broader hemispheric integration (the Free Trade Area of the Americas) promises yet more radical environmental change over the next ten years. Taken together, these factors offer the sector promising opportunities. However, they also present formidable challenges.

Rapid market growth within MERCOSUL over the next ten years offers a valuable, and probably unique, opportunity for the sector to restructure itself within the context of expanding output. With enterprises on a firmer financial footing and demand growing, the sector will be in a position as never before to address its two principal structural weaknesses: technological conservatism and excessive diversification. Provided enterprises are able to maintain market share over the period, expanded demand should make enhanced specialization not only possible but, in fact, the most profitable course. At the same time, more favourable demand prospects should give rise to a more favourable climate for longer-term investments in production facilities and R&D. Whether enterprises take advantage of the opportunities and follow this course of action will depend in large part on the role of the state. If the state acquiesces in increased merger activity and enhances those policies directed at improving technological capabilities within the sector, then the prospects for effective structural reform seem promising. On the basis of recent evidence, there are grounds for optimism on both counts. In the absence of such interventions, however, the prospects are bleaker given the likelihood that enterprises might use short-term market improvements to postpone urgently needed reform.

A crucial determinant of the sector's long-run prospects will be its ability to contain the erosion of its market share within MERCOSUL by European, North American, and Asian imports. Taking the MERCOSUL market as a whole, the import coefficient in total sales of capital goods has been steadily rising. Provided the sector restructures sufficiently rapidly there is no reason why this process should not be halted or, at least, retarded. Failure to contain accelerated imports risks seeing losses of market share turn into absolute declines in output. In the longer run, the sector will have to redouble its efforts to become more internationally competitive given likely developments in trade policy. At present, Brazilian capital goods producers enjoy levels of tariff protection which, while substantially lower than in 1990, still greatly exceed international averages. However, the possible signing of the Free Trade Area of the Americas agreement in 2005 would exempt North American capital goods imports from MERCOSUL's common external tariff. This would have the effect of exposing the sector head-on to intense competition from technologically sophisticated US and Canadian enterprises. At the same time, the possibility of a European Union–MERCOSUL free trade agreement within the next ten years also serves as a warning that more radical trade liberalization is still to come.

In order to respond to these challenges and their associated opportunities, it has already been made clear that further gains in competitiveness are required. In addition to selected (and limited) state interventions, the role of foreign capital will be crucial in achieving this objective. Although foreign capital already has a strong presence within the industry, it tends to be highly concentrated within the electrical energy equipment sub-sector. In the other sub-sectors, by contrast, its presence is far more limited. Not coincidentally, these sub-sectors constitute the areas where the need for reform, better management, increased specialization, and capital injections is most pronounced. The greater entry of foreign capital into these sectors could be of great benefit to their competitiveness provided greater concentration and technological upgrading were the end results. However, in the interests of the development of national technological capabilities, policy-makers would need to ensure that domestic innovatory capacities were not displaced in the course of this process. From the perspective of foreign investors, participation in these sectors would have its attractions. Many of the enterprises constitute grossly underperforming assets. In the context of a rapidly growing and partially protected market, their response to restructuring, capital injection, and better management is likely to prove rapid and positive.

REFERENCES

ABDIB (1979), *Anuário ABDIB*, São Paulo: *Associação Brasileira para o Desenvolvimento das Indústrias de Base* (ABDIB).

—— (1985–94), *Relatórios Anuais*, São Paulo: ABDIB.

—— (1993*b*), *O Setor de Bens de Capital Sob Encomenda: Um Perfil em Perspectiva*, São Paulo: ABDIB.

—— (1993*c*), *Restrições ao Desenvolvimento do Setor Privado no Brasil*, São Paulo: ABDIB.

—— (1994*b*), *Guia de Fornecedores de Equipamentos e Serviços Para Infra-Estrutura*, São Paulo: ABDIB.

—— (1996), *Infra: Programa de Demanda por Infra-Estrutura—Relatório No. 9*, São Paulo: ABDIB.

ABIFER (1993), *Relatório de 1993*, Rio de Janeiro: *Associação Brasileira para a Indústria Ferroviária* (ABIFER).

ABNT (1995), *Certificados Emitidos Sistema de Gestão e Garantia da Qualidade —NBR ISO 9000*, Rio de Janeiro: Comitê Brasileiro da Qualidade—*Associação Brasileira para Normas Técnicas* (ABNT).

Adler, E. (1987), *The Power of Ideology: The Quest for Technological Autonomy in Brazil and Argentina*, Berkeley: University of California Press.

Amsden, A. (1989), *Asia's Next Giant*, New York: Oxford University Press.

Andrade, M., Cunha, L., and Vieira, J. (1994), 'A Siderurgia Brasileira no Contexto Mundial', *Revista do BNDES*, no. 1, Aug.

Araújo, J. T., Corrêa, P. G., and Gatilho, M. R. (1991), *Oportunidades Estratégicas de Indústria Brasileira nos Anos 90*, Rio de Janeiro: *Instituto de Economia Industrial-Universidade Federal do Rio de Janeiro* (IEI-UFRJ).

Arrow, K. (1962), 'The Economic Implications of Learning by Doing', *Review of Economic Studies*, 29, June.

Baark, E. (1991), 'The Accumulation of Technology: Capital Goods Production in Developing Countries Revisited', *World Development*, 19/7, July.

Baer, W. (1972), 'Import Substitution and Industrialisation in Latin America: Experiences and Interpretations', *Latin American Research Review*, spring.

—— (1989), *The Brazilian Economy*, New York: Praeger Publishers.

—— and Paiva, C. (1995), 'O Plano Real' in W. Baer, *A Economia Brasileira*, São Paulo: Nobel.

Balasubramanyan, V. N., and Lall, S. (eds.) (1991), *Current Issues in Development Economics*, Basingstoke and London: Macmillan.

Bambirra, V. (1973), *Capitalismo Dependiente Latinamericano*, Santiago: Editorial Prensa Latinoamericana.

Belassa, B. (1971), 'Trade Policies in Developing Countries', *American Economic Review Papers and Proceedings*, 61.

—— (1980), 'The Process of Industrial Development and Alternative Development Strategies', *World Bank Staff Working Papers*, no. 438.

Bell, M. (1984), 'Learning and the Accumulation of Indigenous Technological Capability in Developing Countries', in M. Fransman and K. King (eds.), *Technological Capability in the Third World*, Basingstoke and London: Macmillan.

—— Ross-Larson, B., and Westphal, L. (1984), 'Assessing the Performance of Infant Industries', *World Bank Staff Working Papers*, no. 666.

Bergsman, J. (1974), 'Commercial Policy, Allocative Efficiency and X-Efficiency', *Quarterly Journal of Economics*, 78/3.

Besant, J. (1991), *Managing Advanced Manufacturing Technology: The Challenge of the Fifth Wave*, Oxford: Basil Blackwell.

Bhagwati, J. (1962), 'On How to Decide What to Import and What to Produce', *Oxford Economic Papers*, Feb.

BNDES (1988), *Questões Relativas á Competitividade da Indústria de Bens de Capital: Bens de Capital Sob Encomenda e Maquinas Ferramenta*, Rio de Janeiro: Banco Nacional de Desenvolvimento Economico e Social (BNDES).

—— (1990a), *Capacitação Tecnológica na Indústria*, Rio de Janeiro: BNDES.

—— (1990b), *Liberalização e Comportamento Das Importações Brasileira: Uma Analise Prospectiva*, Rio de Janeiro: BNDES.

—— (1992–4), *Relatórios De Atividades* (Annual Reports), Rio de Janeiro: BNDES.

—— (1993b), *Emprego, Produtividade e Salários na Indústria Brasileira: Desempenho (1976–1992) e Perspectivas para o Futuro*, Rio de Janeiro: BNDES.

—— (1994b), 'Exportação de Bens de Capital Finamizáveis no Período de 1986 a 1992', Rio de Janeiro: BNDES (unpublished preliminary working paper).

—— (1995), *Relatório Setoral: Bens de Capital*, Rio de Janeiro: BNDES.

—— (1996), *A Experiência do BNDES na Exportação de Bens de Capital*, Rio de Janeiro: BNDES Website (www.bndes.gov.br).

Bonelli, R., Franco, G. H. B., and Fritsch, W. (1992), *Macroeconomic Instability and Trade Liberalization in Brazil: Lessons from the 1980s to the 1990s*, Rio de Janeiro: Pontifica Universidade Católica do Rio de Janeiro (PUC-RJ) (Working Paper no. 278).

Borges, J. C., and Da Silva, C. L. (1993), 'Indústria da Construção Naval: A Crise e Recuperaçâo', *Conjuntura Econômica*, July.

Braga, H. C., and Tyler, W. G. (1990), *Trade Policies in Brazil*, Rio de Janeiro: IPEA.

Branco, F., Cançado, I., and Filho, J. (1992), *Uma Proposta de Ação Conjunta*, Brasília: BNDES.

Brasil em Exame (1990), 'Bens de Capital: O Gigante na Corda Bamba', *Brasil em Exame*.

—— (1993), 'Bens de Capital: O Dinheiro do BNDES pode ser a Salvação', *Brasil em Exame*.

Brown, W. (1957), 'Innovation in the Machine Tool Industry', *Quarterly Journal of Economics*, 406–25.

Bruton, H. (1985), 'On the Production of a National Technology', in J. James and S. Watanabe (eds.), *Technology, Institutions and Government Policy*, Basingstoke and London: ILO/Macmillan.

Buchanan, J., Tollison, R., and Tullock, G. (1980), *Towards a Theory of the Rent Seeking Society*, College Station, Tex.: A&M University Press.

Bulmer-Thomas, V. (1994), *The Economic History of Latin America since Independence*, Cambridge: Cambridge University Press.

Buslik, S. A. (1994), *Energia Elétrica: Setor Emergencial*, Rio de Janeiro: IPEA.

Cardoso, F. H. (1973), 'Associated Dependent Development', in A. Stepan (ed.), *Authoritarian Brazil*, New Haven: Yale University Press.

—— and Falleto, E. (1979), *Dependency and Development in Latin America*, Berkeley: University of California Press.

Carvalho, M., and Machado, J. B. (1994), 'A Escalada Tarifária na Reforma Aduaneira', *Revista Brasileira de Comércio Exterior*, no. 30, Mar.–July.

CEPAL (1993), *Comercio Exterior de Bienes de Capital en America Latina 1985–1991*, Santiago: Comissão Comisión Econômica para América Latina e o Caribe (CEPAL).

Chava, F. N., and Nachmas, D. (1992), *Research Methods in the Social Sciences*, London: Edward Arnold.

Chudnovsky, N., Nagao, M., and Jacobsson, S. (1983), *Capital Goods Production in the Third World*, London: Francis Pinter.

Clarke, R., and Kirkpatrick, C. (1992), 'Trade Policy Reform and Economic Performance in Developing Countries: Assessing the Empirical Evidence', in R. Adhikari, C. Kirkpatrick, and J. Weiss (eds.), *Industrial and Trade Policy Reform in Developing Countries*, Manchester: Manchester University Press.

CNI (1991), *Abertura Comercial e Estratégia Tecnólogica: A Visão de Líderes Industriais Brasileiros*, Rio de Janeiro: Confederação Nacional de Indústria (CNI).

—— (1995), *Custo Brasil*, Rio de Janeiro: CNI.

Colcough, C., and Manor, J. (1991), *States or Markets? New Liberalism and the Development Policy Debate*, Oxford: Oxford University Press.

Colman, D., and Nixson, F. I. (1994), *The Economics of Change in Less Developed Countries*, London: Simon & Schuster.

Corbo, V. (1988), 'Problems, Development Theory and Strategies of Latin America', in G. Ranis and T. Schultz (eds.), *The State of Development Economics*, Basingstoke and London: Macmillan.

Corrêa, P. G. (1995), *Taxa de Câmbio, Impactos Setorais e Desempenho Exportador: Algumas Considerações Preliminares*, Rio de Janeiro: BNDES.

Corrêa do Lago, L., Lopes de Almeida, F., and de Lima, B. (1979), *A Indústria Brasileira de Bens de Capital: Origens, Situação Recente e Perspectivas*, Rio de Janeiro: Instituto Brasileiro de Economia/Fundação Gérulio Vargas (IBRE/FGV).

Correio Braziliense (11 Dec. 1994), 'Finep Amplia Projetos com o Plano Real', *Correio Braziliense*.

Cruz, H. (1983), *Mudança Tecnológica no Setor Metal Mecânico do Brasil Resultados de Estudos de Casos*, Tese de Livre Docência, São Paulo: University of São Paulo.

—— and Da Silva, M. E. (1990), *A Situação do Setor de Bens de Capital e Suas Perspectivas*, Campinas: Universidade Estadual de Campinas (UNICAMP).

Dahlman, C. J., and Frischtak, C. R. (1993), 'National Systems Supporting Technical Advance in Industry: The Brazilian Experience', in R. Nelson (ed.), *National Innovation Systems: A Comparative Analysis*, New York: Oxford University Press.

Dantas, V. (1993), 'Modernização Defensiva', *Automação e Indústria*, no. 46.

Departamento de Comercio Exterior (1980–9), *Comercio Exterior do Brasil: Importações*, Rio de Janeiro/Brasília: DECEX.

Dos Santos, T. (1978), *Imperialismo y Dependencia*, Mexico City: Ediciones Era.

Edquist, C., and Jacobsson, J. (1988), *Flexible Automation: The Global Diffusion of New Technology in the Engineering Industry*, Oxford: Basil Blackwell.

Eletrobrás (1994), *Plano Decenal de Demanda de Equipamentos e Materiais: Vol II Subestações, Vol III Linhas de Transmissão, Vol IV Sistemas de Distribuição*, Brasília: Eletrobrás.

Erber, F. S. (1978), 'Technological Development and State Intervention: A Study of the Brazilian Capital Goods Industry, University of Sussex', unpublished Ph.D. thesis.

—— (1982), *Technology Issues in the Capital Goods Sector: A Case Study of the Leading Industrial Machinery Producers in Brazil*, Geneva: UNCTAD.

—— (1986), 'The Capital Goods Industry and the Dynamics of Economic Development in LDCs: The Case of Brazil', in M. Fransman (ed.), *Machinery and Economic Development*, London and Basingstoke: Macmillan.

—— and Vermulm, R. (1993), *Ajuste Estrutural e Estratégias Empresariais*, Rio de Janeiro: IPEA.

Feldman, G. A. (1928), 'On the Theory of Growth Rates of National Income', translated and reproduced in N. Spulber (ed.), *Foundations of Soviet Strategy of Economic Growth: Selected Soviet Essays 1924–1930*, Bloomington, Ind.: Indiana University Press.

Felix, D. (1978), *Some Problems of the Import Substituting of Capital Goods in a Technologically Dependent Economy*, São Paulo: Conselho Nacional de Pesquisa (CNPq) (CNPq paper).

Ferraz, H. P. (1993), 'Uma Visâo Otimista do Futuro', *Conjuntura Econômico*, July.

Ferraz, J. (1984), 'Technological Development and Conditioning Factors: The Case of the Brazilian Shipbuilding Industry', University of Sussex (unpublished Ph.D thesis).

—— Rush, H., and Miles, I. (1992), *Development Technology and Flexibility: Brazil Faces the Industrial Divide*, London and New York: Routledge.

Filho, M. P. (1983), 'Theoretical Influences on Capital Goods, Dependency and Underdevelopment', University of Manchester (unpublished MA thesis).

Financial Times (22 Mar. 1995), 'Brazil Seeks New Ways to Turn the Lights On' by A. Foster, *Financial Times*, p. 3.

—— (1 Dec. 1995), 'A Powerful Presence' by A. Baxter, *Financial Times*.

—— (25 Mar. 1996), 'Latin American Finance and Investment: A Survey', *Financial Times*.

—— (23 July 1996), 'Blade Runner' by S. Wagstyl, *Financial Times*, p. 14.

Fishlow, A. (1990), 'The Latin American State', *Journal of Economic Perspectives*, 4/3.

Fleury, A. (1991), 'Flexible Automation in Brazil', in S. Watanabe (ed.), *Micro Electronics in Third World Industries: Quality, Competition, International Division of Labour and Employment*, Geneva: ILO.

—— (1995), 'Quality and Productivity in the Competitive Strategies of Brazilian Industrial Enterprises', *World Development*, 23/1.

Folha de São Paulo (29 May 1994), 'Especial: Privatizar, por que e até Onde?' *Folha de São Paulo*.

Forsyth, D., McBain, N., and Solomon, R. (1982), 'Technological Rigidity and Appropriate Technology', in F. Stewart and J. James (eds.), *The Economics of New Technologies in Developing Countries*, London: Francis Pinter.

Franco, G. H. B. (1990), *A Regulação do Capital Estrangeiro no Brasil: Analise da Legislação e Prospectas de Reforma*, Rio de Janeiro: PUC-RJ (Working Paper no. 246).

Fransman, M. (ed.) (1986), *Machinery and Economic Development*, Basingstoke and London: Macmillan.

—— and King, K. (1984), *Technological Capability in the Third World*, Basingstoke and London: Macmillan.

Freeman, C. (1982), *The Economics of Industrial Innovation*, London: Francis Pinter.

—— (ed.) (1984), *Long Waves in the World Economy*, London: Francis Pinter.

Fritsch, W., and Franco, G. (1991a), *Foreign Direct Investment in Brazil: Its Impact on Industrial Restructuring*, Paris, OECD.

Fritsch, W., and Franco, G. (1991b), *Trade Policy Issues in Brazil in the 1990s*, Rio de Janeiro: PUC-RJ (Working Paper no. 268).

—— —— (1991c), 'Industrial and Trade Policy Reform in Brazil: An Interim Assessment', unpublished paper given at the seminar 'Progresso Técnico e Competitivo: Oportunidades para o Brasil' at the Fundação Getúlio Vargas, Rio de Janeiro, July 1991.

Furtado, A. (ed.) (1994), *Capacitação Tecnológica, Competitividade e Política Indústrial: uma Abordagem Setorial e por Empresas Líderes*, Rio de Janeiro: IPEA.

GATT (1993), *Trade Policy Review: Brazil*, i and ii, Geneva: GATT.

GEIPOT (1985), *Anuário Estatístico dos Transportes*, Brasília: GEIPOT-Ministério dos Transportes.

—— (1992), *Anuário Estatístico dos Transportes*, Brasília: GEIPOT-Ministério dos Transportes.

—— (1994), *Anuário Estatístico dos Transportes*, Brasília: GEIPOT-Ministério dos Transportes.

Ghatak, S. (1986), *An Introduction to Development Economics*, London: Allen & Unwin.

Gowland, D. (1985), *Money, Inflation and Unemployment*, Brighton: Wheatsheaf.

Greenaway, D., and Milner, C. (1993), *Trade and Industrial Policy in Developing Countries*, Basingstoke and London: Macmillan.

Grunwald, J. (1970), 'Some Reflections on Latin American Industrial Policy', *Journal of Political Economy*.

Hayward, J. (1986), *The State and Market Economy*, Brighton: Wheatsheaf.

Helleiner, G. K. (1975), 'The Role of Multi National Corporations in Less Developed Countries' Trade in Technology', *World Development*, 3/4, Apr.

Hilpert, U. (1991), *State Policies and Techno-Industrial Innovation*, London: Routledge.

Hirschmann, A. (1968), 'The Political Economy of Import Substituting Industrialisation in Latin America', *Quarterly Journal of Economics*, no. 1, Feb.

IBGE (1981–94), *Indicadores Da Produção Física 1991–1994*, Rio de Janeiro: *Instituto Brasileiro Geografia e Estatística* (IBGE).

—— (1981–94), *Indicadores das Pessoas Empregadas na Indústria 1991–1994*, Rio de Janeiro: IBGE.

—— (1981–94), *Indicadores das Horas Pagadas na Indústria 1991–1994*, Rio de Janeiro: IBGE.

IBS (1995), *A Siderúrgia em Numéros*, Rio de Janeiro: *Instituto Brasileiro de Siderúrgia* (IBS).

IEI-UFRJ (1992), *Boletim de Conjuntura*, Dec. edn.

—— (1994), *Boletim de Conjuntura*, Oct. and Dec. edns.

IE-UNICAMP, IEI-UFRJ, FDC, FUNCEX (1993a), 'Sistemas de Apoio Fiscal-Creditício ao Risco Tecnológico e á Competitividade', in *Estudo da Competitividade da Indústria Brasileira*, Campinas: IE-UNICAMP, IEI-UFRJ, FDC, FUNCEX.

—— (1993b), 'Estímulo Competitivo e Política Tarifária', in *Estudo da Competitividade da Indústria Brasileira*, Campinas: IE-UNICAMP, IEI-UFRJ, FDC, FUNCEX.

—— (1993c), 'Competitividade do Setor Maquinas Ferramenta', in *Estudo da Competitividade da Indústria Brasileira*, Campinas: IE-UNICAMP, IEI-UFRJ, FDC, FUNCEX.

—— (1993d), 'Poder de Compra do Governo e Competitividade', in *Estudo da Competitividade da Indústria Brasileira*, Campinas: IE-UNICAMP, IEL-UFRJ, FDC, FUNCEX.

IMF (1995), *International Financial Statisitics*, Washington: IMF.

Indústria e Produtividade (1991), 'Retração Estatal Asfixia Bens de Capital Sob Encomenda', *Indústria e Produtividade*, Mar.

—— (1994), 'Especial: Perfil Atual e Perspectivas', *Indústria e Produtividade*, June.

IPEA (1989–94), *Boletim Conjuntural*, Sept. 1989, July 1991, July 1994, Oct. 1994, Rio de Janeiro: *Instituto de Pesquisa Econômica Aplicada* (IPEA).

Jacobsson, S. (1988), 'Intra-Industry Specialisation and Development Models for the Capital Goods Sector', *Weltwirtschaftiches Archiv*, 1/124.

James, J., and Watanabe, S. (eds.) (1985), *Technology, Institutions and Government Policy*, Basingstoke and London: ILO/Macmillan.

Jenkins, R. (1987), *Transnational Corporations and Uneven Development: The Internationalisation of Capital and the Third World*, London: Methuen.

Jornal do Brasil On-Line (8 Feb. 1996), 'Maior Acionista do Verolme-Ishibrás é Forçado a Vender Imóveis para Pagar Dívida', *Jornal do Brasil On-Line* (www.jb.com.br).

—— (24 May 1996), 'Empresários Protestam Contra Política Econômica do Governo', *Jornal do Brasil On-Line* (www.jb.com.br).

Kalecki, M. (1972), *Selected Essays on the Socialist and Mixed Economies*, Cambridge: Cambridge University Press.

Katz, J. M. (ed.) (1987), *Technology Generation in Latin American Manufacturing Industries*, Basingstoke and London: Macmillan.

—— (ed.) (1996), *Estabilización Macroeconómica, Reforma Estructural y Comportamiento Industrial*, Santiago: CEPAL.

Kay, C. (1989), *Latin American Theories of Development and Underdevelopment*, London: Routledge.

Kirkpatrick, C., Lee, C. H., and Nixson, F. I. (1984), *Industrial Structure and Policy in Less Developed Countries*, London: Allen & Unwin.

—— and Nixson, F. I. (1983), *The Industrialization of Less Developed Countries*, Manchester: Manchester University Press.

Kirschner, T. C. (ed.) (1993), *Modernização Tecnológica e Formação Técnico-Profissional no Brasil: Impasses e Desafios*, Rio de Janeiro: IPEA.

Krueger, A. O. (1985), 'Import Substitution Versus Export Promotion', *Finance and Development*, 22.

—— (1990), 'Government Failure in Economic Development', *Journal of Economic Perspectives*, no. 3.

Lal, D. (1983), *The Poverty of Development Economics*, London: Institute of Economic Affairs.

Lall, S. (1987), *Learning to Industrialise*, London and Basingstoke: Macmillan.

—— (1991), 'Explaining Industrial Success in the Developing World', ch. 7 in S. Lall and V. N. Balasubramanyan (eds.), *Current Issues in Development Economics*, Basingstoke and London: Macmillan.

—— (1994), 'The East Asian Miracle: Does the Bell Toll for Industrial Strategy?' *World Development*, 22/4.

Larrain, J. (1989), *Theories of Development*, Cambridge: Polity Press.

Leff, N. (1968), *The Brazilian Capital Goods Industry, 1929–1964*, Cambridge, Mass.: Harvard University Press.

Little, I. M. D. (1982), *Economic Development: Theory, Policy and International Relations*, New York: Basic Books.

—— Scitovsky, T., and Scott, M. (1970), *Industry and Trade in Some Developing Countries*, Oxford and New York: Oxford University Press.

Mahalanobis, P. C. (1953), 'Some Observations on the Process of Growth of National Income', *Sanklya: The Indian Journal of Statistics*, 12/4.

Malcher, J. M. G. (1987), 'A Indústrial Mecânica Peasda no Brasil: Concorrência e Capacitação Tecnológica', Rio de Janeiro: UFRJ (unpublished MA thesis).

Marx, K. (1945), *Capital*, i and ii, Calcutta: Saraswaty Library (Indian edn.).

Matesco, V. R. (1994a), *Esforço Tecnológico das Empresas Brasileiras*, Rio de Janeiro: IPEA.

—— (1994b), *O Comportamento Estratégico das Empresas Industrais Brasileiras: Inovodoras Versus Não Inovadoras*, Rio de Janeiro: IPEA.

—— and Hasenclever, Lia (1996), 'Indicadores de Esforço Tecnológico: Comparações e Implicações', *Pesquisa e Planejamento Econômico*, 26/3, Dec.

Merhav, M. (1968), *Technological Dependence, Monopoly and Growth*, Oxford: Pergamon Press.

Meyer-Starmer, J. (co-ord.) (1993a), *Comprehensive Modernization on the Shop Floor: A Case Study of the Brazilian Machinery Industry*, Berlin: German Development Institute.

—— (1993b), *What is Wrong with Technology Policy in Brazil, and What can be Done About it?* São Paulo: *Instituto Latinoamericano de Desenvolvimento Economico e Social-Friedrich Ebert Stiftung* (ILDES-FES).

—— (1995), 'Micro-Level Innovations and Competitiveness', *World Development*, 23/1.

Mitra, J. D. (1979), *The Capital Goods Sector in LDCs: A Case for State Intervention?* Washington: World Bank Staff Working Paper no. 343.

Motta, M. T. (1992a), 'A Indústria de Bens de Capital e o Setor Elétrico', *Carta Mensa*, 37/442, Jan.

—— (1992b), 'Planos de Estabilização Heterodoxos', *Carta Mensal*, 38/449, Aug.

—— (1994), 'Tecnológia', *Carta Mensal*, 40/476, Nov.

—— Knaack de Souza, J. O., and Paim, G. (1994), 'Indústria de Bens de Capital: Analise e Perspectivas do Setor Metal-Mecânico', Rio de Janeiro: unpublished consultancy report.

Nelson, R. R. (1981), 'Research on Productivity Growth and Differences', *Journal of Economic Literature*, 19.

—— (1993), *National Innovation Systems: A Comparative Analysis*, New York: Oxford University Press.

—— and Winter, S. (1977), 'In Search of a Useful Theory of Productivity Growth', *Research Policy*, 6.

Nishimizu, M., and Robinson, S. (1984), 'Trade Policy and Productivity Change in Semi-Industrialised Countries', *Journal of Development Economics*, no. 16.

Oliveira, G. (co-ord.) (1993), *Condicionantes e Diretrizes de Política para a Abertura Comercial Brasileira*, Rio de Janeiro: IPEA.

Pack, H. (1981), 'Fostering the Capital Goods Sector in Less Developed Countries', *World Development*, 9/3.

—— and Todaro, M. (1969), 'Technical Transfer, Labour Absorption and Economic Development', *Oxford Economic Papers*, Nov.

—— and Westphal, L. (1986), 'Industrial Strategy and Technical Change', *Journal of Development Economics*, 22/1.

Papageorgiou, D., Michaely, M., and Choksi, A. M. (eds.) (1991), *Liberalising Foreign Trade: Lessons of Experience from Developing Countries*, Oxford: Basil Blackwell.

PBQP (1994), 'Programa Brasileiro da Qualidade e Produtividade: Subprogramas Setorais da Qualidade e Produtividade—Complexos Industriais, IBK—Indústria de Bens de Capital', *Programa Brasileiro da Qualidade e Produtividade* (unpublished indicators furnished by ABDIB for PBQP survey).

Perez, C., and Soete, L. (1988), 'Catching up Technologies: Entry Barriers and Windows of Opportunity', in G. Dosi, C. Freeman, and L. Soere (eds.), *Technical Change and Economic Theory*, London: Pinter Publishing.

Perez, W. (1993), 'Transferência de Tecnológia em Bens de Capital', *Revista de Administração*, 28/1.

Petrobrás (1993), *Relatório Anual de 1993*, Rio de Janeiro: Petrobrás.

Pinder, J. (1982), *National Industrial Strategies and the World Economy*, London: Croom Helm.

Pinheiro, A. C., and Almeida, G. B. (1994), *Padrões Setoriais da Proteção na Economia Brasileira*, Rio de Janeiro: IPEA.

Porteous, M. (1986), 'Recession and Technical Change in the Brazilian Machine Tool Sector', University of Sussex: unpublished D.Phil thesis.

Porter, M. (1990), *The Competitive Advantage of Nations*, Basingstoke and London: Macmillan.

Portos e Navios (1993), 'Retomada de Crescimento', *Portos e Navios*, Jan.

Prebisch, R. (1970), ch. 2 in *Development Problems in Latin America: An Analysis by the United Nations Economic Commision on Latin America*, Austin, Tex.: University of Texas Press.

Raj, K. A., and Sen, A. K. (1961), 'Alternative Patterns of Growth under Conditions of Stagnant Export Earnings', *Oxford Economic Papers*, 13, Feb.

Ramalho, J. (1995), *Restructuring of Labour and Trade Union Responses in Brazil*, Manchester: University of Manchester International Labour Studies Group Working Paper.

Ranis, G. (1984), 'Determinants and Consequences of Indigenous Technological Activity', in M. Fransman and K. King (eds.), *Technological Capability in the Third World*, Basingstoke and London: Macmillan.

Revista Ferroviária (1994), Dec. edn.

—— (1995), Jan. edn.

—— (1995), Dec. edn.

RFFSA (1995), *Relatório da Administração: Exercicio de 1994*, Rio de Janeiro: Rede Ferroviária Federal (RFFSA).

Robson, M., Townsend, J., and Pavitt, K. (1988), 'Sectoral Patterns of Production and Use of Innovation in the UK 1945–83', *Research Policy*, 17.

Rosenberg, N. (1963*a*), 'Capital Goods, Technology and Economic Growth', *Oxford Economic Papers*, 15/3.

—— (1963*b*), 'Technological Change in the Machine Tool Industry 1840–1910', reprinted in N. Rosenberg (1976), *Perspectives on Technology*, Cambridge: Cambridge University Press.

—— (1969), 'The Direction of Technical Change: Inducement Mechanisms and Focussing Devices', *Economic Development and Cultural Change*, 18, Oct.

Rosenberg, N. (1982), *Inside the Black Box: Technology and Economics*, Cambridge: Cambridge University Press.

Scherer, F. M. (1982), 'Inter-Industry Technology Flows in the United States', *Research Policy*, 11.

Schmitz, H. (1982), *Manufacturing in the Backyard*, London: Francis Pinter.

—— (1984), 'Industrialisation Strategies in Less Developed Countries: Some Lessons of Historical Experience', in R. Kaplinsky (ed.), *Third World Industrialisation in the 1980s: Open Economies in a Closing World*, London: Frank Cass.

—— and Cassiolato, J. (eds.) (1992), *Hi-Tech for Industrial Development: Lessons from the Brazilian Experience in Electronics and Automation*, London and New York: Routledge.

Schmookler, J. (1966), *Invention and Economic Growth*, Cambridge, Mass.: Harvard University Press.

Schonberger, R. (1986), *World Class Manufacturing*, New York: Free Press.

Shapiro, H. (1992), 'The Public-Private Interface: Brazil's Business-Government Relationship 1950–90', unpublished paper presented at a conference on States and Markets, University of Notre Dame, Apr. 1992.

—— and Taylor, L. (1990), 'The State and Industrial Strategy', *World Development*, 18/6.

Sirlin, P. (1997), 'An Appraisal of Capital Goods Policy in Argentina', *CEPAL Review*, 61, Apr.

Soligo, R., and Stern, J. (1965), 'Tariff Protection, Import Substitution and Investment Efficiency', *Pakistan Development Review*, 5, summer.

Stewart, F. (1976), 'Capital Goods in Developing Countries', in A. Cairncross and M. Puri (eds.), *Income Distribution and Development Strategy: Problems of the Developing Countries; Essays in Honour of H. W. Singer*, London and Basingstoke: Macmillan.

—— (1984), 'Facilitating Indigenous Technical Change in Third World Countries', in M. Fransman and K. King (eds.), *Technological Capability in the Third World*, Basingstoke and London: Macmillan.

—— and James, J. (1982), *The Economics of New Technologies in Developing Countries*, London: Francis Pinter.

Stewart, J. (1991), *Econometrics*, Hemel Hempstead: Philip Allan.

Stone, A. (1994), *Complex Transactions under Uncertainty: Brazil's Machine Tool Industry*, Washington: World Bank Policy Research Working Paper no. 1247.

Strachmann, E. (1993), 'Competitividade da Indústria de Equipamentos para Energia Elétrica', in *Estudo da Competitividade da Indústria Brasileira*, Campinas: IE-UNICAMP, IEI-UFRJ, FDC, FUNCEX.

Strassman, P. (1959), 'Interrelated Industries and the rate of technological change', *Review of Economic Studies*, 27, Oct.

Suzigan, W. (1992a), *A Indústria Brasileira após uma Década de Estagnação: Questões para Política Industrial*, Campinas: UNICAMP Working Paper.

—— (1992b), *Política Comercial e Perspectivas da Indústria Brasileira*, Campinas: UNICAMP Working Paper no. 13.

—— and Villela, A. (1997), *Industrial Policy in Brazil*, Campinas: State University of Campinas Institute of Economics.

Tadini, V. (1986), 'O Setor de Bens de Capital Sob Encomenda: Analise do Desenvolvimento Recente (1975–83)', São Paulo: University of São Paulo (unpublished paper).

—— (1993), *Perspectivas do Setor de Bens de Capital Sob Encomenda no Brasil*, unpublished paper presented at the National Forum of Advanced Studies Sector Strategy Workshop Brasília, 5 Aug. 1993.

Tarifa Aduaneira do Brasil (1995), *Tarifa Aduaneira do Brasil*.

Teubal, M. (1973), 'Heavy and Light Industry in Economic Development', *American Economic Review*, 63/4.

—— (1984), 'The Role of Technological Learning in the Exports of Manufactured Goods: The Case of Selected Capital Goods in Brazil', *World Development*, 12/8.

Thorstensen, V. H. (1980), 'O Setor de Bens de Capital, O Estado Produtor e O Estado Planejador: Conflito ou Cooperação', Fundação Getúilio Vargas São Paulo (unpublished Ph.D thesis).

Tidd, J. (1990), *Flexible Manufacturing Technology and International Competitiveness*, London: Francis Pinter.

Torres, S. D., Esteves de Carvalho, M., and Torres Filho, E. T. (1994), 'Exportações Brasileiras de Bens de Capital: Desempenho nos Anos Recentes', *Revista do BNDES*, 1/1, June.

Tyler, W. (1981), *The Brazilian Industrial Economy*, Lexington, Mass.: Lexington Books.

UNCTAD (1985), *The Capital Goods Sector in Less Developed Countries: Technological Issues and Policy Options*, New York: United Nations.

—— (1994), *Directory of Import Regimes. Part I: Monitoring Import Regimes*, New York: United Nations.

Unger, K. (1994), *Ajuste Estructural y Estrategias Empresariales en México*, Mexico City: CIDE.

UNIDO (1992), *Industrial Competitiveness in Brazil: Trends and Prospects*, Vienna: United Nations Industrial Development Organization.

United Nations (1982–94), *Commodity Trade Statistics: Brazil*, New York: United Nations.

Vermulm, R. (1993), 'A Crise da Indústria de Bens de Capital no Brasil', *Informações FIPE*, May.

Villela, A. (1994), *Tendências da Produtividade e do Emprego: Panorama Internacional e Reflexos no Brasil*, Rio de Janeiro: BNDES.

Watanabe, S. (ed.) (1991), *Micro Electronics in Third World Industries: Quality, Competition, International Division of Labour and Employment*, Geneva: ILO.

Weiss, J. (1988), *Industry in Developing Countries: Theory, Policy and Evidence*, London and New York: Routledge.

—— (1992), 'Trade Policy Reform and Performance in Manufacturing: Mexico 1975–88', *Journal of Development Studies*, 29/1: 1–23.

Wirth, J., Nunes, E., and Bogenschild, T. (1987), *State and Society in Brazil: Continuity and Change*, Boulder, Colo. Westview Press.

World Bank (1987), *World Development Report 1987*, New York and Oxford: Oxford University Press.

—— (1994), *World Tables 1994*, Washington: World Bank.

Yeats, A. (1996), 'Does Mercosur's Trade Performance Justify Concern About the Effects of Regional Trade Arrangements? Yes!', World Bank, mimeo.

INDEX